A TRAILS BOOKS GUIDE

THE GREAT MINNESOTA TOURING BOOK

30 SPECTACULAR AUTO TRIPS

Thomas Huhti

TRAILS BOOKS
Black Earth, Wisconsin

Library of Congress Control Number: 2003115108
ISBN: 1-931599-36-X

Editor: Stan Stoga
Photos: Thomas Huhti and Tim Bewer (except where noted)
Cover Designer: Kathie Campbell

Printed in the United States of America.

09 08 07 06 05 04   6 5 4 3 2 1

Trails Books, a division of Trails Media Group, Inc.
P.O. Box 317   •   Black Earth, WI 53515
(800) 236-8088   •   e-mail: info@wistrails.com
www.trailsbooks.com

Tour Guide

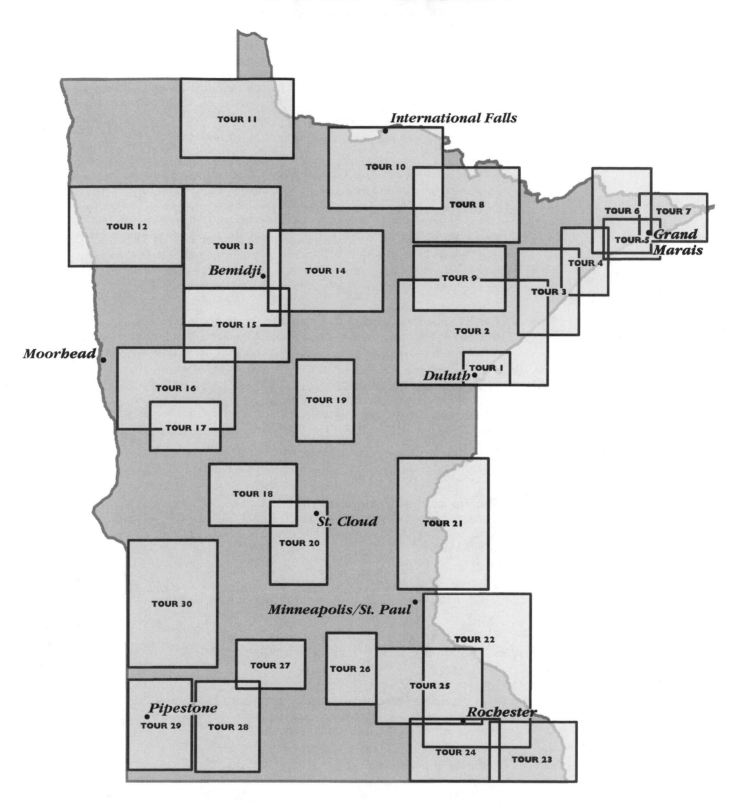

International Falls

TOUR 11

TOUR 10

TOUR 8

TOUR 6   TOUR 7

TOUR 12

TOUR 13

TOUR 14

Bemidji

TOUR 5   Grand Marais

TOUR 9

TOUR 4

TOUR 3

TOUR 15

TOUR 2

Moorhead

TOUR 16

TOUR 19

TOUR 1

Duluth

TOUR 17

TOUR 18

St. Cloud

TOUR 21

TOUR 20

TOUR 30

Minneapolis/St. Paul

TOUR 22

TOUR 27

TOUR 26

TOUR 25

Pipestone

Rochester

TOUR 29   TOUR 28

TOUR 24   TOUR 23

Contents

Introduction

"Land of 10,000 Lakes." "Land of Sky-Blue Waters" (from the original translation of the Dakota word *Minisota,* "Land of Sky-Tinted Waters"). "Star of the North."

These state mottoes (official and otherwise) and license plate slogans are apt descriptions of the wonderland known as Minnesota. Mention the state to most people, and they will imagine icy-blue forest lakes dotted with canoes, moose lumbering through dense stands of tamarack along thousands of shorelines—and, of course, waist-deep snow and bone-chilling cold. Then there are images of ice fishers stomping their feet atop two feet of ice, with snowmobiles whipping by, or the aw-shucks "yup" that's uttered so frequently and convincingly in the Midwest.

And yet Minnesota is *so* much more, culturally and geographically. Should your only "Minnesota" experiences or coffee-table-book-based mental images be those of hiking carpeted forestlands, trolling for smallmouth bass from john boats, trudging through Arctic-sized piles of snow, or perhaps traips-ing the Mall of America, then good news: You will be happily surprised by what you *don't* know of the state . . . yet. I hope that this book helps you encounter many happy surprises—as it did for me.

The Land and the People

The word *diverse* can be at times a travel-writing cliché when it describes a destination or its population. Minnesota, though, proves happily that clichés often develop because they're absolutely true. The state has a lot to offer vagabond motorists, and I hope this book helps guide them to some of the most scenic byways and most noteworthy attractions along the way.

But first, the land. North to south, between its borders with Canada and Iowa, Minnesota stretches roughly 400 miles. East to west, the width of the state varies from 175 miles all the way to 367 miles! With more than 84,000 square miles, it's the 12th-largest state in the Union; but within all those acres, it boasts about five *million* acres of water area—the most of any state!

The Mississippi River from along the Great River Road. Thomas Huhti

View of Lake Superior from Split Rock Lighthouse. Tim Bewer

tually every small town (and many urban neighborhoods) offers visitors a hands-on education in the waves of immigrants that have settled in the state over the years. Ethnically, Minnesota is a mixed salad, with large numbers of Native Americans, French, Norwegians, Germans, Czechs, Finns, Dutch, and (lately) Hmongs making their home here. But no matter when these groups arrived, their traditions and culture are still celebrated and colorfully displayed throughout Minnesota. And the tours in this book show you many of them.

To turn Gertrude Stein's famous quote on itself, "There's a whole lot of there, there." Minnesota offers sublime diversity for the road tripper, and this book is your guide to its many wonders. The superb Lake Superior uplands of the North Shore trace the massive Niagara Escarpment, where Minnesota's modest peaks (its highest point, Eagle Mountain, is here) offer commanding views of the greatest of the Great Lakes. Winding their way north from *Gitchegumee,* blue highways plunge into the first stands of Minnesota's astonishingly large carpets of forest. These roads all lead to the crown jewel of the state, the Boundary Waters Canoe Area, truly a national—not just state—treasure. Here, primeval glacial lakes, as countless as the stars in the sky, dot the never-ending greenery. The swaths of green seem to stretch forever, or at least down to central Minnesota. That's a lot of trees! Along with them are historic villages (of both the authentic and reconstituted varieties), sublime parklands, some of the country's best recreation (one claim, for example, states that Minnesota has one boat for every six residents—very likely true, if this author's experiences are typical!), and—a favorite—wildlife viewing unparalleled in the U.S. This guidebook is an attempt to show you the way to a few of these in the form of compact and convenient loop tours.

The guide doesn't forsake the area scrunched between Lake Superior and the stands of pine to the south. The highways here make a foray into human and economic history in the Iron Range. Few public relations brochures tout it, but this region helped build America, as hardy immigrants toiled in subterranean caverns, extracting iron ore from one of the richest deposits on the planet.

Northwest Minnesota has its own set of unique attractions. After tracing the gorgeous Rainy River along one of the nation's most precious scenic byways, we discover that Minnesota contains the northernmost spot in the continental United States, the Northwest Angle (see Tour 11 for details). In this section of the state, we get to see one of Minnesota's longest and most important (and loveliest) rivers, many more of those crystalline lakes, and one of North America's largest lakes, Lake of the Woods.

Lakes and forests give way slowly to prairies in western and southern Minnesota. One can almost stand near the Red River of the North and see clear to Wyoming. It's hard not to notice that this oft-neglected area of the state is one of the most agriculturally rich regions on earth.

Granted, the state does not feature any *National Geographic*-worthy Rocky Mountain backdrops or shimmering desert palettes. But just about every other kind of topography awaits the motorist up to the task of exploring the best that Minnesota has to offer. Its landscapes *are* diverse, more so than those of any of its neighbors. But typical of America's breadbasket region, its geography, attractions, and even people do not call attention to themselves; they require a bit of slowed-down effort to appreciate fully (perfect for our tour of winding roads and off-the-beaten track destinations). Those willing to put forth the effort will discover a state that is truly its own, with a fusion of landscapes, attractions, and people unlike any other in the United States.

Minnesota's population of 4.7 million ranks much nearer the middle on the U.S. population density scale (20th largest), but what a lovely human mosaic there is. Few states maintain ties to ethnic heritage as faithfully as does Minnesota; vir-

In this guidebook, we'll take you to many of Minnesota's rivers, which sometimes get short shrift because of those ubiquitous lakes. And yet, how could we forget that the area southwest of Bemidji is the birthplace of the mighty Mississippi, and that the state forms the western boundary of the nationally designated Saint Croix Riverway? And in the south, there's the meandering Minnesota River, flowing east and then bending north on its journey to the Mississippi.

The glaciers that scoured the Upper Midwest and pitted the landscape with countless lakes millennia ago stopped in southeastern Minnesota, in what is now called Bluff Country. Here, gumdrop-shaped hills lead our blue highways into gentle rises and falls, making for some exciting driving opportunities. It's one of the state's most active driving areas, and we'll take you there.

The Beginning . . . and What It Led To

The license plates say "10,000 Lakes," and that's pretty much all I knew about Minnesota as I loaded up my father's truck for the long drive from southern Wisconsin to Duluth for the start of my freshman year in college. Now, you may ask, how on earth does a cheesehead who spent his first 18 years in the Badger State cross the border in search of . . . what?

The simple answer is that I had never really traveled much and, come high school graduation, I vowed to see what else was out there. Part of "there" turned out to be the University of Minnesota–Duluth. Despite never having been to the school, I chose it because I could pay in-state tuition (thank you, reciprocity), I was offered a University of Minnesota system scholarship, and, most important, it was far away from home.

I was enraptured from the first morning following my parents' departure. Awakened by—of all things—the bellowing of a foghorn, I happily drifted down to Duluth's waterfront on my bike and sat happily along the harbor, watching the behemoth freighters floating through banks of fog. It was just the first week of September, but it was bone-chillingly cold, and I was giddy with delight. On one of the freighters, a crew member grinned at me and waved. That, I believe, set my wanderlust off to fever pitch.

Mornings and evenings, and often even after classes in the afternoon, I would set out on my trusty Bianchi 12-speed to attempt to ride portions of Duluth's Skyline Drive, the first glorious tour in our book. Easily most of my homework was written or read somewhere in those bluffs overlooking Gitchegumee.

Gradually, my friends and I expanded our Minnesota meanderings. Monthly trips gave way to weekly road trips up Highway 61 along the North Shore for beachcombing and smoked-fish munching. The experiences have led me to regard the area as one of my favorite places in the world.

There followed explorations into the nether regions of northern Minnesota to find out if the state's slogan of "10,000 Lakes" was accurate. (I never came to any conclusions but suspect the figure is an underestimate.) Here also I discovered a preference for "blue highways," those ribbony country roads that are much preferable to frantic interstates and other four-lane highways. Much to my delight, northern Minnesota has few of *those* roads. And parts of it have nothing *but* blue highways, with names like Gunflint Trail and Echo Trail, both of which have found their way into this guide.

Countless other trips followed. A pilgrimage to Bob Dylan's birthplace in Hibbing led to the fortuitous discovery of the birthplace of the Greyhound bus—the wanderer's best friend in the United States. A visit to the U.S. Hockey Hall of Fame in Eveleth every opening weekend of college hockey season became an annual event. Poking around extant iron mines. Swimming in what seemed like

Gently rolling and boundless prairie—the hallmark of western Minnesota.
Tim Bewer

Celebrating the heritage of the state's early residents near Saint Cloud. Tim Bewer

half of Minnesota's 10,000 glacial lakes. And on and on. . . . Roughly half my life has been spent on the road, looking first for the "beaten path" and then meandering off it in search of the Other Place—then trying somehow to write it all down in book form. Sadly, at some point I began to confuse an accumulation of miles with an understanding of Place. One day, on the craggy coast of Newfoundland, I literally ran out of road. An epiphany ensued: it was time to go Home, a revelation that eventually led to writing this book.

Part of going Home was a return to all those familiar Minnesota destinations that had impressed me years before. It was like seeing old friends—and meeting some of the friends they had met while I was gone. Traveling the state again struck old cords and at times reinforced the notion that I knew the state "like the back of my hand." But how joyously misguided I was. Half the time after revisiting an old haunt—a favorite hiking trail or tiny town somewhere—I would find myself somewhere completely unknown. My joyful reaction: "Oops, never saw *this* before."

And so the 30 tours in this book are the result of my new-found joy in getting reacquainted with Minnesota's familiar attractions, as well as discovering new and invigorating places and attractions. I hope you find the trips as pleasing and edifying as I did.

Why These Tours?

The only prerequisites for choosing the tours for the book were that they had to form a loop of some sort, present a rich array of places to visit and roads to drive and, if possible, be able to be completed in one day. Of course, the last factor is arbitrary. You can spend two, possibly three days, on some of the tours if you stop at every site mentioned and take a leisurely approach to the road—both highly desirable goals, by the way.

Perhaps the premier reason for assembling these tours was to get you, the motorist, to experience the variety of Minnesota's scenic roads. The state already has a nationally renowned Scenic Byways system—20 gorgeous routes of historical, cultural, and geographic interest. Each is quite worthy in its own right, yet Minnesota simply resists the need to pigeonhole it according to one theme. The research for *this* book is so rich with Minnesota sites that it wound up with 30 tours, all more varied than any other guidebook out there! In one winding road traipse, to cite just one example, we may take in a Great Lake scenic drive, then drift into roads rutted with the history of mining and homesteading, all via some of the nation's most precious national forestlands.

I hope each tour offers an inviting balance of attractions and highlights, with equal parts geography, human and natural history, scenic driving, recreation, and wildlife mixed in. My goal was to include tours that whisked the reader/traveler from a stately, antique-laden mansion, for example, to a wildlife refuge to a farm machinery museum to a tranquil hiking path, with sightings of rivers, woodlands, prairies, fauna and flora along the way. To spice things up, I added an occasional dollop of kitsch to the mix (the delightful Spam Museum in Tour 24 being the most obvious). And in keeping with the book's adventuresome spirit, each tour contains at least one Quick Trip Option, which provides travelers with some off-the-beaten-path jaunts. A couple of them are on gravel roads, so be alert on them.

One thing the book tries to avoid are interstates (busy or otherwise) and four-lane roads in general. Sometimes, they were unavoidable. But I've made a conscious effort to steer you to those two-lane gems that slow you down, that make you appreciate the state's rich variety of scenery and attractions, that allow you to connect with people.

These roads can be fun in their own right. Their practical and original purpose continues to be to get people and goods from one place to another. Many of the routes in this book trace logging or farm-to-market roads that have been slightly widened and blacktopped over the past century, but they still bend and twist with the terrain (glacial hills, lakes, and rivers are Nature's best attempt to thwart road engineers). And more than a few run arrow-straight across prairies that never seem to end. County blacktops, federal four-laners, local gravel roads, state and national scenic byways, logging roads, and more—they're all here.

No matter which of these you travel (and I hope all of them), enjoy them to the fullest. And remember that getting sidetracked is part of the fun. This, after all, is The Road, isn't it? The destination is only partly the thing. The journey is just as important. People going from point A to point B may travel

A frequently seen and hard-to-miss sign on Minnesota rural roads. Thomas Huhti

down the same "road," but each of us experiences it differently. I hope that this book helps you enjoy the destination as well as the journey.

One reason to be ever vigilant on Minnesota roads. Thomas Huhti

Practicalities

Tourist Information: The main *Minnesota Office of Tourism*, (651) 296-5029 and (800) 657-3700 (www.exploreminnesota.com), is at 500 Metro Square Building, 121 Seventh Place E, Saint Paul, 55101. The regional *state visitor information centers* are located along main highways near Albert Lea, Beaver Creek, Dresbach, Duluth, Fisher's Landing, Grand Portage (May–October), International Falls, Moorhead, Saint Cloud, Saint Croix (I-94), and Worthington. They are usually closed on major holidays.

Parks and Forests: The *Minnesota Department of Natural Resources*, (651) 296-6157 (www.dnr.state.mn.us), is the first place to go for information on all those acres of forest and lake awaiting you! If you're planning a foray into national forest lands, then the Chippewa National Forest's *Supervisor's Office*, (218) 335-8600, in Cass Lake or the Superior National Forest's *Supervisor's Office*, (218) 626-4300, in Duluth are the best places to start. Both national forests have camping reservation hotlines at (877) 444-6777.

Driving Conditions: The Department of Transportation has road condition information online at www.dot.state.mn.us and at (800) 542-0220.

Fall Color Information: The Minnesota Office of Tourism and DNR both update their Web sites with fall color reports. You can also phone them at (888) 868-7476 for up-to-the-minute reports.

Seat Belt/Child Restraint Laws: Seat belts required for all children in front seats and those under 11; child restraints necessary for children under 4.

Motorcycle Helmet Laws: Required for individuals under 18 and those with a learner's permit.

Radar Detectors: Permitted.

Population: approximately 4.7 million.

Capital: Saint Paul.

Area: approximately 84,000 square miles (12th largest).

Admitted to Union: May 11, 1858, as the 32nd state.

Nickname: Gopher State, North Star State.

Motto: Star of the North.

Time Zone: Central Standard Time, DST.

Highest Point: Eagle Mountain, 2,301 feet.

Lowest Point: 601 feet, Lake Superior.

Holidays: January 1; Martin Luther King Jr. Day (third Monday in January); Presidents Day (third Monday in February); Memorial Day (last Monday in May); July 4; Labor Day (first Monday in September); Veterans Day (November 11); Thanksgiving; Christmas.

Taxes: State sales tax is 6.5 percent, with local options totaling 1 to 3 percent more.

30 SPECTACULAR AUTO TRIPS

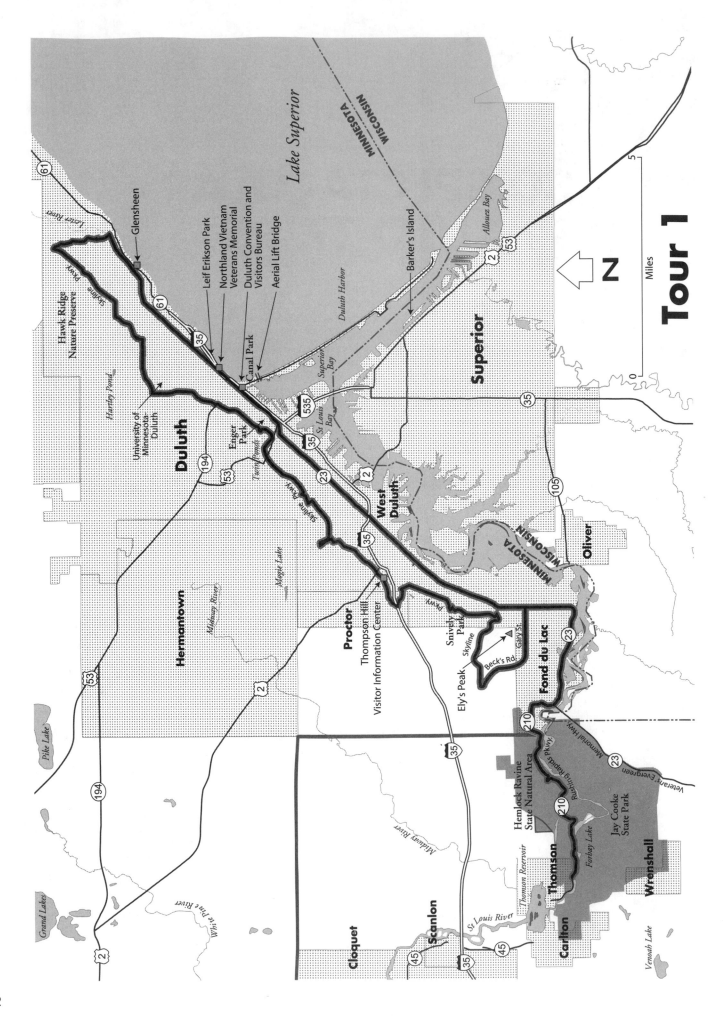

Tour 1

N

Miles
0   5

Lake Superior

MINNESOTA
WISCONSIN

Glensheen

Leif Erikson Park
Northland Vietnam
Veterans Memorial
Duluth Convention and
Visitors Bureau
Aerial Lift Bridge

Canal Park

Barker's Island

Allouez Bay

Hawk Ridge
Nature Preserve

Lester River

Seven Bridges Pkwy

Duluth Harbor

Superior Bay

Superior

Duluth Harbor

St Louis Bay

University of Minnesota-
Duluth

Enger Park

Hartley Pond

Twin Ponds

Skyline Pkwy

Mogie Lake

West Duluth

Oliver

MINNESOTA
WISCONSIN

Hermantown

Miller Creek

Proctor

Thompson Hill
Visitor Information Center

Snively Park

Skyline Pkwy

Ely's Peak

Beck's Rd

Gary St

Fond du Lac

Pike Lake

Grand Lakes

Whiteface River

West Pine River

Midway River

St Louis River

Cloquet

Scanlon

Hemlock Ravine
State Natural Area

Rushing Rapids Pkwy

Thomson Reservoir

Thomson

Forbay Lake

Jay Cooke
State Park

Carlton

Wrenshall

Veronah Lake

Veterans Evergreen

Memorial Hwy

Tour 1
Hawks and Harbor Vistas

Duluth—Jay Cooke State Park—Skyline Parkway—Duluth

Distance: approximately 40 miles

Skyline Parkway, which falls within Duluth's city limits, has a distinct wilderness flavor. That's because Duluth has one of the largest expanses of municipal greenspace in the United States, most of it along the gorgeous bluffs that abut Duluth Harbor, and overlook its more staid Wisconsin sister city, Superior. The nearly 40 miles of Skyline Parkway trace the high ridge above the tiny twin cities and provide superb views: enormous iron ore carriers, Duluth's famed Aerial Lift Bridge, some of Minnesota's most eye-catching historic architectural districts, and hundreds of acres of parkland, including one of Minnesota's favorite state parks— Jay Cooke (with its own brief, but thrilling, scenic tour). Birding along the Skyline Parkway is superb—one ridge is legendary for hawk watchers. The parkway is also a favorite outlet for Duluth joggers and bicyclists.

Duluth's too-often-ignored sister city, Superior, across the harbor in Wisconsin, also makes for an intriguing jaunt with its greenspace and historic attractions. Or, visitors can cross the legendary lift bridge—hopefully witnessing an ore carrier passing beneath—and take in one of the many natural wonders of the bay: the sandbar spits that divide Minnesota and Wisconsin. For those looking for a break from driving (those twisty roads may not be for the weak-stomached), Duluth also boasts a downtown walking zone with some of the Great Lakes' best freshwater charter fishing, the world's only all-freshwater aquarium, and famed events. Wolves and moose have been known to wander through town.

After years of being a bridesmaid to other, better-known "hip" destinations, blue-collar Duluth is finally receiving its kudos: In 2001, it was chosen by *Outside* magazine as one of the country's 10 "Dream Towns," described as "perfect places to live big, play hard and work (if you must)." *Money* magazine rated it one of the top four Midwestern small cities, based on livability.

Perhaps most aptly described by the Depression-era WPA guide *Minnesota* as a "Lilliputian village in a mammoth rock garden," it has all the graces of a small town. Its rocky bluffs, towering some 600 to 800 feet above the harbor's steely waters, lend an intimidating beauty to the city. These ancient rock formations—some of the oldest in North America—also provide challenging hills and winding city streets, perfect for serious road trippers. In some areas, the street grade is ski-slope steep, however, so use extreme caution when driving in winter.

The city had French *voyageurs* poking around it as far back as the late seventeenth century. Daniel de Greysolon, Sieur du Lhute—note the title—showed up in 1679, landing at Minnesota Point. Duluth's namesake helped establish the town as a crucial conduit for the northern Great Lakes' traders and trappers. Oddly enough, however, this flurry of activity didn't prompt permanent settlement until the 1850s.

Start your tour in downtown Duluth at the *Duluth Convention and Visitors Bureau (DCVB)* information office. One of three tourist offices in the downtown area, this one (Endion Station) is located at 100 Lake Place Drive, (218) 722-1322 or (800) 4-DULUTH (www.visitduluth.com), where Canal Park begins to jut into Lake Superior. The chatty and helpful folks can provide you with the highly useful "History of the Skyline Parkway". Other nearby offices are located opposite the Duluth Entertainment Convention Center (the

The Hardest-Working Harbor on the Lakes

The city, the harbor, an overlooked river valley—all linked topographically and historically in Duluth. Visitors certainly can't miss what gave rise to the city's early—and continuing—success. The gaping harbor leads to Lake Superior and, thus, to most of the planet's waterways via the 2,342-mile-long Great Lakes/Saint Lawrence Seaway. (Duluth has a foreign-trade zone run by the Port Authority of Duluth). Northwest of the city are some of the world's richest iron ranges. Leading in interlake cargoes of iron, grain, coal and stone, these resources help make Duluth-Superior the top-volume port on the Great Lakes, with a total of $250 million in annual economic impact—not shabby for a couple of small towns with fewer than 150,000 people between them. (Perhaps this would help explain why Duluth once was home to more millionaires per capita than any other city in the world.) Over 1,000 ocean-going and Great Lakes freighters call at the Twin Ports annually.

View of Duluth's harbor and Aerial Lift Bridge from Skyline Drive. Thomas Huhti

arena-looking structure) and in the Depot (see below).

In summer, Duluth's downtown trolley service makes visiting top attractions much easier. Visitor offices provide maps, trolley stop location information, and up-to-the-minute lowdown on fares.

Leave the DCVB office and walk to the pathway skirting the harbor. This 4-mile-long walk takes in a host of attractions that show what the city has to offer. If you head east, you'll pass the *Duluth Sculpture Garden,* which features works from sister cities in Sweden, Russia, Canada, and Japan. Farther along, you'll come to *Leif Erikson Park,* with its resplendent gardens, including 40,000 lushly colored roses, and the *Northland Vietnam Veterans Memorial.*

Backtracking westward, take the lake walk along more stone-and-sand beaches. The walk leads to one of the town's biggest draws, the *Duluth Canal,* which lake- and ocean-going ore carriers navigate several times daily. Show up just about anytime and you'll find one of these behemoths sliding along the canal, like a floating skyscraper, awaiting the famed *Aerial Lift Bridge* to rise. The carriers announce their arrival with an earth-shaking horn blow, giving bystanders an added rush of excitement.

Ship-spotting can be a contagious diversion and a cool road trip hobby. Educate yourself on ship types and find out how and when to greet arriving ships by picking up a copy of the *Duluth Shipping News* at one of the area's several visitor information centers.

At the western end of the canal, at the entrance to the lift bridge, sits another major draw for lake lovers. The *Lake Superior Maritime Visitor Center,* (218) 727-2497, offers an outstanding way to survey the history and economics of Great Lakes' shipping. Among the featured subjects are the U.S. Army Corps of Engineers and its Herculean efforts to tame the harbor. Mock-ups and replicas of ships and shipboard life allow for grand wandering; engineering types will enjoy the functional steam engine. The center is open from Memorial Day weekend to Labor Day daily, 10 a.m.–9 p.m., reduced off-season hours; free admission.

Just north and west of the Maritime Visitor Center is the *Minnesota Slip Drawbridge.* Interested in fishing? Walk north to the charter fishing marina, where you'll find a host of charter boat captains eager to take you out on the lake for some unforgettable fishing.

On the marina's west side sits the gargantuan and silent *William A. Irvin,* (218) 722-7876. Once the flagship of U.S. Steel's Great Lakes "Silver Stack" fleet, this ore boat carried luminaries and industry heavyweights in addition to its massive daily haul. Everything on the boat has been maintained or reappointed. Tours also include a look at a U.S. Army Corps of Engineers' tugboat. Hours for the *Irvin* are May–October daily; times vary; admission. Adjacent to the ore carrier is Duluth's *Omnimax Theater,* (218) 727-0022, an IMAX dome theater. Check out the combination *Irvin*/Imax tickets.

Another way to soak in the pleasures of Lake Superior is a sightseeing tour. For tickets, head south to the *Duluth Entertainment Convention*

Center (DECC)—the ticket office and departure point for the *Vista Fleet* Sightseeing Tours, (218) 722-6218. Daily trips are offered mid-May to late October. When your boat glides under the *Aerial Lift Bridge* en route to the heart of the harbor, have your camera ready. In one grand sweep you take in grain elevators, ore docks, massive ships, tugboats—the whole parade that is a busy Great Lakes port. You can also choose to go on a lunch or dinner cruise. The Sunday "Fun Cruise," serving pizza and sundaes, is a real kid-pleaser. Overall, food is great, but hope for calm conditions.

After returning to land, head west on the boardwalk to Duluth's second major waterfront attraction: the *Great Lakes Aquarium*, 353 Harbor Drive, (218) 740-FISH (www.glaquarium.org), in Bayfront Festival Park. With more than 70 species of freshwater fish—native and exotic—on permanent display, the Great Lakes Aquarium is the country's only all-freshwater aquarium.

The aquarium's hands-on displays give kids of all ages a wet—and fun—source of learning. Visitors can dunk themselves in some of the aquarium's 120,000 gallons of watery exhibits. One of the most popular is the "Sensory Immersion Experience."

Perhaps the most educational for everyone are the five habitat exhibits based on locations around Lake Superior, from Isle Royale to Pictured Rocks (Michigan)—an excellent slice of the lake's natural history. A laundry list of other participatory exhibits is also available. Hours are Memorial Day weekend to mid-September, Monday–Thursday, 9 a.m.–9 p.m.; Friday–Sunday, until 6 p.m.; reduced off-season; admission.

A new highlight located diagonally from the aquarium is the *Lois Palucci Pavilion* in Bayfront Festival Park. This littoral natural amphitheater has wonderful views—not just of the musical acts that pop up regularly, but also of the massive ships drifting by.

Head north a few blocks across I-35 to Duluth's downtown, in the vicinity of West Michigan and Superior Streets. You can get there easily from the aquarium either on foot (it's a 10-minute walk) or in a vehicle. From the harbor area, you can hop a trolley up to Superior and Michigan Streets, the city's main drags. The crown jewel of non-water-oriented activities in this section of town is *The Depot*, (218) 733-7590, 506 West Michigan Street. This lovingly refurbished old railroad hub is home to the *Saint Louis County Heritage and Arts Center* and the wonderful *Lake Superior Railroad Museum*. The latter features the Midwest's largest collection of historic railroad engines and memorabilia, including one of the world's largest steam locomotives. Don't miss the oldest-known steam rotary snowplow; no others are known to be extant. Also impressive is *Depot Square*, a life-sized mock-up of downtown Duluth, circa 1910. The *Duluth Art Institute* features rotat-

ing exhibits in art galleries as well as performances by the Duluth Playhouse. The entire complex is well worth a visit. Hours are Memorial Day to Labor Day daily, 9:30 a.m.–6 p.m.; reduced off-season hours; admission.

The Depot is also the departure point for another grand transportation-oriented trip: the 1.5- to 6-hour tours aboard the *North Shore Scenic Railroad*, (218) 722-1273 or (800) 423-1273. You chug out of the station aboard vintage coaches pulled by early-model diesel engines and skirt the Lake Superior shoreline heading toward the majestic North Woods region. Shorter trips head to the Lester River area. If you splurge for the longer trip, you'll take in the Two Harbors area.

Recharge yourself—and fuel yourself for more exploration—in Duluth's trim downtown district, east of the Depot. With its funkily anachronistic red-brick streets and fully enclosed walkways (for those winters, doncha know), it makes for a fun day of browsing in shops and sampling the cuisine at a host of cozy eateries.

From the area in downtown Duluth near Michigan and Superior Streets, go to West 1st Street, which is also State Highway 23; turn southwest on 23 and take it for approximately 14 miles to Highway 210, passing through West Duluth and Fond du Lac and following the frequent signs to *Jay Cooke State Park*. Turn right on 210 and follow it to the park. Jay Cooke is a jewel for road trippers in search of a lovely beginning to a drive. Its *Rushing Waters* (or *Rushing Rapids*) *Parkway* winds its 9-mile way through the park's verdance and ancient river valley topography—root beer-colored water slashes through multi-epoched rock beds, highlighted by one enormous gorge. Nearly 50 miles of hiking trails and 13 miles of biking trails allow for a

day-trip or even multi-day explorations; several trails lead to a photo-op-worthy swing suspension bridge, likely one of the most popular spots for Duluth-area shutterbugs. Thomson Cemetery is a short walk off Highway 210 and is historically interesting. Carlton at the western end of the park has canoe outfitters. The rapids of the Saint Louis River are so challenging that whitewater competitions here are used as qualifying events for international competitions.

For the exercise-challenged, take the Willard Munger State Trail from Jay Cooke to West Duluth (access at Indian Point Park, Grand Avenue at 75th Street W). It's 14 miles of gently sloping pavement, perfect for a slow bike ride or challenging walk. Along the path one can see residuals of devastating early twentieth-century forest conflagrations.

Quick Trip Option 1: Jay Cooke State Park's Rushing Rapids Parkway can be combined with the longer *Veterans Evergreen Memorial Highway* to provide a picturesque jaunt all the way to Askov, about 50 miles to the southwest. The trip is notable because it's bookended by two great state parks: Jay Cooke and Banning. Follow Highway 23 south from its intersection with Highway 210, and you'll see why it's often described as the "scenic route to Duluth." The namesake evergreens were planted along the highway as a lasting tribute to fallen U.S. soldiers, but you'll also find tracts of maples and other hardwoods.

A heady mix of Scandinavian ethnicity is also apparent on the route: Askov was settled by Danish immigrants, and the town still sports its heritage on shop signs and architecture. The cheery burg was long known as the Midwest's rutabaga production center, but became even more legendary as one of the country's most successful examples of a co-operative community; it was carefully platted and organized, and its cultural folkways school preserved Danish heritage in the newly settled U.S. And it was purportedly so polite that they never bothered to build a jail!

Among the other flyspeck towns on the route—most under 100 in population—*Kerrick* was most recently highlighted nationally, used by Hollywood filmmakers to shoot parts of *Iron Will* and *Far North.* Show up on a Sunday and be bumper to bumper with other leaf-peepers or wearied urban escapists. At the Banning State Park end, type-T personalities will be happy. In addition to the park's hiking, river fishing, and canoeing opportunities, kayakers love the Kettle River and its Hell's Gate rapids. (Know what you're doing before you try this.) For less adrenaline-inducing endeavors, streams and creeks criss-cross the route, and you'll find some blue ribbon-quality trout fishing (particularly the Nemadji and South Fork Rivers near Jay Cooke State Park). Also near Jay Cooke is the *Veteran's Memorial Overlook,* with a breathtaking vista of the Saint Louis River Valley.

From Jay Cooke State Park, go east on Highway 210 and take it back to Highway 23. Continue east, then north, for about 3 miles to Gary Street. Turn left (west) and go 1 mile to Beck's Road. Turn right (north) and drive 2 miles to the western end of the *Skyline Parkway.* Turn right and proceed for about 5 miles to I-35. The roadway leaving Jay Cooke State Park is a slight letdown, scenery-wise, compared to the park's charming, churlish waters, swaying bridges, and dense carpets of greenery. However, as the road approaches the Skyline Parkway, it begins to loop, doing sworls around hillocks that seem to be growing by the minute and skirting Ely's Peak. You pass through Magney Park and Snively Park—forests, really, in the midst of a city. You then begin to get peeks of Lake Superior, a comforting sight.

Cross I-35 and stop at the *Thompson Hill Visitor Information Center on the frontage road.* This facility, (218) 723-4938, just north of the interstate, has a staff that must have PhDs in Skyline Parkway tourist assistance. And clean restrooms, too!

Follow the frontage road across U.S. Highway 2 and proceed up the hill. After 1 mile, at a five-way stop, take the second road to the right. A little less than 1 mile later, follow 40th Avenue as it links with the Skyline Parkway. The parkway is a treasure by any standard. It's supposedly only 30 miles long, but this author has never used fewer than 40 tracing its length. The road's quality is as varied as the views it offers: Narrow grade in disrepair in some spots and smooth, wide, blacktop in others, with, every minute or so, delightful sights or fork-in-the-road explorations. The road affords you amazing Lake Superior vistas, what with the 600-foot promontories every which way. But you should also be on the lookout for wildlife: bear, deer, and even the occasional moose are found up this way—within the city limits! The parkway is marked by signs, yet some of them are small and easy to miss, while a few others are missing. Be prepared to backtrack or ask directions; but isn't that, after all, part of the fun?

Observation points are offered at regular intervals and offer breathtaking views; make sure to avail yourself of each of them. *Gitchegumee* is not the only highlight: Some little ribbony side roads lead to nearly-hidden rock canyons with gurgling streams, and even the odd cascade or two.

By way of a little parkway background, in the 1870s, enthusiastic city planners envisioned a pair of parallel parks along the lakeshore and Duluth's natural terrace, both linked regularly by existing ravines and creek beds. Yet, somehow, it took until the summer of 1929 until the upper parkway, as it exists today, was completed and christened. The parallel parks idea really never reached fruition until the downtown lake walk was constructed, about 100 years later than the early visionaries had anticipated, but splendid timing for us.

Once on the Skyline Parkway, jog to your right almost immediately. Keep going to another multi-street intersection and proceed straight ahead to *Enger Park*. The highlight of Enger Park—indeed of any spin along the Skyline Parkway—is *Enger Tower.* Overlooking the harbors, it was dedicated by Crown Prince Olav of Norway in 1939. A Japanese temple bell and flower gardens in a riot of color surround the 75-foot-tall tower, along parkland stretching toward the water. Officials report that the view from atop the tower is a whopping 31.4 miles on a clear day; ship captains still use the light beam atop the tower as a navigation aid. By the way, Enger Park also has a public golf course—and a good one at that—one reason why *Golf Digest* rated Duluth the country's number-one place for public golf.

Be forewarned that roads in the Enger Park area seem to split off in all directions. But that's a good thing, because you'll have a chance to explore to your heart's content, wowed by some lovely views no matter which way you go.

After circling the tower area, take the Y-intersection to the right; eventually you should wind up at Mesaba Avenue. Turn left, continue through the stoplight, then turn right immediately. Proceed through the Chester Park district to 19th Avenue E; take a left here and go to the four-way stop at College Street. Turn right on College and go on to Woodland Avenue. Turn left again and continue to Snively Road. Along the way, in the area around College Street and Woodland Avenue, you'll see not one but two institutions of higher learning: the College of Saint Scholastica and the University of Minnesota-Duluth. On the UMD campus is the *Tweed Museum of Art,* (218) 726-8222, with nine galleries of modern and historical art (pieces date from the sixteenth century). The Tweed museum is especially well-known for its international ceramics. The facility makes for a nice leg-stretch during the drive. Hours are Tuesday, 9 a.m.–8 p.m., Wednesday–Friday, 9 a.m.–4:30 p.m., and weekends 1-5 p.m.; admission.

Return to the Woodland Avenue and Snively Road intersection. Turn right and continue to Glenwood Avenue; turn right, take a quick veer left, and go for about a mile to *Hawk Ridge Nature Preserve*. This observation point could well be the most sublime part of the trip. Because Hawk Ridge acts as a natural funnel for tens of thousands of migratory birds, it's aptly named: The birds, which loathe to fly over open water, waft their way along the bluff line, all channeling to this point. The eponymous raptors get all the glory, but you'll also find eagles—lots of

Enger Tower on the bluffs overlooking Duluth. Thomas Huhti

them at times—and every other imaginable bird of prey. No wonder, then, that the place is dubbed "hawk highway" during migration seasons. It also explains the National Audubon Society's fascination for the place.

Leave Hawk Ridge on Skyline Parkway and return to Glenwood; turn left and drive about 2 miles to Occidental Boulevard (sometimes known as the Seven Bridges Road). Turn right and continue to Superior Street; turn right and drive a short distance to 60th Avenue E. Turn left and go a block down to London Road; drive about 4 miles to Glensheen. This is the grand dame of Duluth's extant millionaire residences, 3300 London Road, (218) 726-8910 or (888) 454-GLEN. Known as Congdon

Mansion, this seven-acre estate features a 39-room Jacobean-style home with original furnishings and detail. If not taking an informative guided tour, the grounds make for a lovely stroll with their manicured lawns and artist's-palette colored flower gardens. Hours are summer daily 9:30 a.m.–4 p.m., reduced off-season hours; admission. Before you reach Glensheen, and if you need additional travel information, stop at the North Shore Association information booth on London Road. It's a tiny building, but the staff makes up for it in friendliness and helpfulness.

Quick Trip Option 2: Pity poor Superior, Wisconsin, the topographically challenged little sibling to postcard-quality Duluth. Local citizens deny any inferiority complex over being pretty much ignored by road trippers whipping through to take in Duluth's magnificent bluffs and harbor. In fact, the residents of the little city with the grand name should feel proud of its attractions. Superior is easily accessed from Duluth via the U.S. Highway 53/I-535 bridge over the harbor; then exit and follow 53 as it traces the water.

Just past the Highway 2 junction, look to the left for a jetty of land and one huge boat. That land would be *Barker's Island,* the nucleus of Superior's shipping heritage. The island has lodgings, eateries, a marina, and walking paths, but the highlight is the *SS Meteor*—(715) 392-5742 or (800) 942-5313—a maritime museum of gigantic proportions. This is the only remaining whaleback freighter of the type Superior's shipyards developed and built in the city's early shipyards, and is a direct progenitor of the beasts that power through the Great Lakes today. Tours are offered mid-May to late September, daily 10 a.m.–5 p.m., until 6 p.m. in July; admission. The marina at Barker's Island also offers sightseeing boat trips around the harbor.

The most recent addition to the island's growing list of attractions is the *Richard I. Bong World War II Heritage Center,* at the junction of Highways 2 and 53, near the Barker's Island entrance. Bong was a local boy (from Poplar, Wisconsin, not far from Superior) who shot down a remarkable 40 Japanese planes in his P-38 Lightning (nicknamed *Marge*) in the Pacific, earning the moniker "Ace of Aces." Long

neglected, the plane has been refurbished and will be located at the new heritage center, which will also house a World War II historical display.

Across Highway 2/53 sits *Fairlawn Mansion,* (715) 394-5712, 906 East Second Street, an eye-catching Victorian crown jewel. The 42-room cornerstone of local tourism features detailed period furnishings and appointments—even the carvings and etchings were painstakingly redone. Hours are year-round daily 9 a.m.–5 p.m.; admission.

Superior may look somewhat drab compared to Duluth, but it actually bests everybody else in the country in terms of green space within the city limits. That's right: *Superior's municipal forest* is believed to be the largest urban expanse of public land in the U.S. To get there from the Old Firehouse Museum, backtrack on Highway 2/53 to 28th Street, and turn left. After about 4.5 miles, you will reach the forest and, ultimately, winding Billings Drive, which traces the edge of the forest and overlooks the Saint Louis River Valley. Great picnicking, hiking, dog jogs, and naps.

Superior—well, actually Douglas County—boasts a couple of dramatic waterfalls that are well worth a visit. (Northwestern Wisconsin can lay claim to being the state's unofficial waterfall capital. The state's northeastern quadrant has the numerical superiority, but this area wins the crown based on aesthetics and sheer majesty.)

One of the best is at *Amnicon Falls State Park,* approximately 12 miles southeast of Superior via Highway 2. Also, include time to visit to *Pattison State Park,* located a little more than 10 miles south of the city along Wisconsin Highway 35. To get there from the municipal forest, head east on 28th Street to Tower Avenue and turn right. This splendid park is home to the epic 165-foot Big Manitou Falls, the highest waterfall in Wisconsin, and one of the highest east of the Mississippi River. With the whitewater juxtaposed against the fall's black rocks, it makes for awesome photos. The park is also home to 10 miles of great hiking trails and a backpacking camp area. If you do hike, you may be blessed enough to spy a timber wolf.

From Glensheen, turn left onto London Road and drive about 3.5 miles to downtown Duluth, where this tour began.

Tour 2
Mines and Pines:
The Lower North Shore

Duluth—French River—Knife River—Two Harbors—Cloquet Valley State Forest—Fond du Lac State Forest—Cloquet—Duluth

Distance: approximately 150 miles

From Duluth, the scenery turns downright breathtaking along, as Bob Dylan droned, "Highway 61." The North Shore's south shore is, in fact, a national treasure—a federally-designated "All American Road."

Though private property does, of course, exist, travelers will happily note the relative dearth of fenced-off or prohibitively signed land along this picturesque route. It's fairly easy to sniff out a path down to the lake to skip some stones or get your feet wet (Signs or no signs, however, curious travelers should always explore with care.)

Virtually every 300 yards there's a stop-off for a scenic view, a county park/wayside, fishing access, paved bikeways, a gorgeous lighthouse, hiking trails, canoe routes. The sights seemingly never end.

Sadly, nobody gets *off* this road. The main road to Little Marais is now a whooshing, efficient artery in the beginning, but the old Minnesota Highway 61 is still there and makes for a great side road tracing the coast. The back route into the interior along Highway 1 to the tiny town of Finland rivals this, taking travelers to a wonderfully quaint anachronism populated by settlers who *didn't* follow the masses into the mines and instead logged and farmed. Here also are our first tastes of Minnesota's epic swaths of forested green.

The tail end of the tour gives a taste of what attracted immigrants to Minnesota's arrowhead region: timber and rivers. West of Duluth is a region that gets a bad rap ("On a bad day you can smell Cloquet," a Duluth local once remarked). Yeah, it may not be eye candy, but it is historically and economically relevant. And it gives travelers a glimpse into what's ahead.

Start your tour in Duluth, at the Lake Superior North Shore Association information booth, where Highway 61 (London Road) meets Lester River Road. Located on the far eastern edge of Duluth, this facility is open seasonally. For more information, check www.northshore scenicdrive.com

Drive northeast on Highway 61 for less than 7 miles to *French River*. When Highway 61 splits into two separate roads soon after you've left the information center, keep right and head to "old" Highway 61, bypassing the newfangled swoosh of the four-lane monstrosity that starts kicking up dust a handful of miles northeast of the city limits. Longer? Perhaps, but along the way you take in the wonderful smells of the lake breeze, rows of smoked fish houses, mom-and-pop shops, and infinitely less stress. As you drive, make a stop at *Brighton Beach* and *Kitchi Gammi Park*, where you'll get your first real glimpses of the rugged and rocky shoreline that defines Lake Superior.

As you travel north, you'll see more growling surf, a trio of roadside pull-offs (one with facilities), the odd hole-in-the-wall shop and, ultimately, shoreline fishing access in French River; this is also a fine place to access the shoreline. This diminutive community also has a *DNR state fish hatchery*, and impromptu tours can be arranged weekdays.

Continue northeast on Highway 61 for about 2 miles to Bluebird Landing. This public access, prior to the Sucker River, offers great Lake Superior shoreline access. *Tom's Logging Camp*, (218) 525-4120, 5797 North Shore Drive, recreates life of more than a century ago with replica buildings of a nineteenth-century northern Minnesota logging camp. Most of the tools and equipment are authentic, having been scavenged and saved from regional homesteads. Kids love the pygmy goats and tame deer and, if not, tire them out on the short nature trail. Hours are May–October, daily; hours vary; admission.

But the highlight is directly across the road from Tom's Logging Camp. *Stoney Point* is likely the most superb beachcombing spot along the southern North Shore. Take the mile-long loop roadside trip; it's great for a picnic (unless the wind is howling).

Proceed northeast on Highway 61 for 3 miles to Knife River. Along the way, Buchanan Wayside offers easy beach access to the lakeshore. Knife River is a pleasant understated village just off the expressway. Want to land a big one? The *Knife River Marina* offers charter fishing tours. May through mid-July you can surface fish for lake trout, steelhead, and salmon; eventually, the boats follow the migrating salmon as they swim their

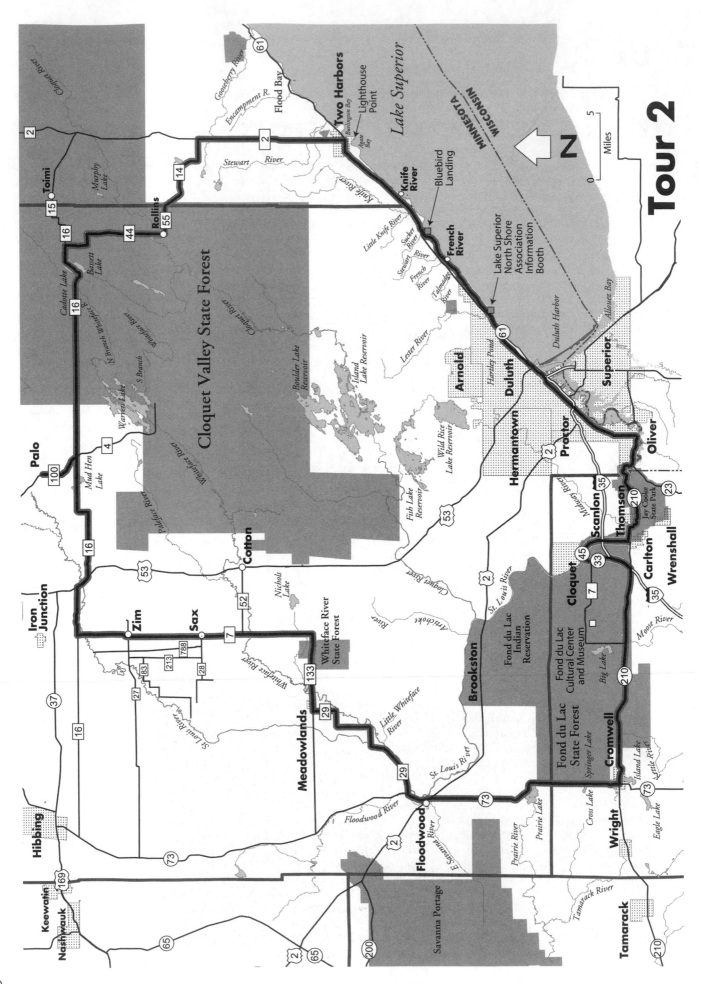

way north. In August and September you can count on big king salmon and lake trout. Knife River is worth the trip, just for the smoked fish. Because of the Knife River's outstanding spring trout fishing—and awesome smelt fishing—the community is heralded as the smoked fish capital of the North Shore. Pick up some savory fish, then bop down to the agate beach to wander about.

Continue northeast for another 8 miles into Two Harbors and the *R. J. Houle Information Center.* The center, (218) 834-4005 (www.two harbors.com), is just northeast of downtown, on Burlington Bay, a block north of the intersection of Highway 61 and 6th Street (also County Road 2). Also, the chamber of commerce's main office is located nearby at 603 East 7th Avenue, (800) 777-7384 or (218) 834-2600. These information centers are particularly good resources if you're interested in spending the evening at one of the numerous local inns, resorts, B&Bs, or motels.

Rolling in, gaze upon the gargantuan jutting finger of an ore dock just south of town. The No. 1 dock in Two Harbors was once among the world's largest at over 1,300 feet long, and it was from here that the very first shipment of iron ore left Minnesota.

From the R. J. Houle Information Center, head a short distance to Waterfront Drive (it was once called 6th Street) and turn left (south) on the less-than-2-mile-long scenic byway (marked by signs) along the harbor.

Two Harbors Happenings

You never lack for something to see or do north of Duluth. May's fishing opener brings loads of wide-eyed landlubbers hoping to bring in a monster lake catch.

Grandma's Marathon in late-June does make it up this far. Mid-July brings Two Harbors' Heritage Days, four days of family-oriented fun. The must-see: the lutefisk toss.

Around the same time, the Lake County Fairgrounds (north of Two Harbors via County Road 2) hosts the Wolf's Head Motorcycle Rally, a weeklong blowout of polite bikers. Lengthy motorcycle tours, smoke shows, bonfires, and the highlight—the bike rodeo. Simultaneous is the Two Harbors Folk Festival. Arts and crafts mix with music; you'll likely wind up dancing a jig.

The Two Harbors Kayak Festival is held in early August. Races are for watching, clinics are for experiencing here. If you know zilch about this cardiac sport, this is the place to learn.

The Two Harbors city band's free concerts, held summer Thursdays at 7:30 p.m. in Owens Park, are absolutely precious. Even more fun may be the ice cream socials that take place just before.

Two Harbors, a town of 3,600, has more than enough sights to take up a morning or afternoon (or, really, day), and most of them are clustered around Agate Bay, one of the two bays that give the town its name.

Probably the best place to begin is at the *Lake County Historical Society depot* (better known as "the Depot"), (218) 834-4898, located along South Avenue, just to the east of Waterfront Drive.

The Edna G., moored in retirement, off Waterfront Drive in Two Harbors. Thomas Huhti

Housed in the former depot for the Duluth and Iron Range Railroad, it's home to, naturally, train artifacts and memorabilia.

The real jaw-dropper, however, is the Mallett, one of the world's most powerful steam locomotives. It's a gargantuan, sweaty-looking thing. The metallic menagerie's other highlight: the first train engine used in the North Shore region. The *North Shore Scenic Railroad* makes a stop here on its trip up the North Shore from Duluth. Hours are May–October, daily, 9 a.m.–5 p.m.; admission.

Just to the southwest of the Depot on Waterfront Drive (a walkable distance) is the retired tugboat *Edna G.*, an I-think-I-can workhorse over a century ago. Christened in 1896, she dutifully served until 1982. The *Edna G.* chugged massive freighters into and out of the ore docks next to which the valiant little boat now rests. She also spent a brief spell guarding U.S. shores on the East Coast during World War II. Tours are offered, generally from Memorial Day to Labor Day, but hours were set to change after publication of this book; admission. If you're here in summers, two days a week the *Grampa Woo*, (218) 226-4100, sightseeing boat departs the dock near this museum for trips to Encampment Island; they depart Thursday and Friday and tickets may be purchased on board or at the Depot museum.

Continuing your trek either by car or foot along Waterfront Drive (which bends to the right), you'll come to the *3M Museum*, (218) 834-4898. Believe it or not, the Minnesota Mining & Manufacturing Company (now 3M, of course) was started here in 1902. The ore the founders expected to unearth turned out to be worthless, and the company nearly went bankrupt right off the bat. Somehow, the company survived. Exhibits and memorabilia from the early years of this Minnesota economic mainstay are in original offices. Open Memorial Day–late October, Monday–Saturday, 9 a.m.–7 p.m., Sunday, 10 a.m.–3 p.m.; admission.

Your trip along the bay culminates at *Lighthouse Point,* at the end of 3rd Street, where you can clamber to the top of one of the oldest lighthouses (built in 1892) on Lake Superior and the only active one on the North Shore. Hours are Monday–Saturday, 9 a.m.–5 p.m., Sunday 10 a.m.–3 p.m., Memorial Day weekend to late October; admission. In addition, photo buffs will love the original pictures in the renovated assistant lightkeeper's cabin, which is part of the museum complex. There is even the cozy Lighthouse B&B in the refurbished keeper's quarters. It may well provide the most memorable B&B experience of the tour. And it's available year-round.

Whiskey Row

In a rough-and-tumble land that was northeastern Minnesota, Two Harbors rivaled any other for its, er, entertainment offerings to the hardened immigrants working the land. The environs of Lighthouse Point were known locally as "Whiskey Row," and you can pretty much guess why. Nearly two dozen saloons and dance halls were found here, slaking the thirst and appropriating the payday pennies of hard-working, lonely workers.

From the waterfront, return to Highway 61 and 6th Street (also County Road 2; proceed north on CR 2 for about 10 miles to County Road 14. Before you leave the town limits, on your right is a wonderful 6.2-mile city-maintained *trail complex*. This is the only lighted ski trail complex for over an 18-mile radius. In summer, if you don't mind dodging golf balls (the trails wend through the Lakeview National Golf Course), you can hoof it out into the hills as well.

Once out of Two Harbors, you'll pass over the Gooseberry River and probably notice that the woodland is becoming denser (and the elevation rising). You're splitting two of northeastern Minnesota's seemingly endless tracts of public lands, the Cloquet Valley State Forest to the immediate west and, should you continue north, the Finland State Forest.

At CR 14, turn left (west) and drive for about 10 miles to Rollins (CR 14 changes to County Road 55 in Saint Louis County). Notice the certain rise in elevation here. One may think of Minnesota as relatively flat, but that's a bit misleading. Remember, the Superior Hiking Trail was founded in part to take in the magnificent aeries that this "bluff country" offers. As you wing through the tiny community of Wales, you're at about 1,640 feet above sea level—not Rockies-esque, but impressive—in a Midwest sort of way.

In Rollins, head north on County Road 44 and drive for about 10 miles to County Road 16. Just north of Rollins, in the far northeastern corner of the Cloquet Valley State Forest, you'll find isolated semi-rustic camping. (Another is southwest of town via CR 44.) Campgrounds here are found along the Cloquet River on an established *state canoe route*, so don't be surprised to see a flotilla of canoes strapped to cartops as you explore the area. Campgrounds also have group camp areas, picnic sites and, usually, swimming access with docks. The former Rollins site also has four walk-in campsites for more privacy.

One stretch of County Road 16 is good gravel, though it may be paved by the time you read this. When you end at CR 16, you'll find yet another campground just to the west and still another to the east, just east of Toimi.

Quick Trip Option: If you wish to partake of some of the local Finnish culture (which the area has in abundance), take a quick jog over to Toimi (about 4 miles east of County Road 44 on County Road 16, then 15), and stop by the *Toimi School*. Built in 1913 and home to 100% Finnish culture till its closing in 1942, the school represents a slice of nineteenth-century Finnish-Minnesotan life, when nearly three-quarters of the state's Finns lived in the surrounding areas. Note the decidedly Scandinavian architecture!

At CR 16, turn left (west) and drive for 18 or so miles to County Road 100. Look for the sign to the town of Palo and turn north (right). If you're around in winter, plan to be in the vicinity the first full weekend of February for the wondrous *Laskiiainen*, or Finnish Sliding Festival. The festival's traditional centerpiece: whooshing down huge slides onto an icy lake, all for luck. Legend has it that whoever slid the farthest would be most blessed in the following autumn's harvest. Hard to beat that! Inside the community center you'll also find heritage craft demonstrations and lots of stick-to-your-ribs fare.

Drive south back to CR 16 and continue west. Almost immediately, near the County Road 4 junction, you can get a look at more Minnesota immigrant heritage. The *Eli Wirtanen* farm, (218) 638-2859, was homesteaded in 1904 and all 16 original buildings on site were hand-built by the eponymous bachelor farmer. Self-guided tours are a treat—note the bathhouse, the only "smoke hole" bathhouse in the region (those Finns love their saunas). Open June 1 to early September; hours vary; free.

Continue west on CR 16 for about 12 miles to U.S. Highway 53. The two highways merge for a couple of miles, then 16 turns west again. Take CR 16 for just under 5 miles to County Road 7. Should you need travel information assistance, just south of here on Highway 53 is a Minnesota Travel Information Center.

Turn left (south) on CR 7. Almost immediately the road bisects the Saint Louis River. The topography is a mix of agrarian patchwork and river valley, with town names—Zim and Sax, among others— still reflecting the ethnicity of the founders. Consider a stop anywhere along here on County Roads 28, 788, and/or 213. Any or all will do as the whole region is covered by the wondrously unique *Sax-Zim Bog*, a rarest of the rarities—an accessible conifer bog. The aforementioned county roads criss-cross the soggy landscape and give an outstanding up-close view of the 200-square-mile bog. In the spruce, tamarack, and northern white cedar you can spot great gray owls and pine warblers, among many others. Bring your binoculars. If you're up for it, contact the *DNR Ecologist*, (218) 744-7448, in Eveleth for pointers on how to spot rare bog vegetation or for recent bird sighting information—you won't be sorry!

You may never give diminutive Cotton (just east of CR 7 on County Road 52) a second thought, but if you're here in summer you may be lucky enough to hit the *Minnesota State Old Time Fiddle Championship*, held the fourth weekend of August. Here, foot-stompin' musicians come from all over the world to participate. Even more, the community holds ethnic dances the first weekend of each month, June to October. If this isn't enough, a couple of dog-sled tour operators work out of Cotton, leading mush-trips into the Cloquet Valley State Forest.

Continue south on CR 7 for around 8 miles to County Road 133. Turn west. The landscape turns forested and then, *poof*, the greenery is gone. Yes, you've just crossed into (and out of) the *Whiteface River State Forest,* the state's tiniest—so small that it has no mention in the state's official databases other than, "Yup, there it is."

Continue on County Road 133 for 4.5 miles to County Road 29. Turn left (south) and drive south and west for around 15 miles to State Highway 73. Tracing the Whiteface River (and, on the odd bend or two, the Saint Louis River), the road mirrors the residual geology that carved the region. In Floodwood, the highway cuts across Highway 2—the Great Northern, one of the first ribbony transcontinental highways opening up this great country to auto-borne snoopers. We'll take in delicious samples throughout our tours.

Turn left (south) on Highway 73 and cruise for 19 miles to Cromwell. Turn east (left) onto State Highway 210. Just east of Cromwell sits another thumbnail-sized state forest—*Fond du Lac State Forest*. No facilities for tenters to be found, but two miles east of Cromwell is a wonderful, well-maintained ski trail complex, offering more than 12 miles of groomed cross-country ski trails.

Head east on Highway 210 for 20 or so miles to I-35. Turn north and, after a short distance, get off on State Highway 33, heading into Cloquet. Sometimes, you just can't escape those super-quick, efficient roadways. Thank goodness it lasts just one exit's worth.

On Highway 33, look for Big Lake Road (County Road 7); turn left (west) and go to

Cloquet's Conflagration

Trees and their sundry byproducts have always ruled Cloquet, a sawdust city if ever Minnesota had one. In the mid-twentieth century the city had massive wood processing plants, among the largest in the world.

The region's endless fields of trees have also brought great pain to Cloquet, particularly one warm night in 1918. On October 12, 1918, 70 mph winds fanned localized forest fires—estimates vary from a few dozen to 75—into a massive conflagration that scorched more than 2,000 square miles. Somehow, ferociously hard-working (and quick-thinking) citizens managed to save all but five people in Cloquet (some 400 died regionally). Losses in the region totalled $23 million, astonishing for the time. Phoenixlike, a new city arose from the ashes and was, despite the region's wealth of timber, built mostly from brick.

Frank Lloyd Wright-designed gas station in Cloquet. Tim Bewer

Return to Highway 33 and head north into downtown Cloquet. This diminutive town is often, undeservedly, unconsidered by the city dwellers nearby. Too bad. It's a trim, friendly little place with more attractions than even native Minnesotans seem to know about. East of Cloquet are some picturesque forestland and river valleys along the Saint Louis River. It is also an access point for the long *Willard Munger Bike Trail* (see Tour 1), with bike shops offering rentals downtown. First stop might be at the *Cloquet Area Chamber of Commerce*, 225 Sunnyside Drive, (800) 554-4350 (*www.cloquet.com*). Drive.

Continue to the junction of Highway 33 and State Highway 45. There sits what surprises absolutely every road tripper to the area: the *Frank Lloyd Wright gas station*. Supposedly the only gas station the famed Wisconsin architect ever designed, this working Phillips 66 station (Clindholm Oil) was part of Wright's ambitious "Broadacre"—a grand, utopian community plan, most of which, obviously, went unrealized. Note the second story, designed to be a waiting area (though not used for this). The original design called for overhead fuel lines, which also don't exist. The station, (218) 879-4666, is open to the public, generally daily 7 a.m.–6 p.m., though if a tour group is planning to descend on the place, it'd be nice to ring first (or to check on hours).

One block southeast, Cloquet also has a *county historical center,* (218) 879-1938, with various exhibits and historical items. Don't miss the exhibits detailing the 1918 conflagration which destroyed much of the county (and town). Hours are generally weekdays 9 a.m.–4 p.m.; free.

From Highway 45, travel south through Cloquet to State Highway 210 (about 6 miles). Head east on Highway 210 for about 4 miles to *Jay Cooke State Park*. This park (covered in detail at the end of Tour 1) is a jewel, a sublime way to finish this trip.

the *Fond du Lac Indian Reservation Cultural Center and Museum.* The Fond du Lac reservation, 1720 Big Lake Road, (218) 878-7582, abuts the eponymous state forest to the west, the Saint Louis River to the north, and Cloquet to the east. Established by the La Pointe (Wisconsin) Treaty of 1854, it's one of six Minnesota Ojibwe tribes. The cultural center has an array of historical exhibits and tribal items on display. Call ahead for specific, ongoing exhibits and events. Hours vary.

From Jay Cooke State Park, head east for about 6 miles on Highway 210 to State Highway 23 (Veterans Evergreen Memorial Drive). Follow Highway 23 into downtown Duluth (a total of about 11 miles), where it becomes East 3rd Street. At North 12th Avenue E, turn right, go a few blocks to Highway 61. Turn left and follow Highway 61 (which soon becomes London Road) for about 5 miles back to the North Shore Association information booth and the start of this tour.

Tour 3
Falls, Finns, and The Lighthouse: The Upper North Shore

Two Harbors—Gooseberry Falls State Park—Split Rock Lighthouse State Park—Beaver Bay—
Silver Bay—Tettegouche State Park—Finland—Finland State Forest—Two Harbors

Distance: approximately 120 miles

We see just a sliver of the North Shore on this tour, but what a sliver it is. Quite likely, the stretch of Highway 61 north of Two Harbors to Tettegouche State Park is the most heavily traveled of the entire North Shore, given the popularity of its three superb state parks, including Split Rock Lighthouse State Park, easily the most photographed sight in northeastern Minnesota. We also have the chance to stop off and trace the mouth of the Gooseberry River as it empties sublimely into Lake Superior in a series of cascades. Perhaps the most ambitious and eye-pleasing hikes are found at the last of our state park trio—Tettegouche.

Given the hordes that descend on these parks, you can also count on them to *slow traffic down* (nearly to a crawl) at times, so do take care when driving. Always expect a lighthouse peeker to be stopped around the next curve, or camera-laden tourists paying more attention to the vistas than oncoming traffic.

After the strenuous park-hopping, we finish with a stroll into Minnesota's ethnic heritage. Center stage are the sturdy Finns, who settled the country in search of the epic forest tracts, which lured so many northern Europeans in the nineteenth century. We'll be just a couple dozen miles away from Lake Superior, but the roads narrow, the tree density leaps upward, and, at times, it will feel as though we're rolling through land that time forgot.

From Two Harbors, head northeast on Highway 61 for just over 1 mile. Again, it's hard not to keep the right eye pegged on the steely waters of Lake Superior. Almost immediately, pull off at the *Flood Bay State Wayside Rest Area.* Here you'll find a picnic area and a gravel beach, awash with colorful stones, agates, and driftwood; the rock-hounding here is some of the North Shore's best. (Hint: This is a great way to occupy the kiddies.)

Continue northeast on Highway 61 for approximately 5 miles to *Silver Creek Cliff.* Sweeping upward on your left—it seems as if from nowhere—is a granite escarpment, clearly touting its glacial history. Today the 1,400-foot-long Silver Creek Tunnel whooshes travelers efficiently (but spectacularly nonetheless) through this sheer precipice. From this cliff face, Lake Superior extends nearly *400 miles* to the east (drivers, keep your eyes on the road; passengers, ogle at will). In 1679, Daniel de Greysolon, Sieur Duluth, passed by here. Later that century, Marquette would land at the Apostle Islands (in Wisconsin, 34 miles east), which you can also see from here on a clear day. The original roadway was breathtaking—both for its beauty and its dangerous edge. Nature eroded the thin, adrenaline-inducing ribbon, so highway engineers blasted the new, safer tunnel.

Continue on Highway 61 for about 3 miles. Here, you'll pass over the *Encampment River*, which shares its name with the surrounding forest, part of which was saved a half century ago by landowners who, perhaps prescient to the North Shore's potential (or to the rapid development quickly encroaching), refused to allow their lands to be logged. Nearby is the imposing *Lafayette Bluff*, with another take-your-breath-away drop down to Superior's icy waters. A steamer of the same name was wrecked here in 1905, and, gazing at the ominous waters below, it's no surprise why. Here, too, Highway 61 had to be tunneled out of million-year-old volcanic formation. Perhaps not quite as road-warrioresque, but certainly safer.

Drive northeast for 6 more miles to *Gooseberry Falls State Park.* Along the way, you'll pass the tiny community of Castle Danger, which shares its name with another marine tragedy. The ship *Castle* was wrecked on reefs near shore, giving the point its name. The area features well-placed rest facilities and, despite the name, plenty of ship traffic can be seen from the road.

Three miles beyond that is the first of the road trippers' North Shore grails—*Gooseberry Falls State Park*, (218) 834-3855. It boasts nearly 1,700 acres of forest—on both sides of the highway—and offers tough beach walks along Lake Superior, rolling forestlands heavy on aspen and birch, and, best of all, five Gooseberry River waterfalls near its mouth along Gooseberry Gorge. Historic stone and Depression-era log structures built by the Civilian Conservation Corps dot the park's interiors along the many hiking trails. The

Agate Hounding
Those who don't know a stone from a rock can still have fun rock-hounding on the North Shore. Agates are plentiful in these parts and rightfully legendary. Just look for the reddish-orange stones with white bands!

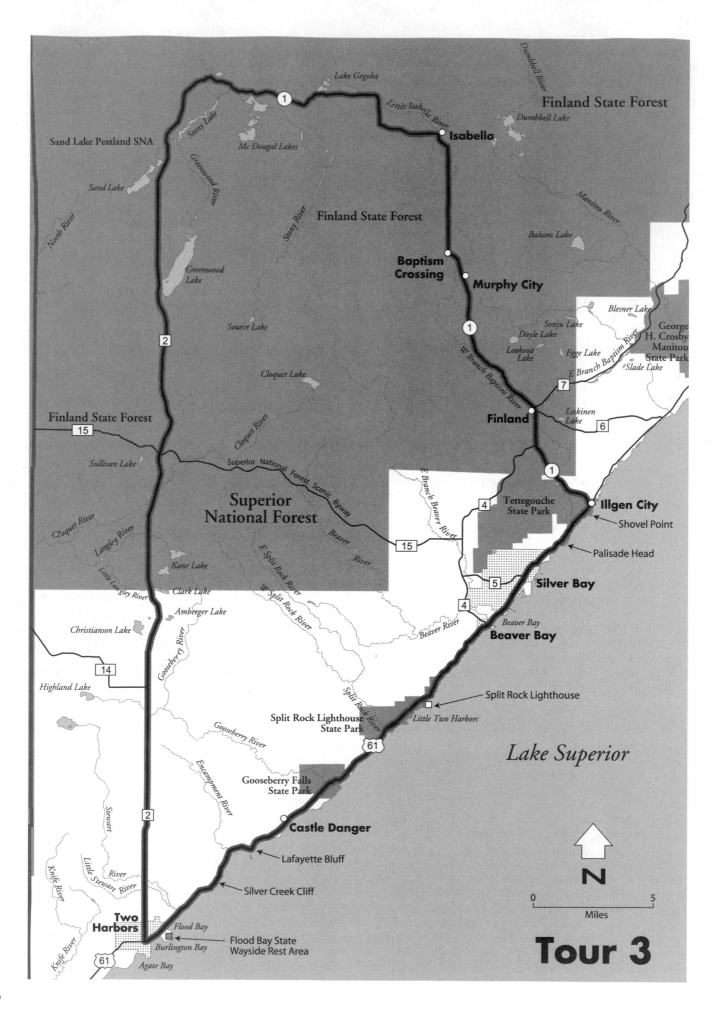

Tour 3

Superior Hiking Trail also makes an appearance, connecting a couple of the cascades. Mountain bikes are welcome along some trails. The 70 campsites are popular but, outside of weekends, you can often find a spot to pitch a tent. The interpretive center should be your first stop, with displays on the natural history of the park and loads of practical information.

Continue on Highway 61 for 7 miles to *Split Rock Lighthouse State Park.* Get your camera ready. Then prepare to go shoulder-to-shoulder—friendly jostling isn't unheard of on particularly crowded holiday weekends—for *the* photo-op of the North Shore: Split Rock Lighthouse, (218) 226-6377. This little structure was among the U.S. lighthouses memorialized on postage stamps in the early 1990s (not bad for a lakeside location). The station was built in 1910 atop a 130-foot promontory (supposedly the geology in the area screwed up mariners' compasses) and, to this day, retains a dignified, workmanlike air. Costumed guides lead wide-eyed tourists around the light keeper's house, the fog-signal building and, naturally, the lighthouse itself.

Spanning 2,000-plus acres around is the state park of the same name. The park features a small but lovely campground, 12 miles of hiking trails (including a chunk of the Superior Hiking Trail), and 8 miles of cross-country ski trails. Mountain bikes are also allowed on some trails. All allow access to the breathtaking shoreline and picnic areas. Given the curious hordes who visit the lighthouse, it's remarkable how few of them actually visit the surrounding parklands.

The park is also a work in progress. Most recently, Gold Rock Point was purchased and added to the park. It allows visitors to get close to the site where the *Madeira* and five other ships sank (nearly 30 more were damaged) in a frightful storm in 1905—prompting the building of the lighthouse. The state is in constant negotiations to add contiguous sections of land of natural or historical importance.

The park's annual *Open House* in early June is a perfect time to visit. From 9 a.m. to 6 p.m., the park is free and welcomes visitors with (also gratis) tours of the light stations, films detailing local history, and many exhibits. The park also hosts a free Children's Day (well, mom and dad pay; kids 12 and under get in free) a couple weeks later.

Continue northeast on Highway 61 for 5 miles to Beaver Bay. One of the oldest towns along the North Shore, phlegmatic Beaver Bay was, prior to the Civil War, the sole remaining community between Duluth and Grand Portage. The other towns couldn't ride out the lean years. This scrappy little town, however, buckled down and hung on. The town boasts an Indian cemetery with the grave of John Beargrease, a legendary Native American mail carrier (he inspired Duluth's eponymous sled dog marathon festival). Fish lovers

Perhaps the most photographed lighthouse in the Midwest—Split Rock Lighthouse. Tim Bewer

flock here for the smelt runs; don't miss spring's (dates vary) famed smelt fry. Delicious!

Beaver Bay is also the departure point for the *Grampa Woo* excursion boat, (218) 226-4100. Scenic cruises run late June to Labor Day to Split Rock Lighthouse and just north to Palisade Head, the latter among the most impressive geological sights on the North Shore. It sits 315 (or so) feet above Lake Superior atop a sheer precipice, the face of which is speckled by an array of hues—highlighted magnificently by the late-morning sun. Tours are offered daily except Thursday and Friday (when they leave from Two Harbors) at noon. A host of other options are available, including dinner cruises, nighttime Split Rock Lighthouse pass-

Baptism River Falls at Tettegouche State Park. Thomas Huhti

bys (once per summer), trips to Thunder Bay, Ontario, even scuba diving trips.

Continue on Highway 61 for another 3 miles to Silver Bay. Drivers, keep your eyes on the road. Everybody else, try to spot Wisconsin's Apostle Islands for the next dozen miles—if the day is clear enough. The views are spectacular from your lofty highway perch. These are the *Lake Superior palisades*, which stretch nearly 40 miles. The crown jewel of the aeries is Palisade Head, northeast of Silver Bay on Highway 61, where you can drive up, park, and walk a mere 25 feet to a spectacular view of, it seems, the entire world.

Whereas Beaver Bay boasts a long and storied history, Silver Bay claims the distinction of being the youngest North Shore community (dating from as far back as 1954). It owes its existence to taconite mining. While trolling around town, you'll spot a statue devoted to taconite ore and a tiny *history center.* Hours vary, but if it's open, do stop in and get directions to the many walking/hiking trails in the area; many offer commanding views of the lake and beyond. Also, ask if *Northshore Mining* is offering its occasional tours.

Sport fishing is big in these parts as well. A few charter operations will take you out on *Gitchegumee* to try to land a trophy. Generally, most operate out of Two Harbors or Knife River, but in the last two weeks of July, a couple relocate operations here to surface fish for trout and salmon.

Quick Trip Option: In Silver Bay you have a lovely option that will afford you the chance to travel the *Superior National Forest Scenic Byway*, a recently established state scenic road that links this tour with the Iron Range (Tours 8 and 9) in Aurora. Along this 54-mile route, you'll find oodles of lovely places at which to stop and gawk or walk. From Silver Bay, just follow the signs, starting at County Road 5, west to County Road 4, north to County Road 15, west to County Road 16, to County Road 110. Glorious scenery is evident everywhere along the route, but highlights are found mostly near the western end in Aurora. (See Tour 9 for details).

From Aurora, you can leave this tour and venture out on your own. Or you can return to Silver Bay the way you came. If you choose the latter, allow plenty of time to get back. You'll no doubt want to stop at sights you didn't catch the first time.

From Silver Bay, continue on Highway 61 for 4 miles to *Tettegouche State Park.* The scenery along this stretch of road gets more topographically challenging with every mile. Then, you'll soon arrive at another tour "must-see": Tettegouche State Park, (218) 226-6365, may offer the widest array of sights along the North Shore, most centered on the fast-flowing Baptism River. Consider the options: *Baptism River Falls* (one of the highest in the state); four wilderness lakes; and 22 miles of trails (including, once again, the Lake Superior Hiking Trail). The trails' semi-mountainous terrain is challenging for those needing exercise, but not too difficult for day-hikers.

The highlight for scenery-seekers is *Shovel Point,* located nearly 200 feet above the lapping lake. The picturesque promontory can be accessed via many area trails. This bedrock on a sheer declivity formed when lava steamed out and formed the Sawtooth Mountains and the entire North Shore. History buffs adore the isolated extant logging camp on *Mic Mac Lake*; these four cabins are tough to get to, but they can be rented and what an awesome place to sleep! Even a short mountain biking trail is here. Campers love Tettegouche. In addition to the one established campground, you'll find a kayak campsite.

From Tettegouche State Park, head northeast on Highway 61 a short distance to Minnesota Highway 1. Turn left (north) and cruise for about 12 miles to the small community of Finland. At the junction of Highways 61 and 1, Illgen City beckons motorists with a sign that says, "Illgen City: Population 4, room for lots more." Stop and sink a line for an animated trout in the nearby Baptism River, a long-time popular fishing spot.

Highway 1 runs toward Finland through the heart of green forests, not unlike those of a century or more ago. Even today, one can see residuals of early twentieth-century logging, right down to unused (or, for some, less used) logging roads. (Caveat: Should you choose to meander down one, you may be trespassing and, worse, the road may be in horrific shape.)

Finland is also one of the Midwest centers of the small but proud Suomi population. At one time during the Great Depression, the area had upwards of 180 Finnish families, most engaged in logging and farming, the latter no longer in evidence. (Today, the region is driven by the three T's: timber, taconite, and tourism).

Finnish activities and events of all sorts can be found within a tight geographic circle around the town. Northeast of Finland, about 1 mile via County Road 7, you'll find the *Finland Area Recreation Center*, where all things happening festival-wise in the area take place. There's a nice little park here, too. To the east, by way of County Road 6, the local folks are continuing to develop the *Finland Heritage Center*, a historical site displaying life in early Finland. Plans are to have costumed docents leading demonstrations of Finnish folkways along with exhibits and crafting displays. Hours vary but are generally late June to Labor Day, daily 11 a.m.–4 p.m. Also, check out *Saint Urho* at the corner of Highway 1 and CR 7. The patron saint of the Finns, Urho stands a towering 22 feet above the road.

If you're looking for action, recreation trails are found in all directions around Finland. During the winter, snowmobiling predominates, but the paths become multi-use in summer. Semi-rustic campgrounds are ubiquitous in the area; you should have little trouble finding a place to pitch your tent. The closest are southeast of town, via Highway 1 and/or CR 6.

Finland hosts the *Tori Celebration*—feting Finnish fun—in late June. Food and general carnival activities are the highlights here. Can't make it in June? Then head here in late September for the *Finn Booya Fest* at the Finland Recreation Hall; lots of great food. Another favorite is the *Saint Urho's Day Festival and Parade*, held March 15. In addition to lots of ethnic (and modern) music, food, a parade, and a fun scavenger hunt, you can help vote vocally in the "Miss Helmi" contest—always a hoot! If it's Saint Urho's Day, don't forget to wear green and purple. The colors, by the way, are based on the legend that the saint drove swarms of grasshoppers out of Finland (green) and saved the grape crop (purple).

Finally, about 7 miles northeast of Finland via CR 7 is an undiscovered gem of the North Shore, *George H. Crosby Manitou State Park*. (See Tour 4 for more on this gorgeous and rugged slice of wilderness).

From Finland, head north, then west on Highway 1 and cruise for about 29 miles to County Road 2. Not too far outside of town and within a handful of miles of Lake Superior, the

Great Lakes Finns

In successive waves, Europeans—northern Europeans mostly—repopulated the Upper Midwest and Great Lakes regions. Just look at Minnesota's professional football team—the Vikings—for a clue about who gets the lion's share of the historical footnotes for settling Minnesota.

They were by no means alone, however. As you bend to the west off the North Shore, it's certainly difficult to overlook the odd place names that can only mean that there are Finns in the area. Embarrass (in the Iron Range) is the nucleus; in this tour we have Finland (natch); previously we've been to Palo and its aw-shucks fun winter sliding carnival.

More than a quarter-million Finns left their homeland for the United States up through 1920. That's no number to sneeze at when you consider the smallish population producing the immigrants. The first large numbers of Finns sailed into Ellis Island around the time of the Civil War. Finland had for centuries been conquered and reconquered by the two mighty nations contiguous to it, Sweden and Russia. Add to that a strict system of primogeniture—basically meaning first son gets everything, tough luck if you're second or later—and many native sons set out for the New Land.

Most Finns were originally drawn to Michigan's Upper Peninsula region, which had an active miner recruitment program; others trickled toward mining and logging in northern Wisconsin and northeastern Minnesota. To many of the previous agrarians, mining was brutal, unfamiliar work. All those epic tracts of virgin forest, however, reminded them of home. So many took to logging.

What most folks don't realize is that Finns were among the first hardy immigrants in the New World. In 1683, William Penn was already writing about the Swedes and Finns and their husbandry skills. More than that, English colonists were constantly amazed by the Finns' love of the use of wood. In fact, the Scandinavian-style log house—sans iron as much as possible—became the one thing that Finns can boast about as much as anything. That and the ubiquitous saunas, of course.

The rock-strewn Baptism River near the town of Finland. Tim Bewer

topography gets challenging, quickly rising some 600 feet. The roadway parallels the Baptism River and the heights on the left rise upwards of 2,100 feet. In the thick of *Finland State Forest,* the modest highway serpentines through thick spinneys of spruce, which at times seem to encroach on the road. Along the way, you pass Murphy City—don't blink, you may miss it. Soon, the Finland State Forest dissolves into the Insula Lake State Forest. (Even most native Minnesotans don't know this exists). Then, you suddenly plunge into the happily named community of Isabella. As you continue west between Isabella and the junction with CR2, consider pitching a tent at one of two state forest semi-primitive campgrounds found right along Highway 1.

Turn south on CR 2 and proceed back for about 45 miles to Two Harbors, the starting point of this tour. On your long, leisurely drive back to Two Harbors, you'll pass through two state forest tracts; a few more rustic campgrounds (the one near Greenwood Lake, just south of the CR 2 and Highway 1 junction, is a good choice); and over the now-familiar Cloquet and Gooseberry Rivers. What you won't see are any of those vestiges of civilization known as "towns." There just aren't any here. Those same heights we chugged up earlier now give us a relaxing roll downward into Two Harbors, no doubt allowing our thoughts to dwell on thoughts of pies at *Betty's Pies,* 1633 Highway 61, (218) 834-3367, a worthy reward for a long day of exploring.

Tour 4
Peaks, Forests, and a Taste of the Boundary Waters

Little Marais—Taconite Harbor—Schroeder—Temperance River State Park—Tofte—Sawbill Trail—
George H. Crosby Manitou State Park—Little Marais

Distance: approximately 95 miles

Think of this tour as the Unknown North Shore. Small and generally overlooked by travelers headed toward more famous stops to the north and south, the area covered by this tour is the underappreciated gem of the North Shore.

From a tiny, cheery anchor town, we roll into a little, but picturesque, "marsh" that was once a gateway to the new land for thousands of European immigrants. From here, limber up the leg and shoulder muscles, as recreation is what this tour is mostly about. Mountains, hills, and dense tracts of forests are chock-full of trails that range in difficulty from easy to challenging. The stately-named Temperance River State Park gets most foot traffic, but there's so much more. We pass the region's highest climbable point—Carlton Peak—and, amazingly, even the highway waysides have gorgeous riverine trails.

Next, a highlight of our tour is a slow roll along the Sawbill Trail, a county road unlike most others in the United States. A spike into the core of wilderness, it leads directly to the Boundary Waters Canoe Area. Even if you don't have the time to undertake the federal regulations to access this region (permit reservations are required), in one short afternoon drive along the Sawbill Trail, you'll encounter more navigable lakes than you've likely seen in your life. (Not to mention the fact that you haven't *done* a Minnesota North Shore "tour" until you've done an afternoon of gravel-pavement-gravel-pavement driving.)

Begin this tour on Minnesota Highway 61 in Little Marais, about 7 miles northeast of Tettegouche State Park. The flyspeck town's name translates as "Little Marsh." Gazing upon the topography, imagining why early settlers affixed such a name isn't hard. Little Marais was a disembarkation point for droves of Finns and other northern Europeans heading into the backcountry logging camps. Mining later gave the town some life, though that has pretty much waned. Today, resorts and gift shops dominate this friendly town.

Continue northeast on Highway 61 for approximately 3 miles to the Caribou Falls State Wayside (left side of road). Every opportunity to stop and stretch your legs on this stretch of the North Shore is worthwhile. This one actually has quite a bit of greenery to poke around in—for a wayside, anyway. In fact, a trailhead here leads into some relatively rugged country. A relatively easy trail from the wayside leads along the Caribou River to Caribou Falls. From here, you can link up with the Superior Hiking Trail, though most wander back to the parking area to continue with the trip. Also from this wayside, a couple of miles to the north, is another pull-off trailhead. *Sugarloaf Trail* is an easy mile-plus ribbon, which runs through forest and along a ledge to Sugarloaf Beach.

At the beach, kids love to romp and look for stones; parents simply love the views and the wind, blowing in the cool, relaxing gusts.

Continue northeast about 9 miles to Taconite Harbor. By the name, you can pretty much guess what you're going to see. Yup, there's a scenic observation area overlooking the harbor where you can watch the ore loading. Even if you know beans about the process, watching the monstrous freighters being gorged on mineral wealth is transfixing.

Taconite Harbor isn't much today, however. As recently as the 1960s, it once thrived. Then the mining industry swooned, and lots of the infrastructure—homes and businesses—was moved completely out of the area. The ore-loading terminal is about all that remains.

One more nugget: Taconite Harbor has an excellent rest area with spotless facilities!

Drive 2 more miles on Highway 61 to Schroeder. In this sister city to Taconite Harbor, you can visit the granite *Father Baraga Cross* at the base of the Cross River. Father Baraga, another intrepid Jesuit forg-

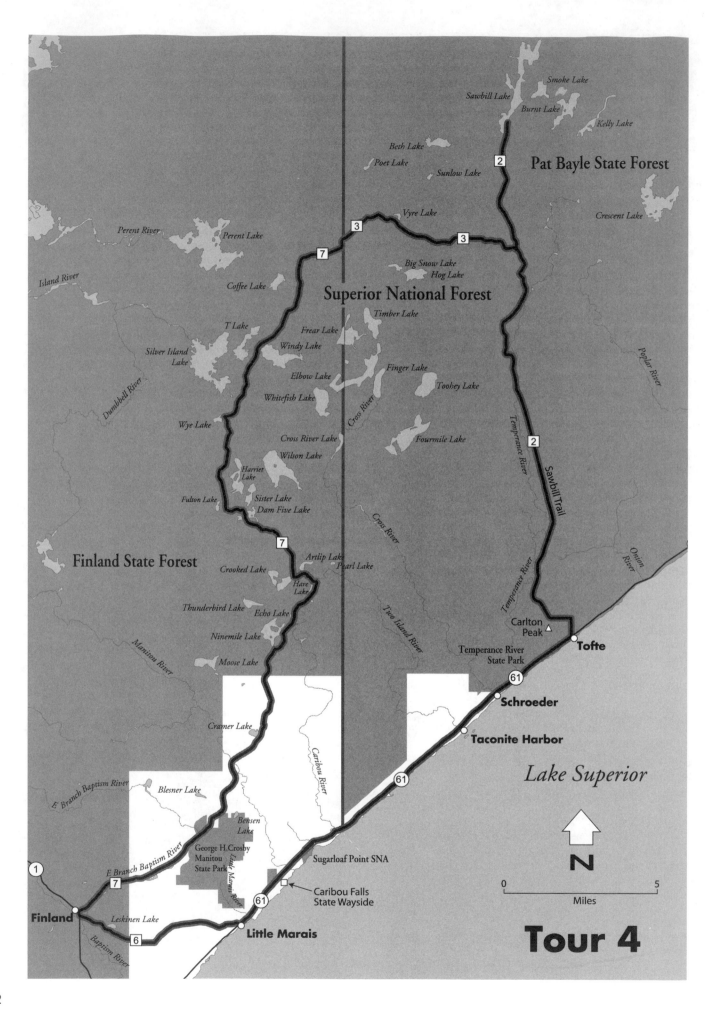

Waves pounding Lake Superior's shoreline—a scene repeated up and down the North Shore. Tim Bewer

ing his way into the New World to spread the word of Christ, is immortalized in the Lake Superior region with a few memorials and even a town's name in Michigan's Upper Peninsula. He erected a cross here to thank the Lord for surviving a frightful canoe trip across Lake Superior in 1846 during a thunderous storm. Later, a permanent granite memorial replaced the wooden original. The Cross River here supposedly got its appellation from this event.

Not far from Highway 61's highway bridge, you can get a pleasant view of a waterfall and a minor, but picturesque, river gorge. A half-mile hiking trail departs from a wayside in Schroeder, leading up a slight incline along the river into the gorge, and revealing worthwhile views. Many make the easy hike from here to Temperance River State Park.

If you're around Schroeder in late June, stop for the town's *John Schroeder Days*, which pays homage to the founder of the town. Minnow races for the kids are always great fun. You'll find dozens of activities and other events in a family carnival atmosphere.

Continue northeast for a little more than 1 mile to *Temperance River State Park*. The park, (218) 663-7476, is highlighted by the river roiling through an ancient gorge chock-full of geological potholes and oddball formations gouged by the angry water. The drop is relatively minor—only 162 feet—but it happens in less than half a mile, which accentuates the effect. Three falls are accessed via trails: two cut gorges are north of Highway 61, while one blasts through toward Lake Superior from south of the highway. This latter cascade is definitely trip worthy, as it drops 100 feet from its mouth at the big lake.

Along the nearly 24 miles of hiking trails, you reach several stone overlook areas built in the 1930s by the Civilian Conservation Corps where, once again, you can link up to the Superior Hiking Trail. This is also a popular cross-country ski trail destination. Snowmobilers have 7 miles. That's short by North Shore standards, but it links up to the North Shore Corridor State Trail—a snowmobiler mecca. A regular campground has 55 sites, but you can also get three cart-in sites for more privacy. There's now even a kayak site along Lake Superior.

Continue northeast on Highway 61 for about 3 miles to Tofte. In the land of Scandinavians, this is the North Shore's epicenter of Norwegian culture. You'll find a small visitor information center along Highway 61; its summer hours are planned, but haphazard. Here, workers can give you precise directions to area sights. One sight, right inside the visitor information center, is a must-see: the *North Shore Commercial Fishing Museum*, (888) 616-6784, built across the road from two original community fish houses. This replica is a faithful mock-up of the 1905 original Hans Engelson fish houses and sports an enormous variety of artifacts from fishing's bygone days. Note the fascinating display on Isle Royale (situated less than 20 miles from shore, but technically in Michigan waters) in fishing history. Generally open June to October, 9 a.m.–7 p.m.; until 5 p.m. the rest of the year; admission.

Why "Temperance"?

The word *temperance* means "habitual moderation or total abstinence in drinking liquor," according to Webster (and Merriam). So what in the world does this have to do with a state park? Well, the mouth of the Temperance River is the key. Note that it doesn't have a sandbar. Bar—get it? No bar.

From Tofte, turn north onto County Road 2 (the Sawbill Trail). Before even settling comfortably into your vehicle for this segment of the tour, realize that you'll have to stop soon to take a closer look at *Carlton Peak*. With its imposing position overlooking the lake and highway, the peak is the region's highest. Standing at 927 feet above lake level (1,529 feet above sea level), it absolutely beckons one to clamber up.

The easiest way to do that is to drive north a short distance on CR 2, the start of the 23-mile-long *Sawbill Trail*, a good paved-and-some-gravel track and one of the main access points into the Boundary Waters Canoe Area Wilderness. About 2.5 miles north of Tofte is a parking area. From here you can take a shorter 3.5-mile or a more ambitious 5-mile trek up to Carlton Peak. Don't be surprised to see rock climbers scaling the craggy walls. By the way, more ambitious trails leading up to the peak are found from the south on Highway 61.

The parking area also serves as another trailhead. The *Britton Peak Hiking Trail* is a short but steep hike up to an aerie with superb Lake Superior views. Do be careful as footing can be dicey here. All in all, these two hikes may offer the most hiking bang for the buck along the North Shore.

Continue north on the Sawbill Trail for about 24 miles to Sawbill Lake. Note that the paved road you start out on ultimately gives way to good gravel and that it dead-ends at Sawbill Lake, where you'll have to turn around. But that's all right!

Tracing the entire length of the Sawbill Trail is great fun—just to say you did it! Along the way, the state forest has primitive campsites: one at the midway point of CR 2, and three whose access roads branch off eastward from CR 2. All are likely to be full. Before leaving Tofte, you can ask about the likelihood of finding an open spot.

Along the Sawbill Trail you'll pass by large stands of northern hardwoods and fir, with occasional glimpses of the Temperance River. Be on the lookout for bears. More likely are any number of smaller mammals or a sun-dappled array of hues from the diversity of bird life. You head through *Pat Bayle State Forest*, where you'll find a precious few hiking opportunities. Yet what everyone is here for is the cornucopia of paddling in the Boundary Waters Canoe Area Wilderness—the mecca of canoeing in the United States. Tofte and its environs have a number of outfitters offering guided trips, rentals and/or lodging. The visitor information center offers all the details you need.

Park the car for a few days, and experience one of the most splendid trips imaginable. Nothing in the Lower 48 exists like this. It's a preternatural way to experience wilderness. (And even if you loathe the natural world, the outfitters have an uncanny way of making creature comforts less of a problem than when you do it yourself.)

Note: technically, a couple of forest roads lead eastward and westward from the Sawbill Trail. But if you're tempted to try one of them, it's best to ask about specific routes in Tofte before attempting any cross-forest drive. These roads may look intriguing on a gazetteer, but one never knows how much Mother Nature may have altered things.

From Sawbill Lake, return back on CR 2 for about 5 miles to County Road 3. Turn right (west) and drive for about 7 miles to County Road 7. CR 3 makes a long, leisurely bend to the west and south through the heart of the area's wilderness. You'll pass hundreds of glacial pools of various sizes and limitless shapes, many with names that are self-explanatory (Big Snow, Sunlow) or those that pique the imagination (Hog, Poet, Coffee).

Turn left (south) on CR 7 and drive for approximately 30 miles. Being careful to stay on CR 7 and not succumb to the temptation to strike out on your own via one of the forest roads, you'll generally head in a southerly direction. About two-thirds of the way along this stretch, CR 7 jogs east before a tight westward bend, and you may start to wonder where you are. That's when you should find yourself at a semi-rustic campground of the *Finland State Forest*, near Ninemile, Moose, and Crooked Lakes.

About 10 miles after that you'll come face to face with a lovely—and well-kept—secret of North Shore explorers. With Highway 61 efficiently channeling the crowds destined for Split Rock Lighthouse, it seems few people get around to checking out *George H. Crosby Manitou State Park*. Donated by an iron magnate, it was established in 1955 as Minnesota's first park devoted primarily to backpacking, and thankfully, it has remained so. No established campground here—just primitive sites found along rugged trails into the gorgeous interiors of the 6,682-acre park. The sights within include crystalline waterfalls carving through millennia upon millennia of volcanic rock; old-growth stands of fir, cedar, spruce, and northern hardwoods; 24 miles of tough but rewarding trails; wolves and moose sharing quadrants with resident bears; streams and the central body of water, Benson Lake, rife with trout and even splake, an oddball offspring, the result of a bit of miscegenation between a brook trout and a lake trout. For more information on the park, contact Tettegouche State Park, (218) 226-6365.

Continue southwest on CR 7 for 7 miles to State Highway 1 in Finland (see Tour 3). Turn left (south) and drive a short distance to County Road 6. Turn left (southeast) on CR 6 and head back into Little Marais, a distance of 7 miles. Along the way you'll come across the one-of-a-kind *Wolf Ridge Environmental Learning Center*, (218) 353-7414, an accredited environmental education center with intense but fun programs that allow for up-close-and-hands-on natural educational experiences. It isn't just for adults, either; kids love it, too.

Tour 5
North Shore Heights

Tofte—Oberg and Leveaux Mountains—Lutsen—Cascade River State Park—Grand Marais—Eagle Mountain—Tofte

Distance: approximately 85 miles

Mountains. In these parts, the word certainly doesn't conjure up images of Mount Everest. No craggy peaks piercing low-slung clouds, no mountain majesties engendering patriotic songs.

Then again, like always, the Midwest understates itself very appropriately. What Minnesota lacks in vaunting rises, it more than makes up for in equability and just-rugged-enough terrain. The stretch of the North Shore from Tofte to Grand Marais may be the Upper Great Lakes' most impressive range of modest, but lovely, "mountains." Chief among them is Eagle Mountain, the state's highest peak. No world atlas will ever highlight it, but at 2,301 feet that's pretty impressive—in a Midwest sort of way. Less ambitious rises look like rough chocolate drops covered in mint. The hiking is superb. It may require some sweat and sturdy shoes, but the views at the top—the steely waters of Lake Superior and its licking, white-topped waves—are world class.

If you have some energy left, there's still a "major" North Shore community to explore. Grand Marais may seem a sleepy town by lower-state standards, but up here it is *the* nucleus of "culture" and special nights out. Snug at the southern end of the famed Gunflint Trail (see Tour 6), here in the largest town between Two Harbors and Thunder Bay, you'll find rustic cabins and beer-and-pizza joints just down the road a piece from luxurious inns and chichi bistros. And everybody has a canoe strapped to their vehicle. A good place to rest and recharge batteries after days of exploring the wild and wonderful North Shore.

Begin your tour in Tofte on State Highway 61. Drive northeast about 3.5 miles to the *Ray Berglund State Memorial Wayside.* On the left-hand side of the road, along the Onion River, are semi-secluded picnic grounds that make for a nice respite if you've been hiking all day (or even if you've just made the short jaunt from Tofte). Actually, you could do more hiking if you wish, as there is a moderately difficult half-mile trail paralleling the Onion River from the parking area. You're almost guaranteed to be alone, and the scenery along the river is beautiful—a near-perfect sensory accompaniment to the sound of the gurgling water next to you.

Continue northeast on Highway 61 for a little more than 1 mile to Forest Road 336; turn left and drive 2 miles (at the most) to a parking area for the *Oberg and Leveaux Mountain National Hiking Trails.* For some challenging gumdrop-mountain clambering, check out these trails. Most people have never even heard of them before. But try them out and you'll likely return, as these two trails offer some lovely North Shore views, particularly in autumn, when the surrounding valleys are an absolute riot of blazing colors.

The Oberg trail is only 2.2 miles, but what a couple of miles! Along the way to gorgeous views of the eponymous lake, you'll get other grand vistas of Lake Superior and Moose Mountain. Be careful at the top of this trail, though, as there are some difficult steep sections. Leveaux rises some 1,000 feet above Lake Superior along a ridgeline and offers some equally impressive views.

Return to Highway 61, turn left and drive for 5 miles to Lutsen. The near-legendary place to see (and partake of the fun) in these parts is *Lutsen Mountains,* (218) 663-7281. It's officially known as *Sawtooth Mountain Park at Lutsen Mountains*— a long name for a place with a lengthy list of recreational activities. It has a gondola up Moose Mountain and chairlift up Eagle Mountain—great for seeing the sawtoothed peaks in abundance. Bicyclists are thrilled with the Lutsen Mountain Bike Park's 50-plus miles of trails; some trails snake through extremely challenging terrain. Kids go bananas for the Alpine Slide, a summer luge run, and for pony and horseback rides at the park's stables. It has hiking trails, too.

The Lutsen Mountains are also a favorite among alpine skiers. One of the Midwest's most highly respected operations, it boasts the region's largest and highest alpine ski center. For rest and refueling, skiers can stop at the Mountain Top Deli at the summit of Moose Mountain.

Paul Bunyan's Tears

One story in the local Paul Bunyan lore has his logging crew shedding gargantuan tears—and not because they were getting in touch with their sensitive side. Purportedly, wild onions were so plentiful in the area near the Onion River, which meets Highway 61 4 miles northeast of Tofte, that the Giant of the Northwoods had to check the tears of his crew as they cut, lest they swell the river and cause it to overflow its banks.

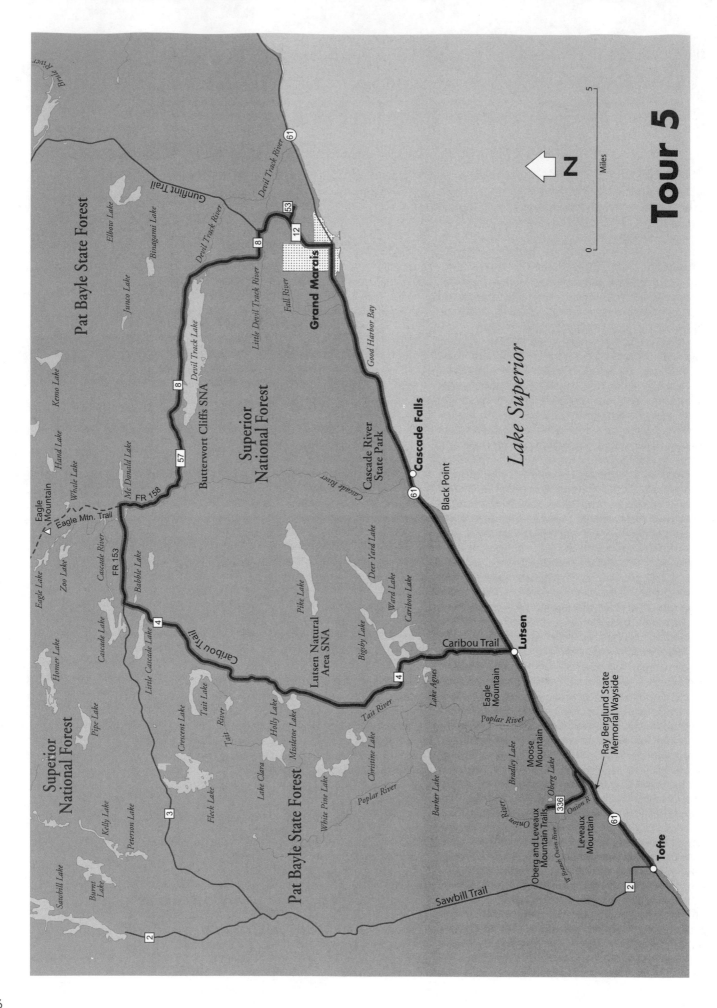

The North Shore's Highway 61—never far from Lake Superior. Minnesota Office of Tourism

From Lutsen, continue northeast on Highway 61 for about 8 miles to *Cascade Falls.* Along the way, a short distance from Lutsen at milepost 97, is *Kahneetah Gallery,* (218) 387-2585. Its cozy gallery features Minnesota artists working in pottery, sculpture, landscapes, forged metals, stained glass, and more. If you're looking for a place to hang your hat for the evening, you can also lodge in one of the sybaritic cottages, all of which feature smashing lake views, cobblestone fireplaces, and direct access to the Superior Hiking Trail. The gallery is open all year.

Cascade Falls is a redundantly named water drop of the more appropriately named Cascade River, just east of Black Point. *Cascade River State Park,* (218) 387-1543, subsumes a long stretch of forestland on either side of the river (about 12 miles, north to south) as it rolls into Lake Superior through a serpentine, rocky gorge. The churning water drops through a series of rapids as it descends some 225 feet in just under a mile, over 900 feet in its final 3 miles. The Superior Hiking Trail runs along the river, giving easy access to the cascades. Along the way, you'll find low-lying topography that remains isolated, even on summertime-busy days. The riverside trail offers a cool, even chilly, walk in mornings and evenings.

If you have more time, approximately 18 miles of hiking trails spiderweb into the backwoods areas. Come wintertime, these trails expand into a full 30 miles for cross-country skiing. Locals also tout the good fishing in the waterways here. In addition to a drive-in established campground,

backpackers have five wilderness sites from which to choose—all bursting with flora and fauna, from aspen, birch, fir and spruce to hawks, salamanders, deer, pine martens, bears . . . even moose and wolves. The park office has information and checklists of the natural wonders you'll see here.

Quick Trip Option. If you want to dive into some of the heavily forested areas that Highway 61 has been skirting, turn left onto County Road 4, a.k.a. the Caribou Trail, about 1 mile past Lutsen. The main tour will follow this road later, after a spin up to a lovely state park and Grand Marais. However, you could head north here now and explore the Pat Bayle State Forest and other forest lands before returning to Highway 61.

Also along CR 4, a few miles north of Lutsen, is the moderately challenging *White Sky Rock Hiking Trail,* the terminus of which offers a fine view of Caribou Lake—a triple-thick treetop canopy emblazoned with fall colors!

From Cascade Falls, continue north on Highway 61 for about 9 miles to Grand Marais. Soon after you depart Cascade River State Park, you'll come to *Good Harbor Bay Panorama,* just east of Thomsonite Beach (as Highway 61 bends left). Suddenly, you're afforded glimpses of Good Harbor Bay, Seagull Rock, and Grand Marais. A small wayside rest area lets you hop out and admire the views, which are truly inspiring. If you're inclined to rock hounding, be aware that fragments of thomsonite can be found in the area. And locals say you can also find basanite (a type of black jasper) and hovlandite (rare), along with the regionally pervasive agate.

Continue into downtown Grand Marais to Broadway, turn right (south), and proceed for a block to the *Grand Marais Visitor and Information Center.* Fully staffed and serviced, the center at 13 North Broadway, (888) 922-5000 (www.grandmarais.com), is a godsend of information on the entire North Shore.

One of the things you may learn is that early twentieth-century guidebooks made note of Grand Marais' lovely natural harbor, remarking on the carpet of floating logs awaiting shipping and processing. While somewhat somnolent, this place is the nerve center of the North Shore: perfectly located for day-trippers and weekenders from Duluth and even points somewhat south of there. More important, it is the southern node of the famed Gunflint Trail—by far the most popular access route into the Boundary Waters Canoe Area Wilderness.

Such a quiet, lovely town is Grand Marais that it's also an artist's haven. Wisconsin Street downtown is lined with galleries—many of them focusing on Minnesota and Great Lakes artists. The city even has *Artist's Point*, a spit of land jutting into Lake Superior offering gorgeous views that artists never tire of painting or sketching. Artist's Point is easy to get to; it's near the end of Broadway, south of the visitor center mentioned earlier.

In fact, park your car and take a stroll along the lovely harbor. An easy half-mile walking/nature trail takes in lake vistas so inspiring to local artists and then passes by the *Grand Marais lighthouse.* Grand Marais' *Municipal Recreation Area* here is a wonderful spot for travelers: It has an RV park with dumping station and more walking trails, the most popular being Sweethearts Bluff Trail. It's short—only a mile—but it ranges from easy to a tad challenging, so be forewarned.

Grand Marais, in addition to the lovely artwork offered in galleries, has the *Arrowhead Center for the Arts,* housed in a quaint old church, 11 West 5th Street, (218) 387-1284; it's home to a number of local arts community members. With its 300-seat theater, the center features a challenging and year-round series of theatrical performances by the *Grand Marais Playhouse*, the highlight of which may be the *Minnesota Shakespeare Festival*, held in late June and early July. The center houses two other artistic endeavors. The *Grand Marais Art Colony* is a half-century-plus-old community of artists; it offers workshops for writers and visual artists, along with educational programs. The *North Shore Music Association* has a series of concerts—maybe bluegrass, maybe folk—throughout the year, as well.

There's more! Folkways and ethnic arts are highlighted at the *North House Folk School*, (218) 387-9762. Situated on the Lake Superior shoreline, this is a real hands-on school, where you can learn to make tools, carve wood, build a canoe, live off the land, or many other fascinating and disappearing heritage skills.

After all that, don't forget that the town does have a tiny *historical museum* as well, located south of the visitor information center.

In Grand Marais, go north on Broadway a short distance to 5th Street. Turn left (west) and drive 5 blocks to 5th Avenue W (County Road 12). Turn right (north) (it's also the beginning of the Gunflint Trail). Drive for about 1.5 miles to County Road 53. Turn right and go a short distance. Here, you can avail yourself of the various lengths and loops of the *Pincushion Mountain Hiking Trails*, which offer trails of up to 15 miles and a couple of superb overlooks. The circle trail to Pincushion Mountain passes through the Devil Track River Gorge and offers inspiring vistas of Lake Superior; from here it's an easy connect to the Superior Hiking Trail. All trails are easy to moderate.

Return to CR 12, continue north, and go about 1.5 miles to County Road 8. Turn left (west) and proceed north, then west again, for about 6 miles to County Road 57. Continue on CR 57 for about 6 miles to Forest Road 158. About a third of the way into this

Grand Marais Festivals and Events

With a population of just a smidge over a thousand, Grand Marais isn't exactly an urban behemoth, even though it's the largest town in this section of Minnesota. But the community certainly lives up to part of its name when it comes to lively festivals and events. Some activities take place year-round; in particular, local galleries and artist collectives have displays and/or events, and the local playhouse (see below) always has something on tap.

In winter, Grand Marais hoots it up with its *Winterfest* and the *Grand Portage Passage Sled Dog Marathon.* Another legendary dogsled race—the *John Beargrease Sled Dog Marathon*—takes place in February.

With late spring and summer, Grand Marais really gears up for festival season. It offers the lovely *Scandinavian Days* festival in late June during which, the wooden boat show is not to be missed. Scandinavian crafts are also taught. At about the same time the local playhouse brings the *Minnesota Shakespeare Festival* to town; performances are great, but the workshops (write a sonnet!) are even more fun.

In mid-July artists flock to the *Grand Marais Art Fair and Festival,* with a juried art show, arts and crafts for sale, and workshops.

Another favorite is the *Grand Marais Birding Festival* in late October, which started in 2001 and will likely be an annual event, given its popularity. Field trips are conducted throughout the area and are highly successful. More than 100 species of birds were observed in the inaugural event. Another similar event is the Gunflint Trail's *Boreal Birding Days* in late May and early June.

A vestige of the past in Grand Marais. Tim Bewer

stretch, you'll pass the east shore of *Devil Track Lake,* then an established Boundary Waters seaplane base (note the pontooned aircraft here). There's plenty of good fishing in these parts of the lake, and you'll pass by an established campground. Most noticeable of all is the *length* of the lake—it seems never to end. (And be on the lookout for herons and lots of geese.)

Go north on FR 158 for about 3 miles to Forest Road 153. At the junction, you'll find the trailhead and a parking lot for the *Eagle Mountain Trail,* which leads to Minnesota's highest point, towering 2,301 feet above sea level. The 6-mile round trip is rugged and at times extremely rocky, with an elevation gain of over 500 feet. There are plenty of streams and cliffs along the way, and the view from the top of the peak is spectacular.

Note: Two-thirds of this trail is technically within the borders of the Boundary Waters Canoe Area, and self-issued day permits must be obtained (they're available at the trailhead); entry point 79 serves this trailhead. Two camping spots are available: one at the base of the mountain, another at

Whale Lake; camping permits also must be obtained for this (available at the trailhead but, remember, all the permits may have already been allocated). In order to keep up with the latest camping regulations, it's recommended you check the Web site www.canoecountry.com/permits before striking out. Better, ask in Grand Marais for up-to-the minute details.

Drive west on Forest Road 153/170 (signage varies a lot, and annoyingly so) for about 4 miles to County Road 4 (the Caribou Trail). Turn left (south) and drive about 18 miles to Lutsen. The Caribou Trail offers more wilderness access into the Boundary Waters and national forestlands. Along the way you pass by the *White Sky Rock Hiking Trail* (mentioned in an earlier Quick Trip Option) a few miles north of Lutsen; it's only a mile long, but what a view of Caribou Lake!

In Lutsen, turn right (southwest) onto Highway 61 and cruise for 9.5 miles back into Tofte, the starting point of this tour.

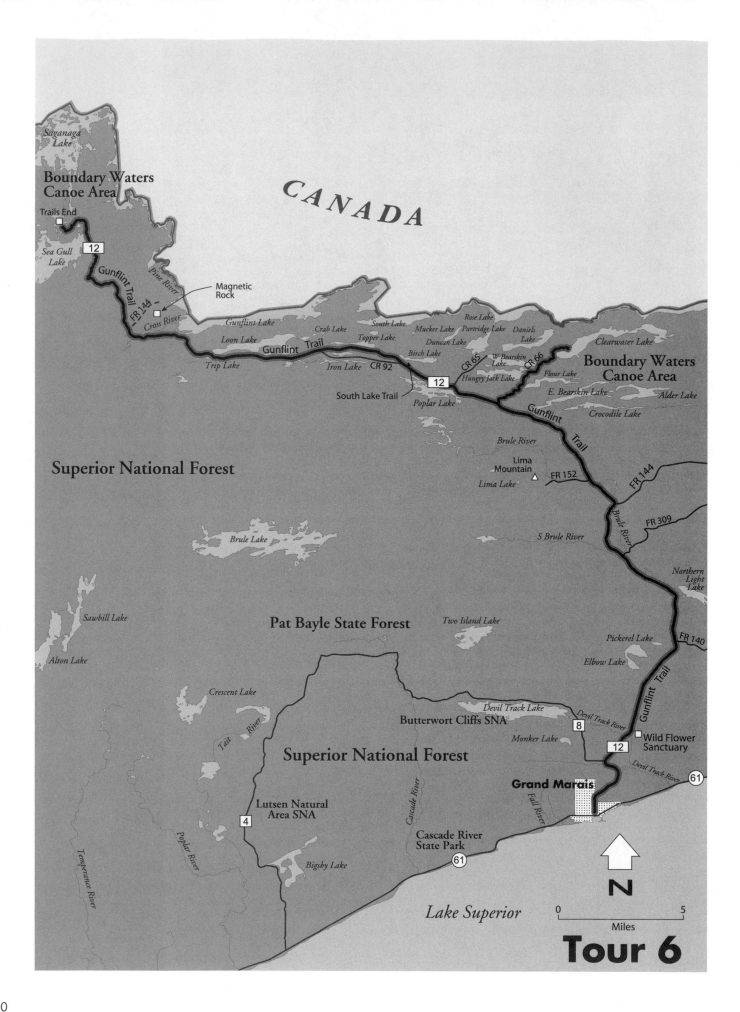

Saganaga Lake

Boundary Waters Canoe Area

Trails End

Sea Gull Lake

CANADA

12

Gunflint Trail

Pine River

FR 144

Magnetic Rock

Cross River

Gunflint Lake

Crab Lake

South Lake

Mucker Lake

Rose Lake

Partridge Lake

Daniels Lake

Clearwater Lake

Loon Lake

Topper Lake

Duncan Lake

Gunflint Trail

Birch Lake

CR 65

W. Bearskin Lake

CR 66

Boundary Waters Canoe Area

Trip Lake

Iron Lake

CR 92

12

Hungry Jack Lake

Flour Lake

E. Bearskin Lake

Alder Lake

South Lake Trail

Poplar Lake

Crocodile Lake

Gunflint Trail

Superior National Forest

Brule River

Lima Mountain

FR 152

FR 144

Lima Lake

Brule River

FR 309

Brule Lake

S Brule River

Sawbill Lake

Northern Light Lake

Pat Bayle State Forest

Two Island Lake

Pickerel Lake

FR 140

Alton Lake

Elbow Lake

Gunflint Trail

Crescent Lake

Tait River

Devil Track Lake

Butterwort Cliffs SNA

Devil Track River

8

Superior National Forest

Monker Lake

12

Wild Flower Sanctuary

Lutsen Natural Area SNA

4

Grand Marais

Fall River

Devil Track River

61

Poplar River

Cascade River

Cascade River State Park

61

Bigsby Lake

Temperance River

Lake Superior

N

0   5
Miles

Tour 6

Tour 6
Into the Singing Wilderness: The Gunflint Trail

Grand Marais—Gunflint Trail—Trails End—Grand Marais

Distance: approximately 125 miles

Unlike the other tours in this book, this one actually ends not where it begins, but where it . . . well . . . ends. For this departure from the norm (and possibly common sense), blame Minnesota's variegated terrain. That and the wondrous Boundary Waters Canoe Area Wilderness, the very existence of which precludes road building. With this tour dead-ending among massive tracts of trees at, literally, Trails End, you may wish to paddle and portage your way out. But since you've brought your vehicle, that doesn't seem like a sensible alternative, although it may cross your mind once you've sampled the area's natural delights.

Gunflint Trail. The name drips with history—buckskinned *voyageurs* tamping down gunpowder, awaiting their roast beaver around a smoky maple fire. Though this is one of Minnesota's most heavily traveled "back" roads, with the dense forests and absolute pervasiveness of wildlife, it feels like you've stepped back in time.

If you have the opportunity, take the trail—and enjoy it. When crystalline waters beckon, park the car and get into a canoe to explore the Boundary Waters Canoe Area. You'll be glad you did—for a lifetime.

Don't have an affinity for water? No problem. Get out the hiking boots. While sharing a trail with a muskrat or a bluejay, you'll also likely stumble across residuals of early settlement history: a stone foundation here, a decaying dam there.

The 63 miles of the Gunflint Trail may well be Minnesota's best. Born of a bush-walking trail for Native Americans and, later, buckskin-clad voyageurs, it has superbly transformed into a well-paved ribbon leading into a place most Americans could never believe still exists. At the trail's south terminus, Grand Marais is the area's supply center, with a woodsy chic complex, where nouvelle cuisine and flannel shirts are not incongruous, and where one can experience Shakespeare immediately after a week in bear country.

Here, some of Minnesota's wildest lands are preserved, the proverbial heart of darkness as the road pierces northward. In addition to the usual zoological suspects, add moose, timber wolves, and maybe an elk. You may see residual logging tracks (likely used as canoe portages or hiking trails),

crumbling stone foundations of forlorn settlements now resting wearily in the weeds, or one-eyed shotgun shacks of long-gone pioneers who came and vanished, seemingly into the wilds.

But this is the Land of 10,000 Lakes after all, bespeckled with an ocean of glacial residual holes stretching all the way to Canada. Here people come to find their own wilderness Walden. Paddle, portage, paddle, sleep under the stars, wake to a loon's shrill call. For a few precious days, you are living 200 years ago.

Start your tour in Grand Marais at the *Gunflint Tourist Information Office*, at the junction of Highway 61 and County Road 12. Before leaving home, contact the Gunflint Trail Association, (800) 338-6932 (www.gunflint-trail.com). Also, see the sidebar "Planning for the Gunflint" on page 34 to get the Web address for the Boundary Waters Canoe Area.

Travel north on CR 12 (the Gunflint Trail) for about 4.5 miles. The road immediately rises and bends, a propitious start to a driving adventure. About 10 minutes out of Grand Marais the town of Maple Hill looms, and to the east is a protected *wildflower sanctuary*. A stand of pines (one of millions on this route) and nice hiking are found nearby at the *George Washington Memorial Pines Hiking Trail*. The parking area is marked well from the road. The trail actually follows an old logging road through majestic and well-seasoned red pines, through a swamp (wear high-top boots), to picturesque Elbow Lake. Here the trail turns and follows the creek to jump back into the forest. At 3 miles round-trip, it's not too ambitious and a good warm-up for later exertions.

Continue north on CR 12 for about 5.5 miles to an access road just after Forest Road 140 (Northern Light Lake Road). Here, and elsewhere along the route, don't be surprised to see the roadside curtains of trees interrupted by a raccoon lumbering across the road. The access road leads to a parking lot and a trailhead to the *Northern Light Lake Overlook Hiking Trail*. This half-mile hike up Blueberry Hill (yes, it's hard to resist singing the Fats Domino song at this juncture), is a

Fog-shrouded lake on the Gunflint Trail. Thomas Huhti

tough little nugget—so bring good shoes. Outstanding views are found at the top. What a thrill!

Drive northwest about 12 miles, be alert for Lima Mountain Road (Forest Road 152). Along the way you pass by picturesque Northern Light Lake and over the Brule River; with lots of pull-offs leading to the cerulean waters. If you're really ambitious, Forest Roads 144 and 309 both plunge into the woods toward Greenwood Lake (great fishing).

If you turn left and drive for 2 miles on Lima Mountain Road, you'll arrive at the base of the road's namesake—Minnesota's second-highest named peak. Even if you don't venture all the way to the mountain, bring your binoculars. Hard-core birders say this is one of the best boreal birding spots in Minnesota. Possible sightings include the rare Spruce Grouse and Black-backed Woodpecker, among others; many rare nesting records have been established in this area.

You may also encounter a 'shroomer, one of those happy souls who love to wander the woods looking for the tasty fungi. Consider yourself eminently blessed if you spot a moose in this area as well. It's not a daily happening, but neither is it rare.

From Lima Mountain Road, continue north on CR 12 for about 6.5 miles to County Road 66. Turn right and travel for a short distance (no more than 5 miles) to a succession of hiking trails. *Most trails mentioned hereafter will likely require a self-issued day permit for the Boundary Waters Canoe Area.* Many hiking trail access points will come in quick succession here. Off CR 66, at Flour Lake Campground, you'll find the short, very steep (but rewarding) *Honeymoon Bluff Trail*, with gorgeous sunsets above Hungry Jack Lake. No permit required. From the end of CR 66 at Clearwater Lake it's a less-than-a-mile trail

spur that leads to the *Daniels Lake Trail*, an easy 1.5-miler that's most often used for access to the Border Route Trail.

Return to CR 12 and continue north for about 1.5 miles to County Road 65. Turning into this dark but inviting road, you'll find the lovely but not always populated (it's rated moderate to difficult) *Caribou Rock Trail*. The first mile is on the beaten path, with overlooks of West Bearskin Lake; the next half mile to Moss Lake finds the number of hikers dwindling. Hardy hikers travel on another couple of miles over rugged terrain to Stairway Portage and Rose Lake. Take water and good shoes.

Continue north on CR 12 about 2.5 miles to County Road 92 on the left and the entrance to South Lake Trail on the right. For the entire stretch, Poplar Lake borders the road on the left, and you're likely to see a forest of fishing poles sticking out of car and truck windows. Opposite Rockwood Lodge and Canoe Outfitters is the entrance to the 3-mile *South Lake Trail*—a popular hiking path that wends through stands of old-growth red and white pines, many of which encroach on the trail. When you reach South Lake, you can gaze at the sparkling waters leading into Canada. At Partridge Lake is a developed campsite; hiking and camping permits are required.

Continue on CR 12 for 4.5 miles to where it rejoins CR 92.

Quick Trip Option. And this is a mighty quick option. Just for a lark and to get off the main route for a change, branch off onto CR 92. This is a short jog that parallels the Gunflint Trail, then rejoins it after 4.5 miles. The Iron Lake campground can be seen along the way.

The Gunflint Trail—an easy access to hundreds of inviting lakes and rivers. Thomas Huhti

Continue north on CR 12 approximately 6 miles from the junction of CR 12 and CR 92 to Loon Lake Lodge; look for Forest Road 1416 and follow it past the lodge. Along the way to the lodge, you might want to stop and sample the *Topper Lake Trailhead,* along Forest Road 317. You have a choice of trails ranging from 1.5 to 6 miles that lead to Mucker Lake. They are fairly easy and can also lead to the Border Route Trail. More permits are required.

Loon Lake seems to unfold forever to the northeast, with countless peninsulas inviting you to leave the road and strike off on your own. Just past Loon Lake Lodge is the entrance to *Crab Lake Trail,* an easy 8-miler that leads to the Border Route Trail.

Continue for 5 miles to South Gunflint Lake Road (County Road 50). After running parallel with Loon Lake on the right for most of this stretch, you'll soon arrive at the granddaddy of the Gunflint Trail's northern section—the *Gunflint Lake Trail* system. This moderate-to-difficult trail network totals some 26 miles. Maps (necessary on these trails), information, and access are also found at any of the several resorts in the area.

Two trails on the Gunflint Lake Trail system bear mentioning. *High Cliffs Trail* and *South Rim Trail* have eye-popping views of the historically named lake—on a clear day you can see all the way to Canada. Trails also lead to an overlook of the Laurentian Divide, which separates streams flowing to opposite ends of the continent, some northward, others southward. You'll perhaps notice a thickening of the canopy in these parts, the northern tier of the Gunflint Trail. Prime boreal bird species are in abundance—especially ruffed grouse, woodpeckers, flycatchers, and several warbler species. The High Cliffs Trail is also legendary for birders. The forest beginning here shows signs of the enormous conflagrations that roared through the Boundary Waters in the mid-1990s and the resultant habitat recovery.

Remaining relatively unknown to most hikers, this longish walk stretches 70 miles from the Gunflint Trail to the Pigeon River below South Fowl Lake—on the Canadian border. Spectacular views and rugged terrain, but this trail is not for novices.

Minnesota Moose

Moose are the largest members of the deer family. Standing up to six feet high and weighing up to 1,200 pounds, you'll never forget the sight of one standing onshore as you paddle by in the Boundary Waters. (You'll also not forget it if you hit one with your car. It's serious business, so pay strict attention to road-warning signs.)

Generally, moose are most active at dawn and dusk, though they can appear anytime. They don't slow down in winter. In fact, they love to lick the road salt off the highway. Mature moose have a distinctive hump on the shoulders and a "bell"—the flap of skin that hangs under the throat. Though the males can be differentiated from cows by their wide-swept antlers, they, like whitetailed deer, do lose them after breeding season, generally in December.

Moose prefer to feed in swampy areas where there's lots of chewy green stuff. In fact, "moose" stems from an Algonquin word meaning "twig eater." The average moose eats up to 65 pounds of nutrients per day.

Minnesota was once rife with the ubiquitous twig eaters, but settlement and uncontrolled hunting severely depleted their numbers. Hunting was banned in 1922 and not started again until numbers had rebounded by 1971. Today, the state's northern moose population is estimated at a stable 6,000. These exist in two blanket areas—one in northeast Minnesota (Saint Louis, Lake, and Cook Counties), one in northwest Minnesota. The northeast population is larger, since the topography is perfect for the animal. The northwest population has been dwindling, due possibly to parasites or disease. Remember, watch those boggy areas—moose love to submerge themselves to escape bugs and keep cool, and because they can reach slimy plants that way.

Expect windfalls and fully expect to lose sight of the not-always-maintained trail. Still, some superb views are found here. Campsites are found along lakeshores. Permits are again required.

Continue north on CR 12 for about 4 miles to Forest Road 144 and the sign for *Magnetic Rock Trail.* The trail, the entrance to which is just down the road from the parking lot, is very popular with day-trippers, so expect to see lots of like-minded hikers. The easy 1.5-miler (one-way) leads to a 60-foot-tall spear-shaped rock composed of materials that will definitely cause your compass needle some trouble. Check it out. Along the way, you cross over Larch Creek and through more forest rejuvenation from forest fires—this one from the summer of 1974. If you continue on the Gunflint Lake Trail system, maps are essential.

Across CR 12 is the trailhead (leading west) for the Kekekabic Trail, a 37-mile trail with various loops stretching to County Road 18 near Ely. The "Kek" follows an old 1930s forest firefighters trail to reach fire-spotting towers; after falling into disuse, it was eventually recreated as a hiking trail. This one requires day and overnight permits.

Continue north on CR 12 for approximately 12 miles to Trails End. The traffic thins out decidedly as you feel the End coming. Ultimately, after a 10-minute-or-so drive from the Magnetic Rock trailhead, you find yourself, appropriately enough, at the Trails End Campground (permits required). Here we find Lake Saganaga, which stretches into Canada and provides a yawning, island-dotted (over 600) greeting to your wilderness experience. Birding is a major highlight here. But even if you know zilch about avian life, wander the side trails and witness the magnificent wildflowers, found pretty much everywhere.

Return all the way to Grand Marais on CR 12. Hopefully, you've armed yourself with a gazetteer. If so, this *might* allow you to assemble a personal tour back to Grand Marais, avoiding the redundancy of CR 12 for part of the trip. But for the first third or so of the way back, even alternate routes are not an option. (Unless you take an innumerable hodgepodge of gravel-surfaced forest roads.) Also, be forewarned that, though roads may look perfect on a map, things do change, usually due to weather conditions or federal money for upkeep. Marking is haphazard at best. If signs exist at all, they may (or usually may not) correspond to what's on your map. The best thing to do is ask locally about any forest road you wish to take. The last thing you want to do is spend the night in your vehicle if you're unprepared for the elements.

Planning for the Gunflint

Famed naturalist Sigurd Olson offered perhaps the most apt description of the Boundary Waters Canoe Area: the "singing wilderness." What one would expect in Alaska is found here in a Great Lakes state.

Consider the staggering details, thanks to Olson and other environmentalists' efforts. Extending some 150 miles south from the Canadian border and its own chain of lakes, the BWCA has over a million acres of untrammeled wilderness—virtually no roads save for the watery variety (1,500 miles of them). Best, those annoying, pollution-coughing outboard motors are strictly controlled. (That alone makes it worthwhile for a lot of people.)

How do we find our personal Walden in the wilds? You can do it yourself or let someone else do all the planning. Do your homework six months to a year before you plan to go—entry points are minimal, highly popular, and highly regulated. It's all on a lottery system, so you may not get a permit at all. Familiarize yourself with www.bwcaw.org, a great source of information on regulations.

Dozens of outfitters are found along the Gunflint Trail. Contact the visitor centers in Ely, Tofte, and Grand Marais for details. A travel truism: *The more homework you do prior to a trip, the happier you'll be with the result.* For the day, you can rent a basic canoe ($30-$45) all the way up to plush, fully-appointed outfitting trips (starting at about $275 to infinity). For example, a three-day, two-night trip—plus one night before and after in a rustic cabin at a lodge—with all essentials included basically runs around $3,000-$4,000 (if you're using a Kevlar canoe).

There's plenty for hikers to do here as well. All those epic tracts of green, dotted with aqua pools, can be reached via foot. Note that permits for many trails are required. This may include a day-use permit *and* an overnight permit. These may be self-issued at trailheads or at the U.S. Forest Service office in Grand Marais. Check out www.bwcaw.org for additional information. *It is crucial you follow all rules on permits.*

Even more important: Take good topographic maps and know how to use them. A GPS reader is also dead weight if you don't know what you're doing. Be prepared for tough, sharp, and occasionally slippery rocks. Take enough food and water treatment capabilities for longer than your planned stay. Other essentials: compass (ditto with the know-how); first-aid kit; sunscreen; bug repellent (including, and this is important, a head net); enough layered clothing to keep you dry and warm (how much is up to you but most people under or overprepare—the latter is safer); fireproof matches and/or chemical fire-starting kit; and common sense.

Finally, please practice No-Trace land ethic: leave nothing but footprints, take nothing but memories, as they say. Learn about the etiquette on sanitation and camping near water, two things even seasoned hikers frequently violate.

Tour 7
The Tip of the Arrowhead

Grand Marais—Kadunce River—Judge C. R. Magney State Park—Grand Portage National Monument—Grand Portage State Park—Partridge Falls—Grand Marais

Distance: 115 miles

With this tour through the northeastern tip of Minnesota's Arrowhead region, we'll say goodbye to Highway 61. But it's not the end of the road, because the highway, which has been on display in several of our tours, crosses into Canada and, eventually, Thunder Bay.

With this tour of the state's northeastern tip, we'll encounter waterfalls, epic hiking in the founding spot of the state, even trips to the nation's most isolated state park—options are never limited. You'll find countless opportunities to disembark and clamber along river gorge trails to photograph ribbony cascades, then hike along trails used by Native Americans and later *voyageurs*.

But the heartbeat of the tour is history. If you have any twinge of interest in European exploration and economic opportunism—which would, of course, lead to permanent immigration in the Great Lakes—then make a point of taking the tour as far north as the road goes: the Grand Portage area. The "Big Carry" was the original settlement spot for Europeans in Minnesota, so-called since rough rapids on the Pigeon River precluded canoe travel, requiring hard-nosed beaver-seekers to lug their boats and stores on an epic trail to Fort Charlotte. Walking it in the summer swelter, batting away black flies, is quite likely the state's best living history experience. You can't "feel" history any more than that.

Travel northeast out of Grand Marais on Highway 61 about 9 miles to the Kadunce River. A couple of miles outside of town, Pincushion Mountain looms on the left. Its set of various looped trails (easy to difficult) totals some 10 miles. One loop takes you past a canyon and footbridge; all the way to Pincushion Mountain proffers a view of Devil Track River Gorge and a lovely view of Lake Superior. The best way to access the trails is to take County Road 12 (Gunflint Trail) from Grand Marais about 1.5 miles to the trailhead on the right.

Highway 61 dances along the edge of high cliffs and veers out, tracing the edge of the Cliff Creek promontory. After some breathtaking views, you arrive at the *Kadunce River State Wayside*. Hop out of the car and grab your fishing pole for some terrific stream fishing. A half-mile trail leads along a nice river gorge; it also links to the Superior Hiking Trail.

Continue northeast on Highway 61 approximately 6 miles to *Judge C. R. Magney State Park*. The road settles itself down and we lose sight of the big lake for a couple of segments. Don't worry; we haven't lost it yet! Magney State Park, (218) 387-2929, is best known for the ferocity of the Brule River as it rushes through rapids. It should have a head of steam as it cascades down from the Boundary Waters Canoe Area, crossing the Gunflint Trail at one point (see Tour 6). Take the scenic trail (lots of staircases, so be forewarned) to the *Devil's Kettle*, where one segment of a 50-foot waterfall mysteriously "disappears" into a huge pothole. This trail also connects to the Superior Hiking Trail.

Proceed northeast on Highway 61 for about 20 miles to *Grand Portage National Monument*. This was the location of the first white settlement in Minnesota, dating from 1731; even before then, it was where canoes had to be portaged between Lake Superior and Fort Charlotte along the Pigeon River. The burgeoning fur trade—to supply Parisian dandies with hats made from North American fur—impelled hardy traders to tough out the rough land, including various creepies, crawlers and critters, and occasional hostile reception by indigenous dwellers. (Grand Portage, incidentally, is also home to an Indian reservation.) The location even today seems remote and quite possibly malignant in the summer heat as swarms of black flies fill the air. Yet, near the Pigeon River, it was a perfect location for exploration and transport all the way to Hudson Bay.

At the monument you'll find a restored stockade and great hall, among other reconstructions. The attention to detail is amazing. And if the opulent furnishings are genuine—as is claimed—it boggles the mind to figure how one could live so regally in such a rough environment. Guides tell a detailed, interesting story as you wander about the grounds. Even those jaded on historical stops can't help but be impressed by the herculean fortitude it took to establish such a place.

Diarrhea River?

Gross or not, the Native American word *kadunce* roughly translates as "diarrhea," and stems from the, um, after-effects of high mineral content of the water (or perhaps from the many moose lounging up to their necks in the water upstream, contentedly chewing their cuds, and doing you-know-what in the water). These mineral-rich waters may have pernicious effects on humans, but fish don't seem to care: They grow to a healthy size in these waters.

35

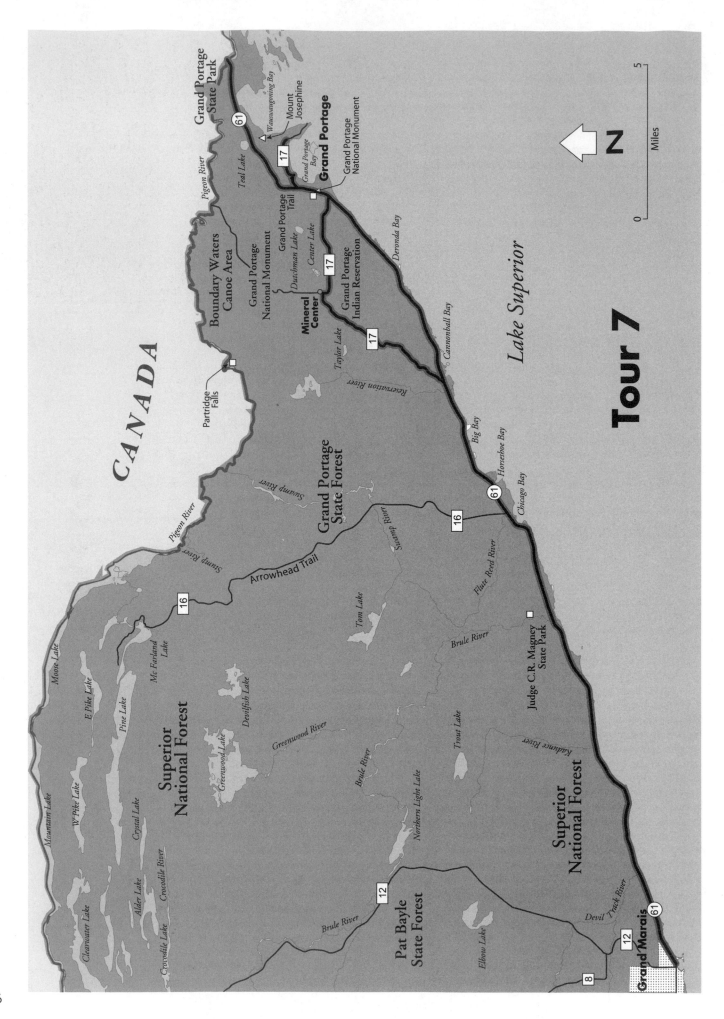

CANADA

Grand Portage State Park

Pigeon River

61

Wauswaugoning Bay

Mount Josephine

17

Teal Lake

Grand Portage Bay

Grand Portage

Grand Portage National Monument

Grand Portage Trail

Boundary Waters Canoe Area

Grand Portage National Monument

Dutchman Lake

Center Lake

17

Mineral Center

Grand Portage Indian Reservation

Deronda Bay

Lake Superior

Partridge Falls

Taylor Lake

Reservation River

17

Cannonball Bay

Pigeon River

Swamp River

Grand Portage State Forest

Big Bay

Horseshoe Bay

61

Chicago Bay

Stump River

Arrowhead Trail

Swamp River

16

Flute Reed River

16

Moose Lake

E Pike Lake

Pine Lake

Mc Farland Lake

Tom Lake

Brule River

Judge C.R. Magney State Park

Mountain Lake

W Pike Lake

Crystal Lake

Devilfish Lake

Greenwood Lake

Greenwood River

Brule River

Trout Lake

Superior National Forest

Superior National Forest

Alder Lake

Clearwater Lake

Crocodile River

Northern Light Lake

Kadunce River

Crocodile Lake

Brule River

12

Elbow Lake

Pat Bayle State Forest

Devil Track River

Grand Marais

12

61

8

N

Miles

0   5

Tour 7

One of the best times to visit is during *Rendez-vous Days*, held the second weekend in August. Not only will you find buckskin-clad re-creators living anachronistically, you'll find an authentic Ojibwe powwow, historical demonstrations, singing, and dancing. Some events charge an admission.

The *Grand Portage Hiking Trail*, a 16-mile round-trip, is a moderately tough hike along a trail used for hundreds of years by Native Americans and, later, European explorers, missionaries and economic entrepreneurs. On the way inland from Lake Superior things get quite dense—with vegetation *and* black flies and mosquitoes. Even more noticeable is the 630-foot rise along the way. On humid summer days, be sure to take *lots* of water and nourishing hiking food. You think you're in good shape? If so, figure on five hours, one way. Campsites at the historic Fort Charlotte on the Pigeon River are free but require a permit, available from the National Park Service.

A much easier trek from the national monument is via the *Mount Rose Trail*, a mere mile up 300 feet of rise (all paved), with awesome views and educational panels along the way. You can sit here, feel a nice lake breeze, and laugh at your friends who decided to hike the Grand Portage Hiking Trail.

The monument, (218) 387-2788, is open daily, 9 a.m.–5 p.m., mid-May to mid-October, though the grounds remain open year-round; admission.

Continue north on Highway 61 just under 2 miles. You're not yet done with Highway 61, though it sure seems finished, at least in spirit. It's super-efficient but seems rather forlorn by this point. Grand Portage village is next. Here you'll also

Devil's Kettle Falls at Judge C. R. Magney State Park, where one segment of the Brule River plunges into a pothole. Thomas Huhti

find a casino/lodge and, more important, next to it—the *Isle Royale Marina*. Boats depart from the marina for Isle Royale, 22 miles out in Lake Superior, the nation's most isolated national park. One mile north of the national monument on Highway 61 is the *Minnesota Travel Information Center*, (218) 475-2592, open 24 hours, May to October. The picnic area has a scenic overlook.

In the village of Grand Portage, take County Road 17 for 1.5 miles to the trailhead for the *Mount Josephine Trail.* This baby is a tough .75-mile-long switchback trail that rises 800 grueling feet to the top of Mount Josephine. You'll be glad you made the hike, though, as you gaze at the

Isle Royale Explorations

Campers should consider a breathtaking backcountry trek in what many consider to be Middle America's grandest wilderness—the wilds of Isle Royale National Park. So magnificent and untouched is Isle Royale that it is considered a living laboratory and has been tabbed as a United States Biosphere Reserve. Although, technically, part of Michigan, the island is much closer to Minnesota.

The isolated, rugged experience is unforgettable. The archipelago is 45 miles long and 9 miles wide at its widest point, totaling 850 square miles (including submerged areas). Some 170 miles of trails snake throughout the wilderness and offer access to 36 campgrounds (often very full, so you may have to double up). As you trudge along ancient rock trails, you'll spot moose, wolves, eagles, and more. And you'll find some of the best fishing you ever encountered. If you're a history buff, you can find historic lighthouses and shipwrecks, even the odd relic from an original voyageur. But be aware that everything that's found in national parks, stays in national parks.

You can travel to Isle Royale by very expensive float plane (though the year this book was researched it had been suspended), but most visitors come on ferries from either Michigan's Upper Peninsula or Grand Portage. Schedules vary year to year, but generally operate mid-June to Labor Day. The *Wenonah* and *Voyageur II* make the trip from Grand Portage. The *Voyageur II* also circumnavigates the island a couple of times a week to drop travelers off, while the popular scenic tours aboard the *Wenohah* leave Grand Portage at 9:30 a.m. and return by 6 p.m. The park itself is open mid-April to late October; admission. A caveat: even on the calmest of days, this ferry ride can be, well, an up-and-down experience. If the wind has its dander up, you'll feel like a fishing bobber out there.

And the park is cold as the dickens—even in summer—so come prepared. This is wilderness, remember, not a cushy state park campground. You had best know what you're doing, hiking and camping-wise. There's no 911 here. *Camping and access rules are strictly enforced, and you should plan well in advance if you wish to camp. Check www.nps.gov/isro, for the latest information.*

amazing vistas of Lake Superior, Pigeon Point, Susie Island, even Isle Royale.

Return to Highway 61, turn right and travel north for about 5.5 miles to *Grand Portage State Park.* Here, at the far northeastern tip of Minnesota, the Pigeon River drops an impressive 200 feet at High Falls. A 700-foot boardwalk helps provide easy access (A wheelchair-accessible overlook is also great). A newer trail—Middle Falls Trail, on which construction started just as this book was being written—begins at the park office and winds scenically over ridge tops, through thick forest, and along the river. It's a day-use-only park with fairly decent foot trails and picnic areas.

Turn southwest on Highway 61 and drive for 5.5 miles back to Grand Portage. Continue for about another 2 miles to County Road 17. Be careful here for two reasons: First, you'll want CR 17 that runs west, not the stretch that you took to Grand Portage to the Mount Josephine Trail, and, second, the road is also known as Mineral Center Road or County Road 72 (whatever the nomenclature, head for the burg of Mineral Center).

Turn right (west) and drive for 3.5 miles to Partridge Falls Road. Turn right and go north about 2 miles to the hiking trail for *Partridge Falls.* Depending on how lost you get, it could take you 10 minutes or it could take you half an hour. Eventually, our grail is a 5-mile round-trip hike along the Pigeon River, ending at a lovely 40-foot waterfall. Canada is just across the river.

Backtrack south on Partridge Falls Road to where County Road 17 continues to the west. Turn right on CR 17 and go about 6 miles to Highway 61. Proceed for about 27 miles back to Grand Marais, the start of the tour.

Quick Trip Option: If you want just one more glimpse of the Boundary Waters, you might want to take a little detour. But be forewarned that it's an 18-mile jaunt (one way on gravel, albeit well-maintained gravel for much of the route). On the way back to Grand Marais, in Hovland, 5 miles south of the junction of CR 17 and Highway 61, is the turnoff for County Road 16, better known as the *Arrowhead Trail.* You bypass several isolated turnoffs to remote boat access points, but that's about it for attractions, other than the sublime solitude that we all crave. If for no other reason, take the little road to its terminus at McFarland Lake to sit and gaze at the remote waters—and Canada, on the other side of the lake.

A Whopper of a Lake

Lake Superior is the second-largest lake in the world (it has more surface area than Lake Baikal in Russia, though the latter is more capacious). With three billion gallons of water, it contains one-eighth of the world's freshwater and would take over a century to drain completely. Lake Superior and its sister Great Lakes account for nearly 20 percent of the planet's total fresh water; fifty million people drink from its basins.

Lake Superior may have avoided the most lethal of Great Lakes' population poisonings (ship captains as late as the 1980s still scooped up Lake Superior's primeval water for *drinking*), but not for long. In 2001, the water levels of all of the Great Lakes dropped to their lowest points in a generation. At Duluth, declining water levels have a woeful impact on shipping. For every inch of draft clearance lost due to shallow channels, a carrier must reduce cargo as much as 270 tons. For a ship owner, that can be a billion dollars per year. Even canoe outfitters along the North Shore say their boats are coming back scratched and dented.

Industrial effluents have been the primary cause of the lakes' ill health—factories dumping at will, though all citizens were to blame. Even today old batteries and freezers can be pulled from the shorelines. Helter-skelter development chewed up crucial marshlands, which had heretofore acted as filters for toxic pollutants. At one point, some 75 percent of Great Lakes' shoreline was hazardous for any use. Up to 20 billion pounds of pollutants were pumped into the Great Lakes annually before we wised up a bit.

The best thing that ever happened to the Great Lakes was the Clean Water Act of 1972. The legislation spurred the Midwest to take stock of its environmental needs, and the Great Lakes were at the top of the cleanup list. A dozen hydrocarbons, pesticides, paper mill and other waste, and agricultural waste are the peskiest toxins still polluting the Great Lakes. Waste effluents from as far away as Russia are claimed to be falling into the Great Lakes. The lethal ingredients read like the periodic chart: PCBs, DDT, HCB, mercury, OC5, and weirdly named but pernicious chemicals like Chlordane, Dieldrin, and Toxaphene. DDT and PCBs are perhaps the most dangerous. As they leach out of industrial fluids, they are ingested by small fish, which are in turn eaten by larger fish, and thus, the vicious cycle has begun. Humans may be at the "top" of this food chain, but we may not wish to be.

Though dead zones still exist in the Great Lakes, all isn't lost. Sportfishing has become a billion-dollar industry and the Clean Water Act really did clean up the lakes overall. A 1986 council of Great Lakes governors signed a ban on all discharges. Intertribal agencies, the EPA and Canada have also begun cooperating to clean things up. Scientists still claim that DDT and PCB contamination has dropped up to 90 percent in human milk. Mercury, cynics counter, is up since 1972. Also, some scientists worry about the quick rise in Great Lakes water temperatures, perhaps owing to global warming. No one disputes water levels dropping and the absolute invasion of nonnative species.

Tour 8
Wolves and Water

Ely—Crane Lake—Orr—Buyck—Vermilion Lake—Tower—Soudan—Ely

Distance: approximately 170 miles

What a ride! The sine-wave tour along Minnesota 1 from the North Shore, gently rising and falling, through vast stands of dark conifer to Ely, seems carved right out of the wilderness. What splendorous solitude it is. This charming little community is the westernmost hub of life for the Boundary Waters Canoe Area, which would alone give it a-head-above-the-rest status. More than that, calling Ely home is a world-renowned wolf recovery center.

Many classic blue highways through the vast Minnesota wilderness beckon, but we mustn't forget that we're also in the Iron Range still. After a hefty number of hours wending through tree-shaded lanes, suddenly we're back spelunking into disused mines—another education in the history of that crucial lifeblood: ore.

Start your tour in Ely at the intersection of State Highways 169 and 1. Here, the *Ely Chamber of Commerce Information Center,* (218) 365-6123 or (800) 777-7281 (www.ely.org), is housed in a cute log cabin built in the late 1930s by Finnish lumberjacks. This should be the first stop for all information on canoe outfitters.

One note of historical interest to Ely visitors: Formerly known as Florence (changed when another Florence, Minnesota, noted it had already used the name), the village once stood at the east end of Shagawa Lake in the area now called Spaulding. When iron ore was discovered farther west, newly named Ely picked itself up, lock, stock and barrel and moved.

Travel one block north of the Highway 1/169 intersection on 17th Street East to Vermilion Community College. There, you'll find the *Vermilion Interpretive History Museum,* (218) 365-3226. Of particular interest is the exhibit on local-boy-done-good Will Steger, the polar explorer who gained fame with his epic trips to the North Pole. Paul Schurke, another explorer, is also profiled. Hours are Memorial Day weekend to Labor Day Sunday, daily 10 a.m.–5 p.m; admission.

Return to the junction of Highways 1 and 169. Turn left and travel two blocks. You'll arrive at one of the most charming stops in northern Minnesota—the *Dorothy Molter Museum,*

(218) 365-4451. The museum's namesake was known as the Root Beer Lady or Lady of the Wilderness, and both monikers were highly appropriate. Originally from Chicago, Molter, a registered nurse, came to the Ely wilderness and lived on the Isle of Pines (on the Canadian border) for more than 50 years (56 of her 79 years, actually.). Her medical skills regularly came in handy, but she really gained fame for offering parched travelers homemade root beer when they stumbled upon her cabins—truly the epitome of traveler karma. The museum buildings are the original buildings, which were moved here. Note the broken canoe paddles: It was considered a blessing if Dorothy used yours to line her gardens. Hours vary but generally are June 1 to August 31 daily 10 a.m.–6 p.m., with reduced hours May and September; admission.

Continue east on Highway 169 for a short distance, following the signs to the *Interna-

Ely's Hidden Treasures

Still looking for something to do in Ely (that is, after the wonderful fishing, splendid hiking, and bracing air)? Here are a couple of spots most folks completely miss. First, turn right from the chamber of commerce onto Highway 169. Go a quarter mile, turn right on Hidden Valley Road, go another quarter mile to the Hidden Valley Ski Jump. Built in 1922, it has a 47- and a 72-meter jump, both of which were used for international competitions. It's presently been mothballed due to budget cuts, but you'll find nice ski trails around it. The Hidden Valley is also good for hiking in summer. (But don't try climbing the ski jumps). Also east of Ely is the Fernberg Trail (County Road 18, after Highway 169 ends), which pierces the Boundary Waters heart for some 20 miles, bypassing two campgrounds, a canoe launch site, and the Snowbank-Old Pines Hiking Trails at the wilderness boundary. Along the way out of Ely along Highway 169, stop by the Hidden Valley Recreation Area, which has a lovely trail system wending through stands of pine, birch, and newer sections of red pine.

From the chamber of commerce office, you could also turn left onto Highway 169, go to the third stoplight, make a right, and go 1 mile. This is the Pioneer Mine Site. Although there's not a lot around here other than the usual detritus of an old mine, it does give one pause to sit and take in the historical atmosphere. Obviously, poking around old mine shafts is fraught with danger, so exercise extreme caution and keep a close watch on the kiddies at all times.

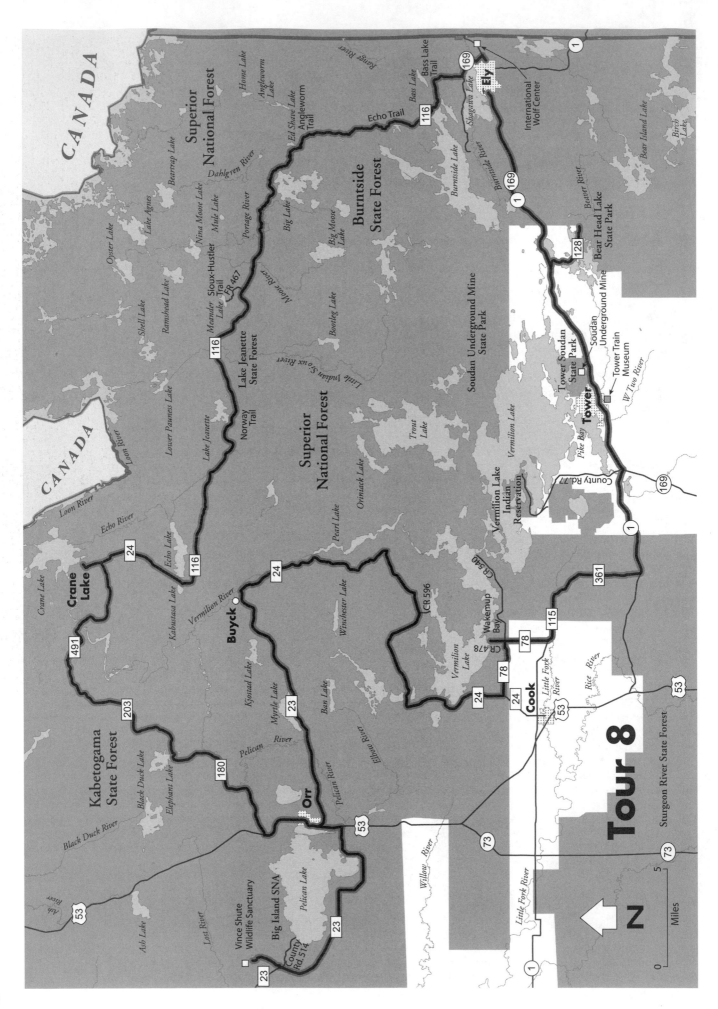

tional Wolf Center. It's impossible to visit this wonderful facility, Ely's main attraction, and not depart awed—or at least changed. Visit the center, (218) 365-4695 or (800) 359-9653, 1396 Highway 169, and its winding path through exhibits detailing the biology and natural history of the wolf. Of particular interest are the displays on the oft-confrontational relationship that the misunderstood mammal has had with humans. But, of course, what folks really come here for is to meet the center's resident wolves. There are usually around a half dozen on site and you'll get close (but behind glass). Be sure to call ahead and get specific times for the educational speeches the staff offers; they're entertaining and highly informative. Even if you think you know a lot about wolves already, you'll come away with newfound knowledge. Hours are July 1–August 31, 9 a.m.–7 p.m. daily, lesser hours mid-May to late-June, October–May; admission. Refreshing is the Trezona Trail, a 4-mile trail departing the center, which circumvents Miner's Lake.

The International Wolf Center is also home to the *Kawishiwi Wilderness Station,* (218) 365-7561, which can provide Boundary Waters information and issue permits. It's open May 1 to September 30, 6 a.m.–8 p.m. daily. Ely also is the home of the district office of the U.S. Forest Service, (218) 365-7600, 118 S. 4th Avenue East, open year-round, 8 a.m.–4:30 p.m., weekdays.

From the International Wolf Center, travel east a short distance on Highway 169 to County Road 88. Turn left (west) and drive for 2.5 miles to County Road 116 (better known as the Echo Trail). Along the way, you'll skirt the eastern shoreline of Shagawa Lake, going north, then bending back to the west. The Echo Trail is a 50-plus-mile, mostly gravel (some paved), backwoods blue highway that runs between Ely and Buyck. Great exercise for those behind the wheel, this road is full of twists and turns. Virtually every topographic feature—trees, marsh, swamp, bog, and meadow—is on display along the way. In the spring, it's a riot of wildflower colors. In the fall, it's a melange of soothing autumnal earth tones juxtaposed with the brilliance of ROY G BIV primary colors. Eyes should be open for moose, deer, bear and, if you're lucky, a wily wolf.

Turn right (north) on CR 116 and go about 2.5 miles, looking for signs marking a trailhead. As you travel, the Superior National Forest is to the right and Burntside State Forest is to the left. No, you can't much tell the difference, but it's nice to know where you are! At the trailhead, hop out and explore the tall grasses and cathedrals of pines on the *Bass Lake Trail,* a moderate and short (5 miles) hop that circumnavigates glimmering Bass lake.

Travel north for about 13 miles to the *Angleworm Trail.* Appearing just north of Beartrap

Denizens of the wolves' den at the International Wolf Center in Ely. Thomas Huhti

Spring Creek, Angleworm is a lengthier trek (13 miles total) than the previous one, and it has its challenging moments. Its rewards include a plunge into the wilderness around a half-dozen lakes.

Continue north on CR 116 for about 12 miles to Forest Road 467. About a quarter of a mile through this stretch, stop and enjoy superb fishing at Big Lake (park at the boat launch). Go for walleye or northern pike, though panfish are also abundant.

At FR 467 (although road signs might not be apparent), turn right and go about 1.5 miles to the *Sioux-Hustler Trail.* The trail begins at appropriately named Meander Lake and continues for a quite a long stretch through some rugged terrain. It's more appropriate for a multi-day backpacking trip, but you may consider a short jaunt up and back on a portion of the trail.

Return to CR 116 and continue west for about 10 miles to *Lake Jeanette.* About a third of the way, you'll enter the Lake Jeanette State Forest, a seamless transition from one state forest to the next. You may want to disembark at the Sioux River for a quick leg stretch, then continue on to

Return of the Wolf

Perhaps no animal better represents the natural world and the North Woods than the timber wolf *(canis lupus),* also known as the gray wolf. Yet, paradoxically, though this grand animal so represents freedom, wilderness, and strength, at the same time it's fought a centuries-old stigma that nearly caused us to exterminate the species.

The timber wolf is related to the dog. (Note: if you swear you saw a wolf, you probably saw a coyote, of which there are hordes in the Midwest. If/when you see a timber wolf, consider yourself blessed.) They are grayish brown with dark patches on their back and neck. Judging by their tracks—3 inches wide by 4 inches long—they're much larger than most dogs and coyotes. The old stories are true: their jaws can snap steel.

Their social life is intriguing. A wolf "pack" consists of a breeding pair—alphas—and their offspring. The unit is incredibly tightly knit (humans should be so responsible). Alphas generally breed each year in February and a litter of up to a half-dozen pups is born in April. Of this litter, two or three will survive to age two, when they leave the family's protection.

Wolf packs live in territories and defend it fiercely. Within this range they live on a diet of deer along with small mammals. Beaver is a delicacy. Turkey, too, which is why wild turkey hunters should pay close attention to their surroundings, since they're covered in camouflage clothing and may be wearing deer scent. The smallest wolf pack territory ranges from 20 square miles to over 120 square miles. But these wolves can travel enormous distances when they disperse to search for pack-free territory. One wolf traveled from Wisconsin to Rainy Lakes District of Ontario, Canada!

There has never been an established report of a wolf attack on a human. All hunters who've had close encounters with them in the 1990s reported wolves moved away very quickly. Nevertheless, most humans don't know that, and this, along with livestock attacks, brought about the wolf's reputation as a varmint. By 1960, the animals had been hunted to extinction in most states (they've been listed as endangered by the United States since 1973). Even the great naturalist Aldo Leopold had considered wolves worthless and hunted them. Then, one day, Leopold's epiphany occurred, which would launch his seminal ecological career. And it happened as he gazed into the dying eyes of a wolf he'd shot.

National awareness started changing in the 1970s, when federal plans were made to reestablish the wolf. (Yellowstone National Park gets all the press, but it happened throughout the upper Midwest. Minnesota gets kudos.)

Many states have angered environmentalists by considering future timber wolf hunts once numbers have rebounded to sustainable levels. Farmers and stock owners would be able to "eliminate" nuisance animals. Later plans could include a brief hunt, with licenses likely being available by a lottery.

Lake Jeanette (complete with campground and boat launch). Also in the area, you'll find another hiking trail: the *Norway Trail.*

Continue north and west on CR 116 for another 11 miles to County Road 24. A mile before the intersection, you'll see long and narrow Echo Lake, another in the endless series of picturesque and serene lakes in the region. And, like many of the others, it comes with boat launch and campground.

Turn right (north) on CR 24 and cruise 8 miles to Crane Lake. The town of Crane Lake is, like Ely, ensconced happily in pristine wilderness. This one is contiguous to both the Boundary Waters Superior National Forest region and Voyageurs National Park. The area is a great spot for birders. If you decide to strike out into the national park waters, near the Northwest Bay beaches on Crane Lake, watch for a *blue heron rookery.* Farther north, Namakan Lake is a primary gull nesting site.

Just northwest of Crane Lake, Gold Coast Road leads to the trailhead of the *Vermilion Gorge Trail,* a mere 1.5 miles, but what a lovely traipse. (Well, it is a three-hour round-trip traipse, but it is fetching.) The front half of the trail, to the Vermilion River from Crane Lake, is graveled and easy; boardwalks cover any messy spots. The tail end of this trail parallels the Vermilion River Gorge, a splendid area of rugged granite cliffs and rock formations.

From Crane Lake, go south about 1 mile to Forest Road 491, turn right (west) and go about 5.5 miles to the trailhead for the *Vermilion Falls Trail.* This leads to a mere 10-minute hike on a well-maintained trail leading to a splendid little cascade. For a meager 10-foot-wide opening, it's an awesome display of energy. Fish for smallmouth bass at the base of the falls. You can easily spend an additional hour or two exploring the area around the falls: Look for the "Chute" and a small wild rice bed.

Continue west on FR 491 for 2.5 miles to Forest Road 203, turn left (south), and proceed for about 22 miles to U.S. Highway 53, joining County Road 180 along the way. Turn left (south) on 53 and go 4.5 miles to County Road 23. Before turning onto CR23, you'll pass through the town of Orr, on the eastern shore of massive Pelican Lake.

Turn right at CR 23, then travel for 13.5 miles (in every conceivable direction but east). After County Road 514 (East Nett Lake Road), go a very short distance, turn right on the first gravel road, and follow it for 2 miles north to the *Vince Shute Wildlife Sanctuary.* Travelers love to come here Tuesdays through Sundays (Memorial Day to Labor Day) for perfor-

Lake Jeanette, along the Echo Trail, northwest of Ely. Tim Bewer

mances by the local residents—black bears. Supported in part by the American Bear Association, this 360-acre sanctuary and former logging camp has a supplemental feeding program that's sometimes visited by as many as 50 bears an evening. From 5 p.m. to dusk you're allowed to watch from elevated platforms as naturalists describe everything that happens below. It's highly educational.

Backtrack to CR 23 and proceed east back to U.S. 53. Turn left (north), go a mile, then turn right (east) onto the continuation of CR 23. Proceed for about 15 miles to the junction with CR 24 in tiny Buyck. Turn right on CR 24 and cruise south, then west, for about 13 miles to County Road 596 (Cedar Road) on the north shore of Vermilion Lake. For most of the stretch along CR 24, the Vermilion River snakes its way northward on your left. The lake of the same name is a wonder to behold. Boreal forest lines the shores (over 1,200 miles of shoreline); sunken islands and massive reefs provide havens for fishers' quarry. Nearly 300 loons reside here, along with osprey, eagles, and a variety of waterfowl. Boaters can explore the 350-plus islands and sandy beaches.

Turn left (south) at CR 596 and go a short distance to the *Black Bay Trail.* This is a gorgeous little trip, and you're guaranteed to be alone (well, usually) as it's the state's only water access-only hiking trail system. (This will require you to rent something if you haven't lugged it along on the roof rack.) This is one of three water launch points on Vermilion Lake; all are shown on maps. The easiest is a 2-mile interpretive trail. You'll also find a slightly longer intermediate/advanced trail. High-

lights? Blueberry and raspberry bushes. Botanists say ferns are aplenty here as well.

Return to CR 24 and continue west, then south to County Road 78 (a total of about 15 miles). Turn left (east) on 78 and proceed for about 3 miles to County Road 478 (78 turns south here).

Quick Trip Option 1: Turn left (north) on CR 478 and go 1 mile to Wakemup Bay, which has a boat launch area and a campground on the southern shore of Lake Vermilion. This is also the fringe of the Sturgeon River State Forest. Return to the junction with CR 78 and turn left (east) onto County Road 540. You'll be rewarded with a leisurely 8-or-so-mile trip along the Vermilion River peninsula, the end of which has a canoe route and access to numerous island campsites (your own boat is required). Return west to the junction with CR 78 and 478.

Continue south on CR 78 for 2.5 miles to County Road 115. Turn left and proceed east for about 3 miles to County Road 361. Turn right and go for 5.5 miles to State Highway 1. The greenery turns soppy as you wend through the Lost Lake Swamp of the Sturgeon River State Forest.

Turn left (east) on Highway 1 and continue for about 7 miles to the junction with State Highway 169. Turn left (north) on 1/169 and proceed for less than 5 miles to Tower.

Quick Trip Option 2: Just after the junction of Highways 1 and 169, County Road 77 breaks to the

Vermilion Falls in the Superior National Forest, near Crane Lake. Tim Bewer

(218) 753-6017. Designed to celebrate the culture of the Bois Forte Ojibwe tribe, it features a variety of exhibits and displays on regional natural history as well as cultural performances. A highlight for all is the re-creation of a wigwam. Hours for the museum are Tuesday–Saturday, 10 a.m.–5 p.m. Thursday till 8 p.m. Near the casino and heritage center is the trailhead for the lovely *Fortune Bay Trail* and its interpretive signs detailing the lake's fascinating history: Native Americans, gold prospecting, early European settlement, and much more. A bit farther on, Highway 77 traces the *very* edge of Lake Vermilion and offers smashing views and guaranteed traffic-less driving. Return to Highway 1/169 and cruise into Tower.

In Tower, at the intersection of Highways 1/169 and 135, go east one block to the *Tower Train Museum.* This represents an eye-catching piece of history, an important hearkening of the mining days, as it was from the Soudan mine to the east that the first ore shipment rumbled to the shipping docks in Two Harbors. The leviathan 1910 steam locomotive on display was built to haul ore, passengers, and food. Today it's chock-full of mining exhibits and memorabilia. For some reason you'll also find a memorial to President McKinley, erected in honor of his assassination in 1901. Open weekends after Memorial Day until mid-June, 10 a.m.–4 p.m., then daily 10 a.m.–4 p.m. through Labor Day; free.

Continue east for 2 miles on Highway 1/169 to Soudan. Turn left on Stuntz Bay Road. Shortly, you'll be at what many might consider the highlight of this tour, a descent into the labyrinth of a half-mile-deep mine (the state's farthest subterranean mine). It feels primevally chilly and damp, much the way it did upon closure back in 1963. *Soudan Underground Mine State Park,* (218) 753-2245, also has tours of extant mine buildings, miles of hiking trails through wildlife restoration habitat, a nature trail circumventing an open-pit chasm, and orientation films. Tours are offered daily Memorial Day to Labor Day, roughly every half hour 10:30 a.m.–4 p.m.; admission, plus state park vehicle pass.

Return to Highway 1/169 and continue east for 7 miles to County Road 128. Turn right (south) and drive for 7 miles to *Bear Head Lake State Park.* Negotiating the serpentine roads will eventually reward you with this isolated and picturesque park, (218) 365-7229. Nature and hiking trails (17 miles total) wind around a calm lake. Sit still and you may see a loon, an eagle, a wolf, even a moose. Eagles' nests are marked by the DNR, and most staff are happy to help point them out, along with other species.

Return to Highway 1/169 and cruise 12 miles back to home base at Ely.

north and leads to the peninsula overlooking Pike Bay, a part of Lake Vermilion. Almost immediately you'll stumble upon the *Pike River State Fish Hatchery,* (218) 753-5692, an operation that keeps Lake Vermilion stocked with its signature fish—walleye. Every spring a number of the local lake walleye make their way up the Pike River to spawn; workers here collect and combine eggs and milk from the walleyes. The take? Some 75 million fertilized eggs. Morning, by the way, is the best time to observe the activities. The state has even built a viewing platform for just that purpose.

As the road dead-ends at the end of the peninsula, you'll find the *Vermilion Lake Indian Reservation,* with its *Fortune Bay Casino,* a well-advertised facility along the route, and the *Bois Forte Heritage Center and Cultural Museum,*

Tour 9
The Iron Range

Chisholm—Hibbing—Eveleth—Biwabik—Aurora—Hoyt Lakes—Virginia—Mountain Iron—Chisholm

Distance: 110 miles

Bob Dylan, the Mesabi Iron Range, Greyhound buses, and a hockey hall of fame. Grim but enormously productive iron mines and incredible stretches of forest and lake. Despite the seeming incongruities of these tour highlights, there is one constant running through the entire region: the legendary lodes of iron that were extracted from subterranean labyrinths and that have played a major role in Minnesota's economy.

Hibbing begat the ore, then later birthed Bob Dylan and even famed basketball player Kevin McHale. Eveleth, a sister ore city, today revels in another aspect of Gopher culture—hockey, as the home of the United States Hockey Hall of Fame. Just for good measure, we get another healthy dose of the Finns and their homesteader culture.

But, no, we never really avoid the ore itself. Unimaginable amounts led to not one but *two* legendary iron "ranges"—the Mesabi and the Vermilion—in Minnesota's Arrowhead Region. No less than 70 percent of the nation's iron ore came from these areas at one time. Today, nature's grandeur gets the lion's share of attention in these parts. But keep in mind what really drew the hordes of immigrants in the first place. These bedraggled, forlorn-looking, cooper-hued hills helped build a nation. They're not pretty, but certainly historically relevant, and worthy of our attention and respect.

The best information source for your trip is the Iron Trail Convention and Visitors Bureau, 403 North 1st Street, Virginia, (800) 777-8497 (www.irontrail.org).

Start your tour in downtown Chisholm at the junction of U.S. Business Highway 169 and State Highway 73. Two blocks north and about three blocks east is the *Chisholm Chamber of Commerce*, (800) 422-0806, 10 NW 2nd Street. Here, you'll get the lowdown on this gorgeous town. Some people, however, would prefer that the qualifier, "for an Iron Range town," follow that assessment.

Go west a few blocks on Highway 73/Business 169 to Memorial Park (a half block from the prominent water tower). Here the *Minnesota Museum of Mining*, (218) 254-5543, 900 Lake Street West, is often overlooked. It's worth a stop, though, fairly well centered downtown with worthy exhibits on mining heritage. If it's not open, you can still clamber aboard early mining trucks, early-twentieth-century steam locomotives, and steam shovels that dot the yard. Most people love the walk down into a simulated underground drift. The museum is open early May to Labor Day, 10 a.m.–5 p.m. daily; admission.

Continue south on Highway 73/Business 169 to Highway 169, turn right (west), and go a short distance to the *Ironworld Discovery Center*. This impressive operation, (800) 372-6437 (www.ironworld.com), is the Iron Range's most popular single attraction. If you're at all intrigued by mining heritage or ethnic mosaics of the Iron Range, this is a must-stop. Located on the edge of the Glen Mine (no longer operational), Ironworld is much more than an astonishing mining museum. It also celebrates the immigrant traditions of the Arrowhead region, including a replica of an Old World Finnish camp and a primitive Norwegian farm building.

Take a load off by hopping aboard an authentic 1920s trolley to get a feel for the miners' lives as you chug along from the open pit overview to the exhibition halls. You'll build up a serious appetite, so head for the great dining room and sample the hearty immigrant food. You can even see Old World fare being prepared in the lower floor of the museum. Wildly popular are the immigrant-oriented festivals that take place in the auditorium here. Especially popular is the Festival Finlandia in mid-August. But European-Americans of all ethnicities have something to enjoy: Slavic Celebration (mid-July), Button Box Music Festival (late July), and the highlight—the National Polkafest (late June).

Just across the road from the Ironworld complex is an 85-foot-tall statue of an iron miner—the country's third-largest freestanding memorial.

Continue on Highway 169/73 south and west for 5 miles to Hibbing. At Howard Street, turn right (west) and drive a short distance. You may want to make your first stop at the cheery *Hibbing Area Chamber of Commerce*, (218) 262-3895, 211 East Howard Street.

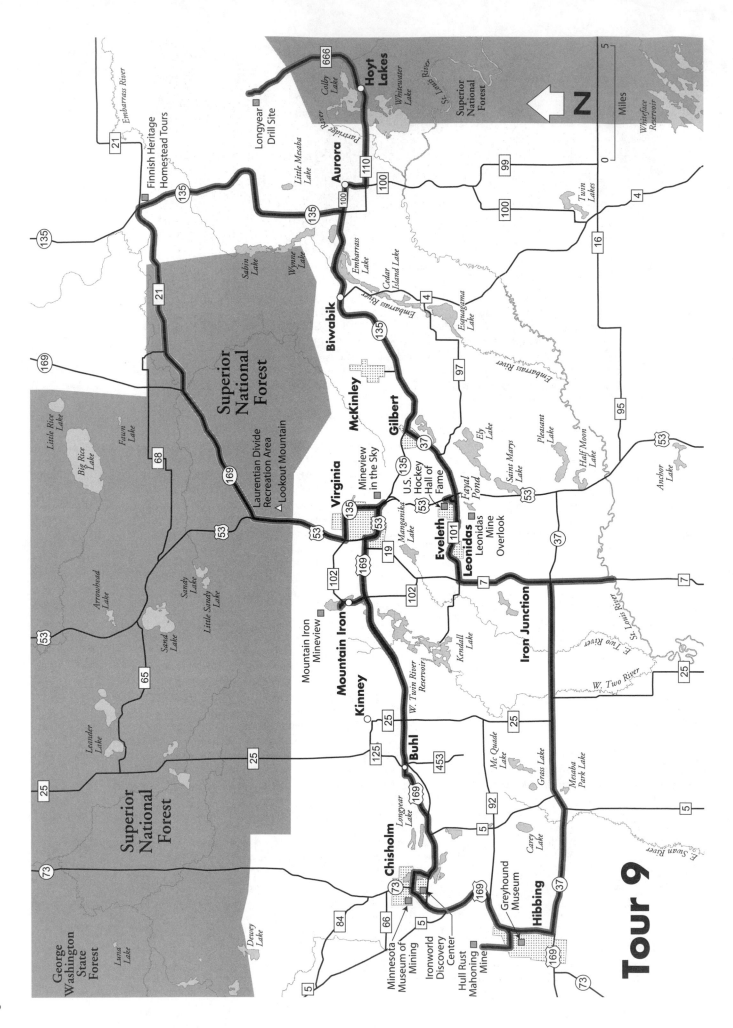

Sod-roofed Finnish dwelling at Ironworld Discovery Center, Chisholm. Tim Bewer

From Howard Street to 3rd Avenue East; turn right (north) and drive about 4 blocks to the *Greyhound Museum.* Hibbing was the birthplace of the Greyhound Bus Company, and the Greyhound Museum, (218) 263-5814, 1201 3rd Avenue East, was established to pay tribute to the fading era of mass bus service. The company started in 1914 as a way of ferrying miners to and from work. Lots of transportation-themed relics are here, but most people go directly to the hangar-sized garage to get a peep at all those old Greyhound buses lined up! Hours are Monday–Saturday, 9 a.m.–5 p.m., Sunday, 1–5 p.m., mid-May to late September; admission.

Continue north on 3rd Avenue East and follow the signs to *Hull Rust Mahoning Mine.* This mine, (218) 262-4900, is the world's largest open-pit iron ore mine. The mammoth operation encompasses more than 2,200 acres and embraces over 50 individual mines that have operated here, most from 1895 and 1957. In total, over 1.4 billion tons of earth have been removed, resulting in what they understatedly call the "Grand Canyon of the North." During the 1940s, as much as one-quarter of the ore mined in the United States came from right here. Today, visitors can view, jaw-dropped, an earth scar some 3 miles long, 2 miles wide, and 535 feet deep. Slide presentations educate visitors on the fascinating history and mining practices. Hours are daily 9 a.m.–6 p.m. summers; free.

Return to Howard Street, turn left (east) and go back to Highway 169/73. Turn right (south), drive for 2 miles to State Highway 37, and turn left (east). Continue for about 16 miles to County Road 7. Turn right (south) and go less than 3 miles to the *Saint Louis River.* Here, a number of nearby canoe access points are available, allowing for easy paddling on the brownish waters. Around here, the sport of choice is fishing, but there are lots of birds about and even a few picnic spots.

Return north on CR 7 for 7 miles, past Highway 37, to County Road 101. Turn right (east) and drive 2 miles to the *Leonidas Mine Overlook.* Here, more mammoth ore production beckons. This time the attraction is the Leonidas Mine (named for Leonidas Merritt, one of seven brothers who developed the Mesabi Iron Range). Opened in 1908, the mine is still in operation, and you'll not be surprised to learn that it is the largest man-made point on the Iron Trail. From the overlook, you get a commanding, 15-mile, 360-degree view, and you can even see the Laurentian Divide, North America's major east-west watershed, on the horizon.

Continue east on CR 101 for about 1 mile to the south edge of Eveleth. Along this stretch on the right, you'll see the gaping maw of the Thunderbird South Mine.

Turn left (north) at Kennedy Avenue, go two blocks to Jones Street, turn right, and go another two blocks to Hat Trick Avenue; turn left and proceed to the *U.S. Hockey Hall of Fame.* What else would you expect on Hat Trick Avenue? You're in the land where ice hockey is a religion, so it's no surprise that Minnesota is home to the Hockey Hall of Fame, (218) 744-5167. (By the way, it's here because the museum's board of directors decided that no U.S. town of comparable size had contributed as much to the sport.) The highlight is undoubtedly the exhibits on the "Miracle on Ice," the gold medal-winning U.S. hockey team's defeat of the Soviet Union in the 1980 Lake Placid Olympic Games. Other highlights include women's hockey (including the U.S. women's own 1998 Olympic championship). Fun is learning about the history of the Zamboni, the puttering ice-resurfacing machines. Hours are Monday–Saturday 9 a.m.–5 p.m., Sunday, 10 a.m.–3 p.m.; admission.

And you can't leave Eveleth without viewing the landmark hockey stick on display downtown. Not surprisingly, it's the world's largest at 107 feet long. It beat out a Canadian rival for the record because the latter was judged by the Guinness Book of World Records not to be a real hockey stick. Eveleth's giant is made of white and yellow aspen.

Return to CR 101, turn left (east) and go a short distance to the junction of U.S. Highway 53 and State Highway 37. Before you get there, pull into *Fayal Pond Park* on the right side. From here you can take a nice hiking/biking trail south into wetlands and residual prairie.

Drive east across Highway 53 to Highway 37, and proceed east for about 3.5 miles to State Highway 135 in Gilbert. Continue for another 8 miles to Biwabik. Probably the town's biggest claim to fame is "Honk the Moose," a character in a children's book written in 1935. The story was set in Biwabik and used actual residents of the town. It was runner-up for the prestigious Newberry Medal and was named one of the 100 best children's books of the twentieth century. Honk now lives in Biwabik's downtown park. A kitschy bit of fun is a photo with Honk!

Continue east on 135 to County Road 100, then into the town of Aurora, a total of 5 miles. At this point the road gets interesting. One second, the view is filled with gorgeous northern Minnesota greenery; the next, gaping remnants of ore extraction—both images emblematic of the region.

Aurora, the self-proclaimed "Star of the North," got its moniker from a particularly brilliant display of the northern lights above the village in 1903. Judging by the quaintness of the place today, it's a perfect story. An autumnal county favorite is *Pumpkinfest*, with craft shows, a quilting demonstration, and lots of kiddie games.

Continue south on CR 100 for about 1 mile to County Road 110. Turn left (east) and proceed for 4.5 miles to the town of Hoyt Lakes. At the stop sign, turn left (north) on County Road 666 and drive 3 miles. Here, you'll view another bit of local history. The *Longyear Drill Site* was the first diamond drill site on the Mesabi Iron Range, dating from 1890. Beginning with the first diamond-tipped drill, which powered down 1,293 feet using steam, E. J. Longyear would eventually drill over 7,000 pits in the region. The company he founded would become a world leader in mining exploration. A nice quarter-mile nature trail is a bonus.

Return to Hoyt Lakes and CR 110. Go west, then north for about 6 miles to State Highway 135 just west of Aurora. Drive north on 135 for about 11.5 miles to the junction with County Road 21. Here, opposite the Four Corners Café is a visitor center for another stop in our Finn-oriented tour—the *Finnish Heritage Homestead Tours*, (218) 984-2084. This is actually an amalgam of historic buildings in the surrounding area. From the visitor center you can pick up brochures for a 15-mile, three-hour circle tour where you'll see lots of log homes, articles, and homesteader equipment. The craft shop near the end is fantastic; over 200 artisans are represented. Tours are offered at 1 p.m. Fridays and Saturdays, May to September; admission.

Where Iron Is King

Following the inadvertent discovery of red-hued ore by Leonidas Merritt near Mountain Iron in 1890, iron soon rivaled timber as one of Minnesota's economic linchpins. At one time Chisholm's mining district had 45 active mines shipping ore. Hibbing was carved out of a forest to get at the ore and plat a town. Virginia straddled both worlds: It had the world's largest white pine mill in the world *and* the biggest ore-producing mine.

It's difficult to dispel the sad stereotypes of ore ranges: windblown, desolate, dusty, not unlike a grim Midwest version of the 49er-esque spaghetti Westerns. However, the massive wealth pulled from the ground had some extraordinary results for the communities that the industry spawned. Historic buildings line the downtown districts. Virginia, for example, has its entire downtown on the National Register of Historic Places. And Chisholm puts the lie to the stereotype of ugly mining town.

Moreover, the money was actually used to benefit the workers. Chisholm's school district was legendary in quality. Hibbing was so wealthy by the turn of the twentieth century that the mines couldn't find anyone who needed relief outside of a handful of widows. All range towns had enormous civic works projects. This was paid for by the mines—owners purportedly faced some 90 percent of local tax burdens. Again, an absolutely mind-boggling thought in our contemporary business climate.

It's still possible to get an up-close glimpse of an erstwhile world from two local mines. It's an amazing sight indeed to see a 30-yard capacity shovel—so big a 4 x 4 could fit into its bucket—next to one of those gargantuan dump trucks, the Tonka truck on steroids. Kids squeal with delight (kids at heart, too). The Minntac Taconite Plant, (218) 749-7469, in Mountain Iron offers tours departing from the town's senior citizen center. Times vary, so call ahead. Tours to the Hibbing Taconite Mine begin from the Ironworld Discovery Center (see above); again, dates and times vary. Note: Clothing requirements and age restrictions vary, so always call first.

Boyhood home of Bob Dylan in Hibbing. Thomas Huhti

Take CR 21 west for 9 miles to State Highway 169, turn left (southwest) and proceed for 7 miles to the *Laurentian Divide Recreation Area*, joining U.S. Highway 53 along the way. This area divides the Red River and Rainy River basins from the Minnesota River and Lake Superior basins. The activity-oriented parkland is a trailhead for the Lookout Mountain hiking/ski trails. The highlight here is the set of backcountry trails (totaling 8 miles) that takes you to the top of Lookout Mountain. The vista is breathtaking.

Continue south on Highway 53/169 for 4 miles to State Highway 135. Look to your left as you travel for a glimpse of the massive complex of the Ispat Inland Mining Taconite Plant, the nucleus of which is the yawning Minorca Pit (surrounded by other mining chasms).

Turn left (east) on Highway 135 and follow it for 1 mile into downtown Virginia. Virginia was known as the "Queen City." This was due to its social progressivism (funded by enormous mining wealth). The postcard aesthetics help, too. (As you drive around, one can't-miss sight is the world's largest floating loon sitting contentedly atop Silver Lake right downtown.) *Olcott Park*, North 9th Street and 9th Avenue, is home to a modest historical museum. Gardeners will love the *Virginia Greenhouse*, (218) 741-1136, which features a lovely landscaped garden amidst 40 acres of manicured grounds. Hours for the park are daily 8 a.m.–dusk; the greenhouse is open daily 7 a.m.–7 p.m., June–August; greatly reduced hours the rest of the year. The park/greenhouse are free; the museum has an admission charge.

Kaleva Hall downtown was the nucleus of "Finntown" in the early twentieth century. A social spot for homesick Finns fresh off the boat (or railroad), the place has been lovingly refurbished to its original grandeur and is worth a stop.

Not far from Kaleva Hall (at the east end of 3rd Street N, three blocks north of Chestnut Street) is the *Finntown Overlook Park*. Here, you can view, astonishingly close to downtown Virginia, the Rouchleau group of mines: 3 miles long, a half mile wide, and 450 feet deep. More than 300 million tons of iron ore were taken from here in the heydays of mining. You can walk out on a 50-foot caged

Bob Dylan Slept Here

If you're looking for a Robert Zimmerman—a.k.a. Bob Dylan—experience, there's a lot in Hibbing, but it's not very centralized, or even recognized much on a civic level. Dylan was seven years old when his family moved here in 1948, and he stayed in Hibbing for most of his life until he departed for stardom. His family home lived most of that time at 2425 7th Avenue East. (The house still stands but it is private property, so be respectful.) Bob Dylan and Kevin McHale (an ex-University of Minnesota and Boston Celtic great) attended Hibbing High School, and tours of the auditorium are possible; contact the school (via the chamber of commerce; see above). The *Hibbing Public Library*, (218) 262-1038, 2020 East 5th Avenue, has a copy of the yearbook from Dylan's graduation year—1959. The library also houses a modest collection of Dylan memorabilia. If you crave a lot more Dylan-oriented stuff, head downtown to *Zimmy's/The Atrium*, (218) 262-6145, a local restaurant on Howard Street. Here you'll find more exhibits on the singer, including the piano he belted out songs on at Hibbing High School so many years ago.

The ultimate in off-road vehicles—a 240-ton capacity mine truck at Mineview in the Sky, Virginia. Thomas Huhti

and drive for 2.5 miles to County Road 102 at Mountain Iron. Turn right (north) and, heading toward the water tower, go 1 mile to Main Street. Turn left (west), go two blocks, and take a right onto Mountain Avenue, then one block to Locomotive Street. Here you'll find *Mountain Iron Park* and the *Mountain Iron Mineview*. Credit this humble town with the origins of the iron boom. In August 1891 a massive tornado leveled much of the county. A couple of months later, John Nichols, who was working for Leonidas Merritt and his brothers, happened upon reddish-tinged ore in the uprooted wilderness and, *voila*! Logging was suddenly supplanted by eager immigrants digging for darker gold. Nowadays, most people come simply to gaze at the hole in the ground where history was made. But they can also view mining equipment, a 1910 locomotive in the park, and a massive statue of Leonidas Merritt just down the street.

safety bridge for a superb view. Even better—a paved recreation trail (the Mesabi Trail) has a trailhead here, so strike out into the heart of the wilderness.

Continue south 1 mile on Highway 135 to the junction with Highway 53 and *Mineview in the Sky*. This is a must-see—an awe-inspiring view of one of the wonders of the local ore industry. From a 20-story overlook, you get an even better view of the Rouchleau Mines than from the Finntown Overlook. Near the observation deck, you can get a great up-close look at a 240-ton, 21-foot-high mining truck, called "King of the Lode". You'll find equally leviathan rail cars, production trucks, a kids' playground, and a visitor information center. Open May to September, 9 a.m.–6 p.m.; free.

Go back through Mountain Iron and return to Highway 169. Turn right (west) and proceed for 9 miles to Buhl. The road here is different from others we've seen on this tour—not a hint of forests or mines. Just south of Buhl on County Road 453 (Morse Road) is the *Great Scott Wildlife Management Area*, which sports a diverse cross-section of northern Minnesota wildlife: moose, bear, deer, wolves, osprey, loons, fishers, and more. Also, you can hike on three miles of grassy trails. The small lake you walk around is super for migratory waterfowl viewing.

Continuing on Highway 169, cruise for about 6 miles to where Business 169 turns into Chisholm. Follow that to the junction with Highway 73, where you began this tour.

Take Highway 53 west and north for about 2 miles to U.S. Highway 169. Turn left (west)

Superior National Forest Scenic Byway

There is a quick, yet scenic, way to get from the Iron Trail to Silver Bay on Minnesota's North Shore. The Superior National Forest Scenic Byway (its official name as of its 2003 grand opening) runs from Aurora to Silver Bay through the magnificent Superior National Forest. The entire flora and fauna of northern Minnesota appear on this gorgeous roll—bears, moose, wolves, and about a dozen other prime species. On a straight run, one could make it in around an hour. But it could easily take all day, as the route follows County Roads 110, 16, then 15 on its way to Silver Bay.

There are numerous scenic attractions along the byway south of Hoyt Lakes. Approximately 5 miles south is the Bird Lake Recreation Area, with 9 miles of hiking and cross-country trails through dense stands of spruce, aspen, birch, and conifer; you may even see a moose or two. It surrounds lovely Pequaywan Lake. Just north is the one-of-a-kind Timber Arch Bridge, a three-pine bridge crossing the Partridge River.

You have over the next miles lots of turnout options—one to picnic areas at Norway Point (look for century-old Norway pines). Stone and Big Lakes are lovely—the former has wild rice and waterfowl; the latter is great for walleyes! Eight miles south of Hoyt Lakes, the Skibo Vista offers unparalleled, 20-mile views of the Laurentian Divide. Keep an eye out for migrating hawks. At Jenkins Creek, check out the Jenkins Creek Hiking Trail, a ruffed grouse habitat. Eventually, you'll pass over the Saint Louis River, which offers excellent canoeing opportunities.

Tour 10
The Nation's Icebox . . . and Voyageurs National Park

International Falls—Voyageurs National Park—Orr—Littlefork—Smokey Bear State Forest—Grand Mound—International Falls

Distance: approximately 180 miles

International Falls is cold. How cold is it? It's so cold. . . .

You can probably fill in the rest with any number of punchlines, but there is an element of truth to the levity. That's because it does get a mite chilly in these parts come January and February (when temperatures nearing 40°F below zero are not uncommon). That's why you'll find a great big thermometer in downtown International Falls, and why television weather casters across the nation love to talk about the city as if it were in Siberia (which viewers in Florida and Arizona get a special kick out of). But heck, International Falls is usually a bit chillier than the rest of the continental United States any time of the year. And, thus, its residents take a lot of pride in the town's nickname, the Nation's Icebox.

But, depending on what statistical method one chooses to use, a couple of other towns vie with International Falls for this distinction. So, even if the town isn't the nation's coldest, it's darn close! Actually, you'll find the Falls to be a lovely town on the Rainy River, as it flows out of Rainy Lake to Lake of the Woods. Actual falls once existed here, but they were submerged by a reservoir in 1905.

But the area is so much more than just wintry popsicle life. To the east is the sublime Voyageurs National Park, equal in majesty to the Boundary Waters Canoe Area Wilderness. (And a really quick drive!) To the west, the first leg of the Waters of the Dancing Sky Scenic Byway stretches along the Minnesota-Canada border with nearly 50 established stop-off points for look-sees.

Start your tour in downtown International Falls at the junction of U.S. Highway 71 and State Highway 11. Here, you'll find the *International Falls Chamber of Commerce and Convention & Visitors Bureau*, (800) 325-5766, 301 Second Avenue (www.rainylakemn.com), while across the street is a *Minnesota Travel Center.* Take your pick. Both are full of helpful information. From here, it's probably a good idea to park the car and walk to the first couple of attractions.

If you're *really* up for an interesting trip, consider the *Rainy Lake Bike Trail*, one of the most scenic bike paths you'll ever take. This one traces the Rainy River eastward from the center of downtown International Falls to near the Rainy Lake Visitor Center entrance in Voyageurs National Park, a total of 11 miles.

Walk west on 3rd Street for a couple of blocks to 6th Avenue. Here, at 214 6th Avenue, is what most folks come here to see. First off, there's the big thermometer, easily the photo op of the entire tour (yes, even if it's a frigid minus-30 degrees Fahrenheit). Then, there's the popular *Smokey Bear statue*, which likely gets as many shutterbug visits as the big mercury stick. If you're taking notes for postcards, Smokey stands in at a whopping 26 feet high, and he weighs some 82 tons. Wow!

Giant thermometer in downtown International Falls— a show of civic pride in the city's frigid reputation.
Thomas Huhti

51

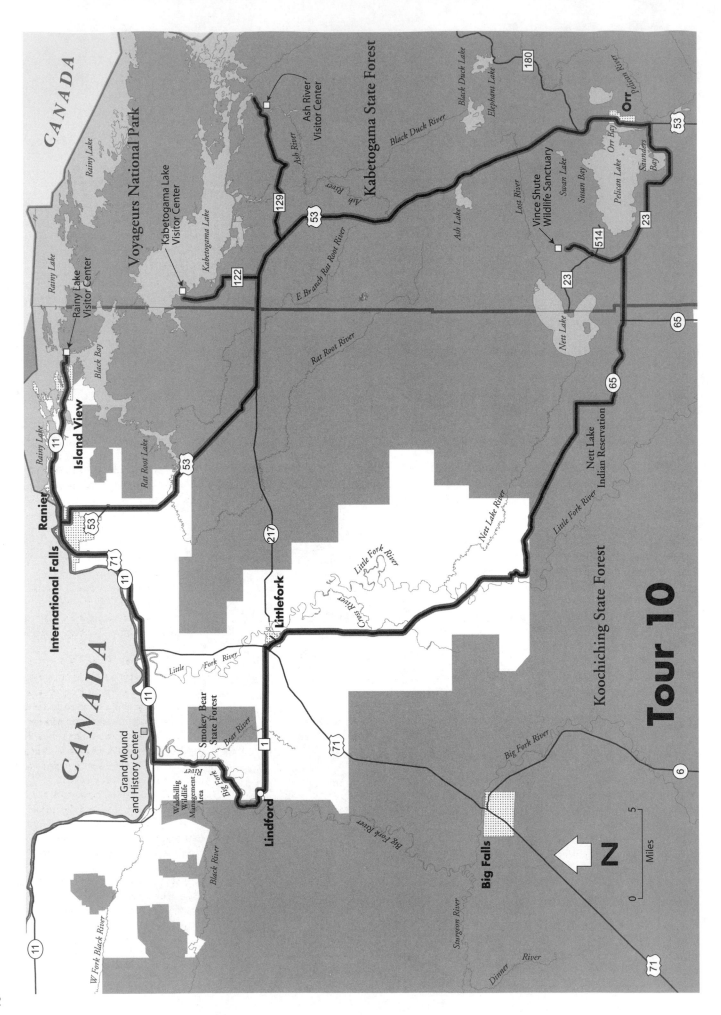

CANADA

Rainy Lake

Voyageurs National Park

Kabetogama Lake
Visitor Center

Rainy Lake
Visitor Center

Kabetogama Lake

Rainy Lake

Black Bay

Island View

Ranier

International Falls

CANADA

Grand Mound
and History Center

Waldbilling
Wildlife
Management
Area

Smokey Bear
State Forest

Bear River

Lindford

Littlefork

Rat Root River

Rat Root Lake

Little Fork River

Big Fork River

W Fork Black River

Black River

Big Falls

Ash River
Visitor Center

Ash River

Ash River

E Branch Rat Root River

Kabetogama State Forest

Black Duck River

Black Duck Lake

Elephant Lake

Orr Bay

Orr

Pelican River

Susan Lake

Vince Shute
Wildlife Sanctuary

Susan Bay

Lost River

Pelican Lake

Saunders Bay

Ash Lake

Nett Lake

Nett Lake River

Nett Lake
Indian Reservation

Little Fork River

Little Fork River

Cross River

Koochiching State Forest

Big Fork River

Sturgeon River

Dinner River

Big Fork River

Tour 10

N

Miles

0   5

52

What most people don't realize is that the park housing these two is also home to the *Koochiching County Historical Center and Bronco Nagurski Museum*, (218) 283-4316. You'll find a mother lode of historical detritus from the county-with-the-coolest-name here, tracing the area's natural and human history, including nice stuff on the fur trade. More, famed local boy and ex-NFL great Bronco Nagurski (one of the best names in the history of football) called the International Falls area home, and he's celebrated with his own wing. Open weekdays, 9 a.m.–5 p.m.; admission.

Walk east and north to the corner of 2nd Street and 4th Avenue. How about a gander at the world's largest, fastest paper machine? You'll find it at the *Boise-Cascade Corporation Mill*, (218) 285-5011, called by *Touring America* magazine as one of the top 20 plant tours in the United States. It's an astonishing sight to see the behemoth machinery involved in putting out the plant's 1,400 tons of paper per day. You get to see the whole process, from pulp to paper. Note: Modern technology has made the once-cacophonous paper-making process much tamer. It's amazing how quiet (well, relatively speaking, of course) the process is. Tours are offered weekdays June to August, other times by reservation. (It's a good idea to inquire at either visitor center if tours are being given that day. No children under 10 or cameras are allowed. Free.

Return to your parked vehicle. Get on Highway 11 and drive east for 15 miles to the entrance to *Voyageurs National Park*. This stretch marks the eastern end of the Waters of the Dancing Sky Scenic Byway, which runs for some 200 miles from its origin in western Minnesota. Here, the road seems to touch the banks of the Rainy River, then the water suddenly ends—flowing into the watery wilderness of Rainy Lake.

Along the way, your first stop might be to the *City Beach*, just north of Highway 11, a nice spot to picnic on the shores of Rainy Lake. You could also follow side roads to the east and snoop around *Birch Point* and *Crystal Beach*, both of which follow along the route. You can spend hours just poking down roads leading to scenic spots along the big lake. Your adventuresome spirit will be rewarded with dozens of delightfully tiny county "roads" leading out onto fingery peninsulas, with some roads so narrow that turning the vehicle around might be a bit problematic. Just sit on the car hood, sip coffee, and gaze at the islands dotting the liquid horizon before you.

But don't worry about getting lost, as all roads lead to Rome, er, back to Highway 11. You'll also notice lots of snowmobile trailhead parking. No surprise in these snowy lands.

The road dead-ends at the *Rainy Lake Visitor Center*, (218) 286-5258, of the Voyageurs National Park. This soggy but no-less-magnificent national treasure borders Canada and is perhaps best repre-

sentative of the Land of 10,000 Lakes. Within its boundaries are some 30 lakes—from thumbnail-sized ponds to massive bodies. Its four primary lakes were carved by glacial machinations on four occasions; the salmon-and-gray-colored bedrock is a colorful residual effect.

Keep in mind that this is an activities-oriented park, with over one-third of it water. So virtually no matter what you do, you're going to have to brave a boat of some kind. Many tours are available (see "Touring Rainy Lake" sidebar, this page); all are great fun. To do it yourself, a plethora of outfitters can be found in the four gateway communities of Ash River, Crane Lake, International Falls, and Lake Kabetogama. Avail yourself of the visitor center's exhibits and naturalist-led educational talks (a couple have trails leading off from the main buildings) if you're more of a landlubber. The best part of the park may be that it's blessedly free, outside of a few boat rental charges. The park has 214 first-come, first-served campsites (free) scattered along the many acres of water.

The Rainy Lake Visitor Center features a short nature trail, along with a set of cross-country ski trails. This is the one center at the park open all year. Hours are daily 9 a.m.–5 p.m., mid-May to late September, lesser hours thereafter. On Little American Island is a quarter-mile loop trail with exhibits on the local gold rush at the tail end of the nineteenth century.

From the visitor center, take a boat across the Black Bay Narrows to Perry Point and the Black Bay Ski Trails. To the south of these trails is the *Chain of Lakes Scenic Trail*, which traverses the Kabetogama Peninsula. Interesting little side detours here include a nice nature trail and a water-accessible-only picnic area in a lovely rock garden area. If you're here in winter, you're in for a thrill. The Kabetogama Peninsula is accessible in winter by the *Rainy Lake Ice Road,* a 7-mile-long road built atop, well, Rainy Lake. Not for the hydrophobic, to be sure.

If you have the money, one thing that really sets Rainy Lake apart are the houseboats. You can see them trolling along the lake. They are a popular and relaxing way to experience the scenery.

Backtrack west on Highway 11 to Highway 53 in International Falls, turn left and travel south and east for 25 miles to County Road 122, passing through the

Touring Rainy Lake

Boats are about the only way to experience Rainy Lake and Voyageurs National Park. If you're not a do-it-yourself boater, other options exist.

The park has three visitor centers: Rainy Lake (the main center), Kabetogama Lake, and Ash River. The former two offer a whole range of summer tours. Rainy Lake offers a Grand Tour, which includes a bit of hiking, along with lots of nature watches. It also offers a fascinating North Canoe Voyage (also offered through the Ash River Visitor Center) wherein you pile into a 26-foot-long canoe du Nord and sample the rugged life of a voyageur.

The most unique tour offered by the Kabetogama Lake center is the Kettle Falls Cruise, which takes you to the historic Kettle Falls Hotel for a picnic lunch and nearby exploration. This is probably the only water-accessible-only hotel you're ever going to experience. This fascinating complex was once home to hundreds of transients—lumbermen, moonshiners, trappers, and supply runners, among others. The spruced-up original buildings make for a true anachronistic atmosphere.

To make all boat tour reservations, call (888) 381-2873.

tiny town of Ray along the way. Turn left (north) onto 122 and drive for 2.5 miles to the *Kabetogama Lake Visitor Center.* This facility, (218) 875-2111, situated on the shore of its namesake, is another access point for Voyageurs National Park. Kabetogama Lake is extraordinary, with more than 25,000 acres of glistening glacial backwash and some 500 miles of rocky shoreline. Clambering over the big old stones could make for an entire day. The center is open seasonally.

Along the nearby peninsulas you have ample opportunities to hop on hiking or nature trails, camp on an island, or head for a boat launch/picnic site. By the time you read this, a tough, long new trail should stretch from here to the Ash River Visitor Center, our next destination.

Return to Highway 53, turn left (southeast) and drive 3 miles to County Road 129; turn left (east) and, following the signs, proceed for 10 miles to the *Ash River Visitor Center.* This facility, (218) 374-3221, is also open seasonally and has car access to several hiking trails. The *Kabetogama Lake Overlook* is short and proffers a particularly nice view, while the *Blind Ash Bay Trail* is a picturesque 2.5-mile-long hike with inspiring vistas and guaranteed solitude (ask for directions to this one at the center). Visitors can also take a private boat across to the Kabetogama Peninsula and head for the three trails accessed only by water. There is also a state forest campground near the center. Note the structure's lovely architecture. Built in 1935, the facility was known formerly as the Meadwood Lodge, and it shows the typical characteristics of North Woods construction.

Return to Highway 53, turn left (south) and cruise 25 miles into Orr. On the way south, you can't help but notice the soothing monotony of the drive, broken only by the appearance of little Ash Lake on the right, which, sadly, disappears almost as soon as it comes into view.

As you approach Orr, massive *Pelican Lake* begins to appear to the west. This 12,000-acre lake has more than 50 miles of shoreline to explore, along with four dozen islands. You'll need to rent a boat. Bring binoculars; you might get a close-up view of an osprey on this big lake.

The chummy little burg of Orr has a relaxing pace and is a great spot for a road-break. Just watch along Highway 53 for the *Orr Visitor Center,* (800) 357-9255 (www.orrmn.com), which has a trailhead for the *Orr Wetlands Boardwalk,* a half-mile-long loop through all of northern Minnesota's wetland types: spruce bog, cattail marsh, tamarack swamp, and ash swamp.

From the center of Orr, continue south on Highway 53 for 2 miles to County Road 23. Turn right, then travel for 13.5 miles (in every conceivable direction but east). After County Road 514 (East Nett Lake Road), go about .1 mile, turn right on the first gravel road, and follow it for 2 miles north to the *Vince Shute Wildlife Sanctuary.* Tuesdays through Sundays (Memorial Day to Labor Day) the local residents—black bears—wow visitors. This 360-acre sanctuary and former logging camp—supported and supervised by the American Bear Association—has a supplemental feeding program that's sometimes visited by as many as 50 bears an evening From 5 p.m. to dusk, you'll get a lifetime's education on bruin life.

Return to CR 23, turn left (south) and drive 2 miles to Palmquist Road; turn right (west) on 23. In about 4 miles, you'll come to State Highway 65. Follow 65 in a northwesterly direction for about 38 miles to Littlefork. Here, the road, which at various times runs west, north, and northwest, goes through the Nett Lake Indian Reservation and the northern tier of the Koochiching State Forest. Highway 65 is a straight-line road through unbelievably vast tracts of trees, which makes for some picturesque but occasionally monotonous driving. Nett Lake is barely visible to the right, then disappears too soon. Even a rise in the road, this one 10 miles beyond the lake, is a welcome change of pace. Nine miles south of Littlefork, a road sign informs you of the distance, and you relish the thought of a town, any town. Thank goodness the road is straight as a preacher, giving you the opportunity to hit the pedal a little harder.

Littlefork provides a bit of a respite from the surrounding greenery. Have your picture taken with the town's hand-carved "Jackpine Savage," maybe stop for gas and some coffee.

On the west edge of Littlefork, turn right on U.S. Highway 71 and go a very short distance to County Road 1. Turn left and drive west, then north for 20 miles to Highway 11. CR 1 leads first through the southern fringes of the wonderfully named *Smokey Bear State Forest.* About midway through this stretch, the road does some serious twists and turns as it parallels the Big Fork River on the right. This section is an established paddling route, so if you've brought your own canoe, put it into the water and have a go. Accesses are found all along the road. After Highway 1 makes a serious northerly bend at teeny-tiny Lindford, you'll pass through the *Waldbillig Wildlife Management Area,* bordered by the Black River on the west. No established viewing areas here, but the region is rife with critters of all kinds. Watch for bear! Just before you arrive at the junction of CR 1 and Highway 11, you can take a self-guided auto tour of the *Boise-Cascade Company forest.* This is an up-close look at a "working forest."

At the junction with Highway 11, turn right (east) and go a short distance. You'll arrive at the *Grand Mound History Center,* (218) 285-3332. Grand Mound is the largest prehistoric burial mound in Minnesota and is thought to have been

Burial mound at the Grand Mound History Center along the Rainy River. Tim Bewer.

put here by the Laurel Indians, who lived in the region as far back as 200 B.C. Fine detailed exhibits tell the story of the area. This center, run by the Minnesota State Historical Society, is an overlooked gem. The nature trail to the burial mound also makes for an awe-inspiring day. Hours are daily, 11 a.m.–5 p.m., Memorial Day weekend to Labor Day, reduced hours May and September–October.

Continue on Highway 11 for 20 miles back to International Falls, where this tour began. This slice of the Waters of the Dancing Sky Scenic Byway (which has to be one of the most poetic names to ever grace a highway) proffers gorgeous slices of dense forest matched in equal parts by the hints of big sky country and prairies calling from the west. If you can arrange it, this jaunt to International Falls is best driven in the morning, with the sun beckoning you from the distant horizon. But an evening drive has its own rewards—a setting sun scintillating off the Rainy River. Truly, either time you pick, a sublime conclusion to this trip awaits you.

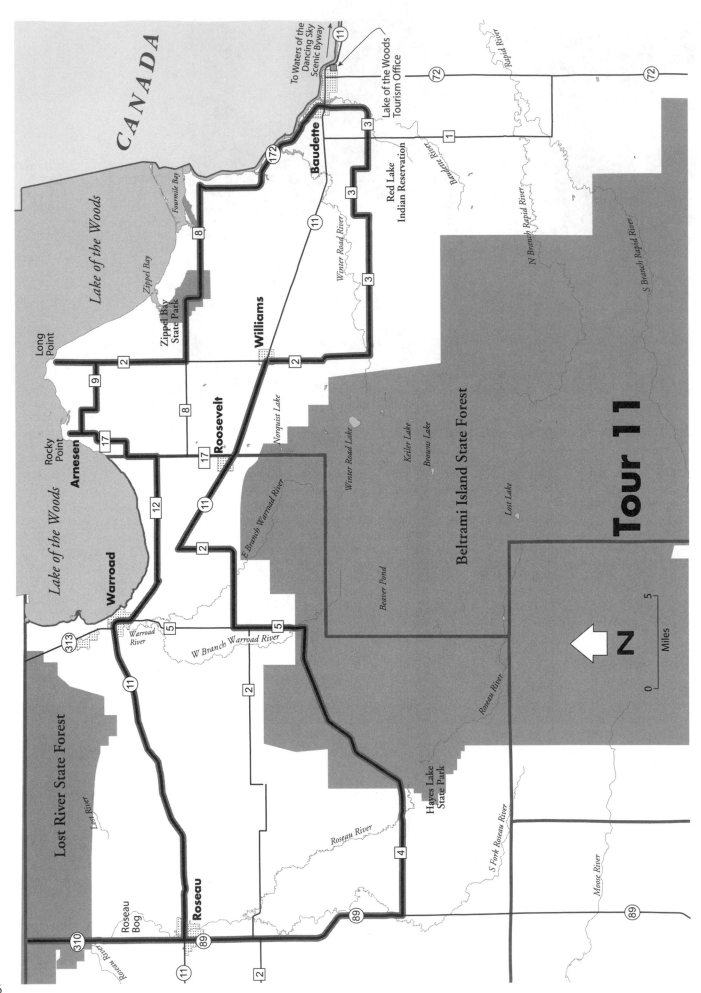

CANADA

Lake of the Woods

To Waters of the Dancing Sky Scenic Byway

11

Baudette

172

Lake of the Woods Tourism Office

72

72

3

1

Red Lake Indian Reservation

Baudette River

Rapid River

N Branch Rapid River

S Branch Rapid River

3

Fourmile Bay

8

Zippel Bay

3

Winter Road River

11

Zippel Bay State Park

Williams

2

2

Long Point

9

8

Norquist Lake

Winter Road Lake

Keiler Lake

Browns Lake

Beltrami Island State Forest

Rocky Point

17

Roosevelt

17

Lost Lake

Tour 11

Arnesen

17

Lake of the Woods

12

11

E Branch Warroad River

Beaver Pond

N

Warroad

5

5

Roseau River

0   5

Miles

313

Warroad River

W Branch Warroad River

2

Hayes Lake State Park

Roseau River

Lost River State Forest

11

4

S Fork Roseau River

Moose River

Lost River

Roseau

2

89

89

Roseau Bog

310

89

11

2

Roseau River

Tour 11
Lake of the Woods

Warroad—Lake of the Woods—Zippel Bay State Park—Baudette—Beltrami Island State Forest—Hayes Lake State Park—Roseau—Warroad

Distance: approximately 180 miles

Water does, indeed, dominate this tour, but it isn't simply because of the presence of Lake of the Woods, the enormous transnational body of water separating Minnesota from Canada. Sure, the massive lake—one of the world's largest—does dominate the mindset around these parts, with its oceanic (or, perhaps, minor Great Lake) horizons. And there's something evocative about taking a side trip through Canada to get to Minnesota (more in a bit).

Still, it isn't just the lake. This tour partly follows the Waters of the Dancing Sky Scenic Byway (State Highway 11), a roadway that stretches for nearly half the length of the international border and offers nearly 50 established stop-off points. The edges of the Rainy River, which stretches for nearly 80 miles from Rainy Lake (see Tour 10) to Lake of the Woods, are a possibility if you're really looking for a side trip. If you're into fishing, Lake of the Woods and Rainy River have copious walleye, northern pike, bass, muskie, and even sturgeon.

For most of us, the byway is simply an awe-inspiring mosaic of everything this great state has to offer. Pasturelands in the west give way to forested outcroppings. Then the river appears. Yawning, it widens, looking for all the world like the lake we've just left. The horizon, one would swear, does seem to grow larger as the road rolls on. And if you're traveling at night, gaze skyward. You may be in the right spot to get a view of the Northern Lights.

Water eventually takes a backseat, as it were, as we turn south into rough farmland to which most folks never pay a second thought. The enormous Beltrami Island State Forest is not an island as such, but it does subsume an Indian reservation—the northern section of the Red Lake Indian Reservation (the southern half will be covered in a later tour). Wildlife is abundant everywhere and all critter viewers will be thrilled.

For more information on this entire tour, contact the *Lake of the Woods Tourism Office*, 930 West Main Street, Baudette, Minnesota 56623, (218) 634-1174 or (800) 382-FISH (www.lakeofthewoods mn.com). Also, communities in the region have partnered to create the *Pine to Prairie Birding Trail*, a 200-mile-long mosaic of natural areas highlighted by excellent birding from Warroad to Fergus Falls. Details are available from the above contact or log onto www.exploreminnesota.com.

Start your tour in Warroad on State Highway 11. A good place to begin is at the Warroad Chamber of Commerce on Highway 11 at Elk Street NW, (800) 328-4455.

There you'll learn, among other things, that Warroad, on the shores of Lake in the Woods, bills itself as being famous for "Windows, Walleyes, and Hockey Sticks."

The first claim to fame: The town is home of Marvin Windows. The second: This is walleye country. And, the third: Is, unfortunately, not as true as it once was. That's because in 2003 the well-known hockey stick factory run by the Christian brothers (three Olympic gold medal winners, incidentally) closed its doors. No longer do hockey nuts make pilgrimages here to see how state-of-the-art sticks were made. Despite this, Warroad's love affair with hockey will never flag.

Many people also remember Warroad as, surprisingly, a town of petunias—folks here plant them by the thousands in summer. Actually, the flower theme is apt, as Highway 11 sports a 75-mile-long corridor near Warroad legendary for wildflowers, featuring more than two million orchids. Seemingly as many showy pink lady-slippers, Minnesota's state flower, are found along the route as well. (Self-guided tour maps can be obtained at the Warroad Chamber of Commerce.)

Further natural highlights abound. Warroad is the northernmost node of the *Pine to Prairie Birding Trail*, which stretches more than 200 miles. The chamber of commerce has maps and brochures. Bring fishing gear, too; pretty much every other vehicle around here is towing a boat. If you don't have your own, the chamber maintains a list of guides and outfitters.

Many people stop by the *Warroad Public Library*, 202 Main Street, (218) 386-1283, in the center of town. The new facility also doubles as a heritage center with exhibits on the region's natural and human history. Check out the mink ranching exhibit. The center also has brochures for a 2.5-mile-long historic walk around town. For some solitude, visit *Highland Park* (Lake Street North and Jean's Avenue), which has an Indian burial ground.

Other local flavors include a summer-stock theater troupe that puts on a big show at the local high school. Just east of town via Highway 11 sits a private buffalo herd, though this tour forgoes that route.

Quick Trip Option 1. When checking a Minnesota map, you'll probably notice that a chunk of the state actually appears to sit in Manitoba, at the head of the Lake of the Woods. The *Northwest Angle* (and accompanying islands) is some 60 miles north of Warroad (one way), and several modern (and rustic) resorts are found there, along with a decidedly laid-back lifestyle. More intriguing are the resorts on the numerous islands—reached by boat, plane, or even snowmobile. The most common point of highway entry is at Warroad, a 24-hour border crossing accessed via County Road 313 off Highway 11. Once in Canada, follow Highway 12 to Highway 308. Note that the first 40 miles in Canada are paved, then the road turns to gravel; nowhere is it impassable but it *is* still a longer drive than you might imagine and *nothing* is between Warroad and the Angle. (Before you go, get the latest information on crossing regulations and traffic from the Warroad Chamber of Commerce at (800) 328-4455.

So how in the world *did* Minnesota get to have a slice of real estate so far north (accessible by road only if you take a leisurely jaunt through Manitoba)? Well, blame seemingly illiterate and/or innumerate early surveyors, and quite likely a government that wanted action before all the facts were known. In order to divvy up U.S. and British territory following the French and Indian War, a line was drawn to the ultimate source of the Winnipeg River, which discharges into Hudson Bay. Trouble was, they had wanted to run a line to the ultimate source of the Saint Lawrence River. Ultimately, the "lake of the woods" was designated as due west of the Mississippi River, when in fact the source of the big river is *far* south of here. The problem was discovered soon enough, but when the British proposed negotiation, the United States refused—no doubt because it would have lost much of northeastern Minnesota.

Once in the area, you'll probably want to check out some local resorts. You can also enjoy a sightseeing or supper cruise on the *Lake of the Woods Island Passenger Service,* (218) 223-8261 or (218) 223-8011, at *Flag Island Resort;* offered during the summer only. Many take the boat just to see reconstructed *Fort Saint Charles* on Magnuson's Island on the north side of the Northwest Angle. It's built on the original site of a fort built by Pierre La Verendrye in 1732. Saint Charles was the most northwesterly settlement of Europeans anywhere North American.

From Warroad, drive east on Highway 11 for 3 miles to County Road 12. Turn left (east) and go about 8 miles to County Road 17. Turn left (north) and follow CR 17 north and east for about 8 miles to Arnesen on the Lake of the Woods. Along the way, you'll probably be the only person on the two county roads as you draw nearer to the massive lake. A long, straight shot is followed by a series of quick jogs left and right. The air seems to cool after the first left turn, auguring a temperate microclimate nearby.

Typical sign in Lake of the Woods country. Tim Bewer

Willie Walleye in Baudette's Bayfront Park. Thomas Huhti

Arnesen, better known as Rocky Point, is a great hidden spot from which to view Lake of the Woods and contemplate its extraordinary dimensions. The lake is the 100th largest in the world, with 65,000 miles of shoreline (it's 90 miles long and 55 miles wide) and 14,582 scenic islands.

Backtrack about 1.5 miles to County Road 9. Turn left (east) and follow it east and north for 5.5 miles to County Road 2; turn left (north) and cruise about 1 mile to Long Point. This is another chance to take in the vastness of the lake and inhale the enlivening lake. If nature's solitude is your thing, this part of the tour is for you. And don't miss Birch Beach for a similar experience.

Drive south on County Road 2 for 9 miles to County Road 8; turn left and follow it east, south, and east again for 6 miles to County Road 34. Turn left (north) to the headquarters for _Zippel Bay State Park_. This state park, (218) 783-6252, has 2,766 acres of rocky shoreline and forest; a harbor and picturesque beach have the best avian views. Tough-to-spot scarlet tanagers and lots of wood warblers flit about. The trails here are great for beachcombing and feeling the cool lake-effect wind. The trails are even more popular with cross-country skiers. Northeast of the park are a couple of state Scientific and Natural Areas (SNAs) on deserted islands that are devoted to protecting the piping plover, one of the few remaining nesting sites in Minnesota. You can also spot bald eagles and American white pelicans here.

Return to CR 8, turn left (east) and cruise for 6 miles to State Highway 172. Turn right (south) and drive for 11 miles to Baudette. Along the route, at the junction of CR 8 and Highway 172, signs invite you to Wheelers Point, which is where the Rainy River briskly empties into the Lake of the Woods. It also affords a great, albeit often fog-shrouded, view of Canada across the river. As elsewhere along in these parts, the smells are sublime.

The first place to stop in Baudette is the _Lake of the Woods Tourism Office,_ 930 West Main Street, (800) 382-3474; hours are generally daily in the summer, weekdays in the winter. Hours vary but figure on 9 a.m.–4:30 p.m, year-round, with more hours in summer.

While Warroad boasts its "windows, walleye, and hockey sticks" trinity, Baudette is unequivocal in its object of adoration: It claims to be "the walleye capital of the world." The statue of a giant walleye in a downtown park shows Baudette's pride in this claim. The nearby Rainy River is rife with the gamefish, and anglers from all over North America come here to this fishing paradise. The Willie Walleye statue in Bayfront Park pays tribute to the largest spring walleye spawning run in the world. (But don't overlook the fact that the Rainy also has one of North America's greatest smallmouth bass populations.)

Willie weighs in at 2.5 tons and comes in over 40 feet long. As the locals say, it's fairly appropriate in the home state of Paul Bunyan. Stop by for Willie's festival day in June, when the town holds a celebratory blowout feting the lake's most famous "catch."

Angling for plentiful walleye and smallmouth bass in the Rainy River east of Baudette. Tim Bewer

At 119 8th Avenue you can also see some serious history at the *Lake of the Woods County Museum*, (218) 634-1200, with exhibits on the Lake of the Woods, Lake Agassiz, Native-American cultures, fishing, and more. A highlight is the exhibit on the great forest fire of 1910, something which many native Minnesotans know little about. Open May to September, 10 a.m.–4 p.m.; free.

Quick Trip Option 2. It's a bit out of the way, but one nice little stop exists equidistant between Tours 10 and 11 on the Waters of the Dancing Sky Scenic Byway. Approximately 28 miles east of Baudette, just north of Highway 11, is the isolated, underpopulated but wholly worthwhile Franz Jevne State Park. It's so unvisited, in fact, that you have to go through the folks at Zippel Bay State Park (see above) for additional park information. However, Franz Jevne is worth a visit, with its tranquility, great fishing, hiking, and scenery. In fact, the reason the state obtained the land from a lawyer and his family was for its aesthetic superlatives; its 118 acres may be small, but they're gorgeous.

Trails throughout the park allow views of Ontario and the Rainy River; one picnic area overlooks Sault Rapids—a nice spot for a sandwich. Other paths lead through extensive peat land; this whole region was once covered by glacial Lake Agassiz. Its resultant topography is so unique that some have called it the last true wilderness in Minnesota. Others debate that, but hey, where else can you find endless sedge mats? Keep an eye out for bear, beaver, wolf, and moose. Rustic campsites exist, and they're usually not filled up, save for peak periods. If you're really in for a side trip, continue south into the Pine Island State Forest. At about 878,000 acres, it's the state's largest established forest. Seeing primevally pure bogs with fens and conifer islands is a jaw-droppingly beautiful experience.

From the west side of Baudette, take County Road 1 for less than 5 miles south and west to County Road 3. Continue west on CR 3 for about 16 miles to County Road 2 at the eastern edge of Beltrami Island State Forest. This huge green carpet is the second-largest state forest in Minnesota, covering three counties with its 669,000 acres. In addition to the numerous recreational opportunities, you'll find excellent berry picking. Otherwise, tramp through marshes, bogs, and sand ridges.

Your best bet to navigate this daunting bit of real estate is to visit the Lake of the Woods Tourism Office (see above) to pick up a "Wilderness Drive Map". The map highlights several tours: a "big drive," a historic homesteader drive, a forest management drive, and a berry-picking drive! Flower watchers will love virtually all of the routes. At the southern edge of the forest, you can also follow signs to the Norris Camp, a 1930s-era CCC camp aging gracefully in the weeds.

In this same area, Beltrami Forest is contiguous with the north border of the *Red Lake State Wildlife Management Area.* It has a quarter-million acres of wilderness with lots of bog lakes and well-mapped trails. Birders love the place, with more than 300 species spotted within the confines of the area. Once again, you may spot the endangered piping plover.

Note that in both the state forest and wildlife area, roads can be dicey once, or if, you decide to lurch onto a less-maintained side road. Rains make these roads treacherous at times.

There are a couple of ways to get to our next destination, Hayes Lake State Park, but none of them are direct or particularly efficient. Let's pick up from the intersection of CR 3 and CR 2. Go north on CR 2 for 7 miles to Highway 11 at the tiny town of Williams. Turn left (northwest) and go for about 13.5 miles to County Road 2 (not the same CR 2 that you left back in Williams). Turn left on CR 2 and follow that south and west to County Road 5, a total of 8.5 miles. Turn left (south) on CR 5 and go for 4.5 miles to County Road 4. Turn right (west) and drive for about 12 miles to the park. On the western perimeter of Beltrami Island State Forest is *Hayes Lake State Park*, (218) 425-7504, snug along the north fork of Roseau River. Few people, lots of picnic areas, and plenty of unspoiled territory to snoop around. There are a dozen miles of trails to stroll—popular in fall, when wildlife comes awake. By the way, if you've come this way via CR 4, you'll pass by Bemis Hill Camping Area. Water sports abound here, along with cross-country skiing. Yet those in the know say that the real reason to come here is the great sledding hill.

Take CR 4 west for 9 miles to State Highway 89. Turn right (north) and proceed for 15 miles to Highway 11 at Roseau. This tiny town is friendly as can be and is known mostly for *Polaris Industries*, the world's largest snowmobile manufacturer (and employer of 1,800 locals). They also make all-terrain vehicles. To see what the company is all about, visit the *Polaris Experience Center*, (218) 463-3212, a 5,000 square-foot collection of displays, interactive demonstrations, and sundry other exhibits showing the history of the snowmobile pioneer. It's located in the Reed River Trading Company building, 205 5th Avenue SW, just north of Polaris's main facility; it's open daily, noon–8 p.m. (to 6 p.m. on Sundays). Tours of the plant are also conducted daily at 4 p.m.

From Roseau, take State Highway 310 north for about 10 miles to near the Canadian border. About 4 miles into this stretch lies the amazing *Roseau Bog Owl Management Unit*, (218) 463-1557. This 9,000-acre bog and forest area has some of the most sublime vegetative cover conducive to bird life in Minnesota, and owls are the prime draw. You'll find the great gray owl, the northern hawk owl, boreal owl, and northern saw whet owl, and of course, the grandest, the great horned owl—all this on pure peat bog covered with black spruce and tamarack.

In a few more miles, you'll enter the *Lost River State Forest*, a 63,000-acre preserve stretching for 25 miles along the Manitoba border. It's backwoods and pretty much original. The flora and fauna is primitive, meaning old growth, or as close as you get to it nowadays. Nothing is "developed" for engaging in touristy activities, but you're welcome to park the car and enjoy the unspoiled beauty of it all.

Head back to Roseau and Highway 11, then turn left (east) and cruise for 22 miles back to Warroad, the starting point of this heavily woodsy tour.

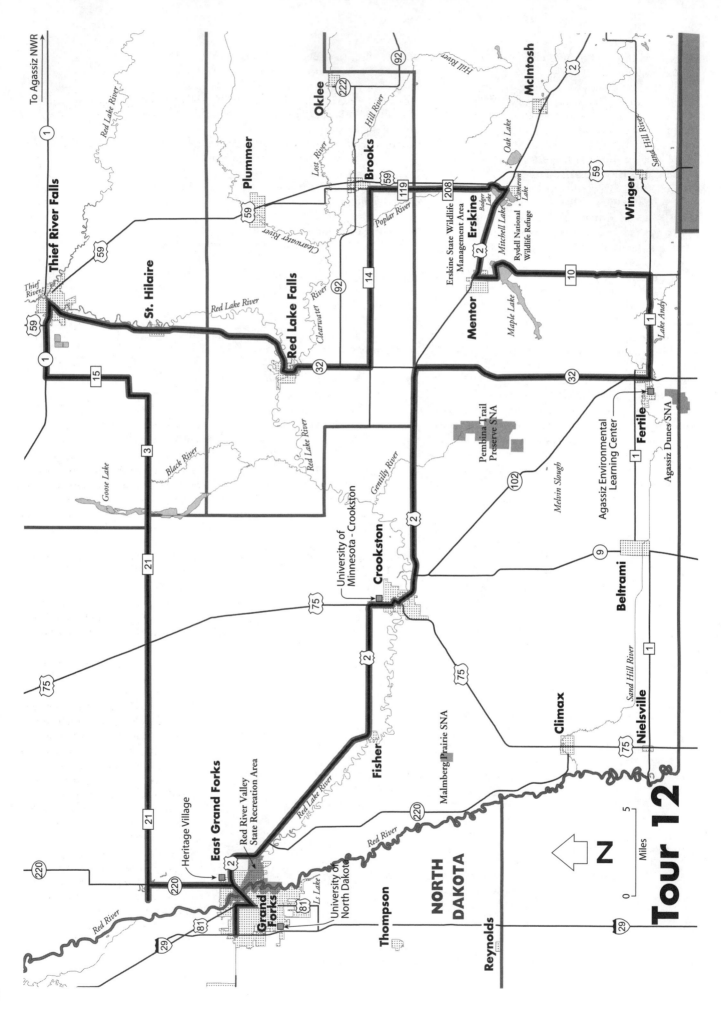

To Agassiz NWR

Thief River Falls

Oklee

Plummer

Brooks

McIntosh

Erskine State Wildlife
Management Area

Erskine

Winger

Oak Lake

Badger Lake

Mitchell Lake

Cameron Lake

Rydell National
Wildlife Refuge

Mentor

Maple Lake

Lake Andy

St. Hilaire

Red Lake River

Red Lake Falls

Clearwater River

Poplar River

Lost River

Clearwater River

Hill River

Sand Hill River

Thief River

Red Lake River

Black River

Goose Lake

Pembina Trail
Preserve SNA

Fertile

Agassiz Dunes SNA

Agassiz Environmental
Learning Center

Melvin Slough

Beltrami

University of
Minnesota - Crookston

Crookston

Gentilly River

Red Lake River

Climax

Nielsville

Sand Hill River

Fisher

Malmberg Prairie SNA

East Grand Forks

Heritage Village

Red River Valley
State Recreation Area

Grand Forks

University of
North Dakota

Red Lake River

Red River

 Its Lake

Thompson

NORTH
DAKOTA

Reynolds

N

Miles

0   5

Tour 12

Tour 12
Snowmobiles and Joe DiMaggio

Grand Forks (North Dakota)—East Grand Forks—Crookston—Fertile—Erskine—Red Lake Falls— Thief River Falls—Grand Forks

Distance: approximately 155 miles

Most folks never give this region of Minnesota a second thought—even native Minnesotans. This is the land of the Red River of the North—famed for its northward flow—not to mention its devastating flooding in 1997, nearly destroying Grand Forks, North Dakota, to the west.

Yet there's so much here. In one brief tour we manage to take in a thriving (based on prairie comparisons) dual-state-sister-city "metro" area, a historic treaty spot, Joe DiMaggio's bar, breathtaking wild rice beds, a massive snowmobile manufacturing operation, and, as if that weren't enough, some of the Midwest's grandest wildlife viewing options.

Start your tour in Grand Forks, North Dakota, at the junction of I-29 and U.S. Highway 2. Here, on the western outskirts of the city, you'll find the Greater Grand Forks Convention and Visitors Bureau, (800) 866-4566 (www.visitgrand-forks.com), which has tons of free information (available in a convenient box outside for after-hours pick-up, as well) and great discount coupons for local businesses.

In a book about Minnesota travel, starting a tour in North Dakota might be unorthodox, but the geography, attractions, and human values of both states in this region are quite the same. The North Dakota side dominates the geography of the place, although East Grand Forks, across the Red River of the North on the Minnesota side, can hold its own. The region has long been a commercial center, not surprising, given the confluence of the Red River and the Red Lake River. Native Americans had used it as a trading and negotiating center even before the French trappers came and affixed the new moniker "la Grande Fourches," which, later Anglicized, stuck as Grand Forks.

Drive east on Highway 2 (Gateway Drive) for 2 miles to North Columbia Road; turn right (south) and go less than 1.5 miles to University Avenue. Turn right (west) into the *University of North Dakota* campus. The university offers several sites to visit, and it's small enough that you can park your vehicle and wander about. For a serious workout, the university has a lovely 10-km fitness trail that stretches south from Highway 2 at the English Coulee south through the campus, and down to 32nd Avenue South, near Columbia Mall.

Another sports-related attraction is the luxurious $100 million *Ralph Engelstad Arena*, (877) 91-SIOUX, home to the perennial collegiate hockey power, North Dakota's Fighting Sioux. This astonishing facility is the envy of many NHL teams, judging by its ornate whirlpools, hand-carved wooden seats, and fastidiously built player locker rooms. The whole operation is astonishing, especially in a university setting, and an indication that hockey is taken pretty seriously in these parts.

Also on campus is the *North Dakota Museum of Art*, (701) 777-4195, an award-winning art space with regional, national, and international art. Free parking too—use the 'A' lot. The *UND Aerospace Center*, (701) 777-2791, features a planetarium and art exhibits in a fun Aero Heritage Room. You can tour flight operations centers, a flight simulator, and even aircraft. Tours are generally offered Tuesdays and Thursdays at 3:15 p.m.; call first.

Drive back east on University Avenue for about 1 mile to U.S. Highway 81 (South Washington Road). Drive south for about 1.5 miles to 24th Avenue South; turn left (east) and drive a short distance to Belmont Road. At the intersection, you'll find the *Myra Museum and Campbell House*, (701) 775-2216, dating to 1879 and now dedicated to the heritage of pioneer women. You'll find a re-created one-room schoolhouse and the original Grand Forks log post office. Hours are mid-May to mid-September daily, 1–5 p.m; free.

Drive north on Belmont Road less than 2 miles to 5th Street N;

From the Floods

Few can forget the horrible images of the floods that devastated the Red River Valley in 1997. Entire neighborhoods were submerged. And worse than water damage, electrical systems shorted, causing ferocious fires. An entire realm of historic architecture was lost.

Still, with the resilience that only a hard-working community can muster, the Greater Grand Forks area picked itself up, dried itself out, and set out to rebuild— and, if possible, learn from the horror. Perhaps the golden "phoenix" rising from the destruction is the Red River Valley State Recreation Area, one of Minnesota's newest state recreation areas. Following the destructive flooding, more than 300 houses were heavily damaged. Instead of rebuilding—always a dicey proposition in a floodplain—the decision was made to revert the area to greenspace, some 2,200 acres in all. The 300-person campground has access to the biking/hiking trails, fishing spots, historic sites, and an interpretive center providing an overview of the area's natural and human history. Individual campsites are named after the families who lived in the area prior to the flooding.

The wide-open spaces of western Minnesota.
Tim Bewer

turn left (northwest) and then take an immediate right onto DeMers Avenue. At this point, it may be prudent to park your car somewhere and wander about the contiguous North Dakota-Minnesota downtowns. To your right in Grand Forks, you'll see the *Empire Arts Center*, (701) 746-5500, a 1919 theater newly restored with an art gallery that regularly changes exhibits and features lots of regional art. Free. Just northeast of the center is the Town Square, a quaint little historic district of gentrified buildings and a new children's museum. Also, don't miss the Farmers Market on Saturday mornings, where you'll find vendors and farmers selling luscious produce.

Downtown East Grand Forks is famed for its lifelike art statues by J. Seward Johnson. Pay attention, or you may find yourself talking to one of these bronze pieces. On the east side of downtown is *Cabela's*, 210 DeMers Avenue NW, (218) 773-0282, legendary manufacturer of outdoors clothing and sporting goods. It's absolutely enormous. Just wander about the open-air place and get a look-see at the trophy animals and huge aquariums! Be careful, though, as it's quite hard to walk out without purchasing anything!

Whether in Grand Forks or East Grand Forks, get on DeMers Avenue and go northeast a short distance to State Highway 220; follow 220 north for less than 1 mile, heeding the signs to *Heritage Village*. This historic site, (218) 773-0406, preserves the history of the Red River Valley with original buildings relocated and reconstructed here from throughout the region. Most folks love to come during Heritage Days, the third week of August, when you can get a look-see at steam-driven threshing machines, demonstrations, and much more.

Return south on Highway 220 and turn left (east) onto U.S. Highway 2. Drive southeast for 25 miles to Crookston. About halfway through this stretch, you'll come to a *Minnesota Welcome Center* should you still require information and/or advice.

Crookston gets overlooked by most travelers on the Highway 2—the Great Northern Highway. Too bad, as this friendly community has quite a bit to offer. Named after a pathfinder and later railroad builder named Colonel William Crooks, the city of

8,200 sits languidly, but happily, on the banks of the twisting Red Lake River.

Just north of Crookston, right after Highway 2 turns south, drive into the campus of the University of Minnesota-Crookston on the left. It's a short hop off the road and is worthy if for no other reason than for its flowerbeds. It would be hard to imagine more cultivated loveliness on a college campus. The dean, it would seem, was serious when he claimed that he wanted every University of Minnesota school to follow UMC's lead in beautification projects. (Wander about—signs are ubiquitous to educate you about the plants.)

Students, however, might be drawn to the school for a different reason: technology. UMC was the first university in the country to issue all its students notebook computers. This was in part the reason why *US News & World Report* cited it one of the best universities nationwide two years in a row and it was named as a hot university by any number of techie-oriented media.

Just west of Highway 2 and near the university is a tranquil little *natural history area* with great bird-watching. Though nobody seems to know about it, it's a wondrous little detour from the four-lane swells. Call (218) 281-8131 for information. This is, by the way, not included in the city's 17 parks. Not bad for a city of its size.

Continue south on Highway 2 for about 2 miles into downtown Crookston. Main and Broadway Streets are the main drags in town. The best thing to do is continue on either one to Fletcher Street and find a parking spot (look for the post office). You should be able to see the *Crookston Area Chamber of Commerce*, 118 Fletcher Street, (218) 281-4320 or (800) 809-5997. The staff can give you all the necessary information on the town.

From here, take a walking tour. The town has a great sense of history. It's Norman Rockwell without any gimmicky gentrification. North of the chamber office at 124 East Second Street, stop for a flick at the *Historic Grand I & II Theater*, (218) 281-1820, which is the oldest continuously operating movie theater in the United States. Turning north and east you'll come to the local *swimming pool*, (218) 281-1180, an Olympic-sized pool with a diving tank.

Return to Highway 2 (Robert Street at this point) and go southeast for about 1 mile. Just outside the city limits, you'll come to the *Polk County Museum*, (218) 281-1038, and the world's largest ox cart. A replica of the types that used to travel between Saint Paul and nearby Fort Garry, this one is a bit larger. (Inside the museum is a more modest example.) This cart is such a big deal that Crookston holds a four-day celebration, August Oxcart Days, that features everything from bed races to beauty pageants. Don't miss the lumberjack contests and classic car shows.

Also on site are lots of re-creations of pioneer living—a blacksmith shop, a pioneer kitchen, and,

Outside Crookston, the Polk County Museum's tribute to the ox cart, a key mode of transportation during the region's early development. Tim Bewer

the real draw, an 1890s Little House on the Prairie mock-up. New is a room devoted to rural fire equipment. Open daily May to September.

Continue east on Highway 2 for 16 miles to State Highway 32. Turn right (south) and drive for 16 miles to the town of Fertile. Establish this wonderfully named town as your base to explore the area's rich variety of preserves, prairies, and other natural attractions. The area is a prime route on the trans-northern-Minnesota *Pine to Prairie Birding Trail*. The endless fields to the south of Highway 2 include no fewer than six protected areas home to an enormous variety of birds (and other critters): the Pembina Trail Preserve SNA; Pankratz Memorial Prairie; Tympanuchus Wildlife Area; Burnham Creek Wildlife Area; Rydell National Wildlife Refuge; and Agassiz Dunes Scientific and Natural Area. This last site has the *Agassiz Environmental Learning Center*, (218) 945-3129, less than a mile west of Fertile on Summit Avenue W. Here you'll find lots of backwoods trails and, even better, a rustic campground.

From Fertile, go east on County Road 1 for 7 miles to County Road 10. Turn left (north) and proceed for 10 miles to the center for the *Rydell National Wildlife Refuge*. This is spectacular driving country, if you're into open country: enormous tracts of golden fields of grain interspersed with aqua pools. On the east side of Maple Lake, the refuge has marshes, deciduous woodlands, and lots of open meadows. The best times to visit are May to June and August to October; you can get lots of views of trumpeter swans, passerines, sparrows, and finches. A checklist is available from the refuge office, (218) 687-2229, generally open weekdays 7:30 a.m.–4 p.m. This is a new refuge, and the staff ask that you report all wildlife sightings.

Continue north on CR 10 for about 3 miles back to Highway 2. Turn right (east) and drive for 6.5 miles to tiny Erskine. The road skirts the east shore of Maple Lake for a few miles, a welcome sight after traveling through the prairies to the west. A legendary New York Yankee is somehow connected to Erskine (see "Joe DiMaggio: The Yankee Gopher?" sidebar below), but it also has a couple other items of interest. First, there's a nice *public beach* on the local lake and, just off the highway, you can't miss the *world's largest northern pike*. Good kitschy photo op!

Travel north from Erskine on County Road 208, then County Road 119, for 10 miles to County Road 14. First skirting Badger Lake just north of Erskine, you'll drive through yet another wildlife area, this one the *Erskine State Wildlife Management Area*. No established viewing areas exist, but it makes for a leisurely drive through

Joe DiMaggio: The Yankee Gopher?

Many years ago, a guy named George went to college in Minnesota with a Bronx-born Joe DiMaggio—no relation to the Bronx Bomber (who was from San Francisco, by the way). Upon graduation, both became teachers, Joe D. in tiny Erskine, Minnesota. Ultimately, he opened a corner bar and you-know-what just had to be the name. (Why not? He always got wrong numbers on the telephone anyway.) Obviously, many travelers along Highway 2 (the Great Northern) screeched to a halt to find out just what was going on and, ultimately, a regional legend was born. You would never find Joltin' Joe of Yankee lore inside, but there was plenty of memorabilia regarding his career plus a host of other baseball-themed stuff.

Things got so big that the two old college friends eventually reconnected and went into business together. Joe DiMaggio's became a trademarked restaurant name and now you'll find one in Red Lake Falls, Grand Forks, North Dakota, and even one near Minneapolis in Fridley. Interestingly, the original building in Erskine still exists, although the name has changed several times. No matter what the name, however, it has always been followed by parentheses with the reassuring message "Joe D's" inside, just because that's what people come here to see.

pretty agrarian/rustic country. If you get lost, just head east and you'll link up with U.S. Highway 59 to lead you to larger highways.

Turn left (west) on CR 14 and drive for 12 straight-as-an-arrow miles to State Highway 32. Turn right (north) and proceed to Red Lake Falls, 5 miles away.

This town has always been known for canoeing, kayaking, and tubing on the Red Lake River: 180 miles long and the only river flowing out of the 289,000-acre Upper and Lower Red Lake. Each year some 30,000 people come to the falls to experience the rolling, cool waters of the Red Lake River. Many stay at the Voyageur's View Campground 4 miles north of town. This is where the river drops the most during its middle section, making for rapids just serious enough to make a water trip fun. Rentals are available.

If water isn't your thing, the city's surrounding area has historical attractions in abundance, from gravesites of *voyageurs* to residual spots where the shoreline of glacial Lake Agassiz can be seen. The highlight is likely the *Old Crossing Treaty Monument,* west of Red Lake Falls along County Road 11. This is where the Pembina and Red Lake bands of Ojibwe ceded some 11 million acres of land to the U.S. government. History comes alive here the last weekend of August, when the Afran Club (a Red Lake Falls civic group devoted to preserving Francophone heritage) holds its chautauqua, with walleye dinners, fiddling competitions, storytelling histories, and more.

Finally, Red Lake Falls has become a stopping point for those road trippers looking to visit Joe DiMaggio's Bar. If you're looking, it's at Park Place Mall, on Highway 32 on the south end of town, (218) 253-2929.

Continue north on Highway 32 for 18 miles to Thief River Falls. There's a story behind how these falls got their intriguing name. Legend has it that a Sioux warrior once camped by the confluence of the two local rivers and robbed passersby, thus impelling the Ojibwe (and unfortunate Sioux victims, too) to dub it "Robber" River in local dialects. It was later Anglicized to "Thief" by the U.S. Army right before they built a dam. They also changed the local term "rapids" into "falls," thus adding the final piece to the nomenclature puzzle. For information on the town, head to the *Thief River Falls Visitors and Convention Bureau,* 2017 Highway 59 SE, (218) 681-3720 or (800) 827-1629 (www.ci.thief-river-falls.mn.us).

The two rivers (the other is the Red Lake) are no longer the prime draw in the city, but they sure could be. Following their shorelines you pass through a half-dozen city parks and two nature trails. Fascinating pictographs are found along the 7 miles of trail.

But folks really come here to see the snowmobiles being built. One of the country's largest man-ufacturers of the machines, *Arctic Cat,* has its main plant at 600 Brooks Avenue South, (218) 681-8558. Its factory tour has been called one of the best in the United States by people who actually keep track of such things. It's not surprising that the residents have something of an obsession with snowmobiling. So accepted are the machines that locals pile onto them and whip them around the city as if they were bicycles. The plant offers daily 45-minute tours, April to November at 1 p.m. You'll also see personal watercraft and all-terrain vehicles being assembled.

Quick Trip Option. This jaunt will add some 45 miles to your trip, but if you're a nature lover, it's worth it. From Thief River Falls, drive east on State Highway 1 to County Road 20/12; turn left (north). Drive to County Road 7 and turn right (east) to the headquarters of the *Agassiz National Wildlife Refuge,* (218) 449-4115; open 7:30 a.m.–4 p.m., weekdays. The headquarters has information and maps on scenic drives and hiking trails in the refuge; it's a good idea to ask first.

In the aspen/parkland transitional zone between the coniferous forest, tall grass prairie, and prairie pothole region of the United States, Agassiz is the largest wildlife refuge in Minnesota, comprising more than 40,000 acres of wetland, 10,000 acres of shrub land, 7,000 acres of forest, 4,250 acres of grassland, and even a few dozen acres of croplands. Additional state land in circumference tops out the total at 83,940 acres. Wetlands have been the primary beneficiary of environmental progress here. Twenty pools have been developed, ranging from 100 to 10,000 acres. Four thousand acres in the northcentral portion has been designated national wilderness under the Wilderness Preservation System. Two lakes in the area were formed by deep peat fires. You can wander about the system and find 280 species of birds, half of which nest in the refuge. And the tens of thousands of migrating waterfowl in May and October are an unforgettable sight. In 1999, bald eagles returned for the first time in 30 years. The park also hosts 49 mammal species, including eastern gray wolves, 12 species of amphibians and more.

From Thief River Falls, travel west on State Highway 1 for about 5 miles to County Road 15; turn left (south) and go 7.5 miles to County Road 3. Turn right (west) and travel for 35 miles to State Highway 220 (after 10 miles or so CR 3 becomes CR 21). In the first third of this stretch, you'll pass two state wildlife management areas (Higinbotham and Pembina), though neither has established viewing areas. They are part of the *Pines to Prairies Birding Trail.*

Turn left (south) on Highway 220 and drive about 6 miles to Highway 2 in the Grand Forks area. Turn right and follow it west to the junction with I-29, where we began this tour.

Tour 13
Paul Bunyan and the Beginning of the Mississippi

Bemidji—Lake Bemidji State Park—Buena Vista—Red Lakes—Clearbrook—Fosston—Bagley—Mississippi Headwaters State Forest—Bemidji

Distance: approximately 185 miles

Two symbols of Minnesota hold our imagination, and their links to a mythical past permeate this tour. You'll see signs of Paul Bunyan's influence everywhere in the Bemidji area. And being near the origin of the Mississippi, another national icon, is a source of profound local pride. Even though Paul was "born" in Bangor, Maine, and was the creation of a couple of newspapermen eager to sell papers, this area is where tales of his fantastic exploits have flourished most vigorously. And though the Mississippi's origin is 30 miles southwest of Bemidji in Lake Itasca State Park (see Tour 15), the myth-laden river flows north into Lake Bemidji, then reemerges on its 2,500-mile journey to the Gulf of Mexico.

In this tour, we head north and west from Bemidji to areas many folks never hear about—the Continental Divide (and, arguably, the real source of the great river); the Chippewa National Forest (the country's oldest); and the Red Lake region, generally accepted as the site of the oldest human habitation in Minnesota. Thus, we'll get more glimpses into the past.

Start your tour in downtown Bemidji, on Bemidji Avenue on the southwest edge of the lake of the same name. You'll know you're there when see one of the biggest Paul Bunyan statues you'll ever see, along with one of his blue ox, Babe. Bring the camera! Note that Paul and Babe are but the first in a "sculpture walk." Just north is another figure, Chief Bemidji—the first Native American that most settlers met moving west. Nearby, you'll also find the *Bemidji Area Tourist Information Office*, (218) 759-0164 or (800) 458-2223 (www.visitbemidji.com). Here you'll get lots of cheery advice and loads of artifacts pertaining to the Bunyan lore. There's also a fireplace built with stones from each continental U.S. state and Canada.

You'll no doubt notice that "Paul Bunyan" is affixed to pretty much everything in the vicinity of Bemidji. Get used to it! First off, the kids will probably scream and holler to sample the first place with Paul's name—the nearby *amusement park*, filled with (cheap, fun) kiddie rides.

Bemidji bills itself as the "First City on the Mississippi," and in Ojibwe, *Bay-may-ji-ga-mawg* means "a lake of crossing waters." Both descriptions are accurate, as Ol' Man River passes through

Lake Bemidji on its long roll to the Gulf of Mexico from its source to the south in Lake Itasca State Park. Bemidji also sits on the western fringes of the Chippewa National Forest, the oldest national forest in the United States.

Bemidji also has a few other noteworthy sights to take in before you hit the highway. It features, for example, the National Register of Historic Places-recognized *Great Northern Depot,* 130 Minnesota Avenue SW, home to the Beltrami County History Center.

This city is for culture lovers, too, and you can participate. In addition to the previously mentioned sculpture walk, Bemidji has the *Paul Bunyan Playhouse*, Minnesota's oldest (another first) professional summer theater, with summer performances Wednesday to Sunday. It's located in the historic Chief Theatre, 314 Beltrami Avenue, (218) 751-7270. In the same complex, the *Headwaters School of Music and Art* has a huge array of concerts, readings, workshops, and performances throughout the year. Local and regional artists are featured at a number of galleries downtown. Particularly interesting is the *Talley Art Gallery*, located on the campus of Bemidji State University and featuring work by the school's students.

Speaking of BSU, this is Minnesota's only lakeside campus and lovely it is—worthy of a stroll. Another education-related draw to the area is the wondrous and famed summertime *Concordia Language Villages*, wherein students are housed in re-created living settings of various cultures, facilitating in language learning.

Follow Bemidji Avenue southeast as it becomes Paul Bunyan Drive. Take it for about 1.5 miles to Roosevelt Road (Highway 8). Turn left (east) and

Bemidji Events
Bemidji always has something going on. One such happening is the twice-a-summer (July and August) International Days, an annual celebration of linguistic achievement and cultural understanding. Guests are free to wander about the language village of Bemidji State University, sampling music, food, and games.

Arts are very big in Bemidji, and the 10-day First City Celebration of the Arts does it up well. Music of every variety is the biggest draw, but the entire city rolls out the red carpet to literary readings, children's theater, craft workshops, and lots more. Art lovers all go to the simultaneous Art in the Park—a three-decade-plus tradition in the Headwaters region.

Winter festivities are equally lively. The Minnesota Finlandia Marathon, for example, features over 600 international cross-country skiers. Later, Bemidji Polar Daze is a fun family event with sled dog races, snow-cross snowmobile races, and lots of kids' games, all poking fun at Old Man Winter.

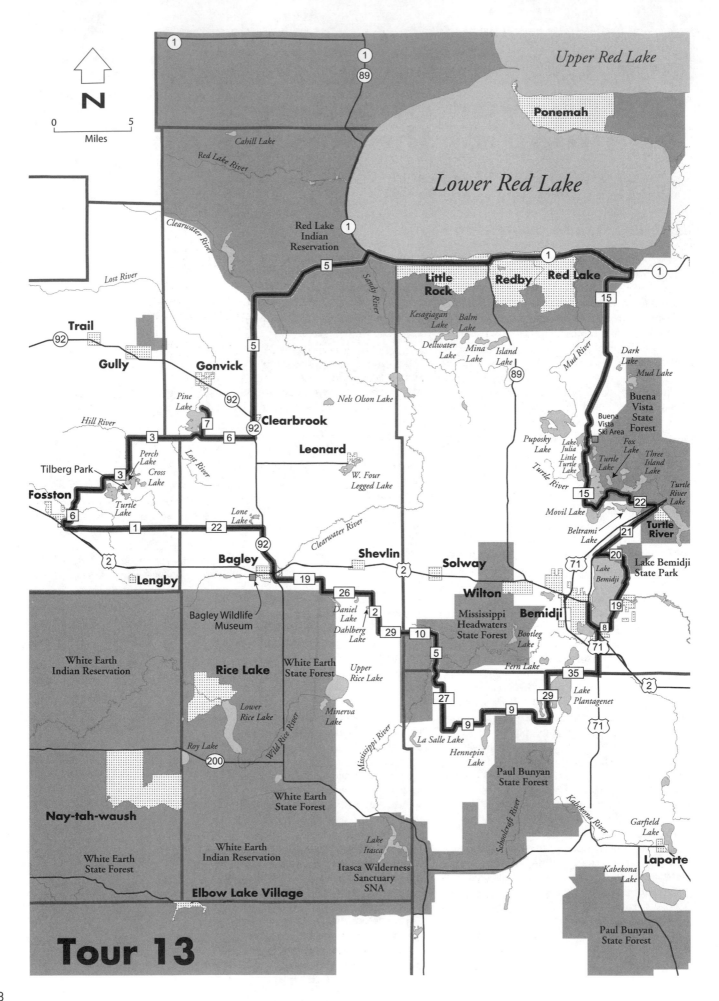

Upper Red Lake

Ponemah

Lower Red Lake

Cahill Lake

Red Lake River

Clearwater River

Lost River

Red Lake Indian Reservation

Little Rock

Redby

Red Lake

Sandy River

Kesagiagan Lake

Balm Lake

Dellwater Lake

Mina Lake

Island Lake

Mud River

Dark Lake

Mud Lake

Buena Vista State Forest

Trail

Gully

Gonvick

Clearbrook

Nels Olson Lake

Puposky Lake

Lake Julia

Little Turtle Lake

Buena Vista Ski Area

Fox Lake

Three Island Lake

Pine Lake

Leonard

Turtle Lake

Turtle River

Turtle River Lake

Hill River

Perch Lake

Cross Lake

W. Four Legged Lake

Tilberg Park

Fosston

Lost River

Turtle Lake

Lone Lake

Clearwater River

Movil Lake

Beltrami Lake

Turtle River

Lengby

Bagley

Shevlin

Solway

Wilton

Lake Bemidji State Park

Lake Bemidji

Bemidji

Bagley Wildlife Museum

Daniel Lake

Dahlberg Lake

White Earth State Forest

Mississippi Headwaters State Forest

Bootleg Lake

White Earth Indian Reservation

Rice Lake

Upper Rice Lake

Minerva Lake

Fern Lake

Lake Plantagenet

Lower Rice Lake

Wild Rice River

Mississippi River

La Salle Lake

Hennepin Lake

Paul Bunyan State Forest

Garfield Lake

Nay-tah-waush

White Earth State Forest

White Earth Indian Reservation

Roy Lake

White Earth State Forest

Schoolcraft River

Kabekona River

Laporte

Lake Itasca

Itasca Wilderness Sanctuary SNA

Kabekona Lake

Paul Bunyan State Forest

Elbow Lake Village

Tour 13

Paul Bunyan and Babe in downtown Bemidji overlooking Lake Bemidji. Thomas Huhti

drive less than 1 mile to Lake Avenue (County Road 19). Turn left (north) and drive about 9 miles to *Lake Bemidji State Park.* This is a great route to take as you circumnavigate Lake Bemidji. At roughly the halfway point along the lake's perimeter, you cross over the Mississippi River as it flows east. (An uncharacteristic direction for a river famed for its southerly flow.) Eventually, following signs, you'll come to picturesque Lake Bemidji State Park, (218) 755-3843, which offers a wealth of swimming, mountain biking, and hiking—including a cool little bog walk. The natural history of this oddball topographic feature is well-detailed at the park's interpretive center. You can also access the Paul Bunyan multi-use trail from here. If you brought fishing gear, be sure your line is strong as the sharp-toothed muskie is prime catch around here. These primeval-looking beasts are hard to hook, but once you do, they fight like a Baja sailfish.

Finally, try and plan this segment of the tour to coincide with the tail end of the day, as Lake Bemidji sunsets are legendarily sublime. So extraordinary that even munching mosquitoes won't detract from it.

Turn left (west) onto County Road 20, which runs through the park, and drive for about 2 miles to County Road 21. Turn right (northeast) and proceed for 6.5 miles to County Road 22, just south of Turtle River. On the way, you'll enter the *Buena Vista State Forest,* where maples and aspens abound. There isn't much to do around these parts, but this is a genuinely lovely drive, particularly in the explosion of

autumn colors. Even a fog-shrouded misty morning can be breathtaking.

A mile south of Turtle River—though this is a mite hard to establish—eagle-eyed travelers will see signs for Old Highway 71. This would be the residual of the Leech Lake-Red Lake Trail, so well-worn that the path was sunk a foot deep into the ground. We'll get a highlight of this historic path a bit farther on. By the way, the birding is good around here; check out the Turtle, Beltrami, and Turtle River Lakes. (The Bemidji Tourist Information Center has avian lists.)

Turn left (west) onto CR 22 and follow it for roughly 10 miles to County Road 15; Turn right (north). This stretch of road is 6 miles as the crow flies, but with hairpin turns, numerous meanderings, and roller-coaster rises and falls, the mileage is closer to 10. This challenging road bobs and weaves, bends and slides and somehow manages to negotiate the labyrinth of Beltrami, Three Island, Fox, Movil, *and* Turtle Lakes. In fall, it's an artist's palette of riotous colors; in summer, it's simply a hoot!

Drive 5 miles north on CR 15 past Little Turtle Lake to Lake Julia; follow the well-placed signs to Buena Vista. Buena Vista is a village—or allegedly it is. Although locals speak of it as a living thing, the Department of Transportation seemingly does not recognize its existence (it isn't on any map). But trust us, it's there. One thing that is definitely there is the *Buena Vista Ski Area,* (218) 243-2231, the nucleus of just about all the activities in the area.

Buena Vista's motto, "Ski Top of the World on the Continental Divide," is but a slight exaggeration when you find yourself atop a cool aerie, looking down on nine lakes. Lake Julia flows north to Hudson Bay, while the Little Turtle Lake flows south to the Gulf of Mexico. On the Continental Divide, the views are spectacular. In addition, getting to the top can be great fun aboard a covered wagon for a bumpy 45-minute trip. You won't be disappointed! Once back at the base of the ski hill, visit the *Lumberjack Hall of Fame*. Paul Bunyan himself would be proud of the place.

Continue north on CR 15 for about 15 miles to State Highway 1. Turn left (west). Here, you'll find yourself face to face with the eastern shore of Lower Red Lake. The huge and weirdly configured Red Lakes (Upper and Lower) are home to the Red Lake Indian Reservation. Archaeologists believe an archaic Native American site on a peninsula separating the two lakes is the oldest human occupation in Minnesota. Given all the attention that mythical lumberjacks and forest recreation get in these parts, the Red Lake area gets overlooked. But if you're seeking something out of the ordinary, consider this from a local tourist publication: "If one felt absolutely compelled to swing that driver, the nearest golf course can be found in Blackduck about 38 miles away."

Our tour along the southern perimeter of Lower Red Lake will likely entice you to further exploration (see Quick Trip Option below). If not, Highway 1 runs close enough to the lake for some good ganders at its impressive size. For the most part, the road is griddle-flat and horizon-stretching, save for a few inadvertent twists in the road and interruptions (and reduced speeds) in Redby and Red Lake, two of the four Red Lake Indian Reservation communities. Redby has the tribe's forest products industry, while Red Lake, the tribal headquarters, features a modest casino and the pow-wow grounds. Soon after leaving Red Lake, Highway 1 bends away from the big lake, leading us into dwindling peat and bog lands and into more traditionally agrarian patchwork lands.

Quick Trip Option. The Red Lakes are the largest body of water in the state, and you'll feel absolutely alone most of the time. This tour skirts the southern fringes of the lower lake (giving plenty of pleasing views of the azure waters), but you could easily spend an entire afternoon circumnavigating the shoreline. Another option is fishing: crappie fishing here is some of Minnesota's best. It's so good that the Waskish Crappie Contest draws ice anglers from all over; check it out in early March. To get the best quick view of the Red Lakes, instead of turning left on Highway 1, as the main tour does, turn right and follow it all the way to

Highway 72; then turn left and follow 72 to Waskish, the epicenter of all Red Lake Area activities. Fishing is huge on the lake, as mentioned, but is especially big near the Tamarack River at Waskish.

But what interests most road trippers is the relatively new (as of 2000), but geologically fascinating, *Big Bog State Recreation Area* that's located approximately 12 miles north of Waskish on Highway 72. This astonishing park was once the lakebed of glacial Lake Agassiz and contains open sphagnum bogs, black spruce bogs, white cedar swamps, and lake beaches. According to officials here, it's the largest, most diversely patterned peat land in the United States. The bog *is* huge: over 50 miles long and 12 miles wide. Portions of the site have been designated a National Natural Landmark.

If you do visit the bog, you have either a *long* loop up and around to the north, or a grudging, but more efficient, backtrack down Highway 72 to Highway 1 in order to link up with the main tour route.

Drive west on Highway 1 for about 22 miles to County Road 5; turn left and proceed south, then west, for 20 miles to Clearbrook (always watching for signs to it). The area in and around Clearbrook is misleadingly plain-looking. Actually, much of the marshy-looking areas are rife with wild rice beds, and with permission you can even harvest rice yourself. In these parts some 50 growers cultivate wild rice, and it accounts for some $50 million of the state's economy. Stop by any store around and check out the wide variety available.

From Clearbook, take State Highway 92 south for about 1.5 miles to County Road 6/3. Turn right (west) and drive for 5 miles to County Road 7; turn right (north) to *Pine Lake*. Here, you'll find the site of a University of Minnesota-Crookston *ornithological research station*—a birders' paradise. Like the Gully Rice Paddies/Gully Fen Scientific and Natural Area just to the northwest, it's an established node on migratory bird ways. Birding in early spring is superb, though after that songbirds are still plentiful. Keep an eye out for tundra swans, peregrine falcons, and snowy and short-eared owls!

Drive back south on County Road 7 to County Road 6/3 and turn right (west). Drive for 6 miles to where CR 3 branches off to the south. Follow that for 3 miles to Cross and Perch Lakes, watching for signs to *Tilberg Park*. The small park, wedged on a spit of land between the two lakes, offers great swimming and a chance to take a break and dip your toes. And enjoy the other lakes in the area; there are plenty.

Return to CR 3, turn left (west) and drive 5 miles to County Road 6. Turn left (south) and

proceed for about 3 miles into Fosston. Here's a pleasant burg with lots of sleepy city parks and a lovely *veteran's memorial garden* downtown. There's also a nice indoor pool in the civic center.

Folks often bypass Fosston for other tourist spots in the region, but people do notice *Cordwood Pete*. Often regarded as Paul Bunyan's little brother, Cordwood Pete (and his donkey Tamarack) is honored by a statue in downtown Fosston. Check out Pete's history at the *East Polk Heritage Center* on Highway 2 downtown. There you'll see "life-sized" Cordwood Pete and Tamarack statues and perhaps learn a bit of the lore. Hours are Tuesday to Sunday, 1–4 p.m. By the way, Fosston is trying to make its formal celebration of the little guy, Cordwood Pete Days, an annual event in June; expect lumberjack demonstrations, games, and lots of hearty food.

From Fosston, drive east on County Road 1, then County Road 22, for 15 miles to State Highway 92. Turn right (south) and proceed for 4 miles to Bagley. Just north of the junction of these two roads sits an established wildlife area at Lone Lake. Bagley is another cheery community, with a nice campsite-equipped *city park*. Just west of downtown on Highway 2 sits the *Bagley Wildlife Museum*, (218) 694-2491, in a low-slung ranch house. As the name indicates, enter and you'll find any number of stuffed critters, most bagged for more than 40 years by the proprietor. This trophy collection is a bit weird, but it's not something you see every day—so enjoy it.

From Highway 92 in Bagley, turn left on County 19 and drive east, then south for 4 miles to County Road 26. Turn left (east) and go for about 3.5 miles. Just to the south are Daniel and Dahlberg Lakes, small by Minnesota standards, but another excellent spot to disembark for some serious wildlife viewing.

Continue east on CR 26 for a short distance to County Road 2. Turn right (south) and drive for 3 miles to County Road 29/10. Turn left (east) and proceed for 4.5 miles to County Road 5/27; turn right (south) and cruise for 8 miles to County Road 9. You'll get a good dose

Cordwood Pete

According to Paul Bunyan lore, Peter DeLang was a four-foot-nine-inch spitfire lumberjack who loved to crow about his physical strength to anyone who would listen in local saloons. The local constable checked this fireplug's background and, lo and behold, he turned out to be Paul Bunyan's brother. Years before, Cordwood Pete left their birthplace of Bangor, Maine, and came to Minnesota to prove himself to his brother. Stealing Paul's axe, he tried to swing it, but couldn't stop himself due to its weight. Spinning for one entire day, he wound up clearing over 100 acres before he wound down. This "legendary" feat got him hired to clear railroad lines and, thus, Bemidji likely owes its existence to Paul Bunyan's little brother.

of twists and turns here, but it's worth the effort, as you're tracing the initial stages of the Mississippi River, just after it has departed its headwaters. In fact, you've entered the confines of the *Mississippi Headwaters State Forest* and, despite the name, the tree quotient certainly outweighs the water quotient. And it offers lovely viewing throughout. You'll pass by any number of campgrounds as you head south. Ultimately, you'll cross over the Mississippi River just before Stumphges Rapids, with a close-by campground and boat access.

Turn left (east) at CR 9 and travel for 11 miles to County Road 29. Turn left (north) and drive for 3.5 miles to County Road 35. For most of the latter stretch, you'll pass Lake Plantagenet on the right, which was described by *National Geographic Traveller* as one of the country's most beautiful lakes, especially when the leaves—aspen, birch, maple, and oak—explode into color come autumn. South of the lake is *Paul Bunyan State Forest,* which leaves us with one last reminder of the big guy's influence around these parts.

Turn right (east) on CR 35 and drive 4 miles to U.S. Highway 71. Turn left (north) and go straight about 4 miles, as the route becomes Washington Avenue in Bemidji, then Paul Bunyan Drive. Continue to Bemidji Avenue and a return to our starting point.

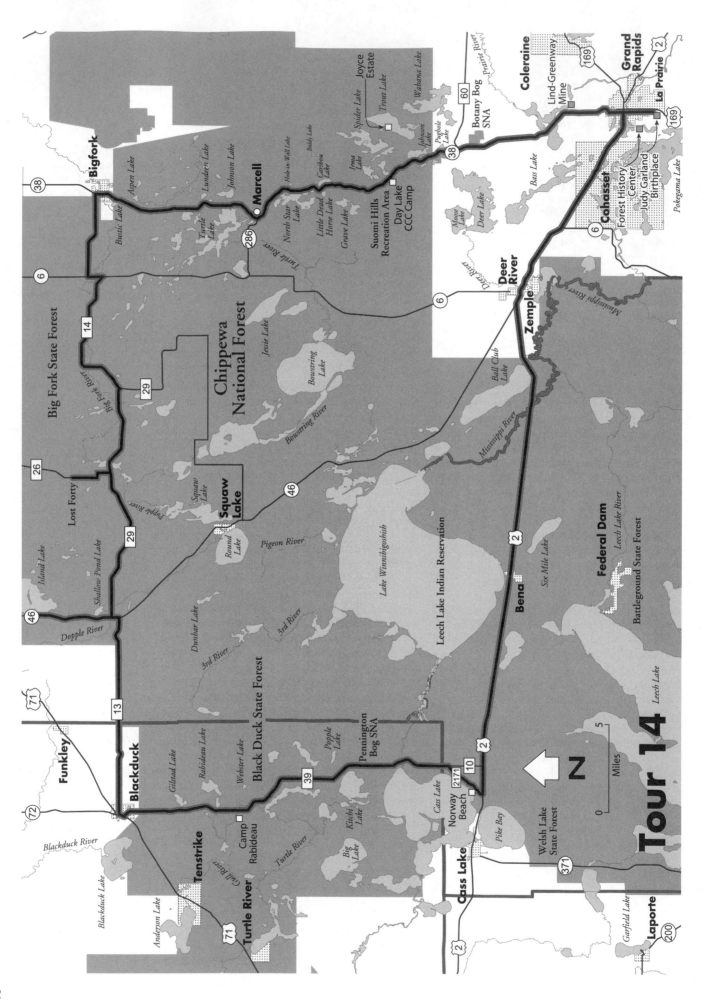

Tour 14

Tour 14
First in Forests

Grand Rapids—Turtle Lake—Chippewa National Forest—Bigfork—Blackduck—Deer River—Grand Rapids

Distance: approximately 188 miles

The Chippewa National Forest takes center stage on this tour, geographically and otherwise. The first U.S. national forest established by Congress, the "Chip" dominates the local ethos. Acre upon acre of isolated backcountry invite endless snooping. For drivers, a must awaits—an established backwoods scenic byway. Along the way, you can't help but notice myriad glacial pools; within the sphere of our tour, you can count (if you're so inclined) over 1,000 residual pockets of glacial tears. Don't overlook the importance of water; this is, after all, the headwaters region of the Mississippi River.

Forests, lakes, rivers—yet we haven't even begun to exhaust the possibilities. Hopefully you've packed your sturdy hiking boots, because the hiking opportunities in the 1.6 million acres of the Big Chip could fill a phone-book-sized list. And this doesn't even begin to cover the canoeing possibilities.

Human culture isn't overlooked. The Leech Lake Indian Reservation sits amidst the enormous national forest and breathes its spirit into the region.

Start your tour in downtown Grand Rapids at the junction of U.S. Highway 2 and U.S. Highway 169. Just south of the junction on 169 (Pokegama Avenue), you'll find the well-run *Grand Rapids Chamber of Commerce*, 1 NW 3rd Street, (800) 472-6366 (www.visitgrandrapids.com).

Grand Rapids was fortuitously platted indeed. Not only close to an extraordinary bounty of timber, it was also the northernmost stopping point for steamships on the Mississippi River. And, of course, a combination of timber and transport was the linchpin of any flourishing North Woods community. By the way, the "rapids" are a historical remnant; construction of a paper mill and a dam flooded the once 3-mile-long stretch of gurgling waters.

Also downtown, a block north of the junction is the *Itasca Heritage Center*, 10 NW 5th Street, (218) 326-6431, in the old Central School Building. Given that movie star Judy Garland was born (as Frances Gumm) and raised in Grand Rapids until age four, it's no surprise to find a yellow brick, er, sidewalk leading up to the door. The 1895 edifice is smashingly well restored inside, and you'll find old storefronts and offices, a bank, a general store,

and lots of Judy Garland memorabilia. Hours are Memorial Day weekend to Labor Day, Monday–Saturday, 9:30 a.m.–5 p.m., Sunday, noon–4 p.m., reduced off-season hours; admission.

Drive south on Highway 169 (Pokegama Avenue) to 10th Street/Golf Course Road (County Road 23). Turn right (west) and drive less than 2 miles to County Road 76, then Forest History Road. There, the *Forest History Center*, (218) 327-4482, 2609 CR 76, is a replica of a late-nineteenth-century logging camp. It's the only one in Minnesota, which is good in itself. Yet travelers find it marvelous, because of its extraordinary design and execution. In-character chatty docents lead visitors about a spacious, wooded complex devoted to the state's forest heritage. You could pretty much while away an afternoon just nosing around the grounds laden with Smithsonian-quality artifacts. A 100-foot-tall restored fire tower offers commanding views. Hours are Memorial Day weekend to mid-October, Monday–Saturday, 10 a.m.–5 p.m.; Sunday, from noon; reduced hours the rest of

Is Paul . . . Tall?

As legend has it, Paul Bunyan was born amidst the smoky interiors of nineteenth-century bunkhouses, as bored and exhausted lumbermen swapped "fish" tales of legendary timber prowess. Eventually, exaggerated lore coalesced into one immense legend.

Actually, the mythology of Paul Bunyan was helped along by journalists paid by the word to create yarns. The first recorded Paul Bunyan tale was put into print around 1910, with many more following. Ribald tales popular for years among lumberjacks suddenly became more family-friendly. A year later, the first advertisement from the Red River Lumber Company featured the legendary lumberman. The ad campaign cemented the Paul Bunyan mythology. William Laughead is credited with writing the stories from the campaign, purportedly basing them on tales he heard years earlier in Chippewa National Forest logging camps. He's also credited with naming Babe the Blue Ox. Other writers and journalists picked up the Bunyan stories as the legend began to grow. Bunyan's fame seemed to hit a zenith in the mid-1920s with publication of the writings of James Stevens.

One thing researchers have never been able to pinpoint: Whence the name Paul Bunyan? No one's ever come up with a good explanation for its origin.

Blacksmith showing off his skills at the Forest History Center, Grand Rapids. Tim Bewer

the year; admission. The interpretive center and nature trails are free during the off-season. If you're really into timber and its effects, stop by the *Tall Timber Days* festival the first weekend in August. You'll find arts and crafts, canoe and foot races, and a host of "timber skill" events, including ever-popular pole climbing!

Return to CR 23 and drive east to Highway 169 (Pokegama Avenue); turn right and go for about 1 mile to the *Judy Garland Birthplace House.* The star of *The Wizard of Oz* is probably the second-largest draw to Grand Rapids. The house, 2727 U.S. 169 S, (800) 664-5839, has been painstakingly restored to its 1925 appearance, using family interviews as a guide. Of course, much of the memorabilia is themed toward her legendary movie role. One acre of themed gardens is nice for a stroll. Picture yourself bopping about with the Munchkins! Hours are mid-May to mid-October, daily 10 a.m.–5 p.m.; admission. Of course, the city celebrates Judy Garland with her own festival, held in June.

Quick Trip Option 1. Let's not forget that we're on the fringes of the Mesabi Iron Range. Those intrigued by the notion of subterranean spelunking have another grand side trip in Calumet, about 15 miles east of Grand Rapids: *Hill Annex Mine State Park,* (218) 247-7215, Highway 169, one of the state's best-preserved historical sites. Tour buses whisk you into the interior of the 500-foot-deep mine for 90 fascinating minutes. Interpreters bring alive the rough life and difficult work of the miners. Keep your eyes sharp, as you may even get a glimpse of some antediluvian fossils in the

rock beds. Fossil hunting tours are offered Wednesdays at noon, and are great fun. Tours depart Memorial Day weekend to Labor Day, daily 10 a.m.–4 p.m.; admission.

Return north on Pokegama Avenue to Highway 2 in Grand Rapids; turn left (west and go two blocks to NW 3rd Avenue (State Highway 38). Turn right (north). Highway 38 is one of those legendary blue highways that poke into pristine wilderness. You're at the door to the *Edge of Wilderness Scenic Byway,* one of the state's loveliest. For 47 miles, virtually every twist and turn reveals an amazing sight. There's so much to see, in fact, that you're never, but never, going to go faster than 40 miles per hour—guaranteed. Gaze at a map; you're about to roll and bend around an astonishing number of glacial lakes. You'll soon discover why locals call this highway "Highway Loop-de-Loop."

After 3.5 miles, at the intersection with County Road 61, look for a parking lot on the northeast corner. Here, you find the *Lind-Greenway Mine,* a now-defunct iron ore mine that once rivaled any other in the area. Most salient is the 200-foot-tall-high "mountain" of tailings—the residuals from extracting ore from rock—one of thousands in the Iron Range. (In fact, this is a spot to hook up with the Taconite Trail, a multi-use trail skirting the site that gets its name from the low-grade ore pulled from the ground.) Today jack pine is most prevalent, slowly growing over the landscape scars. This is the result of Grand Rapids school kids planting trees on the first Earth Day in 1970.

Continue north on Highway 38 for another 8 miles or so to Blue Water Lake Road (County Road 60). Not long after turning back onto Highway 38, on either side of the road, hardly discernible, is one of the region's largest bogs (part of the Botany Bog State Natural Area); this one a black spruce/tamarack variety. In autumn, the tamarack glow a brilliant yellow, set off by the dark hues of black spruce. The tamarack, by the way, is the only conifer to shed all of its needles in the fall. This is only a drive-by visual, however. To protect the environment, no parking/tramping is allowed.

Turn right (east) on Blue Water Lake Road and proceed to the parking area and trailhead for *Trout Lake* and the *Joyce Estate*. The three-mile hike north (one-way) to this magnificent estate (the entire trail system totals about 10 moderately-difficult miles) is well worth the effort. But the word *estate* hardly does justice to the place. Built out of native timber and stone, this massive complex of 40 buildings was put up between 1917 and 1935 by a wealthy Chicagoan who built his fortune in timber. Imagine time-traveling here: You'd see a private golf course, private seaplanes, tennis courts, and telephone line just to serve the main house. Today only four of the buildings have been restored and are short-listed for the National Register of Historic Places. Now managed by the U.S. Forest Service, it's still an astonishing place to explore, and an excellent example of Adirondack timber construction. Information signs on numbered posts along a path help bring the Roaring Twenties and the estate's heyday alive again.

Return to Highway 38 and continue north for 1 mile. It's quick, but it's worth it to stop at the Birch Stand at Pughole Lake, found at a wayside on the highway's east side. Nothing historical here— just a lovely place to stop and take in Mother Nature, especially in autumn. The creamy white trees laced with black really stand out against an evergreen background.

Proceed on Highway 38 for approximately 6 miles. The moniker "Highway Loop-de-Loop" really comes to mind about now. Trees crowd the roadside, and the road seems to dodge the densest tracts of the jack pine. No matter; it gives more flavor to the drive! Get ready to walk, for you're passing along the edges of a sublime spot for history and hiking simultaneously.

On the west side of the highway, you'll see a parking lot for the *Suomi Hills Recreation Area*, with 10 square miles of modest, but picturesque, forest offerings, trails (21 miles) to lakes, and ribbony streams. Several lakes offer good brown and rainbow trout fishing. Hikers will find morel mushrooms in the fall and blueberries in season. Another favorite hike is to the Miller Lake area. This "sunken" or "disappearing" lake has had its topography dramatically changed twice: once when an

earthen dam gave way, and another time when a beaver dam collapsed. An enormous gully remains.

Most folks, however, come to snoop around the gracefully decaying remains of the *Day Lake CCC camp* on both sides of Highway 38. Day Lake was one of President Franklin Roosevelt's Works Progress Administration's development sites. One of only six camps that operated after the Civilian Conservation Corps era, it was also the only one to be used by African-Americans in the CCC program. (German prisoners of war also resided here during World War II.)

Continue north on Highway 38 for 1 mile to a wayside on the right. The terrain has been rising of late; not very noticeable, but certainly appreciable. At the pull-off, you've reached a pinnacle of sorts—the top of the Continental Divide, separating watersheds to the north and south. The Divide reaches as far north as Hudson Bay and as far south as the Gulf of Mexico! The views here are inspiring, especially in autumn.

Keep going on Highway 38 for about 8 miles to Marcell. After 2 to 3 miles, you start to see lots of arbor vitae about. It's officially white cedar, and it was introduced into Europe from North America as far back as the mid-1500s. It was known for its life-saving properties (its name, after all, means "tree of life"), such as providing vitamin C to prevent scurvy on long ocean voyages. Native Americans used it in medicinal ointments, and in building canoes. Today, it's used for decks and fencing, among other things. No parking exists along this jog, however, so we're left to simply ponder this versatile tree.

The road cruises through a labyrinth of North Woods lakes, large and small, with mundane names (Caribou, Forest, North Star), as well as intriguing ones (Hole-in-Wall, Little Dead Horse, Baldy). Nearing tiny Marcell, the road—and the forest—seem to tire. The trees back off and the twisting subsides, as if we all need a rest. Enjoy the break.

Along the way, a mile south of town, look on the east side of the highway where you may spot an osprey nest. The nest has been there for quite a spell now and is gaining local fame. *Marcell Park* on the south side of town has information panels on this community. This town was actually "born" near Turtle Lake north of here in 1901. Unfortunately, the railroad decided to build the spur line through here, not there, so the town had to pick up and move.

Quick Trip Option 2. Here's a lovely little offshoot of our regular route—an already grand and educational natural history drive. This is the *Chippewa Adventure Tour*, a subroute of the Edge of Wilderness Scenic Byway. *Just* north of the Marcell Ranger station, County Road 45 heads east past Ranier and Forest Lakes. If you follow it to County Road 47, then head north on Forest Road 2181, then west on Forest Road 2182, you'll take in nearly a dozen historic or environmentally special stops. Everything is explained in detail at interpretive boards: trees, bogs, eagles, forest management—everything. It's only an extra 18 miles, so you can do it fairly quickly. The route is open May to November only, and the dates vary, so ask at the ranger station if you're not sure if the weather has allowed the roads to open yet. If you follow this route, you'll link up with the next stop below, Jack the Horse Road, at the final point on the Chippewa Adventure Tour.

The Majestic Bird

The Chippewa National Forest is home to the largest breeding population of bald eagles in the continental United States. The Chippewa Adventure side trip has a stop at Burns Lake that explains the remarkable tale of these majestic birds. Now totaling more than 200 eagles, the Chip's population has nearly tripled since the late 1980s.

From Marcell, continue north on Highway 38 for a little more than 1 mile to Jack the Horse Road. A few hundred feet east of Highway 38 is the Gut and Liver Line, an erstwhile section of the Minneapolis and Rainy River Railroad. The name is the key.

Folk legends suggest that it stems from the only food served on the rail. Or worse, it implies what the horrid food effected in you. Or even, too, what covered the front of the engine after it hit the animals that crossed its path.

Proceed on Highway 38 for 11 miles to Bigfork. About a mile into this stretch, look to the east, and you'll start to see a series of glacial eskers, residuals of the massive Wisconsin glacial epoch.

On the south side of Bigfork, a little wayside park has a big story about a local character dubbed "Uncle Tom." This character was legendary for his hospitality, or his version of it, anyway. It seems Uncle Tom loved to entertain guests and serve "chicken" (or so he said to keep people's stomachs easy). Actually, he served whatever game (or varmints) he could shoot.

Bigfork was known for logging and milling, but today you can't help but notice the preponderance of canoes in the area. Every which way, you see either a canoe outfitter for trips on the Bigfork or Rice Rivers, or a canoe construction operation. You can visit a traditional birch bark canoe maker and take a canoe home. But be prepared for sticker shock. The Big Fork and Rice Rivers offer challenging and rewarding canoeing. The former offers 165 miles of somewhat tough paddling (some big rapids beyond the community of Bigfork). Rice River is generally easy as it flows north to join the Bigfork River.

Go north on Highway 38 a short distance to County Road 14. Turn left (west) and continue on this road, which will become County Road 29 after 17 miles. This winding little country route snakes through some dense wilderness; it seems the trees crowd out any lakes. Prepare for some good sights to come. Don't dawdle!

Proceed on CR 29 for about 6 miles to County Road 26. Turn right (north) and go for 2 miles to Forest Road 2240; turn left (west) and go 1.5 miles to the *Lost Forty*. In 1882, a mapping error pegged this 144-acre area as being under part of nearby Coddington Lake, which meant that the virgin pine was left untouched by loggers. The most impressive specimens are found at the east end; most are up to 350 years old and between 22 and 48 inches in diameter. This old-growth section of the Chippewa National Forest is increasingly rare and important for woodland biologists.

Return to CR 26 and then CR 29. Turn right (west) on CR 29 and proceed for 10 miles to State Highway 46. Turn right (north) and cruise for 5 miles to Island Lake. The road is wide, straight and unimpressive. But hold on, an overlooked gem awaits. Island Lake is a largish body of water with prominent Elmwood Island perched in the middle of the azure waters. The island is totally undeveloped and features untouched upland cedar. It's a great day trip. You'll find boat rentals at any of the numerous local resorts on the lake.

Return south on Highway 46 for 6 miles to County Road 13. Turn right (west) and drive for 13 miles to U.S. Highway 71 in Blackduck (CR 13 becomes County Road 30 about halfway through this stretch). Turn left (south) on Highway 71, go a short distance to County Road 39, turn left, and drive for 6 miles to *Camp Rabideau*. CR 39 provides another lush, tree-encroached back road with a wealth of sights to see. Don't let the straightness of the road fool you. Plenty of challenging rises and falls await, and you're likely to see innumerable deer. Camp Rabideau, a CCC facility, was built during the 1930s. Today 15 of the camp's original 25 buildings are preserved. A 1-mile trail has interpretive boards highlighting the history.

Continue south on CR 39 for about 2.5 miles. Look for signs west to the *Gilfillan Area* and east to *Webster Lake*. (For the former, look for Forest Road 2091, where you'll find a parking area.) These two turnoffs appear approximately at the same time, so most travelers will choose one or the other. The Gilfillan Area is an undeveloped zone rife with orchids and a large white spruce seed production area. Webster Lake, somewhat larger, has a highly educational bog walk, a half-mile boardwalk with interpretive signs detailing the bog's ecological diversity. Highlighted are carnivorous plants (kids love this).

Continue south on CR 39 for 10 miles to *Pennington Bog*. Yes, another bog. But this one has an unusually large spread of orchids and extends as far as a contiguous State Natural Area. This region is sensitive, so you'll need to get a free entry permit, available from the regional DNR office in Bemidji.

Long-abandoned barn near the Chippewa National Forest. Thomas Huhti

Continue south on CR 39 for 7 miles to Forest Road 2171. Turn right and drive southwest for 3 miles to U.S. Highway 2. You'll pass the Norway Beach Area, with a campground and swimming beach, and also the Ten Section Area, with old-growth red and white pines. Norway Beach has a summertime visitor center with lots of information on early-twentieth-century conservation movements that helped preserve this area.

Turn left (east) on Highway 2 and head east for about 34 miles to Deer River. Approxi-

mately 8 miles west of Deer River, the Mississippi River crosses Highway 2. Look for eagles soaring overhead. Deer River is where you'll find the *Cut Foot Sioux Ranger Station,* the oldest remaining ranger station building in the U.S. Forest Service's eastern region. Tours are arranged through the Cut Foot Sioux Visitor Information Center, just off Highway 2 in Deer River.

From Deer River, continue southeast for 12 miles to the junction with U.S. Highway 169 in Grand Rapids, where this tour began.

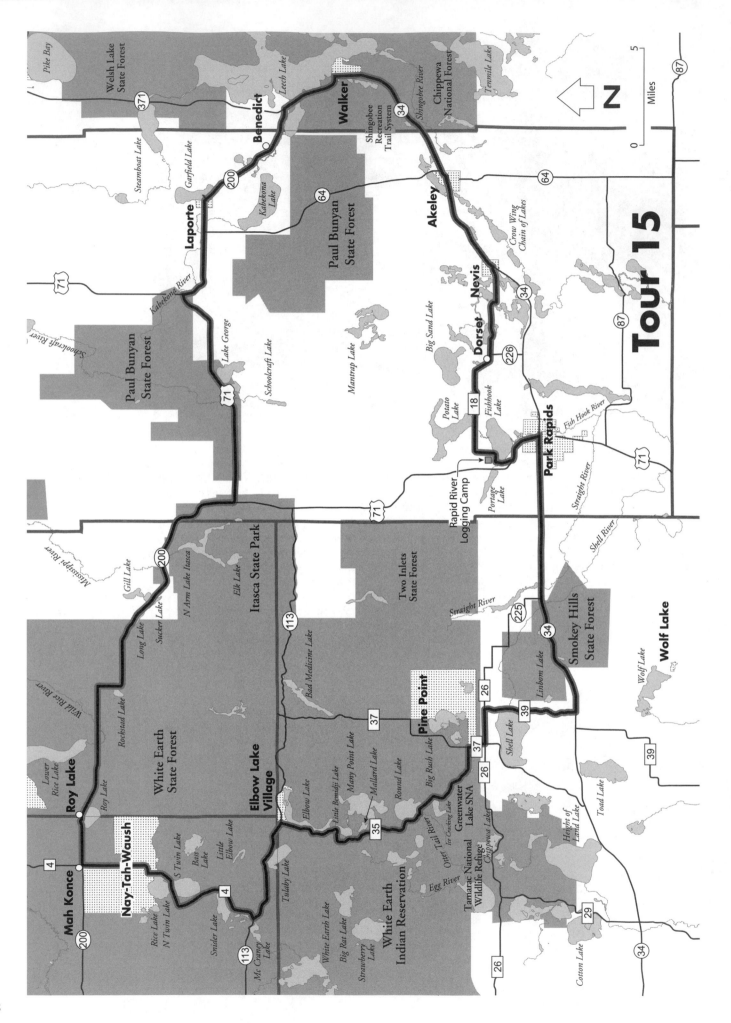

Tour 15
Birthplace of the Mighty Miss

Park Rapids—Akeley—Walker—Lake George—Itasca State Park—White Earth Indian Reservation—Smoky Hills State Forest—Park Rapids

Distance: approximately 138 miles

What a weird thrill, broad jumping the Mississippi River. Well, that's what you can do on this tour, and you don't have to be of Bunyanesque proportions to make the leap. At Itasca State Park, one of the mightiest rivers in the world starts as a tiny ribbon of gurgling water as it begins its 2,550-plus-mile-long roll to the Gulf of Mexico. Even though its dimensions here are puny, you're guaranteed to get a shiver if you contemplate what the river means to our country.

The Mighty Miss, though, is but one segment—albeit the major one—of this traipse through the eastern end of one of the state's many versions of "lakes country." We begin with steam-powered saws and emu hugs, find ourselves fishing for eelpout in the dead of winter, munching on delectable blueberries, and only then can we get an up-close view of the Old Man River. Sounds odd, but read on.

Start your tour just south of Park Rapids on U.S. Highway 71. You'll find all the information you need about the area at the *Park Rapids Area Chamber of Commerce*, (800) 247-0054 (www .parkrapids.com). This is a good resource for Itasca State Park guides or maps to the surrounding areas. Also ask for a map of the *Heartland Trail*. This 49-mile, multi-use paved trail was the state's first rail-to-trail path. You can travel all the way to Cass Lake from Park Rapids, passing through Akeley, Nevis, Walker, and Dorset. Along the way is a nice mixture of pasture, meadow, and pockets of sentinel-like trees.

For information on the entire Itasca Lakes area, also contact the *Itasca Area Lakes Tourism Association*, (888) 292-7118 (www.itascaarea .com).

Drive north on Highway 71 into Park Rapids and the corner of Third Street and Court Avenue. Here, the *Hubbard County Courthouse*, (218) 732-5237, is both the local county historical museum and a great arts center, with a fine collection of historical and contemporary art. One gallery features historical European art; four other galleries feature rotating exhibits of contemporary art. Note the eye-catching architecture of the house of justice, too. Hours are, June to August,

Tuesday–Sunday, 11 a.m.–5 p.m., reduced hours May and September; admission.

Then, just stroll about the trim downtown of Park Rapids. It feels like you're walking through the set of a 1930s picture show; you half expect the locals to be speaking in dated slang. You can belly up for a soda at the original town *soda fountain* before you take in a show at the town's original theater. Even the streets are old-fashioned; check out the center-avenue parking jobs.

Go north on Highway 71 for about 1 mile to *Deer Town.* The highlight of this petting zoo, (218) 732-1943, is an area where the kids get to hand-feed the deer. Families will find the large menagerie of Minnesota species highly educational, and kids love the more, er, exotic species. You'll also find a trout pond, picnic facilities and more. All told, good family fun. Hours are Memorial Day weekend to Labor Day, daily 9 a.m.–6 p.m.; admission.

Continue north on Highway 71 for about 2 miles to County Road 18; turn right and follow the signs to the *Rapid River Logging Camp.* This restaurant-cum-historical-museum, (218) 732-3444, offers three squares served daily, family-style, which means as much as you can stuff in. It's lip-smacking good. Outside, the grounds are equally fun. Nature trails snake around the environs, allowing you great views of the Lady Slipper, the Minnesota state flower. Best of all, a live steam-powered sawmill is fired up Tuesdays and Fridays. This is an experience you won't soon forget.

Continue north, then east on CR 18 for about 15 miles to State Highway 34, passing through Dorset and Nevis along the way. At the beginning of this stretch, you'll zip through some lovely lake-dotted topography. For your driving pleasure, CR 18 adds loops and twists around Fish Hook Lake before taking a serious eastward bend and high-tailing it toward Dorset. Immediately, it bisects Fish Hook and Potato Lakes (great name!) and then makes a run tangentially to another pincushion of smaller lakes.

Just west of Nevis is the *Heart of Minnesota Emu Ranch.* Here you can hug an emu. Then you can learn why emus are the source of many skin care and pain relief products. Everybody learns something on this tour! Tours are offered Thursdays or other days by appointment; call (218) 652-3790, for information.

Just north of Nevis via County Roads 2 and 40 you have another oddball ranch tour—*Northland Bison Ranch*, 22376 Glacial Ridge Trail, (218) 652-3582, has bus tours to meet Big Thunder and his brother, Lightning—the resident heads of the bison herd on this ranch. Tours are generally available daily, though call first to verify.

In Nevis itself, you can't help but notice the local attraction—the enormous fiberglass *tiger muskie,* which gives a pretty good clue as to what anglers come to town for.

Birding near Akeley

You'll find a number of noteworthy and rewarding birding opportunities in the Akeley area. Approximately 4 miles south of town on the west side of State Highway 64 is a great blue heron colony. Another colony is located 12 miles north of town on Highway 64 on the west side of the road. Three miles farther north, also on the west side of the road, near the junction with State Highway 200, you can find an osprey colony. Four miles east of Akeley along Highway 34 you'll come to the Chippewa National Forest's Shingobee Area, with 6 miles of trails winding through upland habitat including mature jack pine, young red pine, oak-birch forests, and a cedar swamp. A huge number of bird species can be spotted here year-round.

Turn left (north) on Highway 34 and travel 7 miles to Akeley. In this cheery community, the *Woodtick Musical Theatre*, (218) 652-4200, on Highway 34, presents a fun array of musical acts year-round. It's heavy on country and bluegrass, though you'll find any number of different styles on any given weekend. Foot stompin' is the rule here! Performances are generally offered Wednesday–Sunday at 8 p.m., with Wednesday and Thursday matinees, mid-June to Labor Day. Advance reservations are always recommended.

But what most travelers will remember is Akeley's enormous statue of Paul Bunyan in the downtown. At 33 feet tall, it's supposedly the largest of its kind in Minnesota (and, therefore, in the world). Paul's hand is intentionally stretched out to cup your rear as you sit for pictures! You can also visit the nearby *Paul Bunyan Historical Museum* or get your kicks at 50-year-old-plus *Paul Bunyan Days* festival, held annually in late June.

For the more adrenaline-inspired, Akeley sits at the headwaters of the Crow Wing Chain of Lakes, 11 interconnected pools that flow into the Crow Wing River, which in turn spills into the Mississippi River. Canoeists describe it lovingly.

From Akeley, drive northeast on Highway 34 for 4 miles. Here, at the *Chippewa National Forest's Shingobee Area,* you can link up with the *North Country National Scenic Trail,* the transnational hiking trail that was born in the Great Lakes (and named in next-door Wisconsin). The trail snakes through Minnesota east-to-west, with nearly 70 miles stretching through the Chippewa National Forest. Ultimately, the epic trail will connect the entire country from New York to the Pacific Ocean *and* will have a link south on the Appalachian and Lewis and Clark Trails.

Continue for 4 more miles on Highway 34 into Walker. This pleasant town is the epicenter of the Leech Lake Area, a prime water-oriented recreation zone plunked on the shores of the eponymous lake. Your first stop here should be at the *Leech Lake Area Chamber of Commerce,* (800) 833-1118 (www.leech-lake.com), located on State Highway 371/200, east of the Highway 34 junction.

Though the main attraction in this area is Leech Lake, save time to visit the *Cass County Museum,* located next to the chamber office at 205 Minnesota Avenue W, (218) 547-7251. It features lots of artifacts that trace local history, highlighted by a reconstructed schoolhouse nearly 100 years old. Hours of the historical museum are, Memorial Day weekend to mid-September, Monday–Saturday, 10 a.m.–5 p.m.; admission.

From Walker, head north on Highway 371/200 for 4 miles to where Highway 200 splits off to the left. Follow it for about 13 miles through Benedict and Laporte. You'll find yourself slicing through another chain of lakes and bisecting the appropriately named Paul Bunyan State Forest. The state forest spreads for more than 72,000 acres with lots of rolling hills, heavy timber, and bog areas. Near Mantrap Lake is a nice 2-mile-long hiking trail.

From Laporte, continue on Highway 200 to *Lake George,* a stretch of about 15 miles. Just outside of Laporte, signs invite you to take a jaunt south to a host of lakes with campgrounds and boat launches. County Roads 93 and 91 offer up a scenic detour if you tire of asphalt. The time-challenged should barrel along Highway 200, which then pairs up with U.S. Highway 71 about 6 miles east of Lake George.

This tiny town sits on the perimeter of the 788-acre spring-fed Lake George, which offers great panfish and walleye fishing, along with several hiking trails through birch and pine forests. The town really comes alive in July, when area residents descend on the town to pick wild blueberries, a local delicacy. Locals can fill you in on where to snoop out the berries, but the best time to come is the last full weekend of July, when the *Blueberry Festival* takes place. Three full days are devoted entirely to this delicious little berry. The fire department has a huge—and filling—ham-and-bean feed, and the senior center has a popular blueberry pancake breakfast. You'll also enjoy the local churches' gospel concert and a quilt show.

Continue west on Highway 71/200 for 7 miles to the intersection where 71 splits off to the left. Watch for County Road 48 going west and for entrance signs to Itasca State Park. Itasca, (218) 266-2114, is Minnesota's oldest state park, established in 1891. This early recognition was amply justified, as this is the place where the mighty Mississippi River gets its gurgling start as a modest, broad-jump-sized brook. But that's just the beginning of what the park offers. Truly, the park's 32,000 acres may be the state's most diverse in offerings: the Mississippi, extant settlement buildings, a pioneer cemetery, old-growth trees, a scenic driving tour, and even one of Minnesota's National Natural Landmarks. Not enough? Well, how about scrumptious food in historic Douglas Lodge. Try, for example, a not-to-be-forgotten meal of blueberries, walleye, and wild rice.

Itasca is an amalgam of the Latin *verITAS CAput* or "truth" and "head" respectively, coined by Henry Rowe Schoolcraft, as he and a missionary companion were shown the source of the river by their Anishnabe guide in 1832. Later in the century, rapacious loggers had already descended on the area when surveyors came to fully establish the river's source. Due to several prescient surveyors, the area was finally put off-limits to development by the Minnesota legislature in 1891; by just one vote, but, still, a fantastically progressive idea at the time.

The park recently christened a new, multi-million-dollar information and interpretive center. Not only is it an amazingly high-tech educational facility, but it's also used as a warming center for the park's hikers and other trail users. At the center, be sure to pick up a copy of the park's "Stepping Stones" guide, with detailed maps and descriptions of the park's highlights. Also, pick up a brochure outlining the park's 16-mile loop auto tour, the "Main Park/Wilderness Drive." More than two dozen super scenic viewing areas and areas of historic interest are highlighted along the way. Note that 8 miles of the drive are one-way only and shared by bicycles; please use extra caution.

Simply put, everyone will find a trail suitable for their needs. Most will want to drive north from the visitor center to the North Arm of Lake Itasca, where you'll find the modest beginnings of the legendary river. But consider any of the wonderful scenic/natural/historic sites along the way. Following your hop across the "river," you can continue your driving tour of the park in a clockwise fashion, with more trails and historic spots ready to be visited. Don't miss the short (half-mile) Bohall Trail leading into the Itasca Wilderness Sanctuary State Natural Area.

Return to Highway 200 and proceed north and northwest about 24 miles to the community of Mah Konce. West of Itasca State Park, the road leads to an astonishing array of sights and attractions for nature lovers. First, you whip by two established *scenic wildlife* areas on Sucker and Gill Lakes. Then, along comes *Long Lake Park*, with a campground and great swimming. Just then you see signs indicating that you're in yet *another* state forest: the *White Earth State Forest*, just south of Zerkel. Eventually, County Road 200 crosses into the *White Earth Indian Reservation*.

There's no need to guess what crop is grown in these parts. Just look at the names on a map: Upper Rice Lake, Lower Rice Lake, Wild Rice River,

and so on. You can see marshy, wild rice beds, drying lots, and storage sheds everywhere. Each fly-speck town has its own local variety for sale in stores. If you're here in autumn, you're in for a treat. This entire stretch is likely among the loveliest in Minnesota, particularly the environs surrounding the junction of Highway 200 and County Road 7 near Roy Lake. The golden grasses juxtaposed with the changing leaves is a spectacular sight.

Mah Konce, a strange and lovely name, is a White Earth Reservation community, and likely the nucleus of the wild rice industry in this area. You can see a large harvest barn here and snoop about the local shops for wild rice packages. (They make lovely gifts and souvenirs, by the way.) A Minnesota tidbit: Perhaps the most famous White Earth tribal member is Winona LaDuke, the vice presidential candidate on Ralph Nader's Green Party ticket in the 1996 presidential election.

At Mah Konce, turn left (south) on County Road 4 for 4.5 miles to Nay-Tah-Waush. This community has an Ojibwe cemetery, but it's difficult to spot. You'll need local directions and, obviously, respect all property.

Continue south on CR 4 for approximately 10 miles to State Highway 113. You enter the *White Earth State Forest* again, as the road twists and turns amid myriad lakes. Looking for all the world like a snake on the map, CR 4 doesn't disappoint anyone looking for some driving thrills.

Turn left (east) on Highway 113 and drive for about 6 miles to County Road 35 at Elbow Lake Village. Turn right (south) and proceed for 16.5 miles to County Road 37. After Elbow Lake village, another classic Minnesota chain of lakes awaits. One by one: Elbow Lake, Little Bemidji Lake, Many Point Lake, Mallard Lake, Round Lake (campground here), and all-time favorite, Ice Cracking Lake.

Muskies, Walleye, and Eelpout

Every community touts its annual festivals, but those in the Leech Lake area warrant special mention. Fishing is key here. One of the world's largest fishing tournaments, the Mercury Walleye Classic, takes place in early June. And the annual Muskie's Inc. Tournament comes to the lake each fall, with more than 800 pro-muskie hunters prowling the waters.

But the top festival—and the one that garners lots of national and international coverage—is the International Eelpout Festival. Held in mid-February, this ice-fishing extravaganza features a search for the lake's ugliest fish. The eelpout has been best described as an eel with whiskers—and even that under-describes its, er, lack of aesthetic appeal. Ironically, the "champion" eelpouts can fetch thousands of dollars (why is anyone's guess). More fun than fishing are the zany sideshow activities that take place—lots of weird races, games, and the like. All in all, it's one of Minnesota's most unique festivals.

At the source—the headwaters of the Mississippi River in Itasca State Park. Tim Bewer

Turn right (south) on CR 37 and go 1 mile to County Road 26. Turn left (east) and proceed for 2 miles to County Road 39. Turn right (south) and cruise 5 miles to State Highway 34.

Quick Trip Option. Off to the right throughout most of this stretch you've been skirting the *Tamarac National Wildlife Refuge.* To get to the heart of the refuge, and pure wildlife viewing joy, turn right on County Road 26 and head west for about 10 miles (the opposite direction from the main tour). At the junction with County Road 29 is the visitor center, where you'll learn that the refuge has 43,000 acres and 200 species of bird life. Even if you're not into birding, you can hike or ski on the Winter Wonderland Trail System, a 66-km-long series of trails through conifer and deciduous woodlands, lakes, bogs, marshes, and prairies. At the center, you can also pick up brochures on a lovely 5-mile-long self-guided auto tour, with interpretive stops along the way. For more information, call (218) 847-2641.

At Highway 34, turn left (east) and drive for 4.5 miles to the *Smoky Hills State Forest.* What with all the established parks around, you're guaranteed to be alone here. The forest features a somewhat ambitious terrain, with moderately steep slopes covering the 14,000 acres of state land within the boundaries. The Shell River and numerous shallow lakes pepper the area, with great shorebird viewing. By the way, the Shell River is a wonderful place for a splash. It lies close to one of the three Shell Prairies, where the glaciers stopped, the result being a transition from pine to prairie. It offers outstanding fishing, too; it's one of the Midwest's blue ribbon trout streams. But kids will love to look for the "shells" for which it's named. The clam shells around here were so lovely that, long ago, a button factory was built in nearby Osage. Today you can find shells that were stamped for buttons, but then discarded for other flaws.

Continue east on Highway 34 for 12.5 miles to Highway 71 in Park Rapids to finish your tour.

Tour 16
Lakes, Prairies, and Birds of a Different Feather

Detroit Lakes—Frazee—Vergas—New York Mills—Maplewood State Park—Pelican Rapids—Barnesville—Rollag—Audobon—Detroit Lakes

Distance: Approximately 190 miles

If you gaze at a map, the Detroit Lakes region defies categorization. Is it "western" Minnesota? "Northern" Minnesota? As we'll soon see, it's a bit of both. To the west, we have the fecund flat plainslike prairies of the North Valley's Red River. And to the east, we have the paint-splatter groupings of one of Minnesota's most picturesque concentrations of glacial pools.

Indeed, it appears that the glaciers did terminate here. These glacial residuals, in fact, are what draws thousands of visitors to the region each season—looking to dangle toes in cool waters or sink a line looking for a prize catch. But the farther west we loop on this tour, the rolling hills of glacial carving give way to a more, well, historic feel—the less ambitious fields of agriculture and prairie. This topography shouldn't be overlooked. Some of Minnesota's last remaining original prairie is here, as are pockets of the Midwest's most precious wildlife habitat.

But coffee-table-book sunsets over tall-grass prairie or glacial lakes notwithstanding, this tour has a lot of other unexpected treats. So many, in fact, that this segment could be called the "Something for Everyone Tour." We'll drift into a community that one could swear comes transplanted directly from the Hudson River Valley, a historical and cultural highlight that many Minnesota natives don't know exists. Among this tour's other inviting draws: turtles, turkeys, bluestems, steam-powered threshers, and spuds. Intrigued? You should be—this amalgamation of varied topography, historic communities, tongue-in-cheek festivals, and more offers the most variety of any of our tours.

Start your tour in Detroit Lakes, at the *Detroit Lakes Regional Chamber of Commerce,* 700 Washington Avenue. The staff at this facility, (218) 847-9202 or (800) 542-3992 (www.visitdetroitlakes.com), will give you the low-down on the sights and events that make this community of about 7,500 the recreational hub of this great lakes region.

Detroit Lakes doesn't derive its name from any Motor City connection, although a lot of highways (U.S. 10, U.S. 59, State 34, and a couple of county roads) intersect here. Rather, an itinerant Jesuit priest purportedly remarked upon the noticeable *detroit* ("straits") in the area, which stuck, after some Anglicization, to the pronunciation. The "lakes" came later and should be obvious—over 400 glacial remnants sit within a day-hop drive radius (25 miles). No surprise, given all these inviting pools, that the region is a *major* resort area. A phone-book-sized list of the family resorts lining the shores of all these lakes is available on the town's Web site. Or the chamber of commerce will mail you a copy.

Water lovers are to come home here, from: casual tubers to kids splashing at city beaches to trout-fixated anglers. If you're around in early to mid-July, kick up your heels at the 70-year-old *Northwest Water Carnival,* a 10-day blowout of family activities, culminating in the largest parade in northwest Minnesota.

A few blocks west of the chamber of commerce (best to park the car and hoof it) at the corner of Summit Avenue and Front Street is the *Becker County Historical Society,* 714 Summit, (218) 847-2938. It has two floors of historical displays chronicling the history of the Detroit Lakes region, including a pioneer cabin and an Ojibwe birch bark wigwam. Hours are Tuesday–Saturday, 9 a.m.–5 p.m.; free.

Drive south on Washington Avenue a short distance to where it turns west and becomes West Lake Drive. Here, on the south end of town, sits *City Park Beach,* a mile-long white-sand beach that's well utilized come summer.

Continue west, then south on Lake Drive, eventually connecting with County Road 24 (South Shore Drive) going east. When the road becomes East Shore, it will parallel U.S. Highway 10 to the right. Along this entire stretch that loops around Lake Detroit, you'll have lovely views and plenty of dead-end roads leading to little peninsulas or public access. It's short enough to cover in less than an hour, and it provides various perspectives on a western Minnesota recreational gem.

Quick Trip Option. Moorhead, 45 miles straight west from Detroit Lakes on U.S. Highway 10, is off our itinerary on this tour, but fans of all things

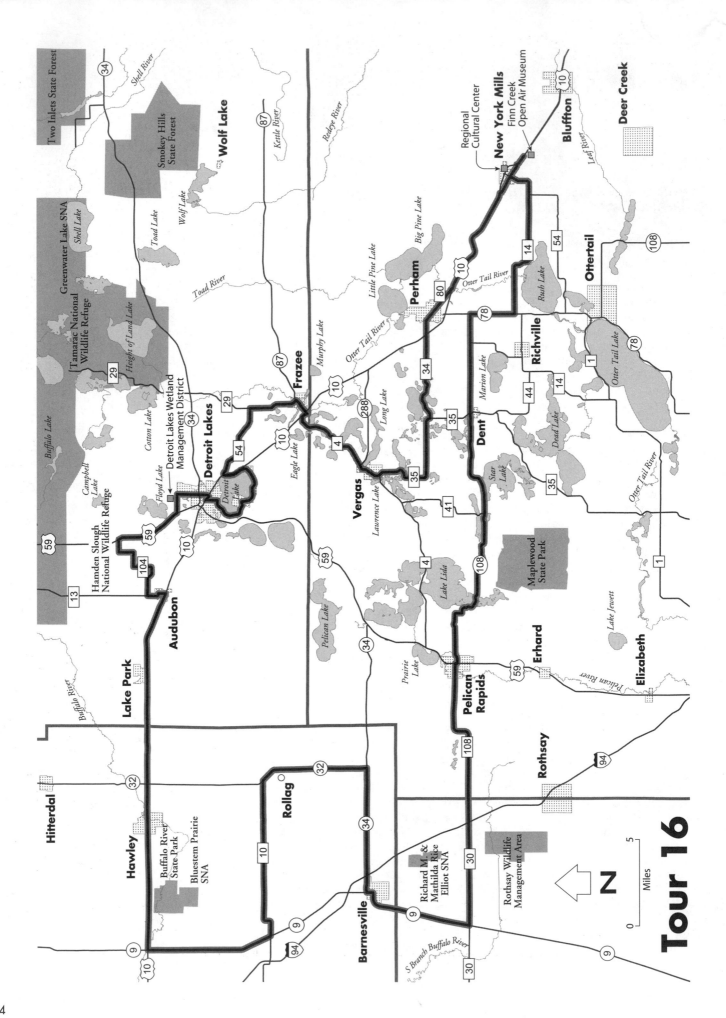

Two Inlets State Forest

Smokey Hills State Forest

Wolf Lake

Greenwater Lake SNA

Tamarac National Wildlife Refuge

Hamden Slough National Wildlife Refuge

Detroit Lakes

Detroit Lakes Wetland Management District

New York Mills

Regional Cultural Center

Finn Creek Open Air Museum

Bluffton

Deer Creek

Ottertail

Perham

Richville

Dent

Frazee

Vergas

Erhard

Elizabeth

Maplewood State Park

Pelican Rapids

Rothsay

Audubon

Lake Park

Hawley

Hitterdal

Rollag

Barnesville

Buffalo River State Park

Bluestem Prairie SNA

Richard M. & Mathilda Rice Elliot SNA

Rothsay Wildlife Management Area

N

0   5
Miles

Tour 16

84

A traveler's best friend checks out the scenery along the Minnesota River. Thomas Huhti

Granite outcroppings are just one of the natural wonders at Big Stone National Wildlife Refuge, south of Ortonville. Thomas Huhti

A sense of tranquility, gorgeous prairie views, and Native American history abound at Pipestone National Monument, near Pipestone. Thomas Huhti

This three-story log cabin is one of the many preserved structures in Mantorville, whose entire
12-block stretch is listed on the National Register of Historic Places. Tim Bewer

An abandoned one-room schoolhouse is silhouetted against the prairie sky near Battle Lake. Tim Bewer

Minnesota never forgets its Norwegian heritage. Here, a replica of a twelfth-century all-wood stave church graces the grounds of the Hjemkomst Interpretive Center in Moorhead. Tim Bewer

One of the joys of auto touring is coming across establishments (and their owners) selling all manner of pre-owned items. Tim Bewer

Another oddball sight: the stately Hooper-Bowler-Hillstrom House in Belle Plaine with one of the country's only two-story outhouses, seen on the left. Tim Bewer

This fearsome Germanic warrior stands atop the 102-foot Hermann Monument in New Ulm's picturesque Hermann Heights Park. Thomas Huhti

The Munsinger Gardens, located along the Mississippi River in Saint Cloud, are a great place to unwind after a day or two touring the area. Tim Bewer

Here, the Mississippi River near Brainerd looks nothing like the mighty waterway it becomes later in its long journey to the Gulf of Mexico. Tim Bewer

The vastness of the western Minnesota prairie is breathtaking, an experience that travelers don't soon forget. Tim Bewer

Nordic will want to save some time before or after this tour for a major cultural highlight of the Red River Valley region.

Moorhead's *Hjemkomst Interpretive Center,* 202 First Avenue, (218) 299-5511, is housed in an unmistakable building—the one that resembles a ship's sail. This is because the museum houses the Viking replica ship *Hjemkomst* (Norwegian for "homecoming"), which was sailed to Bergen, Norway, from Duluth in 1982 by the surviving family members of a man with a dream. Robert Asp had always envisioned sailing a Viking ship. So he built one: a 75-footer that made the epic voyage (sadly, after he had died) of more than 6,100 miles. It's a fascinating story well told by the exhibits. A replica of a twelfth-century Norwegian stave church is also on site. Hours are Monday–Saturday, 9 a.m.–5 p.m., until 9 p.m. Thursday, and noon to 5 p.m. Sunday; admission.

Late June brings the *Hjemkomst Festival* to the complex—all Nordic nations are feted here with dancing, entertainment, folk arts, and lots of food.

Follow East Shore Drive as it crosses Highway 10 and immediately becomes County Road 54. Take that to the right (southeast) for about 5.5 miles to County Road 29. Turn right (south) and drive for about 3 miles to Frazee and the junction with County Road 87. Along the way you'll see lots more lakes; not many fishing hot spots, but boat landings are ubiquitous.

This micro-sized town offers a lot of "interesting" photo opportunities. First, as you come into town on CR 29, look for a left turn before you reach the baseball fields. This will take you to a splendid little *covered bridge.* Stop to snap a few photos and take a stroll inside for a history lesson on the logging days of yesteryear.

Most folks around here, though, know Frazee as a town full of turkeys. Not the *homo sapiens,* mind you, but rather some tongue-in-cheek memorials to the local birds. A couple of blocks southwest of the junction of County Road 29 and 87, on Lake Avenue, you'll see an oversized *turkey statue.* But wait. You ain't seen nothing yet. Continue on CR 87/29 to the junction with Highway 10 on the southwestern fringes of town. Now *here's* a turkey statue. If locals are to be believed, it's the world's largest turkey. Who's going to dispute them—this thing's huge!

Frazee has yet another not-to-be-missed sight. If you return toward the downtown area, just after crossing the railroad tracks, turn right and soon you'll see what *Ripley's Believe it or Not* chose to highlight as one of its Midwest marvels: a bridge over a bridge over a river. The folks at Ripley's said they'd never seen a community besides Frazee that sported such an architectural oddity.

From CR 87/29 in Frazee, head southwest to the junction with U.S. Highway 10. Just past it, continue on CR 29 as it turns to the right. A few miles after that, 29 becomes County Road

Replica of a Norwegian stave church at the Hjemkomst Interpretive Center in Moorhead. Tim Bewer

4 in Otter Tail County. Follow that southwest for about 6 miles to Vergas. You pinball around among a smattering of lakes before finally rolling into Vergas, a tiny and friendly community perched on the far western edge of appropriately named Long Lake. Propped majestically along the shoreline of the lake downtown is another giant community mascot—one of the world's largest (one presumes) *loon statues.*

Continue southwest on CR 4 for 1 mile to County Road 35. Turn left and proceed south for about 8.5 miles to County Road 34. Turn left (east) and drive east for 7 miles into Perham. In the nineteenth century this pleasant little town was a primary node on the Red River Trail, an ox cart path used as a gateway to the Western frontier. The history of the trail is celebrated in August's Pioneer Days celebration. However, see the sidebar "Perham's Turtle Races" on page 86 for the *real* fun here.

Some last-minute preparations at the Perham Turtle Races. Tim Bewer

From downtown Perham, go south via County Road 80 (Main Street) to its merger with U.S. Highway 10, 2 miles later. Continue southeast on Highway 10 for 9 miles into New York Mills. The first thing you notice coming into New York Mills is the Continental Divide monument—another indication of the significance of the watershed between north and south. As for the town name, the first two words indicate the origin of much of the town's lumber barons who came to exploit the wilderness; and *mills* represents the industries they founded.

Finns worked those lumber mills, and the region became a well-known Finnish enclave in northwestern Minnesota. (It, in fact, supported a widely distributed Finnish language newspaper in the nineteenth century.) It wasn't uncommon

Perham's Turtle Races

Perham is well known in these parts as the home of Wednesday Turtle Races, wherein kids race real turtles around the city park during the summer. That's every Wednesday morning, 10:30 a.m.

The tension mounts as registration begins. You don't have a turtle? No problem! The local chamber of commerce will happily provide kids with one. (By the way, all turtles are rescue critters, brought in from certain death on local highways. They're cared for by chamber of commerce volunteers during the summer, then after Labor Day returned to local lakes.)

Turtles are placed in 10-foot circles and race to the outside. Winning times average 9 to 12 seconds. Winning "trainers" get a blue ribbon and a dollar bill. And pooped parents are treated to the Perham Express Train, offering tours about the community.

to walk the streets here and hear much more Finnish than English until well into the twentieth century. That heritage lives on in the *Finn Creek Open Air Museum*, (218) 385-2233 or (218) 385-2230, a collection of extant settler dwellings constructed by some of the area's original Finns. It's located 6 miles southeast of town via Highway 10 and County Road 106; just follow the signs. In late August the town has a celebration for the Finn at heart, with lots of family activities and Finnish food, along with rides and tours of the old farmstead.

Most people come to town today for a wonderful stopoff at the *New York Mills Regional Cultural Center*, 24 North Main Avenue, (218) 385-3339, which you can't miss, given that it's also the local tourist information center. The main floor gallery has nine exhibits annually focusing on local and regional artists, but much national recognition comes here due to its Continental Divide Music and Film Festival. Some prefer another wonderful event, June's Great American Think-Off. It's sort of a quiz show for armchair know-it-alls in which contestants ruminate on thought-provoking topics and a panel judges their final essays. In addition, just about any weekend you show up, you'll find some music, literary, or other cultural events taking place, so it's always worth calling ahead.

From New York Mills, drive south, then west, on County Road 67 for 2.5 miles to County Road 14. Continue west on CR 14 for about 9 miles to State Highway 108. Turn right and follow it north, then west, for about 16 miles, through the tiny town of Dent, to *Maplewood State Park*. The first stretch along CR 14 heads straight before making a quick jog around Rush Lake, the southwest side of which has super wildlife viewing and fishing. Following this, you'll pinball along county roads that seem to be designed on a whim by Mother Nature. And, per usual in these parts, there are all shapes and sizes of lakes on both sides of the road.

If you aren't confused or lost or both by now, you'll soon find yourself on the northern boundaries of Maplewood State Park, (218) 863-8383, which has a tranquil sandy beach, camping, and plenty of hiking. Water lovers have a great time as six gin-clear lakes are linked here. We find yet another outstanding spot to glimpse wildlife, especially birds, on the *Pines to Prairie Birding Trail.*

Continue west for 8 miles west on Highway 108 to Pelican Rapids. Not many pelicans around these parts, you say? Well there's an enormous one right downtown. Yup, here we go again with another world-record fiberglass creature. This one is the *world's largest pelican* at the base of Mill Pond Dam. And, in keeping with the oddball events in other parts of this tour, there's the *Turkey Festival* in mid-July. An enormous turkey barbecue (20 tons) will feed you well, but stick around for the turkey races (yes, they really do race them, and turkeys are fast!). Also, don't miss the Ugly Car contest.

Travel west from Pelican Rapids on Highway 108, which later becomes County Road 30, for about 19 miles to State Highway 9. Not far from Pelican Rapids, the road dips southward to avoid a grouping of lakes five miles west of Pelican Rapids. It straightens out eventually, and you pass by the *Rothsay Wildlife Management Area* just south of CR 30. Here, fields of native mesic and wet prairie lie contiguous with restored wetlands. This is some of northwestern Minnesota's best wildlife viewing, especially for fall and winter birding; native sparrows in October are particularly popular. Note that there are no established trails here and some land is private, so be careful where you tread.

Turn right (north) on Highway 9 and cruise for 7 miles to Barnesville. The hearty potato is honored in this fun town every August (usually the third weekend) at *Potato Days.* You cannot imagine how many different ways there are to celebrate a lowly tuber, but these folks do it well—and with gusto—at this two-day tater blowout. A favorite event is the cook-off competition of lefse—a flat Norwegian type of potato pancake.

At the north edge of Barnesville, turn right (east) on State Highway 34 and go 9 miles to State Highway 32; turn left (north) and go about 6 miles to Rollag. Come late August–early September, western Minnesota really gets a taste of the good old days when throngs descend on tiny Rollag for the wildly popular *Western Minnesota Steam Threshers Reunion,* celebrating its 50th annual hoedown as this book was being prepared.

You'll find 70 *acres* of exhibits and demonstrations: horse-, gas-, and steam-powered machinery of all possible kinds, including some rarities. Other highlights include a turn-of-the-twentieth-century farm, three operational sawmills, and three chug-chug-chugging steam trains. Even nongearheads just shake their heads in wonder here.

Continue north on Highway 32 for 1.5 miles to County Road 10. Turn left (west) and proceed for 11.5 miles to State Highway 9. Turn right (north) and go 8.5 miles to U.S. Highway 10. Turn right (east) and go about 1.5 miles. Just to the right are two scenic natural areas. *Buffalo River State Park*, (218) 498-2124, and the *Bluestem Prairie Scientific and Natural Area* are adjacent and offer smashing examples of original prairie and wetland topography. The state park features the bluegray gnatcatcher, on the periphery of its Minnesota range. The prairie zone has sandhill cranes (a crucial reminder of prairie heritage), eastern meadowlark (interesting this far west), and prairie chickens. The scientific and natural area is recognized as one of the largest and most perfectly preserved northern tallgrass prairies in the United States. A visitor center has trails departing from it, and inside you'll find exhibits on ornithology and a bird feeding area.

Continue east on Highway 10 for 25.5 miles to Audubon. Turn left (north) at 4th Street (County Road 13) and go a short distance to County Road 104 in town; turn right and follow the road in stair-step fashion to the east and north a few miles to the south edge of *Hamden Slough National Wildlife Refuge.* This newly established refuge is the result of ambitious efforts to restore prairie wetlands and grasses. Already flock upon flock of migrating birds can be found here spring and fall. Bald eagles are particularly prominent; even rare species like cattle egret and piping plover have been spotted. For all this, it's considered an important node on the Minnesota Pine to Prairie Birding Trail. From the headquarters office a new trail and overlooks connect the inter-linked wetlands. The office for the refuge is located at the intersection of CR 104 and Township Road 440, (218) 439-6319; hours are 7:30 a.m.–4 p.m. weekdays, and the staff asks that you share all wildlife sightings with them.

Take CR 104 east and north to U.S. Highway 59. Turn right (south) and drive for about 4.5 miles to Tower Road. Turn left (east) and go 1.5 miles. Here you'll find the office of the *Detroit Lakes Wetland Management District,* (218) 847-4431, which is comprised of an impressive 40,000-

Minnesota "Man"?

While U.S. Highway 59 was being constructed in the early 1930s, engineers discovered a skeleton believed to be nearly two millennia old. After anthropologists dubbed it "Minnesota Man," they had to do some backtracking when it was later discovered to be a woman, or, precisely, a young woman approximately 16 years old.

plus acre spread of restored wetlands and prairie, also an important link in the Pine to Prairie Birding Trail across northwest Minnesota. Prior to settlement, the place teemed with bison, wolves, whooping cranes, and other indigenous species. Agriculture siphoned off more than half of the wetlands, dooming the native species. Today, however, the "prairie pothole" topography has returned, and you can view it via the Prairie Marsh Trail, an interpretive foot-stomp through the grasses leading from the main building. Rare bird sightings could fill half a page; less rare are the warbler varieties, but there are more than two dozen of these.

Continue east on Tower Road for about .5 mile to County Road 21, turn right (south) and drive for about 2 miles to Main Street in Detroit Lakes. Turn right (west) and drive a short distance to Washington Street, where we began this nature-filled tour.

Badlands

As the Red River of the North rolls toward Manitoba, it flows through some of the Midwest's most fertile regions. Not surprisingly, agriculture is a major economic linchpin in many towns, all sporting the ubiquitous grain elevator towering above the community's train-loading depot. It wasn't always so, however. Early travelers on the Ox Cart Trail found the land ugly at best, contemptuously barren at worst. Still, it was crucial for transportation, and towns like Moorhead exploded in size quickly. Still, no one could lure agriculture. General Sibley of the U.S. Army, passing through after a western battle, wrote of the region, "It is fit only for the Indians and the Devil." Supposedly, this view held on strongly. One perhaps apocryphal story held that a man walked into a Moorhead bar with a bag of gorgeous vegetables he'd supposedly grown on his stake. The other saloon goers were so dismissive of this claim that he pulled out his gun and shot one of them.

Tour 17
Ottertail Country

Fergus Falls—Inspiration Peak—Clitherall—Battle Lake—Glendalough State Park—Otter Tail Lake—Phelps—Fergus Falls

Distance: Approximately 105 miles

It's unfortunate that relatively few travelers barreling down I-94 to "Other Places" bother to glance up from the map and explore Ottertail Country. But they should. And they should begin in Fergus Falls, the gateway to touring along the mills and dams of the Otter Tail River. Of course, there's outstanding fishing and, best of all, gorgeous hiking (and views)—to the top of the highest point in western Minnesota, Inspiration Peak, for example. You've also got the chance to nose around smoke-belching old farm machinery, pedal throughout the county on one of the state's longest paved multi-use recreational trails, and explore the remnants of a once-thriving Mormon settlement site. Near the end of our tour, we visit Minnesota's newest state park, Glendalough—an ecological experiment in action, where wildlife and water conservation are being ushered into the next generation. We accomplish all this—and more—without leaving the confines of sprawling Otter Tail County.

Start your tour in downtown Fergus Falls at the *Fergus Falls Convention and Visitors Bureau,* 112 West Washington Avenue, (218) 739-0125 or (800) 726-8959 (www.visitfergusfalls.com). You can find all the information you need for Ottertail Country right here, so stop by for maps and advice. And get used to seeing the endless string of things named "Otter Tail" around here. The moniker here is almost as ubiquitous as the Paul Bunyan name is in the Bemidji area.

For example, there's the Otter Tail River, a tributary of the Red River of the North, which flows through the heart of this city of 13,000. Nearby, the convention and visitors bureau office is the perfect spot to access Fergus Falls' lovely *Riverwalk.* Totaling about a half mile, the walk features picturesque tree-lined picnic spots, with lots of flora and fauna to observe. A highlight is the Otter Tail Dam, on Cascade Street between Lincoln and Washington Streets. Here you can inspect a working turbine above the Central Dam Walkway. Otherwise, keep an eye on the buildings: lots of classic renaissance and medieval revival architecture arose when the dams powered mills and money poured into local coffers. (The convention and visitors bureau office has brochures on walking tours of historic districts.) On the east side of downtown, on the opposite side of the river, is an established *waterfowl sanctuary.*

About a block north of the CVB office is the *Center for the* Arts, 124 West Lincoln Avenue, (218) 736-5453, housed in a classic town theater. In addition to traveling theatrical and musical events, the place has a funky old Wurlitzer organ and regular art exhibits of local and regional artists. Eight or so blocks west of the CVB is the downtown's main tourist attraction, the *Otter Tail County Historical Society Museum,* (218) 736-6038, 1110 West Lincoln Avenue. Inside are exhibits of daily homesteading life, with re-creations of a printer's shop, dentist's office, and general store. Another area highlights Native American history. At times visitors can participate in lively historic walking tours of Fergus Falls; the museum also has rental cassette tapes that detail the country's historic sites. They're wonderful if you have extra time to explore. Hours are weekdays 9 a.m.-5 p.m., Saturday 1-4 p.m., Sunday 1-4 p.m. in summer; admission.

From West Washington Street, go east a short distance to Cascade Street. Turn right (south) and drive 1.5 miles to Highway 210. Let's sample a couple of fine natural retreats before we really hit the road. From southeast of the intersection of Cascade Street and Highway 210 spreads the *Prairie Wetlands Learning Center,* (218) 736-0938, a fascinating, 325-plus-acre site dedicated to preserving and rejuvenating native topography. This is the U.S. Fish and Wildlife Service's first residential environmental education center in the nation. Twenty acres of virgin prairie are dwarfed by more than 180 acres of restored tallgrass prairie, wetlands, and oak savanna. You'll also be able to wander about the nearly two-dozen wetlands on 4 miles of trails. Fun are the occasional (and free) naturalist-led jaunts into the fields. Try an evening visit, where you'll find the acreage to be downright halcyon with the setting sun bronzing the landscape.

Just east of the learning center is the Otter Tail County Fairgrounds, and bordering this to the southeast off Highway 210 is the *DeLagoon/Pebble Lake Campground and Recreation Area,* with campsites, a golf course, picnic areas, lots of green-space, and a sandy beach. Two bike trails—lovely

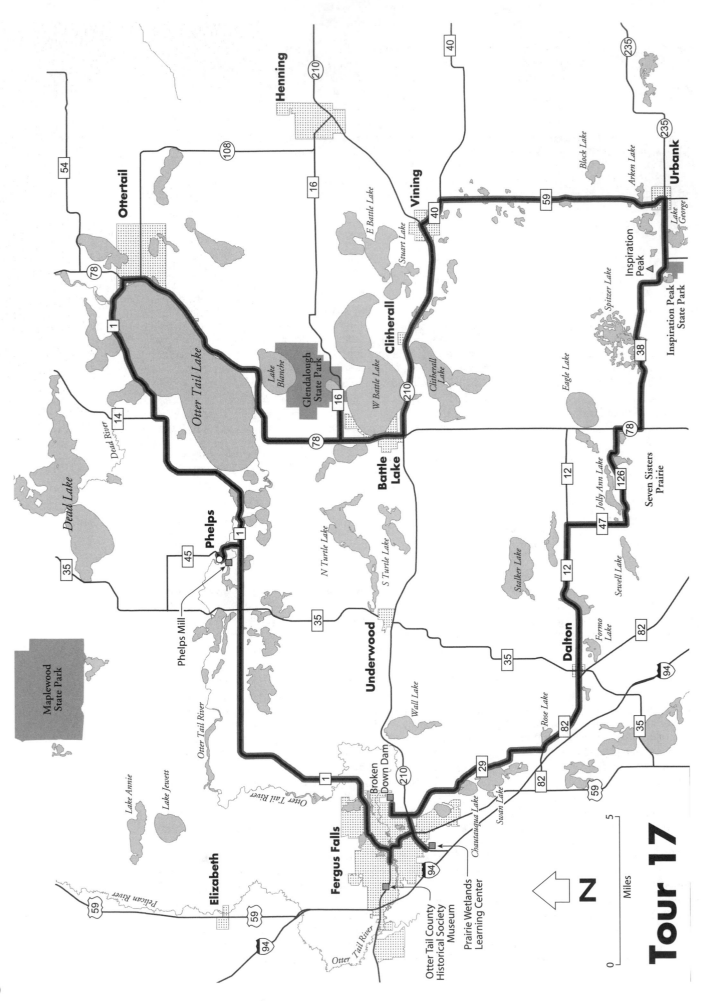

Tour 17

N

Miles

0   5

Henning
Ottertail
Vining
Urbank
Clitherall
Battle Lake
Phelps
Underwood
Dalton
Fergus Falls
Elizabeth

Maplewood State Park
Glendalough State Park
Inspiration Peak State Park
Inspiration Peak

Otter Tail Lake
Dead Lake
Lake Blanche
W Battle Lake
E Battle Lake
Stuart Lake
Clitherall Lake
Block Lake
Arken Lake
Lake George
Spitzer Lake
Eagle Lake
Jolly Ann Lake
Seven Sisters Prairie
Stalker Lake
Sewell Lake
N Turtle Lake
S Turtle Lake
Wall Lake
Formo Lake
Rose Lake
Swan Lake
Chautauqua Lake
Lake Annie
Lake Jewett

Dead River
Otter Tail River
Pelican River
Otter Tail River

Phelps Mill
Broken Down Dam
Prairie Wetlands Learning Center
Otter Tail County Historical Society Museum

54
210
40
235
108
16
78
1
14
35
45
16
78
210
59
38
78
12
126
47
12
35
35
82
29
82
82
35
59
94
210
1
94
59
59
94

90

and not too challenging—also lead downtown and out into the prairie and farmlands toward Douglas County. Plans are to pave this 63-mile stretch all the way to Osakis.

Drive east on Highway 210 for about 1.5 miles to County Road 29 junction; turn left (north) and go less than .75 mile to Main Street and turn right. Watch for signs (at times hard to spot) to the *Broken Down Dam*, a Fergus Falls-owned dam that collapsed in 1909. The resultant ruins are kind of an odd, engaging attraction, fun to poke about. Ponder how crucial dams like this one were to the rise in western Minnesota's fortunes.

Return to the junction of CR 29 and Highway 210. Then follow CR 29 southeast for 7.5 miles to its junction with County Road 82. CR 29 is part of the Minnesota Department of Transportation's *Otter Trail Scenic Byway,* which we will follow for most of this tour. The byway forms a 150-mile loop as it bends and rolls, up and over classic ag-prairie landscapes. Note the mellifluous nomenclature: Chautaqua Lake, Swan Lake, Rose Lake. You forgive them for pushing the road into a maddening series of curlicues. Paralleling you to the right is the Central Lakes Trail, a paved bicycle trail that leads into Douglas County. Plans are to have it paved all the way to Osakis by 2005.

Turn left (east) at CR 82 and drive 4 miles into tiny Dalton. This is an otherwise unassuming burg, but come early September the skies are darkened by the coal fires burning in antique threshing machines at the *Lake Region Pioneer Threshermen's Association Festival.* Antique Case tractors, Waterloo Boy gas engines, and more line the croplands around the town. Hands-on activities are available for kids (they'll love the toy tractor displays). And the whole family will have fun just snooping around the antique machines. This is a bigger deal than most folks realize, with aficianados coming from around the United States to join the fun.

From Dalton, drive east for 6.5 miles on County Road 12 to County Road 47. Turn right (south) and go for less than 2.5 miles to County Road 126; turn left (east) and proceed for about 4.5 miles Minnesota Highway 78. As you drive east on CR 126, you're just north of the *Seven Sisters Prairie*, above it a series of seven thorny buttons—often described as "jewels of a crown" around here—that adorn the top of a 200-foot-tall hill just north of Lake Christina. The plant diversity here is incredible, with a large number of plant species not commonly found elsewhere in Minnesota. Be careful where you tread, when you get out of the car. Some species are so fragile that trampling them could kill them. To play it safe, you may want to confine your viewing to the road. Then enjoy the *road*, a tiny string bean of a pavement cut between hillocks and easing itself

amongst lakes, with numerous flocks of birds in constant motion.

Turn south on Highway 78 and go 1 mile to County Road 38; turn left (east) and continue for 7 miles, following the signs to *Inspiration Peak* just to the north. Here it is, the pinnacle, so to speak, of our tour: Minnesota's second-highest peak. Up we go to the top, for eagle-eye views of numerous lakes and into three counties. Be careful of the *steep* walk up—after all, it's 400 feet to the top. The pathway is paved, and there are plenty of benches to stop and rest. The sunrises and sunsets here are sublime. Bring your camera. And a local tidbit of legend holds that if a couple throws a penny off the top of Inspiration Peak, they'll be married within a year.

Who could resist taking a spin down a road marked like this? Tim Bewer

Return to CR 38 and continue east to for 2.5 miles to County Road 59 in tiny Urbank Turn left (north), following CR 39 to County Road 40; turn left (west) and drive to State Highway 210 at Vining (a total of about 10.5 miles). Turn left on 210 and follow it west for about 5.5 miles to Clitherall. This community was the site of Otter Tail County's first permanent white settlement. Founded in 1865 by a Mormon sect that fled religious attacks in Illinois and Iowa, 30 families arrived by oxcart to found a new community. Not much remains, but there is a new *historical kiosk* on Highway 210 just east of County Road 5 that provides lots of details. You can also find out more at the county historical museum in Fergus Falls and the History Museum of East Otter Tail County in Perham if you really want to see the heritage. Certainly this is a relatively little-known chapter of Gopher State history.

Continue west for 5 miles west on Highway 210 to State Highway 78; turn right (north) into the town of Battle Lake. The Battle Lake area boasts some of western Minnesota's finest fishing. Huge West Battle Lake, which parallels the highway for much of the trip from Clitherall, has muskie (that ferocious predator fish) walleye, perch, crappie, and lots of bass. Not much to do in town, but stop off and get a picture with Chief Wenonga, a brave Ojibwe who, during a fierce

Typical scene on the Otter Trail Scenic Byway. Minnesota Office of Tourism

1795 battle over hunting and fishing grounds in the area, held off a counterattack by the Sioux. By holding them off, Chief Wenonga gave his people time to escape, yet the fight cost him his life.

From Battle Lake, drive north about 2 miles on Highway 78 to County Road 16. Turn right (east) and go less than 2 miles to the entrance to *Glendalough State Park,* **(218) 864-0110.** Glendalough, the state's newest state park and one of its most extraordinary, is one of western Minnesota's last large tracts of undeveloped lakeshore and land—virgin topography in a transition zone from prairie to northern hardwoods. Six lakes (two reserved for waterfowl) and almost 10 miles of undeveloped shoreline are the big draws here.

Intriguing is the plan for the outstanding fishing inside the park. The larger of the park's two lakes—Annie Battle Lake—has been declared a state Heritage Fishery, both for its prodigious fish numbers and how crucial it is to Minnesota's ecological future. Fishing regulations are much stricter on this lake than elsewhere, so be sure you know before you go! For the non-fisher, don't worry, you have plenty of nature and hiking trails, bike paths, canoeing, and swimming to occupy your time as well!

Return to Highway 78 and turn right (north). Follow the road in a northeasterly direction for about 13.5 miles to County Road 1; turn left (west) and proceed for 14.5 miles to County Road 45. For just about the entire stretch, you'll be following the shoreline of *Otter Tail Lake*—and nearly circumnavigating it in the process. All along the way, you can soak in the lovely vistas of this huge lake. If you want to get an extra-heavy dose of the true North Woods, hit this road near sunset—you won't be disappointed. Heck, why not find a place to hang your hat for the night, then catch the sunrise on the west side of the lake? This trek makes for a dazzling fall color tour.

Along the way, you'll find a nice wayside park, with well-done descriptive panels telling about the local fur trade in the early days, plus more information on the lake's great fishing. Otter Tail Lake is included on the Pines to Prairie birding trail, but most people come here to try landing a walleye. It's also great fun to float a tube down the Otter Tail River that feeds into the lake. For the golfer, there are two fine courses in the area.

At CR 45, turn right (north) and go about 1 mile to Phelps and the *Phelps Mill.* Originally called the Maine Roller Mills, this was among the pioneer mills that used roller-milling technology, which didn't debut in the United States until the 1890s. With the growth of mega-mills in Minneapolis near the turn of the twentieth century, the mill and its surrounding community gradually went into decline before dedicated locals started preservation work. Lots of old equipment still can be seen inside, with detailed explanations—very educational. The mill itself may no longer grind out grains, but it retains a dignified air, courtesy of a loving restoration. If you're around in mid-July, stop by for the fun, family-themed *Phelps Mill Festival*, with lots of games and entertainment, plus a juried arts and crafts show. Also, don't miss the lovely county park surrounding the mill, a serene stop-off and great place to decompress from the road.

Return to CR 1 and head west for approximately 14 miles to Lincoln Avenue in Fergus Falls. Turn right (west), go 1 block to South Cascade and turn left (south). Drive another block to West Washington Street, turn right (west), and arrive at the visitor center where this tour began.

Quick Trip Option. For a rewarding trek to the west of Fergus Falls, follow County Road 1 south, then continue west on County Road 2. You'll come to Orwell Reservoir and Dam, a federal dam created for flood control. Ox cart tracks dating to pioneer days still can be found in the grasses around here, and the entire area is now a wildlife refuge and part of the Pines to Prairie Birding Trail. The mix of wetlands, reservoir, brushy grasslands and juniper stands has a few rare birds, including long-eared and northern saw-whet owls and Townsend's solitaire. (Note that there are a couple of No Trespassing Areas inside the refuge.)

Continuing south and west via County Roads 2 and 7, you'll come to the Otter Tail Prairie Scientific and Natural Area, a reserve of native prairie that features lots of owls too. The one-way mileage to this area is approximately 15 miles.

Fish: A Danger to Health?

To eat or not eat that fish you just landed? That's a question that's often asked in the North Woods. Many insist they've eaten lake or river fish their entire lives and not suffered any adverse reactions. Others say toxic environmental pollutants are among the most pernicious, silent health crises in the North Woods today.

Take mercury contamination as an example. Mercury enters the environment from coal burning, chemical plants, medical waste combustion, municipal solid waste combustion, fluorescent light breakage (it's supposedly six percent of the total contamination), and an array of smaller sources. Mercury has clearly been shown to hinder childhood development, perhaps as much as lead exposure. Too much can damage brain and nervous systems. Fetuses and children under seven are particularly affected as their brains haven't developed fully yet. The Centers for Disease Control and Prevention in Atlanta says one woman in 10 in the United States already has dangerous levels of mercury in her blood.

The U.S. Food and Drug Administration is currently debating whether to start maintaining statistics on mercury levels in fish; state and local officials have been arguing for years whether it's necessary. No long-term studies have ever been done on humans. Northeastern Minnesota, oddly enough, has a rather high level of mercury contamination when compared to the rest of the state, due mostly to airborne contaminants.

Women of childbearing years, nursing mothers, and children under 15 should eat no more than one meal per week of bluegill, sunfish, and yellow perch (among panfish), and one meal per month of walleye, northern pike, bass, channel catfish, and flathead catfish (among predators and bottom feeders). Do not eat walleye longer than 20 inches, northern pike longer than 30 inches, or muskellenge.

For men and women beyond childbearing years, the former isn't limited, the latter at one meal per week. If you only eat fish during vacation or sporadically otherwise, you can double these amounts. To increase your chances of eating a healthy fish, eat smaller fish, eat panfish (sunfish, crappies, etc.) rather than predators (walleye, northern pike, etc.), and trim skin and fat.

The Minnesota Department of Natural Resources and Minnesota Department of Health have an excellent brochure listing lakes and waterways with high contaminant levels and what you need to know about it. You can find it at www.health.state.mn.us/divs/eh/fish/index.html.

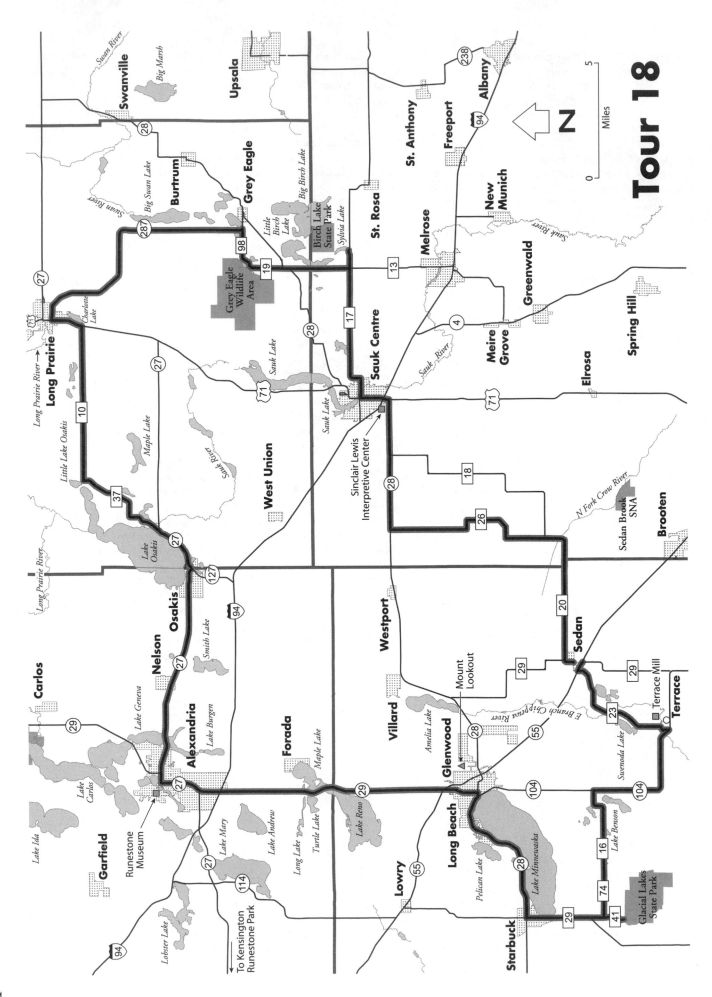

Swanville

Swan River

Big Marsh

Upsala

28

Burtrum

Big Swan Lake

287

Swan River

Grey Eagle

98

Little Birch Lake

Big Birch Lake

Birch Lake State Park

Sylvia Lake

St. Rosa

238

Albany

94

Freeport

St. Anthony

New Munich

Melrose

13

Sauk River

Greenwald

Meire Grove

4

Spring Hill

Elrosa

71

27

71

Charlotte Lake

Long Prairie

19

Grey Eagle Wildlife Area

28

17

Sauk Centre

Sauk Lake

Sinclair Lewis Interpretive Center

10

Little Lake Osakis

27

71

Sauk Lake

71

Sauk River

West Union

37

Maple Lake

28

18

Long Prairie River

Lake Osakis

27

127

26

N Fork Crow River

Sedan Brook SNA

Brooten

Osakis

Nelson

27

Smith Lake

94

Westport

Villard

20

Sedan

29

29

Terrace Mill

Carlos

29

Lake Geneva

Alexandria

Lake Burgen

Mount Lookout

Amelia Lake

28

Glenwood

55

E Branch Chippewa River

23

Terrace

Swenoda Lake

104

104

Garfield

Runestone Museum

Lake Carlos

Lake Ida

27

Lake Mary

Lake Andrew

Forada

Maple Lake

Turtle Lake

Long Lake

Lake Reno

29

Lowry

55

Long Beach

Pelican Lake

28

Lake Minnewaska

16

Lake Benson

74

Glacial Lakes State Park

Lobster Lake

94

27

114

To Kensington Runestone Park

Starbuck

29

41

N

Miles

0 ——— 5

Tour 18

Tour 18
From Main Street
to Lake Wobegon

Sauk Centre—Long Prairie—Osakis—Alexandria—Glenwood—Starbuck—Terrace—Sauk Centre

Distance: approximately 140 miles

If there is a true representative "Main Street," where rock-solid trustworthiness is the norm, there is no better place to find it than in Minnesota. This is the state, after all, that spawned Garrison Keillor's Lake Wobegon (of public radio fame), where "the men are all strong, the women good looking, and the children are all above average."

However, the "other Main Street"—the one Sinclair Lewis depicted in his biting 1920 novel of the same name—flips that on its ear in a bitter social criticism. Both revel in—if not obsess over (as the latter satirizes and the former celebrates)—the classic social setting of tightly knit Midwestern communities.

No tour in this guide better exemplifies Main Street's spirit—its regularity, permanence, benign ordinariness—than this one. It begins in Sauk Centre, birthplace and hometown of Sinclair Lewis, and the basis for his legendary novel of middle America, *Main Street*. Here we view some of the same sights that Lewis did and try to imagine what drove him to depict small-town life as he did. There is no doubt, however, that even as a disaffected native son, he had a genuine connection to the place and its people.

Our tour then rolls through Long Prairie, certainly a rival to Sauk Centre in classic, rock-solid American lifestyle. Nothing could be more representative of a Minnesota vacation than spending lazy days fishing on nearby Lake Osakis, one of the state's most productive fisheries.

But it is not just the heartland's ethos that we come upon in our travels. We also learn about Viking explorers who predated Christopher Columbus, and explore Native American burial mounds. All this before ending at a historic mill, stomping our feet at a heritage music festival, or learning Norwegian rosemaling.

Start your tour in Sauk Centre, at the intersection of I-94 and U.S. Highway 71 (exit 127). Here, you'll find the *Sauk Centre Chamber of Commerce*, (320) 352-5201, sharing quarters with the *Sinclair Lewis Interpretive Center*, (320) 352-5201. The former is packed to the brim with regional information (good maps, too). The latter is an excellent general introductory education into

Sauk Centre's most famous son. In addition to Lewis memorabilia, his books, and his life, you can compress his life via a 12-minute video. It's generally open daily 9 a.m.–5 p.m. summers, weekdays only the rest of the year; free.

For a perfect slice of the region, stop by Sauk Centre's *Sinclair Lewis Days* in mid-July, when folks consider the legendary writer, but quickly refocus on the parades, crafts shows, flea market, auto races, and a treasure hunt.

Drive north about 1.5 miles on Highway 71 (Main Street) into downtown Sauk Centre. Here it is, the original Main Street made famous by Lewis. In the spectral light of a dewy morning or the high-skies of an azure summer day, you might swear things haven't changed much since the period when a young Lewis walked these streets. Look for the distinctive cornice of Main Street Drug, above which Lewis' father had his medical practice. At the corner of Main Street and Sinclair Lewis Avenue you'll see the Palmer House Hotel and Restaurant, where the young author worked (and which supposedly was visited for inspiration by another famous (and disaffected) Minnesota writer, F. Scott Fitzgerald). No doubt a young scribbler would have spent countless bookish hours in a local library, and the *Bryant Public Library*, 430 Main Street S., has a good treat: Its basement houses the *Sauk Centre Area Historical Society Museum*, which has a group of Lewis-themed items. These are but a few of the extant buildings and/or businesses that Lewis would have been familiar with and that, no doubt, formed the basis for settings in his novels. The chamber of commerce has many more ideas and brochures for historical walking tours.

Travel west on Sinclair Lewis Avenue for a few blocks. Not surprisingly, given the street's name, you'll come upon the *Sinclair Lewis Boyhood Home*, 810 Sinclair Lewis Avenue, (320) 352-5359; his birthplace sits across the street. The residence in which he grew up is filled with original family furnishings; half-hour tours are detailed and full of fascinating tidbits on his life before he turned to a life of letters. (Did you know he was nominated for but rejected, the Nobel Prize in 1926? Visit and discover why.). Hours are generally daily except Monday, 9:30 a.m.–5 p.m.; admission.

Return east on Sinclair Lewis Avenue past Main Street and continue out of town on County Road 17, passing County Road 13 and following signs to *Birch Lake State Forest*, about 10 miles from downtown. This quiet retreat is great for fishing on Big Birch Lake. Walleye are plentiful, "if you know what you're doing, of course," said a wizened local angler. You'll also be able to swim and hike on 5 miles of nature trails. A campground also has 30 drive-in sites.

Native Sons

Sinclair Lewis, the first American to win the Nobel Prize for Literature (1931), was born in 1885 and raised in Sauk Centre. His birth and boyhood homes still stand. His 1920 novel *Main Street* (his sixth) garnered him international recognition and a bit of local malice, as his "fictional" town of Gopher Prairie was clearly a representation of Sauk Centre and its citizens. He focused a gimlet eye on self-serving hypocrites found in every community everywhere, but more apparent in a small town. This view drew local ire, then and now—though today this "betrayal" is tempered somewhat by tourist dollars trickling in as a result of the author's legacy.

For many who can overlook the jabs at local hypocrisy, there was and is love in the book. "This is America," began one of the its most famous passages.

It's unfortunate that so much attention on whether or not he betrayed his hometown detracts (at least in these parts) from his other fine work. *Babbitt* is a classic work of literature that added a word to the lexicon, with its eponymous hero representing the shallow materialism of small-town business leaders. *Elmer Gantry* railed against opportunists of another ilk—crusading evangelists—long before late-night cable television brought them into the nation's homes.

It's also fitting that Stearns County, found along our route, is the inspiration for Lake Wobegon, the fictional creation of another native son, Garrison Keillor. A wonderful way to experience Keillor and Lewis and their obsession with small-town America is the new and lovely Lake Wobegon Regional Trail. This 28-mile-long multi-use recreational trail was dedicated in 2001 and takes in Sauk Centre, Melrose, Freeport, Albany, and Avon. Keillor was even on hand for the christening.

You cannot likely find a lovelier way to experience the America that inspired Lewis and Keillor's work than to pedal your way through these small communities. The trailhead in Sauk Centre is located just northeast of the chamber of commerce and the county fairgrounds

To answer the number-one question around here: No, there is no actual Lake Wobegon. Stearns County in its entirety inspired Garrison Keillor in the original Lake Wobegon stories. However, over the years, it's become apparent that a couple of towns do stand out. The Lake Wobegon Trail passes through Freeport, where Keillor and his family lived in the early 1970s. The Freeport Tavern has long since been "spiffed up," but still bears an uncanny resemblance to Lake Wobegon's shot-and-a-beer nerve center. Keillor himself has said that Holdingford, less than 10 miles north of Avon and Albany, is, aesthetically, the "most Wobegonic" of Stearns County hamlets.

Backtrack on CR 17 to CR 13. Turn right (north) and follow the road, which changes to County Road 19 after 2 miles, then County Road 98. When CR 98 turns right (east) follow it for 1.5 miles to State Highway 287. Turn left (north). You pass through the *Grey Eagle Wildlife Area* on CR 98 along the way; lots of deer live around here.

Go north on Highway 287 for about 13 miles to U.S. Highway 71 in Long Prairie. Turn right and proceed a few blocks to the downtown area. Ultimately, after pleasant twists and turns (peculiar to a county back roads tour) and passing enormous rolled hay bales or combines sitting idle, we wend our way into Long Prairie. Or rather, we go from original Main Street to what may truly be a slice of Americana. Long Prairie (talk about imagery of America's Middle West—what a name!) could have been lifted straight from its own nostalgic novel or good-old-days picture show and plopped in westcentral Minnesota.

First, relax by Lake Charlotte beach and Lions Park downtown. Besides the sandy beach, you'll find a fishing pier, boat launch, and lovely shoreline. Incidentally, the Long Prairie River is another of Minnesota's oddities—it flows north. The river offers excellent fishing and even better lazy canoeing.

In the center of this town of about 3,000, the 1903 *Reichert Place* was once an elegant grand hotel. Since converted into affordable housing, the structure boasts a lobby that still has some ornate fixtures, with original stained glass and furnishings. Most people, however, make sure to stop to visit the *Christie House Museum,* Central Avenue and 1st Street S (320) 732-2514. This 1901 Queen Anne was built by a prominent local doctor and has been exquisitely maintained and restored, down to the family's Tiffany lamps, stained glass, Library-of-Congress-worthy rare book collection, and hand-laced Morris leather furniture. Hours for the museum are Memorial Day to Labor Day, Wednesday–Sunday, 1:30–4:30 p.m.; free.

Long Prairie is also home to the *Long Drive In*, one of the original Midwestern drive-in theaters, and it looks—wonderfully—as if not much has changed.

Drive south on Highway 71 to County Road 10; turn right (west) cruise for 8.5 straight-as-an-arrow miles to County Road 37. At the intersection, turn left (south) and proceed for another 9 miles to the town of Osakis, being joined by State Highway 27 about halfway along the stretch. At about the same time, you'll begin to follow the shoreline of impressive *Lake Osakis* on the right. (An alternate route is to follow CR 10 all the way around the lake.) If you've packed your fishing pole, prepare for a field day. Osakis is one of Minnesota's top 10 fishing lakes—bullheads up to 2.5 pounds were reported in the summer of 2002. Otherwise, this lake is known as

One example of the Main Street legacy in Sauk Centre. Tim Bewer

the "Mother Walleye Lake," as the DNR removes females from the lake and strips them of eggs to nurture fledgling fish. The take is so large that they can stock 30 additional lakes before returning the females to the waters here. Northern pike, bass, and crappie fishing is excellent as well. You can participate in the local communities' weekly fishing contest in summer—weekly trophies or even vacations are prizes. If you're not an angler, you frolic on lots of talcum sand beaches. Contact the *Lake Osakis Visitors and Heritage Center*, (800) 422-0785, for more information.

From Osakis, drive west on Highway 27/37 for 10 miles to Broadway Street in downtown Alexandria. Turn right (north). This city of 8,000 sports a famous name, but it is inspired by neither a conqueror nor his namesake city in Egypt. The draw here is lakes. The city is ringed by them—a half-dozen of the 400 or so in the region, more residuals of 20 millennia of glacial bulldozing. Not surprisingly, it's a resort area. Show up here in summer and expect to rub shoulders with the gliterati of the Mini-Apple, Milwaukee, and Chicago. However, it's legendary for a stone. (Hold on! Explanation coming.)

But first, be sure to visit the *Alexandria Lakes Area Chamber of Commerce*, 206 Broadway Street, (320) 763-3161 or (800) 235-9441 (www .alexandriamn.com); it's just a short distance north of Highway 27/37. Stop there for precise directions to local sights. Ask about the status of the *Central Lakes Trail*, an 18-mile multi-use recreation trail that links the county end-to-end. It will eventually link Alexandria and Lake Osakis with Fergus Falls; the plan is to have the whole trail finished by 2005.

Situated at the same location as the chamber of commerce (how's that for convenience) is the *Runestone Museum*, (320) 763-3160, perhaps the most underappreciated museum in Minnesota. As the story goes, one day in 1898 Olof Ohman, a local Swedish immigrant farmer, found a strange stone near the town of Kensington, west of Alexandria. After local historians turned up to look at it—the farmer had been using it as a shed doorstop—all jaws dropped. The "rock" was a flat greywhacke stone with a runic inscription. Dated 1362, it purported to tell the saga of a band of Goths (Swedes) and Norwegians who had passed through. It's not difficult to guess at the uproar this caused in archaeological circles, and though nothing's firmly resolved, the stone has never been disproven. (If it's a hoax, it's a darned good one, according to many experts.)

The stone is still housed at the museum, along with local Scandinavian heritage artifacts, ancient Viking tools, natural history displays, and more. Hours are mid-May to mid-October, Monday–Friday, 9 a.m.–5 p.m.; Saturday till 4 p.m.; Sunday 11 a.m.–5 p.m.; reduced off-season hours; admission.

Also on site (look for the Viking statue) is *Fort Alexandria*, a replica of an earthen settlement fort dating from the Civil War. Hours are the same as the Runestone Museum and admission includes both sites. If you're here during Memorial Day weekend, you should head for that big Viking statue, as it's the nucleus of the *Ole Oppe Fest*, celebrating the Scandinavian heritage of the community.

Quick Trip Option. If you want to learn more about the runestone story, drive to *Kensington Runestone Park,* where the whole history is laid out again. It's an eerie feeling indeed to stand on the ground where Olof first picked up that famous stone. Take County Road 27 west to County Road 15, turn left, and go about 1.5 miles (the entire trip is about 18 miles from downtown Alexandria).

Return to Highway 27/37 (also known as 3rd Avenue in Alexandria) and turn left (east); go a couple of blocks to Nokomis Street. Turn right (south) and drive about 1 mile to 12th Street. You'll be at the *Knute Nelson House*, 1219 Nokomis Street, (320) 762-0382, where one of Alexandria's favorite sons was born and grew up. Nelson was a governor of Minnesota (1892–1895) and a U.S. senator (1895–1923). The buildings and its furnishings seem plucked directly out of a family picture archive and provide a glimpse of the

Glacier's End

Nature came first; that's what this tour shows us. These blood-red barns and somnolent Bessies stand atop geologically profound earth. Thirty millennia (or so) ago, the last glacial advance ground to a massive halt in these parts, in what today we call the counties of Douglas, Stearns, Pope, Swift, and Kandiyohi.

Our tour follows the terminal moraine of the glaciers (specifically, the Wadena Lobe of the Alexandria Glacial Moraine Complex) from Sauk Centre to Alexandria/Kensington, then through Glacial Lakes State Park to Terrace. Should you wish to continue your explorations, there is much more. The Glacial Ridge Trail, an official Minnesota scenic byway, will roll you through a graduate course in glacial topography. The easiest way to link up with it is to simply drive south from Glacial Lakes State Park to Benson, or south from Terrace to Sunburg; each trip is about 15 miles one way.

The Glacial Ridge Trail is not one route, but a network of roads. Though very well-marked (they even tell you when you've successfully made the correct turn!), it's a sprawling spider web of nearly 250 miles of federal, state, county, and township roads (some are gravel, in good condition). Contact the chamber of commerce in any community on this tour and they'll happily mail you a fabulous foldout map for the trail.

Here's a quick topographical primer of terms you see constantly in these parts. First, this glacial end moraine is famous for its "kames" (conical hills of sand and glacially polished stone) and "kettles" (glacial depressions now usually filled with water). You'll also whip by more than a few "drumlins" (narrow hills formed by glacial detritus, usually parallel to glacial flow). Also look for "eskers" (ridges of sand and stone formed by streams flowing through tunnels at the base of glaciers). A lonely-looking boulder in a meadow is probably an "erratic". That is, it was carried a *long* way here by a glacier and dumped. Erratics make great impromptu picnic sites, by the way—sitting atop these original "travelers" is quite a feeling.

Also, just northeast of Sunburg (via County Roads 36 and 115) *don't* miss *Threshing Rig Alley*. Amazingly, you crest the crown of a drumlin—and are suddenly smacked in the eye by post-glacial human detritus: everywhere, weather-beaten threshing machines rusting quietly in fallow fields. It's a graveyard of antiquity, but still eons younger than the land.

early years of Minnesota's statehood. It also houses the Douglas County Historical Society. Hours are weekdays 9 a.m.–4 p.m.; admission.

Alexandria is definitely home to one of the loudest festivals around. The *Vikingland Band Festival*, held in late June, has grown to become one of the Midwest's largest marching band competitions, with nearly 20 drum corps groups and 30,000 spectators descending on the city. The Saturday Drum Corps Classic competition is one of the most amazing musical spectacles you'll see.

Go west on 12th Street to Broadway (also State Highway 29), turn left (south) and drive for 15 miles to Glenwood. About halfway along this stretch, you'll snake through a gauntlet of lakes, including Lake Reno and the smaller Long, Turtle, and Maple Lakes. As you near Glenwood, you'll be wowed by enormous Lake Minnewaska (13th-largest in the state), named for a Native American chief's daughter. Minnewaska and her father are purportedly buried along the lake's northern shore, where a number of native burial mounds are found. To get a commanding view of the lake, and the surrounding countryside, drive to the top of *Mount Lookout*, just northeast of Glenwood, on State Highway 55.

You should plan to get a more up-close view of the shoreline of massive Lake Minnewaska— east or west. Should you choose to drift down the eastern shores, you'll see a swimming beach, public boat ramps, and, best of all, grove upon grove of sugar maples, an absolute must-see when fall colors turn riotous. Native American mounds can be found along here, though they're very tough to spot at times. You can ask for precise directions at the *Glenwood Area Chamber of Commerce*, 200 North Franklin Street, (320) 634-3636.

In downtown Glenwood, follow Highway 29 as it turns right. Almost immediately, you'll come to the *Ann Bickle Heritage House*, 226 East Minnesota Avenue, a turn-of-the-twentieth-century craftsman home. It was in its time the most breathtaking building in the county, according to travelers' accounts.

Continue southwest on Highway 29 for about 3 miles. As the road follows the shoreline of Lake Minnewaska, you'll arrive at the *Minnesota DNR State Fish Hatchery*, 23070 North Lakeshore Drive, (320) 634-4573, which puts out a mind-bogglingly large number of fish to stock a five-county region. We're talking billions in its time. April to May is the best time to come; you can view millions of walleye hatchlings splashing about in pools. Grounds are open daily, dawn to dusk; free.

Another interesting nearby stop off is *Morning Glory Garden*, which is a lovely old chapel with nearly three-dozen flower varieties surrounding it. It's resplendent with color in the early mornings.

Continue on Highway 29 for about 5 more miles to Starbuck. Turn left (south) on 29 and proceed for about 3.5 miles to County Road 41. Go straight on 41 for about 2 miles to *Glacial Lakes State Park.* The park is home to deep pools of ancient water, but also the spot where the forests begin to give way to the prairies and as such, the site of numerous mixtures of flora and fauna communities. Less than one percent of Minnesota's original prairie exists today, and this is your best chance to see it. Also, plenty of hiking trails radiate out into the mixed topography.

Drive north from the park on CR 41, then turn right (east) on County Road 74, which becomes County Road 16 after a few miles. Drive for 7.5 miles to State Highway 104, turn right and go south, then east for about 7 miles to Terrace. Aesthetically, this is an inspiring road. The trees and mazed growing fields are lovely, but this partly follows an established glacial history route—the Glacial Ridge Trail. It's well-marked and local visitor information centers have excellent maps that'll fill you in on what exactly kames, eskers, and the like are.

Tiny Terrace is home to one of the most precious of anachronisms in Minnesota—the *Terrace Mill,* (320) 278-3728. It's actually misleading to think of it as just a mill or even a collection of extant turn-of-the-twentieth-century buildings—a dam, a cabin, an old miller's house, and, of course, the lovingly refurbished mill, whose first incarnation dates to 1870. Today, it's as much the sense of community that seems to radiate from this mill's "heart". Think of it as part cultural center, part living history structure, part regional heritage life giver. Show up and be treated to an art exhibit . . . or a hootenanny with a bluegrass band . . . or a bake sale . . . Throughout the festival season (spring to fall) you're sure to happen upon some sort of family-oriented celebration on any given weekend; the most popular are June's *Heritage Art Festival* (featuring lots of Norwegian rosemaling) and October's *Fiddler's Contest.*

In Terrace, turn left (north) on County Road 23 and go for about 6.5 miles to County Road 29 in Sedan. Turn left (north) and go a very short distance to County Road 20. Turn right (east) and go 6.5 miles to County Highway 26, where you turn left (north). Cruise for 10 miles to State Highway 28, turn right (east) and proceed for 7 miles to U.S. Highway 71 and the intersection with I-94, just south of Sauk Centre, where we began.

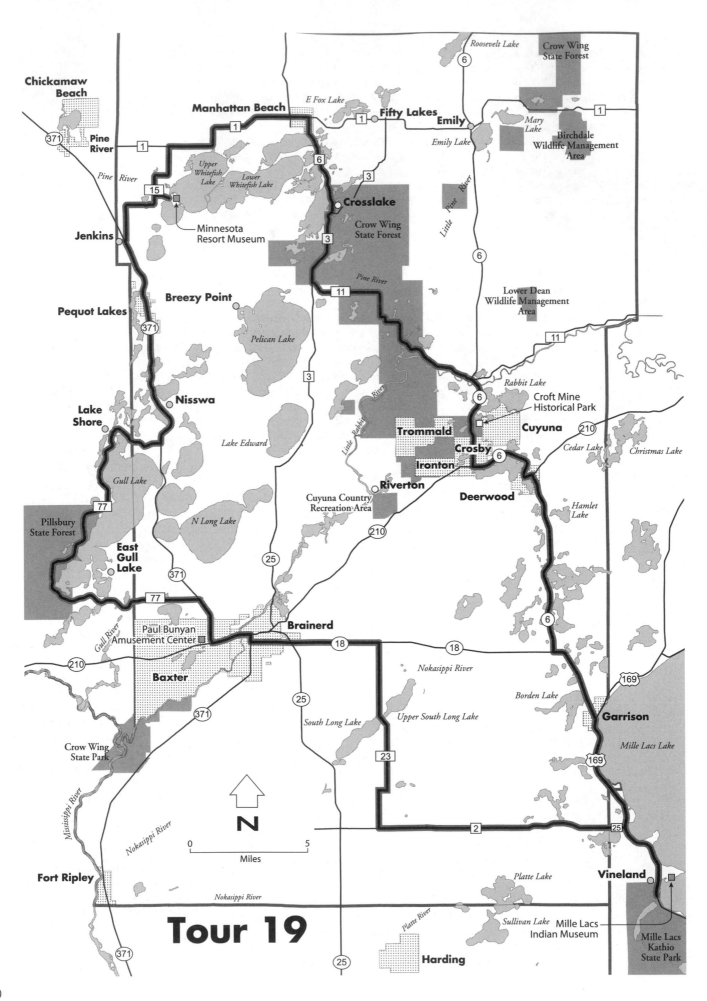

Chickamaw Beach

Pine River

Manhattan Beach

E Fox Lake

Fifty Lakes

Emily

Roosevelt Lake

Crow Wing State Forest

Mary Lake

Birchdale Wildlife Management Area

Emily Lake

Pine River

Upper Whitefish Lake

Lower Whitefish Lake

Crosslake

Crow Wing State Forest

Little Pine River

Minnesota Resort Museum

Jenkins

Breezy Point

Pelican Lake

Pine River

Lower Dean Wildlife Management Area

Pequot Lakes

Nisswa

Lake Shore

Lake Edward

N Long Lake

Little Rabbit River

Rabbit Lake

Croft Mine Historical Park

Cuyuna

Cedar Lake

Christmas Lake

Trommald

Crosby

Ironton

Riverton

Deerwood

Hamlet Lake

Gull Lake

Pillsbury State Forest

Cuyuna Country Recreation Area

East Gull Lake

Paul Bunyan Amusement Center

Brainerd

Nokasippi River

Baxter

Gull River

Crow Wing State Park

Mississippi River

South Long Lake

Upper South Long Lake

Borden Lake

Garrison

Mille Lacs Lake

Nokasippi River

Fort Ripley

Nokasippi River

N

0   5
Miles

Platte Lake

Vineland

Platte River

Sullivan Lake

Mille Lacs Indian Museum

Mille Lacs Kathio State Park

Tour 19

Harding

Tour 19
Brainerd and Mille Lacs Lake

Brainerd—Gull Lake—Nisswa—Crosslake—Crosby—Mille Lacs Lake—Brainerd

Distance: approximately 126 miles

More Paul Bunyan lore begins our trip. How could it not, with a leviathan Brainerd Bunyan who remembers your name? Ah, but there's so much more. The Brainerd Lakes Area—its official name—is laden with refreshing lakes, so much so that it's the number-one resort destination. In fact, if you're toting a brood of young ones, Brainerd is one of the best stops in the state.

But it's the roads we come for, and this tour doesn't disappoint. We're treated to a tour of quick jaunts and side trips—around scintillating lakes and through tracts of trees. Some back-road routes we construct ourselves, others the state has kindly helped us with. We experience North Woods grandeur, the history of mom-and-pop resorts, a thrilling woodsy side tour, and even some mining heritage. This is before we traipse over to the third-largest lake in the state for fish and a glimpse of Native American culture.

Start your tour in downtown Brainerd at the intersection of State Highways 371 and 210. Paul Bunyan and his giant ox Babe may not roam these forests any longer, but given the ubiquity of their names, you'd swear they did. Early guidebooks touted the region as the "Capital of the Paul Bunyan Playground," and to this day Brainerd battles Bemidji for claims to being his birthplace. (Maine disputes them both.)

The Northern Pacific Railroad somehow hacked its way through the leviathan stands trees in the 1870s and founded lumber mills in the area And despite the rapacious appetite of the United States for the forests' resources, the roadways around here are still reminiscent of 150 years ago. Paul Bunyan, indeed.

Within the area are literally hundreds of lakes (466 according to one state bureau) and an even larger number of resorts catering to family fun. The Brainerd region hosts the highest percentage of summer and winter resorts in the state. The parents can get their fill of fun, but the kids have an even larger number of choices to keep them busy. The city itself has a high degree of old-fashioned quaintness, plopped along the banks of the Mississippi River, which is still somnolent here.

Find out more about the area at the *Convention and Visitors Bureau of the Brainerd Lakes,* 124 North 6th Street, (800) 450-2838 (www .explorebrainerdlakes.com). It's right near the Highway 317/210 intersection.

Go west on Highway 271 about 2 blocks to 4th Street. Turn left (south) and proceed for another 2 blocks to Laurel Street; turn right (west) the *Crow Wing Historical Society Museum.* Brainerd at one point had nearly 10,000 lumberjacks and gained a reputation for its legendary rows of saloons catering to the woodcutters' thirsts. Yet, the town also boasted of its lack of intoxicated boisterousness, claiming that women were welcomed and safe at any time, day or night. Get a good dose of this rip-roaring history at the Crow Wing Historical Society Museum, 320 Laurel Street, (218) 829-3268. You enter the refurbished original sheriff's house and county jail—perhaps an appropriate place for a museum detailing the legendary logging exploits of the area! Hours are summers, weekdays 9 a.m.–5 p.m., Saturday 10 a.m.–2 p.m., reduced hours the rest of the year; admission.

Return to Highway 371, turn left (west), and go 3 miles to where the highway splits off from Highway 210 at Baxter. Along the way, at NW 7th Street, you'll pass by signs leading you to one of Brainerd's highlights, the *Northland Arboretum,* (218) 829-8770, also known as *Paul Bunyan's Arboretum* (of course). A host of ecological displays are found here, highlighting the area's diverse habitats. Recreation enthusiasts flock here for the 20-kilometer-long (12.42 miles) lighted trail system on more than 600 acres!

The Brainerd area is the place for kids. At the junction of High-

The *Fargo* Phenomenon

In 1997, Midwesterners, especially those in Brainerd and Fargo, North Dakota, cringed at the release of the movie *Fargo,* a widely acclaimed and Academy Award-winning retelling of a sordid Minnesota kidnapping and murder story. Why the distress? Well, no reason really, save for the thick "Minnesota" accents the characters spoke ("Yah der hey . . . "; "You betcha"), the goofy clothes they wore, etc.

Writers/directors Joel and Ethan Coen in fact are native Minnesotans and certainly didn't mean the film as an insult to anyone. A gentle jab, perhaps, but if you look at bit below the surface, you begin to see that the film is more of a paean to the icier portions of the Upper Midwest, not a mockery.

Rent the video and get a look at the setting; much of it was shot in these parts. Images of Paul Bunyan, of course, show up more than once. A few businesses are recognizable. Otherwise, don't feel embarrassed to ask at the visitor information center for other spots seen in the flick. They're used to it!

Acrobatic bear in downtown Brainerd. Tim Bewer

ation trail stretching north more than 100 miles, passing through six communities and bypassing dozens of lakes and rivers. Boat rentals are available along the route.

Proceed north on Highway 371 for 3 miles, then turn left (west) onto County Road 77. Follow this around Gull Lake for about 20 miles as it loops back to Highway 371. Here's a chance—with another one to come—to get off the beaten path. The lake views along this stretch are awesome—rivaling those found in any of the other tours in this guide. Plus, the recreation options are topnotch, and you have a much lower quotient of passenger vehicles here than on Highway 371.

CR 77 is a sworling curlicue of a county road, as it wraps itself around a half-dozen lakes west of Baxter. As you begin, keep looking for signs to the *U.S. Army Corps of Engineers—Gull Lake Recreation Area*, 10867 East Gull Lake Drive, (218) 829-3334. It's a lovely little spot with a quiet pavilion from which you get a picturesque overlook of Gull Lake; there's also camping and picnicking. Walking trails lead around Native American burial mounds. Also look for heron rookeries.

Next, you'll whiz to a point where the road starts a wide yaw to the north. But if you veer west, you'll come to the *Pillsbury State Forest*, (218) 829-8022, which sports two campgrounds and a handful of day-use areas to go hiking, have a picnic, swim, or launch a canoe. If nothing else, this forest is historic: It was some of the first land logged by lumber companies in the 1880s and some of the first protected by the state government decades later—one reason it seems so healthy now.

At the junction with Highway 371, turn left (north) and drive 3 miles to Nisswa. This charming small town boasts *Pioneer Village*, (218) 963-9998, at the north end of Main Street. Here, helpful costumed guides lead tours around historic buildings, and busy workers perform demonstrations of period craftwork. There is an admission charge. A favorite is Nisswa's early June *Nisswa-Stammen* Festival. This annual regional hoedown is loosely based on the *spelmansstammor* (or "musician's gathering") tradition in Sweden. You'll find tons of Scandinavian folk music, dancing, arts and crafts, and food. A local tidbit: Try the local favorite, "Pork on a Stick," an arteriosclerosis-inducing delicacy cooked up by the local Lion's Club at the fairs around the county.

Continue north on Highway 371 for about 9 miles to County Road 15 in Jenkins. At CR 15, head north, then east, for about 3 miles to Driftwood Lane. Turn right and follow the signs to the Driftwood Resort. Five highways roll into the greater Pine River area today, appropriate enough for a region founded as a network of small trading centers due to the many nearby streams, rivers, and lakes. These waterways later

ways 371 and 210 is the massive, city-state-sized *Paul Bunyan Amusement Center*, (218) 829-6342. The big guy—actually an enormous statue facsimile of him—stands proud and tall, greeting families (he talks and remembers kids' names!). Then, enter the absolute and enjoyable chaos that lies within. Rides and attractions everywhere: slides, swings, go-karts, mini-golf, helicopters, and on and on. The complex brags that it adds new things year to year. Open Memorial Day weekend to Labor Day, 10 a.m. to whenever they can kick the last kid out; admission. (By the way, along our route there's another family fun center run by these folks in Nisswa to the north. It isn't as Paul Bunyan-sized as this one, but it still has outstanding water slides.)

Near this junction is the southern terminus of the *Paul Bunyan Trail*, a multi-use paved recre-

gave rise to resorts—many resorts. The result is that the Brainerd Lakes area offers the quintessential Northern Minnesota family resort experience.

No little surprise, then, that the area boasts of an actual museum celebrating this popular but underappreciated bit of Americana. The *Minnesota Resort Museum*, (800) 950-3540, is actually part of the sprawling and outdoor activity-rich *Driftwood Family Resort*, 6020 Driftwood Lane, (218) 568-4221, one of the state's longest-running family-owned resorts. Even non-guests will gaze appreciatively at the museum's collection of antique fishing equipment, classic water skis, and weathered lake boats. Given the economic status of resorts in northern Minnesota, this collection is quite important. By the way, if you're around the resort, they also offer fun pony rides and escorted trips around on a wonderful 1929 Chevrolet fire truck!

After wandering about the museum, if the day is sweltering, a couple of local spots are ideal for getting out on the water. The Pine River (in and around the small town of Pine River to the north) is a state-designated canoe river; rentals and information are available in several places in town. Another favorite is the park next to the Pine River dam. Great swimming! Each Tuesday at 10 a.m. in summer, this park is also the spot of *free fishing seminars*. Local anglers will help tweak your skills and show you some area hotspots. And note that the *Paul Bunyan State Trail* passes through Pine River.

Quick Trip Option. North of Brainerd, the recently established *Paul Bunyan Scenic Byway* is a 48-mile loop route through some of the most pristine forestland in central Minnesota. Depending on the route, you can either circumnavigate the Whitefish Chain of Lakes or drive along the north shore of Pelican Lake. In either case, the drive lives up to its name by the epic stands of pines (jack, red, and white), spruce and cedar you'll see along the way. You'll also pass by an incalculable number of lakes of all sizes and shapes, along with numerous resorts. Wildlife abounds, with lots of critters spotted at established wildlife management areas. History buffs aren't overlooked, either. Historic structures lie along the route: archaic churches, extant one-room schoolhouses, even old logging smokehouses poking out of the weeds.

There are several ways to travel the route, but probably the main one is to take County Road 16 east and north from Highway 371 to County Road 66. There you make a decision to turn north or south. If the former, take CR 66 to County Road 1 and go west back to 371 at Pine River. If you prefer the second (and shorter) option, take CR 66 south to County Road 3, west on County Road 11 back to 371 at Pequot Lakes. Don't worry, the route is well marked, and it's virtually impossible to get lost! Feel free to pick and choose along the way; it's the best way to do it! One good way to know you're in Pequot Lakes: look for the fishing bobber-shaped water tower.

For lots of good information on the sites—obscure or obvious—along the way, visit www.paulbunyanscenicbyway.org.

Return to CR 15, turn right and follow it north and east for 3 miles to County Road 1; turn right (east) go about 12 miles to County Road 66 in Manhattan Beach. Both CR 15 and CR 1 stair-step their way around the west and north shores of the island-rich Whitefish Chain of Lakes, part of the Paul Bunyan Scenic Byway. Both roads have lots lots of sharp turns. Just east of the CR 15 and CR 1 junction is McGuire's Irish Hills, which is likely Minnesota's most remote golf course. Along CR 1, a handful of wondrous peninsulas jut out into Upper and Lower Whitefish Lakes, perfect for snooping and exploring.

Turn right (south) on CR 66 and go 5 miles to Crosslake. The velvety county road seems built atop nothing but a large embankment, flanked almost impossibly on either side by the lapping waters of eight—at least—gorgeous pools of blue. Look for signs to the *U.S. Army Corps of Engineers Corps Recreation Area*, (218) 692-2025, right along CR 6. You'll find a camping area, swimming beach, and plentiful deer nibbling leaves along the roadways.

For an overview of all the logging and mining in the area's past, take in the *Crosslake Area Historical Society and Log Village*. It contains a replica of several early log buildings and their furnishings; open summer weekends, 11 a.m.–4 p.m.

At Crosslake, take County Road 3 to the right and drive 5 miles south to County Road 11. Turn right (east) and drive about 10 miles to State Highway 6. As you drive along CR 11, the green does seem to darken a bit more. This tells you that you've entered the confines of the *Crow Wing State Forest*. Want a bit of respite from the road? Along both CR 3 and CR 11, you pass established canoe route landings on the Pine River (rentals available pretty much everywhere around here). A campground is located east of Crosslake. And that beguiling slice of blue on the right that you've been following on part of CR 11? That's the mighty Mississippi, just starting to get up some steam on its grand flow.

Turn right (south) on and drive 5 miles to downtown Crosby. This community of about 2,000 is legendary in these parts for its somewhat schizophrenic nature. To the west it's buttressed by all those lakes and stands of timber; to the east, though, lies the Cuyuna Iron Range (which helps explain all the names like "Ironton" around here).

Pine River Duck Races

Every Friday at 1 p.m. (mid-June to mid-August) is the time for one of the hoot-and-holler funnest events in the state—Duck Races on the Pine River, which take place in Pine River, a five-minute drive north of Jenkins on Highway 371. Kids (let's be honest, adults too) flock to the Pine River dam to drop in one or more duck decoys they've sponsored (money goes to local charity); the three fastest floaters get prizes. Just try and not get as worked up as the local kids!

Remnants of the Crosby area's rich mining past at the Croft Mine Historical Park. Tim Bewer

Thus, Crosby had a lot going for it in its heyday. Once a thriving boomtown like so many others, today it's a bit somnolent, but by no means decaying. It thrives due to recreation and antiquing. Yes, it is also known as the Antique Capital of the North Woods (somewhat self-proclaimed), so lots of deal-sniffers are found hereabouts.

Crosby's biggest draw is the *Croft Mine Historical Park,* a complex of buildings, set on an original mine site, celebrating the Cuyuna Range's rich mining heritage. Included among the buildings on a 17-acre site is a museum, miner's cottage, mining equipment, and a replica of the Croft Mine, complete with elevator, tunnels, tramcars, and various mining equipment. Regularly scheduled guided underground tours are available, State Highway 6, just north of State Highway 210, (218) 546-5466.

Just southwest of Crosby on State Highway 210 is the *Cuyuna Country State Recreation Area,* (218) 546-5926. This area is comprised of 5,000 acres of former open-mining pits and rock deposit piles. Canoeing, hiking, and mountain biking opportunities abound among these rugged hills—man-made or otherwise. Amazingly, scuba divers flock to the crystal waters filling the erstwhile gaping pits. More amazing, there's even a blue-ribbon quality trout lake here. (Note that some lands within the park borders are privately owned, so respect all rules.)

From downtown Crosby, turn left on Highway 6 and proceed east, then south, for about 14 miles to State Highway 18; turn left (east) and go for 4 miles to U.S. Highway 169 at tiny Garrison on the shores of *Mille Lacs Lake.*

Most road trippers find their jaws dropping at the immensity of the lake before them: Mille Lacs Lake is Minnesota's third largest. Today many know the western edge of the lake for its enthusiastic gaming industry. But others recall it for its original draw—fishing and other water-related activities. Indeed, this 132,500-plus-acre "pond" (as locals call it) is one of the top walleye lakes in the state (and Midwest), and many a trophy has been landed here. Between 200,000 and half a million walleye are taken from the lake annually. Locals tout the fact that Mille Lacs Lake's mud flats provide for deep-water (and, thus, cooler) fishing. This is important, as walleye fishing in most places finishes with the hot weather of July and August.

Actually, over 40 species of fish call the pond home, yielding fairly large muskies and northern pike. Many come for the walleye's cousin, the yellow perch. Tasty!

"Launch" fishing, once popular all over, remains popular here. Large launches holding six to 50 people loll about the big puddle—a great way to get out and about on the lake, not to mention a way to land a wall-sized walleye.

Drive south on Highway 169 for 10 miles to the *Mille Lacs Indian Museum.* This impressive facility, situated on Indian Point, 1.5 miles north of tiny Vineland, (320) 532-3632, sports a huge (23,000 square feet) exhibit area detailing the cultural history of the Mille Lacs Band of Ojibwe. Of particular interest for travelers is the Four Season Room, where you'll get a guided tour of the band's history, from 1750 to the present. On-site artisans display craftwork. Hours in summer are Monday–Saturday,

10 a.m.–6 p.m., Sunday from noon, reduced off-season hours; admission (not cheap, but worth it).

Quick Trip Option. Just south of the Mille Lacs Indian Museum you'll find *Mille Lacs Kathio State Park*, (320) 532-3523, a 10,000-acre plot of green (the state's fourth-largest state park) nestled among Mille Lacs Lake to the northeast and smaller Ogechie and Shakopee Lakes to the northwest and southeast. The Rum River connects the two smaller lakes as it begins its journey to the Mississippi some 80 miles south. The hills are particularly challenging at times when hiking many of the 35 miles of trails. They seem to rise as if from nowhere, and provide a good workout. Here's the real draw here: white deer. So look carefully for one of the eight (or so) albino deer known to be roaming the park's interiors.

Return north on Highway 169 for 4 miles to County Road 25; turn left (west) onto the road (which soon becomes County Road 2) and go about 13 miles to County Road 23. Turn right (north) and proceed for about 10 miles to State Highway 18. On CR 23, look for signs just after you pass over the unusually configured bridge (engineers appear to have used every inch of the isthmus for bridge supports) crossing the narrow bottleneck of Upper South Long Lake and South Long Lake. At the other end is an established *state wildlife viewing area,* with lots of birding here, though mammals are present as well. No trails exist, and remember to respect private property boundaries.

Turn left (west) on Highway 18 and drive the final 6.5 miles to Highway 371 in Brainerd, the start of this tour.

Bandolier bag on display at the Mille Lacs Indian Museum. Tim Bewer

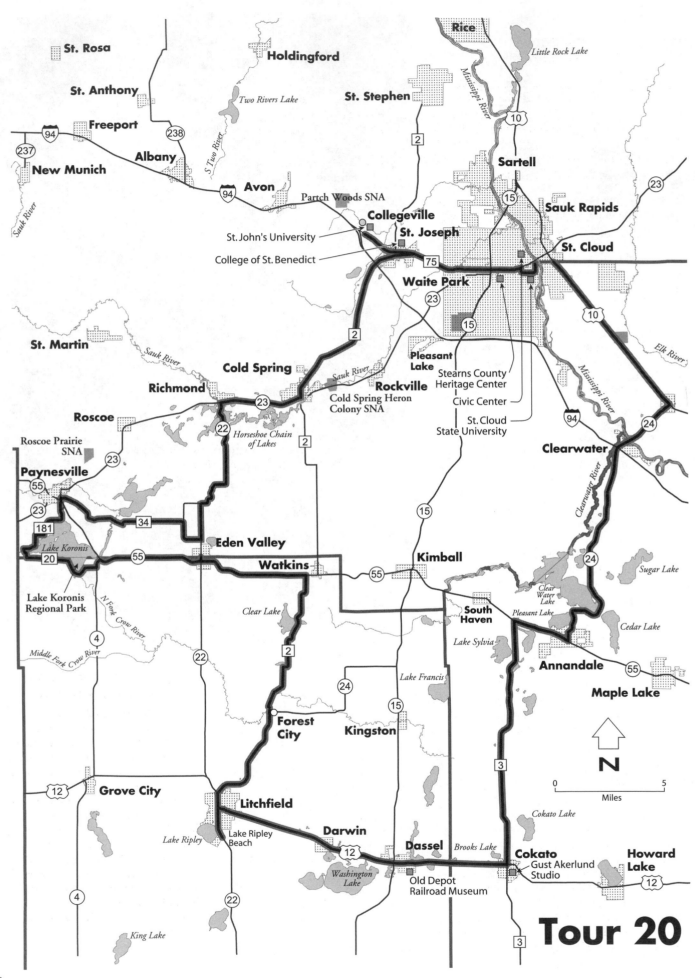

St. Rosa

Holdingford

Rice

Little Rock Lake

St. Anthony

Two Rivers Lake

St. Stephen

94 Freeport

238

Mississippi River

10

237

Albany

New Munich

94 Avon

Sartell

15

Sauk Rapids

23

Sauk River

Partch Woods SNA

Collegeville

St. Joseph

St. John's University

College of St. Benedict

75

St. Cloud

St. Martin

Sauk River

Cold Spring

2

Waite Park

23

Pleasant Lake

10

Richmond

Rockville

Cold Spring Heron Colony SNA

Stearns County Heritage Center

Civic Center

St. Cloud State University

15

Elk River

Roscoe

23

22

Horseshoe Chain of Lakes

2

Roscoe Prairie SNA

Clearwater

Clearwater River

Paynesville

55

23

181

34

Eden Valley

Lake Koronis

20

55

Watkins

Kimball

24

Sugar Lake

Clear Water Lake

Lake Koronis Regional Park

55

55

Pleasant Lake

Cedar Lake

N Fork Crow River

Clear Lake

South Haven

24

Middle Fork Crow River

4

22

Lake Sylvia

Annandale

55

Lake Francis

Maple Lake

2

24

15

N

Forest City

Kingston

3

0   5

Miles

12 Grove City

Litchfield

Cokato Lake

Darwin

12

Dassel

Brooks Lake

Cokato

Gust Akerlund Studio

Howard Lake

12

Lake Ripley

Lake Ripley Beach

Washington Lake

Old Depot Railroad Museum

4

22

King Lake

3

Tour 20

Tour 20
Midwestern Mosaic: Saint Cloud and Vicinity

Saint Cloud—Saint Joseph—Collegeville—Cold Spring—Paynesville—Forest City—Litchfield—Darwin—Cokato—Annandale—Saint Cloud

Distance: approximately 135 miles

What a Midwestern mosaic this tour offers. The environs centered around Saint Cloud resist easy categorization or any attempts to pin them down with catchy marketing phrases. From the cheerily ebullient town of Saint Cloud, blessed with a noticeable intellectual and cultural flair, we make a pilgrimage to two of the state's, if not the nation's, most hallowed spiritual retreats. Perhaps fittingly, an investigation of divine intervention in a precious small town during a scourge of grasshoppers follows—not to mention the town's crystalline waters and frosty suds!

We peer back into a sad chapter of U.S.–Native American relations, reminding us of the history that these routes have seen. Great balls of twine lighten our mood a bit. And, there's a native Minnesotan's unique success story that everyone knows about.

No, this is Minnesota, so we don't (we can't) forsake the water. Gorgeous lakes regularly appear just beyond our windshields, welcome us, then melt away.

Start your tour east of downtown Saint Cloud at the *Saint Cloud Area Convention and Visitors Bureau.* This facility, just south of the intersection of U.S. Highway 10 S. and State Highway 23, (320) 251-4170 and (800) 264-2940 (www.visitstcloudmn.com), is fantastically well stocked with printed info and the staff offers friendly advice.

Saint Cloud was once the northernmost point for major Mississippi River shipping and passenger traffic, auguring a propitious future before the railroads arrived. Its economic base was diverse as well—a strong combination of fecund agricultural production and hard-working lumber mills buttressing the river transit. Despite the Southern, Yankee, and Teutonic immigration patterns, the name Saint Cloud was chosen to represent the area's French history. Saint Cloud is a suburb of Paris.)

Geology was the final piece of the economic puzzle. Some of the finest buildings in the nation have used Saint Cloud's legendarily lustrous colored granite. Among the local stonework examples are those of the numerous colleges and universities in the area, a heady concentration of academia and religious devotion which gives the city a distinctive cultural and intellectual flair.

Saint Cloud is perhaps overlooked by travelers, given the bright lights of the Twin Cities to the south, but maybe not for long. National media consistently rank the Saint Cloud area among the best for quality of life in the United States; its people live longer, according to many studies. Also, the city is attractive and the populace, without stretching things too much, go about their business with a positive spark not uncommon in thriving, friendly Midwest communities such as this. As such, it's gradually becoming one of the fastest-growing cities in the state (and Midwest).

Drive south on Highway 10 and go a short distance to 15th Avenue SE; turn right and go south to 13th Street SE. Turn right (west) and go a short distance to Kilian Boulevard. You'll soon arrive at the *Munsinger Gardens* and *Clemens Gardens,* (320) 650-1050. The Munsinger Gardens are spread along the Mississippi River under stands of hemlock and pine, with an abundance of shaded trails. There you can enjoy more than 75,000 annual plants as you amble through a gorgeous piece of property. Just above Munsinger Gardens, Clemens Gardens features a half-dozen formal gardens. The Virginia Clemens Rose Garden, for example, has over 1,100 rose bushes. The Renaissance fountain at Clemens Gardens is Minnesota's tallest outdoor garden fountain, topping out at a somewhat modest 24 feet. Hours are late May to mid-September, dawn to dusk; admission.

Drive south on Kilian Boulevard a couple of blocks to Michigan Avenue SE. Turn right (west), cross the bridge and go a short distance to 4th Avenue S. Turn right and continue into the campus of *Saint Cloud State University.* Besides having a highly competitive Western Collegiate Hockey Association men's hockey team, the school features a couple of cultural attractions located along the Mississippi River

Slavery and Saint Cloud's Founders

Amidst the usual history of Mississippi River transport and legendary forest wealth, one tidbit of Saint Cloud history stands out: A founding member of the city was a slave-owning Southern army general; another was an abolitionist publisher who wooed fervently anti-slavery Protestant settlers to offset the Southern-leaning alternate settlers. Ultimately, the two enclaves merged, however uneasily, with waves of Germans lured by timber and sawmills to form a community. (Note: No one actually *owned* slaves in the town.)

Saint Cloud's Clemens Gardens, with its impressive fountain in the background.
Tim Bewer

this is the place to come. Hours are weekdays 7 a.m.–5 p.m., though these hours are often extended when the civic center is hosting an event.

Afterward, consider setting off on a historic stroll. While at the convention and visitors bureau, request a map of the city's nearby historic districts. Within these confines, more buildings are listed on the National Register of Historic Places than not. At 913 West Saint Germain Street, for example, is the distinctive and lovingly retouched *Paramount Theatre*, (320) 259-5463, which anchors a district of exquisite architecture. The Paramount hosts cultural events regularly. Other noteworthy edifices include the massive 1922 *Stearns County Courthouse*, unmistakable given its glistening dome and half-dozen, 36-foot-high granite (many-hued Saint Cloud stone) pillars, and *Saint Mary's Cathedral* (more granite), found along a two-block traipse of 8th Avenue North. Virtually every building on 5th Avenue North is on the National Register of Historic Places.

At 2nd Street S. (State Highway 23), the main thoroughfare through downtown, drive west for a little more than 2 miles to 33rd Street S. Turn left (south) and go a short distance to the *Stearns County Heritage Center.* This enormous center, 235 33rd Avenue South, (320) 253-8424, has particularly good displays of German and Luxembourg immigration to this area, among general historical flotsam and jetsam. Kids go bonkers in a miniature circus, as dads dreamily caress classic autos. One entire gallery is devoted to children's education. Hours are Monday–Saturday, 10 a.m.–4 p.m., Sunday, noon–4 p.m.; admission. The parklike surroundings boast nearly 10 miles of hiking trails.

Return north to Highway 23, turn left (west), and follow the road (which becomes County Road 75) for 6 miles to Saint Joseph. The Sisters of the Order of Saint Benedict, the largest grouping of Benedictine women in the world, maintain a rolling and isolated campus here that includes the *College of Saint Benedict.* Not to be missed is the adjacent *Saint Benedict Monastery*, 104 Chapel Lane, (320) 363-7100, with a distinctive 1914 baroque chapel (look for the prominent dome). The Art and Heritage Place and separate Benedicta Arts Center are repositories for the century-plus of Benedictine history and artwork; hours vary. Visit during late September's *Millstream Arts Festival*, with arts and crafts sales and demonstrations, entertainment, and regional cuisine.

Continue west 3 miles on CR 75, to County Road 159 in Collegeville; turn right (north) and go about 1 mile. There, *Saint John's Abbey and University* is the state's oldest center of higher learning, established in 1857, and with nary an interruption since. It has the gorgeous *Abbey Church* (noted for its 112-foot bell tower) and library (with a famed collection of European

that are worth a visit. The *Atwood Gallery*, (320) 255-2205, has a variety of contemporary regional and national artwork, while the *Kiehle Visual Arts Center*, (320) 255-4283, focuses more on local artwork. The Atwood Gallery is open weekdays 7 a.m.–7 p.m. and weekends 9 a.m.–5 p.m.; Kiehle has hours on weekdays, 8 a.m.–4 p.m.

Drive northwest a short distance on 4th Avenue S. to the *Saint Cloud Civic Center* in the downtown area. There, at 10 4th Avenue South, (320) 255-7272, you don't want to overlook the *Minnesota Baseball Hall of Fame*. Though this is a land where hockey is a religion, quite a few major league baseball players have called the Gopher State home. If you know who Harmon Killebrew or Paul Molitor are (or even if you don't) and want to learn more (about them and others),

medieval religious documents, said to be the largest in the world in microfilm form). The grounds are often praised for their melding of traditional and modern, due to the efforts of noted architect Marcel Breuer. A brief introductory slide show at the library is recommended. Hours are generally weekdays, 8 a.m.–4:30 p.m., though these vary; free. The campus does offer tours daily in summer; call (320) 363-2011, for more information. A good time to visit is during the *Swayed Pines Folk Festival* in late April, with artisans demonstrating woodworking, musical instrument making, pottery, quilting, and more; the folk music hootenannies are a joy.

Return to Saint Joseph and County Road 2; turn right and drive southwest for about 12 miles to Cold Spring. Along here is gorgeous prairie country. As you roll through the meadows and hilly stretches approaching Cold Spring, a geology primer seems to reveal itself. Prominent ridges hereabouts are layers of that famed granite.

Cold Spring hints of refreshing liquid, but it's grasshoppers that draw most visitors. Drive east of town along State Highway 23 to a memorial to a miracle. The *Grasshopper Chapel*, (320) 685-3280, is a meditation center devoted to an event of Biblical proportions. On April 27, 1877, a plague of grasshoppers was suddenly (and divinely?) halted by a freak snowstorm. The original chapel was destroyed in the 1880s by a cyclone, but the new edifice impressively sports local granite.

If making a pilgrimage isn't quite your bent, well, then the watery name indicates another landmark. Since 1857, the *Gluek Brewing Company*, 219 Red River Avenue North, (320) 685-8686, (north of the downtown district), has been putting out a refreshing sudsy local brew. Free tours are given in summer, though not regularly. The crystal waters of the underground aquifers—also filling many marketed mineral water bottles—are touted to be even purer than other, much more expensive, bottled waters.

Drive west of Cold Spring on Highway 23 for 4 miles to State Highway 22 in Richmond. Turn left (south) and go about 7 miles to County Road 46. Turn right (west). CR 22 is a diminutive county road well worth the effort of negotiating its many twists and turns. You whip along an almost impossibly narrow isthmus—water, water everywhere, and a splendid view to boot. You're amidst the *Horseshoe Chain of Lakes*, a baker's dozen (plus one) pools of water and a small resort area. (The area around Richmond has more than 40 lakes in a 10-mile radius.). Catfish fishing is king here, by the way.

Continue west on CR 46, which shortly becomes County Road 162, and follow that west and south for about 1.5 miles to County Road 34. Turn right (west) and follow it to Paynesville, a total of about 10 miles. Nearing Paynesville, you bisect the Crow River and split Rice Lake and Lake Koronis, and a modest resort area reveals itself. Paynesville was at the northern end of major skirmishes in the Dakota Conflict of 1862, and *Bicentennial Park* southwest of downtown contains a memorial to the fighting. More history is found at the *Paynesville Historical Museum*, 251 Ampe Drive, (320) 243-7547. It's on the east side of downtown along Highway 23; just follow the signs. Hours are Tuesday–Saturday, 10 a.m.–4 p.m., Sunday 1 p.m.–4 p.m.; admission.

A 12-acre plot of restored prairie, the *Crow River Nature Park* lies just west of downtown along Highway 23 via Burr Street. Three nature trails total almost a mile and wander amongst the grasses and along the river. Tranquil and lovely, you'll be surprised by how alone you are here.

Paynesville is also working beaverishly on a lovely new *nature/recreation trail* stretching eastward from town to Lake Koronis. Eventually, the paved trail will circle Lake Koronis and link a handful of parks and nature preserves, providing an excellent day-trip.

From State Highway 55/4 on the south edge of Paynesville, take County Road 181 south to Lake Koronis. Follow the shoreline south and west via Crest Ridge Road, NW Koronis Road, Breezewood Road, and finally Baywater Road to County Road 20, a total of about 5 miles. Turn left (east) on 20 and go about 5.5 miles to State Highway 4. Turn left and go less than .5 mile to State Highway 55. Turn right (east). (Alternately, you could follow Highway 55/4 south to CR 124, then travel along the lake's eastern shore.) It sounds difficult, but it isn't. Hopefully, by the time you read this the recreation trail around the lake will be finished, which would mean you could park your car at a park on the east side of the lake, then circle on your bike.

Lake Koronis is one of two major resort lakes near Paynesville. From here the Crow River flows north into Rice Lake, then onto the Mississippi River. Numerous parks are found along the perimeter of the lake. The east side has *Veteran's Memorial Park*, with a swimming beach, hiking trails, and excellent lookout tower. The south side has the much larger *Lake Koronis Regional Park*—you can find a campground in addition to lots of boating and fishing. The hiking trails are also worth an amble.

Follow Highway 55 for 13 miles to County Road 2 just west of Watkins. Turn right (south) and drive 8 miles to tiny Forest City, where the road is joined by State Highway 24. The little-known *Forest City Stockade* is a memorial to a September 1862 Dakota uprising. A hastily erected stockade protected settlers during a 10-day siege, while volunteers were mustered into a rescue militia. Many original log structures are still standing, while others have not been so lucky; in 2001 a main log cabin burned, but has been recon-

The center of attention in Darwin: Francis Johnson's giant ball of twine. Tim Bewer

structed. Since, other renovations have been started. The site is eerily appealing, with the wind rustling through the grass and whistling through cracks in the walls. Hours are irregular, but you can usually snoop around on your own.

Proceed south on Highway 24 for 6 miles to its junction with State Highway 22 in Litchfield. Civil War buffs will love a tour of the town's *Grand Army of the Republic (GAR) Hall*, 308 Marshall Avenue North, just east of Highway 24 (320) 693-9811. This distinctive straw-colored structure is Minnesota's sole remaining memorial hall to the GAR. Built in 1885 by Union Army veterans, it was designed to be a meeting hall where erstwhile combatants could enjoy camaraderie and swap war stories. (The organization also helped widows, orphans, and disabled veterans.) Note the chairs and chandelier: They're originals, dating from 1885. The altar is made of wood from the cabin near Acton where the first skirmishes of the Dakota Conflict of 1862 took place. Hours are noon–4 p.m., Tuesday–Sunday; admission.

Drive south on Highway 22 for 1 mile to Lake Ripley. Following the road that bisects Lake Ripley with East Lake Ripley, you'll find a campground, beach, and boat landing. But most impressive is *Anderson Gardens,* an attractively landscaped plot of perennial and annual plants and flowers. It's free and quite lovely.

Return to Litchfield and turn right on U.S. Highway 12; drive east 6 miles to Darwin. Any weary traveler just a bit jaded by one (or 10) too many general county historical museums will be delighted by Darwin's *World's Largest Ball of*

Twine. Whoops, better clarify that. This is not the world's largest ball of twine; it is the world's largest ball of twine *made by one man.*

Apparently in March of 1950 Francis A. Johnson, a local agriculturalist (and son of a U.S. senator) picked up some stray twine in his yard and wrapped the pieces: a small ball formed. Well, one thing led to another and now Johnson—and the world—have this "thing." After he "finished" in 1979, the folks from the *Guinness Book of World Records* crown it the top twine ball in the world—a title it held until 1994. For the record, it's 11 feet high, 40 feet around, and weighs 17,400 pounds. Finally, Darwin has the Twine Ball Inn restaurant and holds the Twine Ball Days festival in early August.

Proceed east on Highway 12 for 5 miles to Dassel. Along Highway 12 is the *Old Depot Railroad Museum,* (320) 275-3876, a refurbished Great Northern Railroad depot chock-full of every imaginable piece of railroad memorabilia imaginable. Parents love to wander about looking at the antiquey things, while kids go loopy ringing the big locomotive bell. Hours are Memorial Day weekend to October, 10 a.m.–4:30 p.m.; admission.

Continue east on Highway 12 for 6 miles to Cokato. At the corner of 4th Street West and Millard Avenue South sits the *Cokato Museum,* (320) 286-2427, with collections providing a general overview of local and regional settlement history. But most people come here to visit the adjacent *Gust Akerlund Studio*. Akerlund was a Swedish immigrant and local photographer whose studio and workshop have been listed as a landmark by the National Register of Historic

Places. The studio's original equipment is fascinating (the 12-foot skylight provides for some lustrous lighting), but even more fascinating are the 14,000—count 'em!—negatives preserved in a database. Tracking through them will hook you for hours. Hours are Tuesday–Friday, 9 a.m.–4:30 p.m., Saturday, 10 a.m.–4 p.m., and Sunday, noon–4 p.m.; admission.

From Cokato, take County Road 3 north for about 14 miles to State Highway 24/55. Turn right (east) and drive 2.5 miles into Annandale. Here, *Saint Mark's Church* is Minnesota's oldest Episcopal church, but most come to visit *Minnesota Pioneer Park*, 725 Pioneer Park Trail, (320) 274-8489. Garbed docents lead visitors about the grounds; you can watch wool being spun or horseshoes being hammered out. Many of the artisans will let you grab hold and help out with the chores. (They probably appreciate the help!) Hours are Memorial Day weekend to Labor Day,

Tuesday–Friday, 10 a.m.–5 p.m. and weekends 1–5 p.m.; admission.

In Annandale, drive north on Highway 24 for about 18 miles to U.S. Highway 10. You'll begin by skirting the shores of Pleasant Lake and Clearwater Lake, two appropriately named bodies of water that provide plenty of boating and swimming opportunities, and then weaving through a small gauntlet of smaller lakes. As you near Highway 10, you'll pass I-94, a sure sign that civilization, in the form of Saint Cloud, is near.

Turn left (northwest) on Highway 10 and follow it for about 12 uneventful miles back to the convention and visitors bureau in Saint Cloud, where we began. Actually, just about any county road leading north from the Annandale area will take you back to Saint Cloud. All whirl around lakes, beaches, campgrounds, and prominent limestone ridges.

Little Falls and Charles Lindbergh

One half hour north of Saint Cloud, Little Falls was the home of Charles Lindbergh, Jr. We all know the story. In 1927, the modest young man flew solo nonstop from New York to Paris. The achievement is one of the best examples of a local-boy-makes-good story in U.S. history and produced one of the most intense of media blitzes in history. For his flight, "Lucky Lindy" won a cockpit full of awards, including the U.S. Congressional Medal of Honor, and his autobiography won the Pulitzer Prize.

Lindbergh never forgot his Minnesota roots and, in fact, he often credited his Midwestern upbringing for giving him the inspiration and fortitude to accomplish his goals. He said once, "I can even connect the Mississippi, here, with aviation."

He was a Renaissance man if ever there was one. Later in life he would become an inventor and conservationist. He became a futurist before the word had been coined, given his worries about the impact of technology on humankind. Of course, later, he would be involved in the second media frenzy of his life, with the kidnapping and murder of his son.

West of the Mississippi River and south of the town center along Lindbergh Drive you'll find, in order, two sites honoring the local lad who became a worldwide hero. The *Charles A. Lindbergh House State Historic Site*, (320) 632-3154, is a modest home set along the Mississippi, where the Lindbergh family spent their summers and some winters. Now renovated to its turn-of-the-twentieth-century look, the site is filled with original family furnishings and lots of artifacts and memorabilia. Noteworthy is that the site doesn't specifically focus on the younger Lindbergh's more famous accomplishments; the elder namesake was a pioneer in his own right and isn't overlooked. Hours are May 1 to Labor Day, weekdays 10 a.m.–5 p.m., and weekends, noon–5 p.m.

Opposite the historic site is *Charles A. Lindbergh State Park*, (320) 616-2525. Spend a few hours "where the river pauses," and imagine yourself a young Lindbergh soaking his feet in the waters and watching open-mouthed as a plane buzzes overhead.

The Lindberghs aren't the town's only draw. Just south of the Charles A. Lindbergh State Park is the *Charles A. Weyerhauser Memorial Museum*, (320) 632-4007. The site was the spot of a fur-trading post (and still possesses something of that air) and it has a strong back-in-time feel. In addition to being the warehouse of county history, visitors will appreciate the natural prairie gardens, a Victorian-era fountain and a gazebo with a splendid river overview. Hours are Tuesday–Saturday, 10 a.m.–5 p.m., and from 1 p.m. on Sunday; reduced off-season hours; free.

The *Minnesota Fishing Museum*, 304 West Broadway, (320) 616-2011, is a fascinating place, with more than 6,000 items on display from anglers around the Land of 10,000 Lakes. Even if you don't much like fishing, you'll appreciate its importance in Minnesota, and everyone appreciates the ecologically oriented sections of the museum. Hours vary; admission.

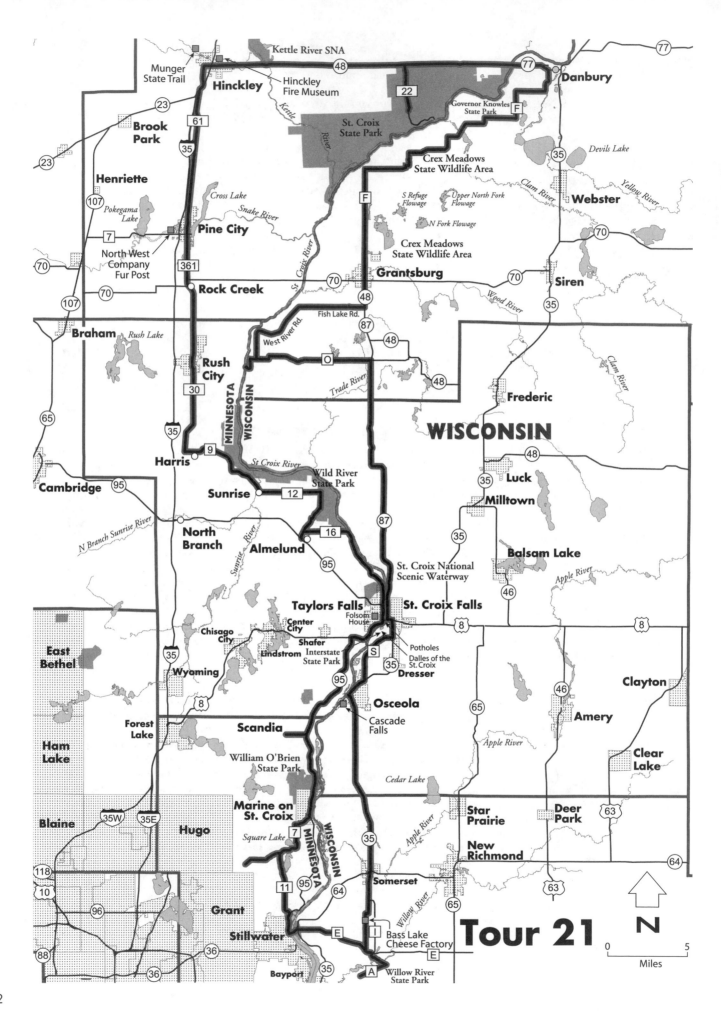

Kettle River SNA

Munger State Trail

Hinckley
Hinckley Fire Museum

Danbury

Brook Park

Henriette

Pokegama Lake

Cross Lake

Snake River

St. Croix State Park

Governor Knowles State Park

Crex Meadows State Wildlife Area

Devils Lake

Webster

Pine City

North West Company Fur Post

Rock Creek

S Refuge Flowage

Upper North Fork Flowage

N Fork Flowage

Crex Meadows State Wildlife Area

Grantsburg

Siren

Braham

Rush Lake

Fish Lake Rd.

West River Rd.

Rush City

MINNESOTA

WISCONSIN

Frederic

WISCONSIN

Trade River

Harris

St Croix River

Wild River State Park

Luck

Milltown

Cambridge

Sunrise

Balsam Lake

St. Croix National Scenic Waterway

North Branch

N Branch Sunrise River

Almelund

Apple River

Taylors Falls
Folsom House

St. Croix Falls

Center City

Chisago City

Shafer

Lindstrom

Interstate State Park

Potholes
Dalles of the St. Croix

Dresser

Clayton

East Bethel

Wyoming

Osceola

Amery

Ham Lake

Forest Lake

Scandia

Cascade Falls

Apple River

Clear Lake

William O'Brien State Park

Cedar Lake

Blaine

Hugo

Marine on St. Croix

Square Lake

WISCONSIN

MINNESOTA

Star Prairie

Deer Park

New Richmond

Grant

Somerset

Bass Lake Cheese Factory

Stillwater

Bayport

Willow River State Park

Tour 21

N

0   5
Miles

Tour 21
Sister States on the Saint Croix

Hinckley—Pine City—Wild River State Park—Taylors Falls—Marine on Saint Croix—
Stillwater—Osceola (Wisconsin)—Saint Croix Falls (Wisconsin)—Danbury (Wisconsin)—Saint
Croix State Park—Hinckley

Distance: approximately 240 miles

Note: This tour really racks up the miles. It may make more sense to overnight halfway and then return on the opposite shore. A day-trip is possible, but exhausting.

The Mississippi River to the south gets the lion's share of glory, but don't forget that the Saint Croix River is officially known as the Saint Croix National Scenic Riverway, a federal designation that translates as "worthwhile." Like the Great River Road, which is shared by Minnesota and Wisconsin and on which we travel for part of the way, our tour takes in the best of both shores—along the Minnesota side to take in the sunrise, returning on the Wisconsin side for great sunsets. This lengthy tour takes in everything one could hope for: picturesque state parks, time-locked river towns, recreation galore, sensitive and lovely natural areas, and a whole lot of gorgeous country roads to explore.

Given the media exposure of the Great River Road, it's surprising (and pleasantly so) to see the lack of vehicles traveling it and less-hyped roads in the vicinity. Even in the rather gentrified, picture-postcard-quality towns of Taylors Falls, Marine on Saint Croix, and Stillwater, tourist swells are rarely heavy (those traffic jams that many experience crossing the Saint Croix River in Stillwater are due mostly to commuters, not tourists). Even the sister Interstate State Parks—truly two of the Midwest's nuggets of natural beauty and geological excitement—have head-scratchingly underpopulated trails.

What this means, of course, is that the roads are almost begging to be utilized, So let's get moving!

Start your tour in Hinckley at the *Hinckley Convention and Visitors Bureau.* Located at exit 183 of I-35, (800) 996-4566 (www.hinckleymn.com), this facility is a mere 86-mile jaunt up the interstate from the Twin Cities. Unofficially the "pit stop" for travelers between Duluth and the Twin Cities, it sits precisely at the halfway point. Incidentally, *Tobies* (open 24 hours, seven days a week) across the parking lot has been serving up legendary caramel and cinnamon rolls for more than a half century—a road food must.

At the *Hinckley Fire Museum,* you can view the little-known story of a disastrous fire (see the sidebar "The Fire of 1894") that swept the area in the late 1800s. Housed in a restored old train depot in downtown Hinckley, 106 Old Highway 61, (320) 384-7338, (the original was destroyed in the conflagration), the museum has wall upon wall of newspaper accounts of the tragedy, along with an eerie videotaped re-creation. It's haunting and unforgettable. Hours are Tuesday–Saturday, 10 a.m.–5 p.m.; Sunday, noon–5 p.m., May 1–mid-October; admission. If you're pressed for time or the museum is closed, right along Highway 23/48, east of I-35, is a fire monument—a historical marker explaining that the disaster is found along Highway 61 northeast of the fire museum.

Hinckley is also the southern terminus of the *Willard Munger State Trail* (see Tour 1), a 70-mile-long paved trail (the longest in the United States).

The Fire of 1894

During the logging heydays of the late nineteenth century, forest fires were a constant threat. Still, the conflagration that devastated the Hinckley area (along with a handful of other communities in east-central Minnesota) was even more ferocious than anyone had imagined.

On September 1, 1894, unusually hot, dry winds swept the area, this after the driest summer in recorded history (a record that still stands). Smaller fires intentionally set by loggers in virgin stands—full of downed, kindling-sized wood—flared larger, joined a few larger fires burning to the south, and created a Hell on earth.

Modern climatology helps explain what followed. Simplified, a cool front moved into the area and created the perfect "vortex" of fuel and air. Given the dryness of the atmosphere and wood chips lying everywhere, the ingredients were ideal for a massive fire not unlike that created by a nuclear bomb.

The enormous fast-spreading fire burned for four hours—completely destroying six towns, blackening more than 400 square miles, and killing over 400 people. The wall of fire was estimated to be 5 miles high and frontal winds gusted up to 100 miles per hour. The air could have thus reached more than 1,500 ° Fahrenheit.

People still talk of the daring train rescues undertaken by the Northern Pacific, Eastern Minnesota, and Saint Paul and Duluth railroads. Most remembered, perhaps, is engineer Jim Root, who backed his train up through walls of flame all the way to Duluth. He saved 350 lives, but his hands literally burned onto the throttle.

From Hinckley, proceed south on Old Highway 61 for 12 miles to Pine City. At times, the route takes you precariously close to I-35, but we don't venture onto it. The name "Pine City" leaves no doubt about the town's roots, and it's a (somewhat mangled) translation of the original Ojibwe word *Chengwatana*. Some erstwhile copper prospectors' mine shafts can also be found in the north bank of the Snake River.

From Old Highway 61 in Pine City, turn right (west) on County Road 7 and go about 2 miles to the *North West Company Fur Post*. At this reconstruction of an original 1804 fur trading post, (320) 629-6356, you see period-clothed tour guides play roles of original inhabitants and demonstrate life on the fort. This author is particularly fond of black-powder gun firings. Hours are May 1 to Labor Day, Tuesday–Saturday, 10 a.m.–5 p.m.; Sunday, noon–5 p.m.; admission.

Quick Trip Option 1. Southwest of Hinckley is the charming community of Mora, named for a sister city in Sweden, and Mora certainly feels Swedish. Downtown the four-foot-wide clock face of the "MoraKlocka" and 25-foot-high Dala horse are both tributes to its Swedish sister city. Early February's Vasaloppet Ski Race brings nearly 3,000 skiers to town to compete in the second-largest cross-country ski race in the United States. From Hinckley, take State Highway 23 southwest for about 18 miles.

Return to Pine City via CR 7. Turn right (south) on County Road 361 and drive for 10 miles to Rush City, then 6 miles on County Road 30 to County Road 9 just east of Harris. Turn left (east) onto CR 9 and follow it for 6.5 miles to County Road 12 at the burg of Sunrise; turn left and continue east and then south for 6 miles to a side road leading east into the main section of *Wild River State Park*. The route may be a bit confusing, but this is a lovely and worthwhile trip. Even though at times it feels like you're getting more and more lost, just knowing that you're tracing the littoral edge of the Saint Croix River sort of fills your soul. Wild River State Park is popular with canoeists. Yet anyone can have fun here. This 6,800-acre park has 35 miles of trails (careful, some of these trails are quite challenging!), a small nature center, and numerous marked historic sites including old homesteading spots. Naturalist programs take place year-round. Watch for the side road. Call (651) 583-2125, for more information.

In Sunrise (the little town with the heartwarming name), you can rent a tube and get a shuttle to splash about on the Sunrise River, which flows into the Saint Croix River.

Continue southwest on CR 12 for another 3 miles to County Road 16 at Almelund. History buffs will love the *Amador Heritage Center*, with an old two-room schoolhouse and Swedish-style immigrant log house.

Turn left on CR 16 and travel east and south for a little more than 10 miles into downtown Taylors Falls. Finding CR 16 is a bit tricky, so stay alert. Taylors Falls used to be called Taylor's Place (no apostrophe today) and is a sister city to Saint Croix Falls, Wisconsin, across the river. Both are the headquarters of sorts of the *Saint Croix National Scenic Riverway*, but, even more so, for the jaw-dropping majesty of *Interstate State Park*.

There's plenty to see in the park and the town, so you might want to first check out the visitor center headquarters, a mile south of town on U.S. Highway 8/State Highway 95, (651) 465-5711. (Note: An entrance permit—required—from one state is good in the other state only at this park. The catch is that this only applies on weekdays and non-holidays. Otherwise, you'll have to pony up the money for each state.)

The most popular Taylors Falls trail leads to humongous glacial potholes. Another favorite is along an old railroad grade that leads into Taylors Falls. All along the trails you're treated to eye-bugging geological highlights of lava cliffs—some of which, your knees will soon note, rise and fall some 200 feet above the water. These are the famed Dalles of the Saint Croix, the hodgepodge geological residuals apparent in the river gorge. Note the preponderance of rock climbers, especially on the Wisconsin side.

Tailor-made for camera-toters are the *Taylors Falls Scenic Boat Tours*, (651) 465-5711, near the Highway 8 bridge across the Saint Croix. These double-decker old-style paddlewheelers—historically detailed—lug tourists again on 50- and 80-minute tours. Schedules vary, but usually five times daily in summer; admission.

Taylors Falls also has some points of interest *off* the water. The *Folsom House Historic Site*, 272 W. Government Street, just north of Highway 8, (651) 465-3125, is, as they like to tell you here, a bit of New England in the Midwest. A wealthy lumberman from Maine, W. H. C. Folsom, built this lovely frame house in 1855, which today anchors Taylors Falls' historic Angel Hill Historic District. Look for the still-in-use Greek revival church and the numerous antebellum clapboard and frame homes in the neighborhood. Tours of the house are generally given Memorial Day weekend to mid-October, afternoons daily, except Tuesday, 1-4:30 p.m.; admission.

Quick Trip Option 2. West of Taylors Falls, Chisago County is rife with pinprick-sized towns. For an entertaining, scenic, and quick side trip, head west of Taylors Falls on Highway 8 to Shafer, Center City, Lindstrom, and Chisago City. Near Taylors Falls, right along the highway, *Franconia Sculpture Garden* invites local, regional, and interna-

Some of the avant-garde outdoor art at the Franconia Sculpture Garden, near Taylors Falls. Tim Bewer

tional artists to construct sculptures in this 14-acre park. The result—an ongoing "experiment" in art—is both eccentric (look at all the forms and materials) and lovely.

In Shafer, follow the signs to the *Yesterfarm,* a farm museum where the family can get an up-close view of (if not a participatory experience in) a turn-of-the-twentieth-century homestead. The *Chisago County Government Center* in Center City has lots of historical exhibits including a fascinating display of a Swedish midwife's life. Nellie Gustafson emigrated from Skane, Sweden, in 1900 and traveled around the county by horse and buggy. Her medical items are quite rare and worth a look. Center City, incidentally, is well-known among Twin Cities antique aficionados. So many reputable antique and arts and crafts dealers are found in the town that travel agents in the Twin Cities organize antiquing coach tours here.

Eventually, you'll pass through the *Carlos Avery State Wildlife Management Area,* a huge tract of protected land stretching from Chisago County into Anoka County, nearly to the fringes of the Twin Cities. Absolutely every turn of the road brings you past a boat landing, campground, or another dense spinney of spruce. For a federal highway, U.S. 8 sure smacks of a ribbony county road! And it's only about 13 miles from Taylors Falls to Chisago City.

From Taylors Falls, continue south and west on Highway 8/95 for 3 miles to where Highway 95 turns left. A mile or so out of Taylors Falls, definitely stop in the marked pullout, which offers a magnificent vista of the Lower Dalles area of the Saint Croix River Valley Gorge!

Continue south on 95 for about 10 miles to State Highway 97, turn right and drive into tiny Scandia, about 1 mile west. Fair-haired Scandia was Minnesota's earliest Swedish settlement. Dala horses—hand-carved and painted horse statues many consider the primary symbol of Swedish culture—are prominently displayed downtown. The magnificent *Gammelgarden Museum,* (651) 433-5053, explores this heritage. The 11-acre museum site has a half-dozen smashingly restored immigrant buildings and a spanking-new (2002) *Valkommen Hus* (Welcome Center). Kids love the old Swedish barn! The grounds and buildings are open mid-May to mid-October, Friday–Sunday, 1–4 p.m.; admission.

The *Midsommer Dag,* or Midsummer Day Festival, is a worthy June festival. You can feast on Swedish fare (the saffron buns are delicious) and watch Swedish musicians and dancers perform. In December the *Lucia Festival* celebrates winter's darker days and the crowning of a young girl with lights is a highlight of eastern Minnesota's festivals. Call far in advance for seating to this event.

Backtrack to Highway 95 and continue south for 3 miles to *William O'Brien State Park.* The park, (651) 433-0500, has a lovely lake connected to the Saint Croix River. Most appealing are the numerous river channel islands. Their isolation and perimeters, ever-changing due to tides and river currents, have given them wonderfully diverse bio-zones.

Continue south on 95 for 1.5 miles into Marine on Saint Croix. From the riparian loveliness of our river drive, suddenly we're in the mid-

View of Stillwater and the Saint Croix River from atop the bluffs. Tim Bewer

ever, you're just a brisk walk away from the legendary lumber mill that established the town in the nineteenth century.

Continue south on Highway 95 to where County Road 7 branches off to the southwest. Follow CR 7 for 4.5 miles to County Road 11. Along the way, take a short jog off the river road to scenic *Square Lake Park*, with a campground and excellent swimming beach.

Turn left (south) on CR 11 and drive for about 4.5 miles to Highway 95; turn right and continue south for another 1.5 miles into downtown Stillwater. The birthplace of Minnesota, Stillwater likes to call itself. It was here in 1848 that a territorial convention agreed to put forth the necessary paperwork to gaining statehood. Following statehood, the town grew rapidly, and by the 1880s it had the largest logging operation on the river and, oddly enough, the state prison.

Today Stillwater is still a "boom" town, yet now its prosperity is the result of a short commute to the Twin Cities and droves of tourists poking around. But neither should detract from your enjoyment of all the things to do and see here. You may have to share quite a bit of sidewalk space with other river rats or leaf peepers, but that's OK; it's a laid-back enough place to handle the congestion.

The *Warden's House Historical Museum,* 602 North Main Street, (651) 439-5956, was home to the first territorial prison in the Northwest Territory. County historical odds and ends predominate, but the intriguing context—being a warden's quarters and all—give it an odd and engaging feel. Hours are Thursday–Sunday, 1–5 p.m., May to October; admission.

The gargantuan edifice just to the north of the warden's house? Indeed, this was the first prison in the Northwest Territory and dates from 1851; it was mothballed in 1914. The walls are still imposing, and a guardhouse and another building still stand. Exhibits detail a fierce battle between the Dakota and Ojibwe of the area in 1839.

Across the street from the prison is the *Logging and Railroad Museum.* It is the terminal for the *Zephyr,* (651) 430-3000, an elegant 1940s train that today takes travelers along the bluffs and valleys of the Saint Croix River Valley on fine-dining excursions.

Travelling south on Main Street (Highway 95), you'll soon arrive at the office of the *Greater Stillwater Chamber of Commerce,* 201 South Main Street, (651) 439-4001 (www.stillwatertraveler.com). The office has detailed historical walking tour maps.

From here, it's a good idea to leave the car and browse. As with every other Saint Croix River Valley town, Stillwater is made to tour on foot. Housed within all the gingerbread architecture you'll find

dle of Currier & Ives. Marine on Saint Croix could, indeed, come from an Americana-themed mail-order catalog, with virtually the entire town historically preserved. Garrison Keillor once quipped that the town highly resembled his "mythical" Lake Wobegon, and Hollywood moviemakers regularly come calling when they need that "perfectly charming" backdrop for a movie.

Don't miss the *Brookside Bar and Grill,* 140 Judd Street, (651) 432-5132—especially its basement, which has a stream running through it, cooling the beer! Also, the town has the wonderful, all-in-one town hall/theater stage/library. At least one member of your party will likely insist on meandering along the streets to window shop. If you're not in the mood to open the wallet, howart galleries and artisan shops every which way. Local businesses also do an admirable job of showing regional artists' works. The shopping is excellent, too, from antiques to books—lots of books.

Stillwater has the privilege of calling itself North America's first official Booktown, as decreed by "King" Richard Booth, the self-anointed regal of the first Booktown in the "movement"—Hay-on-Wye, Wales, Great Britain. Stillwater boasts an almost unreal number of rare and antiquarian bookshops, and the number rises all the time. At last count, nearly a half-million books were for sale in the downtown area. Bibliophiles rejoice!

From Stillwater, go east over the bridge spanning the Saint Croix into Houlton, Wisconsin, and take County Road E east about 7 miles to County Road I. Turn right and go about 1 mile to County Road A. Turn right and go another mile to *Willow River State Park*. Here, three dams create separate flowages and a handful of modest cascades. Trails aren't numerous but pass by some burial grounds. You will find a nature center that doubles as a ski hut come winter.

From Willow River State Park, backtrack on CRs A, I, and E west to 60th Street. Turn right (north) and drive 6 miles. Watch for signs to the *Bass Lake Cheese Factory*, (715) 549-6617. What could be more classic than a visit to a Wisconsin cheese factory in the countryside?

Continue north on 60th Street (which eventually merges with County Road I) for 4.5 miles into Somerset. Here's something weird: Somerset (once famed for moonshine running during Prohibition) is known for frog's legs and pea soup. The former delicacy is served at numerous town restaurants. Pea soup is celebrated with its own festival in summer!

But the biggest thing here? Tubing the Apple River, splashing one's way downstream to the mouth at the Saint Croix River. So popular is this trip that *Life* magazine has celebrated its particular brand of Americana. You'll have no trouble finding rental operations.

From Somerset, drive north on State Highway 35 for 14 miles to Osceola. Here's a little town with a lot to do. Osceola is named for Chief Osceola—look for the large statue of him downtown—but it was originally named Leroy. And Leroy wouldn't allow the change until he was paid off. The price? Two sheep!

The town rests on prime riverine real estate, affording lovely vistas of the Saint Croix River and Osceola Creek. *Osceola Bluff* is an official natural landmark, and right downtown wooden steps lead to picturesque *Cascade Falls*. Farther along river you can explore the historic remnants of old flour, grist, and roller mills. More architecture is available on any impromptu town walking tour. One definite

Rock climbers about to challenge the Dalles of the Saint Croix. Thomas Huhti

stop should be at the renovated barn now known as *ArtBarn*, (715) 294-ARTS, a gallery-cum-workshop and local cultural center.

Connecting Wisconsin with its sister state is the *Osceola and Saint Croix Railway*, (800) 643-7412, an old locomotive-led train chugging into the wilds of the river valley on 90-minute round trips to Marine on Saint Croix, Minnesota.

Continue north on Highway 35 to County Road S. Turn left and follow it until it rejoins Highway 35 and drive into Saint Croix Falls (a total of about 8 miles). South of Saint Croix Falls is a small county information center. This is the southern terminus of the *Gandy Dancer State Recreation Trail*, which heads north into classic river valley country and stretches nearly 100 miles to Superior, Wisconsin, on Lake Superior, crossing over the Saint Croix River into Minnesota. At one point the trail crosses a majestically tall 350-foot-high bridge. A trail pass is required.

Saint Croix Falls is the sister city of Taylors Falls across the river. Here is the Wisconsin segment of *Interstate State Park,* with more epic views of the Dalles of the Saint Croix. These odd-ball topographical wonders of basaltic lava soar 200 feet above the river. The *Potholes Trail* should not be missed, nor should the trail to *Old Man of the Dalles,* one of the most photographed spots in Wisconsin. (You'll know why when you see it.) Interstate State Park was chosen to be the westernmost link in Wisconsin's Ice Age National Scientific Reserve, a chain of nine crucial examples of geological residuals, all linked by the Ice Age National Scenic Trail.

Saint Croix Falls is also the location of the park headquarters, (715) 483-3284, of the Saint Croix National Scenic Riverway.

From downtown Saint Croix Falls, drive north on State Highway 87 for 20 miles to County Road O. Turn left (west) and drive about 11 miles for another glimpse of the Saint Croix River. Backtrack about 2 miles to West River Road; turn left and go north, east, and north again for about 6.5 miles to Fish Lake Road. Take that for about 5 miles to State Highway 48. Through this whole stretch, the driving gets a bit difficult. Wisconsin's famed "nose" of its "Indianhead" region swoops to the west, but this is only geography, not road engineering. Instead, a hodgepodge of tiny community roads heads off into the wilds, all of which will take you precisely nowhere. It's virtually all county or state forestland here. On Fish Lake Road, you're guaranteed to be alone. In tiny Lind, an access road leads to a public boat landing and the trailhead for the Southern Hiking Trail along the Saint Croix River.

You're also in the midst of the *Governor Knowles State Forest*—33,000 acres of rolling topography with outstanding canoeing and hiking. Two hiking trails of 20 miles each trace the bluff line above the river.

Turn left (north) on Highway 48 and head 2 miles into Grantsburg. This is pleasant town has a village hall with an eight-foot-tall talking statue of "Big Gust." This seven-and-a-half-foot-tall giant was the town's lamplighter and town marshal; in his first role, he apparently saved ladder expenses, and the second is understandable when you get a gander at his imposing stature. Very fun is July's Snowmobile Watercross, when local knuckleheads try to skim their machines across a downtown lake.

Drive north, then east, on County Road F for about 12 miles. For nearly the entire stretch, you'll be skirting the *Crex Meadows State Wildlife Area.* Near the fantastically lovely (and large) Phantom Flowage, this 30,000-acre spread has more than 250 species of birds, including nesting herons, sandhill cranes, trumpeter swans, rare colonies of yellow-headed blackbirds; a pack of timber wolves has even reportedly taken up residence here. Some of Wisconsin's only remaining virgin prairie is here, too. A nature/interpretive center has self-guided auto tour maps.

Continue in a northeasterly direction on CR F for about another 17 miles to Danbury. East of town are the fringes of the 11 communities comprising the *Saint Croix Indian Reservation.* Often referred to as the "Lost Tribe" due to its dispersion over four Wisconsin counties (and one Minnesota county), the tribe today holds a festive Wild Rice Powwow in August. East of Danbury is the region of Wisconsin dubbed the "Fishbowl" due to the preponderance of glacial lakes and ponds and the jillions of panfish in them. Good fishing!

From Danbury, head west on State Highway 77 for 3 miles. After crossing into Minnesota, where the road becomes State Highway 48, go for about 8 miles to County Road 22. Turn left (south) and proceed for about 5 miles to *Saint Croix State Park*. At 34,000 acres, plus change, this is Minnesota's largest state park, (320) 384-6591, but size is not its only superlative. In 1997, the park was also federally deemed a National Historic Landmark as its topography and architectural designs represent a "particularly pristine and intact example of recreational demonstration areas." That's government-speak for "lovely" and "historic."

The park is plunked alongside the Saint Croix River, a National Wild and Scenic Waterway. Canoeing is an excellent way to explore these parts. Plenty of area rental and guide outfitters are available; most folks opt for pleasure tour operators located farther south along the river.

Besides the canoeing and kayaking, the park has a plethora of trails (over 125 miles), a swimming beach, six canoe landings, boat/canoe/bicycle rentals, and a huge campground.

Return on CR 22 to Highway 48. Turn left (west) and drive for 15.5 miles back to Hinckley, our starting point.

Tour 22
Rolling on the Great River Road

Hastings—Red Wing—Lake City—Wabasha—Winona—Fountain City (Wisconsin)—Alma (Wisconsin)—Pepin (Wisconsin)—Prescott (Wisconsin)—Hastings

Distance: approximately 140 miles

We've already seen the birthplace of the Mississippi. Then we explored its nascent stages, where it begins to discover its youthful strength. Now, we begin to see it as it gathers steam on its epic flow to the deltas of the Gulf of Mexico.

We also get the best of both states. Once again, our eyes get to drink in the orangish rays of sunrise splashing over the silty Mississippi from Minnesota, and, from the aeries of the Badger state's bluffs, we take in the wearied sun setting over the powerful river.

The towns along the way seem time-locked and we flip through the pages of history with each mile driven. The odometer spins, the engine purrs, and we tick off a perfect day of road-tripping: superb greenspaces overlooking towering riparian bluff lands, charming towns perfect for strolling, and, despite the highway's general popularity with weekend road-trip warriors, a decidedly low-key feel to the whole route.

Yes, this is the Great River Road (hereafter simply, the GRR). Actually, this epic byway is not one "road" but an amalgamation of many federal, state, and local roads on *both* sides of the Big Muddy, which follow its flow all the way to New Orleans. One of the longest (and oldest, dating from 1938) established byways in the United States, this is the most glorious of all small-road alternatives to the frantic interstates. Look for the green-and-white signs with the distinctive pilot wheel; they are frequent and well-placed, easily leading you on your way in Minnesota and Wisconsin. (If you continue along the GRR south of Illinois and Iowa—good luck. Some states thereafter have a baffling if not nonexistent signage system.)

For our purposes, the following Web sites are all one needs to prepare for a jaunt on the Great River Road: www.mnmississippiriver.com (for Minnesota touring) and www.greatriverroad.org (for the Wisconsin side).

Start your tour in downtown Hastings on U.S. Highway 61. Lying at the confluence of the Saint Croix, Mississippi, and Vermilion Rivers, Hastings has a perfect location to make use of all the hydro power. Flour and lumber mills went up as tie-hacks floated enormous loads of logs farther downstream. The mills established Hastings at one point as one of the country's major grain markets.

Hastings *is* history, many folks say. More than 60 structures are on the National Register of Historic Places, and these eye-catching buildings are more than apparent as you stroll the downtown. An architectural walking tour brochure is available at the *Hastings Area Chamber of Commerce*, 111 East Third Street (at the corner of U.S. Highway 61 and West 3rd Street, just south of the Mississippi River), (651) 437-6775 (www.hastingsmn.org). Must-sees downtown include the *LeDuc-Simmons Mansion*, owned by President Rutherford B. Hayes's secretary of agriculture and restored by the Minnesota Historical Society; the copper-roofed Frank Lloyd Wright-designed *Fasbender Clinic*; and the *Norris Octagon House*.

Don't forget the sublime, challenging riparian topography—those basalt rises are a picture-perfect backdrop to this delightful town. Vermilion Falls, southeast of downtown, doesn't lure tourists like Hastings, but it's a lovely little place and the spot of the oldest flour mill in the state.

If you have extra time, then just north of the city along Highway 61, the U.S. Army Corps of Engineers *Lock and Dam No. 2* has an excellent viewing platform from which you can watch river traffic chugging through the 600-foot-long lock. More than six million gallons of water are pumped through the gates to raise craft—from canoes to massive barges—12 feet!

For more active types, the city has the excellent *Hastings Trail System*, a 15-mile-long trail system that loops throughout the city. It offers outstanding views of the Vermilion River, Lake Isabel, Lake Rebecca, and the Mississippi River.

A popular regional event is Hastings' *Front Porch Festival*, held in mid-May. In a city with countless Victorian gingerbreads, most surrounded by sprawling porches, someone had the lovely idea of combining that architecture with the friendly ethos of small-town life. *Voila!* A festival with neighborly chats, rocking chair marathons, and maypole dancing.

Drive east out of downtown Hastings via East 10th Street (which becomes Ravenna Trail, then County Road 54). Follow this route for about 9 miles to County Road 18. Approximately 15 blocks (or five minutes) southeast of the chamber of commerce, you'll pass *C. P. Adams Park*

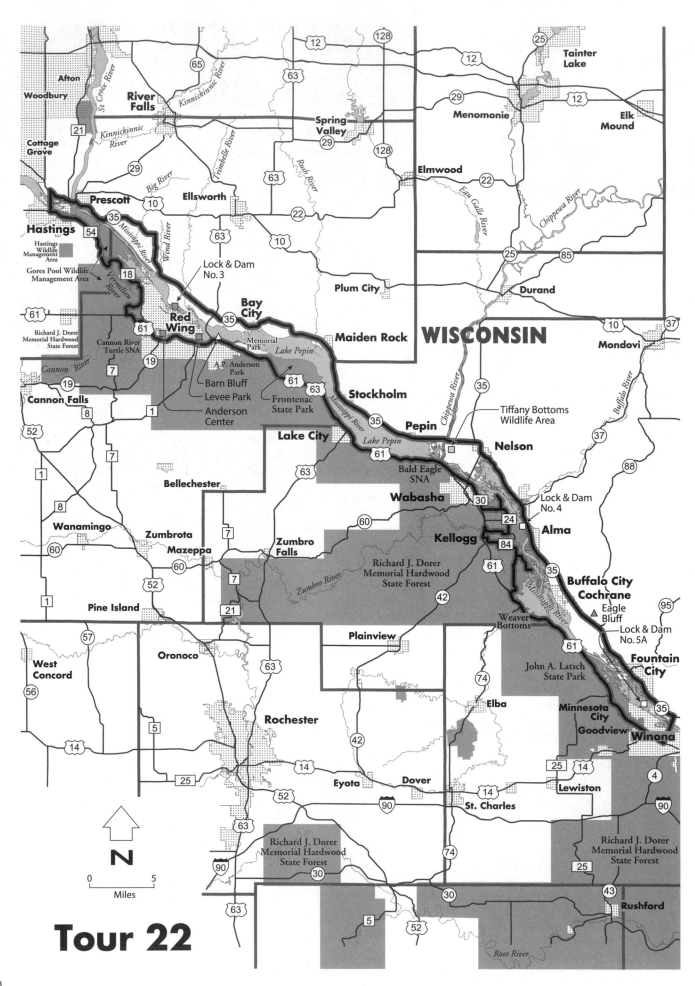

Tour 22

on your right (you'll also see a big lake on the left-hand side). After this, a right turn onto Leduc Road takes you to a forlorn but worthy trio of parks, including *Old Mill Park*. Get an eyeful of the gracefully decaying remains of the oldest mill in the state—Ramsey Mill, which was finished in 1857.

After you leave Hastings proper, you're in for a challenging but rewarding road trip. CR 54 skirts the western side of the Vermilion River—and the road seems to have been deliberately constructed to mimic the river's bight and dip. Slow down and appreciate the greenery!

A scant few minutes upon leaving Hastings you're passing by the *Hastings Wildlife Management Area* and, five minutes farther on, the *Vermilion River Bottoms-Gores Pool Wildlife Management Area*. Both are nodes of the Great River Birding Trail and offer breathtaking river topography, plus warblers, hawks, owls, herons, and bald eagles. Bring the binoculars. It's all public land, and the official government maps encourage you to get out and explore. The land is second-growth maple and basswood forest mixed with excellent examples of floodplain forest.

Turn east on CR 18 and follow it south for about 8 miles to Highway 61; turn left and drive east and south about 9.5 miles to Red Wing. About halfway along the CR 18 stretch, an east turn onto Sturgeon Lake Road will bring you to the U.S. Army Corps of Engineers *Lock and Dam No. 3*, one of the busiest on the Mississippi River. Captains also say that the river bights in the Red Wing area are some of the most challenging to navigate on the Upper Mississippi River.

Craving wildlife viewing opportunities? No problem. To the east is *Cannon River Turtle Preserve Scientific and Natural Area*, and to the west, almost opposite that preserve, is the *Spring Creek Prairie Scientific and Natural Area*. The former is an excellent example of a bottomland forest and, as a bonus, is along the Cannon Valley bike trail, which follows the river, then branches westward along Cannon Creek.

On the western outskirts of Red Wing, look for signs to the *Anderson Center*, at the intersection of Highway 61 and State Highway 19, (651) 388-2009, one of the Midwest's leading and largest arts communities and interdisciplinary studies institutes. Potters, sculptors, poets, and a variety of other artists have set up shop in the former estate of A. P. Anderson; scientists and artists work side by side.

Follow Highway 61 into downtown Red Wing at Broad Street; turn left and go a short distance to *Levee Park*. This charming town is full of history and lots of postcard-worthy vistas. Henry David Thoreau climbed peaks in the area and raved about communing with nature here; Mark Twain steamed by in riverboats and scribbled at length about the sculpted beauty of the river bluffs and the town's handsome skyline.

In the downtown area, turn east toward the river and park the vehicle at the can't-miss-it *Mil-*

View of Red Wing from atop Sorin's Bluff. Thomas Huhti

waukee Depot, which sits at the waterfront Levee Park. Here you have free parking and a chance to visit the *Red Wing Chamber of Commerce*, 420 Levee Street, (651) 388-4719 or (800) 498-3444 (www.redwing.org). Of all the well-informed and well-stocked information brokers on the Great River Road, these folks win hands down.

By the way, this downtown trek assumes you have a good pair of shoes, as hoofing around town is preferred. Levee Park is a longish piece of greenspace with nice views of passing watercraft. Walk to the southwest and you'll come to a nice park on Bay Point and a *historic fishing village*, where fish shanties stand tall as their aged flat paint contrasts with the perikwinkle sky. *Bay Point Park* is perhaps the best place to get an up-close view of Mississippi River barges. The bend at this park is one of the most difficult to navigate, given the strong current and sharp turns.

Backtrack to the chamber of commerce and walk toward the historic *Saint James Hotel*, 406 Main Street (651) 388-2846. The aging (but renovated) grand dame landmark of Red Wing has hosted prime ministers and presidents alongside with everyday traveling folk. Take the elevator to the top of the hotel for a superb view. Also, don't miss the *Sheldon Theatre*, at Third Street and East Avenue, (800) 899-5759—another jewel in Red Wing's architectural crown. This historic performing arts venue was the country's first municipal theater, opening in 1904. Public tours include a multimedia presentation on the city's history. They're offered June to October, Thursday–Saturday at 1 p.m.

For a taste (and sound) of river-town Americana, take in a free concert—Broadway to bluegrass—on a hot July night, Wednesdays at 7 p.m.

If you're into more challenging exercise, the city has superb biking on the *Cannon Valley Trail,* which runs on old railroad tracks along the Cannon River Valley. Three miles outside of Red Wing you rise up to an archaeological preserve (there may be a dig in progress). Otherwise, you bypass gorgeous bluffs and ride through or past parks, prairies, and a few Native American burial mounds.

From Levee Park, return to Highway 61, go two blocks to Plum Street, turn right, go to East Seventh Street, and turn left. Immediately start looking for signs to the imposing, 385-foot-high *Barn Bluff* off to the left. A short access road takes you to the base of this commanding aerie. From here you can walk up. Good luck, though; it's an awfully steep climb. Or just wander about the base and look for steel-armed rock climbers. Some deserted lime kilns can be seen at the eastern base. Otherwise, the bluff is an intriguing mix of wildflowers and goat prairie.

Continue east on Seventh Street a short distance to Skyline Drive and turn right into *Memorial Park* (look for signs to Sorin's Bluff). An even higher, more superb vista is found by driving and winding your way up in your car into the hills here. At the top—*Sorin's Bluff*—you're treated to magnificent views of the entire river valley. When you get to the lookout, you *may* be able to view some natural caves just over the edge (but exercise *extreme* caution if venturing near the edge).

A bit farther to the east, along the waterfront, is *Colvill Park.* This is a prime location for eagle-watching. Year-round you can see these regal birds soaring above the water or majestically perching themselves in park trees. Even in winter, hot-water discharge from the Prairie Island nuclear power plant keeps eagles about.

Return to Highway 61 (now joined by U.S. Highway 63) and continue south of Red Wing. Immediately, massive Lake Pepin begins to form. It widens and widens, stretching for some 30 miles downriver. Think fishing first; it's excellent all along the route. Second, think climate. The widened river body adds a touch of warmth and humidity to the area and is one reason you begin to see so many orchards advertised upon leaving Red Wing. Spring blossom seasons reveal all roads south of Red Wing in riotous color, but August, when apples begin to appear on trees, is also a great time. Minnesota's trademark Haralson apple is a favorite.

Travel for about 11 miles to County Road 2; turn left and proceed into *Frontenac State Park*. Perched high above the northern shoreline of Lake Pepin, this 2,150-acre park, (651) 345-3401, has commanding views from the semi-rugged trails tracing the lake's shoreline. The topography is a mixture of uplands, oak savanna, wetlands, and an adjacent private bison farm. Along the way, you can explore old limestone digs and even a couple of Native American burial mounds. As with most parklands along the Mississippi River, it's excellent for birding (more than 260 species are found here). Turkey vultures and other migrating raptors are found in abundance here. There are several accesses leading to the park.

Nearby, the town of Frontenac is the site of the *Lakeside Hotel,* which dates to 1867 and proudly claims the title of the first resort hotel in Minnesota. "Old Frontenac" has distinctive architecture—including the Westervelt House, Saint Hubert's Lodge, and the most intriguing, Villa Maria, an ex-convent. Interesting is the fact that Old Frontenac has no commercial businesses. New Frontenac, located back on Highway 61, is relatively "new," but is the site of the oldest continually used town hall in Minnesota.

Return to Highway 61/63 and proceed for 6 miles to Lake City. The next town on our Great River Road tour is *long*, seemingly stretching forever along the banks of Lake Pepin. Lake City is credited with being the birthplace of water skiing, which supposedly first took place here in 1922. (Stop by the tiny chamber of commerce office to see replicas of the first pine board water skis.) Naturally, you can also visit during Water Ski Days the last weekend in June; 20,000 folks descend on the area to celebrate the summertime tradition. An even larger festival is *Johnny Appleseed Days* in October, when equal numbers come to chomp and stomp on apples. One-fourth of Minnesota's total apple production—or 700,000 bushels worth—is produced in the Lake City area.

Red Wing: A Household Name

Red Wing is the place where, for years, pottery and shoes bearing the town name have been made. Nationally acclaimed Red Wing Pottery was for generations *the* stoneware for home cooking and preserving. Collectors avidly pursue classic pieces. The original company shuttered in 1969, but the Red Wing Stoneware Company has now rejuvenated the business.

Red Wing has pottery makers at the *Anderson Center* (see above), along with pieces at several galleries and especially antique shops. But the Red Wing Stoneware Company still garners most of the attention. Its industrial operations are located just east of the Anderson Center. Factory tours are given weekdays at 10 a.m. and 1 p.m. in summer, at 1 p.m. only in winter, but you can watch potters at work seven days per week. You can also visit a pottery museum—head for the *Pottery District* by following Old West Main Street, just north of Highway 61 and west of the downtown.

The classic American footwear, Red Wing, is also made here. The factory is west of town, just north of Highway 61 (opposite A. P. Anderson Park). You can also head downtown to La Grange Park, where you can step into Riverfront Center and visit the *Red Wing Shoe Museum*, 314 Main Street, (651) 388-8211.

Lake Pepin, along the Great River Road. Minnesota Office of Tourism.

Marinas and parks, that sums up Lake City. They claim 252 acres of parkland, no mean feat in a small town. The best thing to do is strike out on the 2.5-mile-long *Riverwalk* that runs along the lake. Get set for some wondrous birding along the way. Lake City has been designated by the American Bird Conservancy a Globally Important Bird Area. You may see thousands of migrating tundra swans, 500 bald eagles, and/or three-fourths of the world's population of Common mergansers (late November). Birding societies say that just north of Lake City's city limits, *Hok-Si-La City Park* is the best place to watch birds.

Drive southeast on Highway 61 (63 splits off to the southwest at Lake City) for 12 miles to Hiawatha Drive (County Road 30) on the west edge of Wabasha. As you cruise along here, it feels almost as if you're on top of the water. And the views are majestic, with several opportunities to pull off the road and enjoy it.

After passing through Maple Springs, the *Bald Eagle Bluff Scientific and Natural Area* suddenly appears, with more excellent birding—eagles and hundreds of other species are found from here to Reads Landing.

In tiny Reads Landing, notice the confluence of the Chippewa River across the river; here is where Lake Pepin narrows back into the Mississippi proper. This watery action keeps ice floes from forming and, thus, keeps lots of birds and wildlife active throughout winter. Reads Landing also has the *Wabasha County Museum*, which houses an exhibit on Laura Ingalls Wilder and her "Little House on the Prairie" books.

Established in the late 1830s, Wabasha holds bragging rights as the oldest community in Min-nesota. Fur traders had fronted up as far back as the American Revolution, and this, of course, was itself long after native Dakota had used the river points for canoe landings. Wabasha was also the focal point of one of our country's first forays into ecological protection. The Winneshiek Bottoms, stretching from here to Illinois, was the first refuge to include fur-bearing animals, fish, and plant life. Fittingly, this is among the best places on the Upper Mississippi River to view bald eagles; right in town you'll find an observation deck with high-powered binoculars and scopes (set out only Sun-

Great River Birding Trail

Birders across the nation recently celebrated the publication of the first maps detailing the new *Great River Birding Trail,* based on the original granddaddy of all them all—the Great Coastal Texas Birding Trail. The Great River Birding Trail follows the Upper Mississippi River, and separate maps highlight communities and bird species, of which there are more than 300 found along the river route in Minnesota and Wisconsin. State and local communities generally have maps available at chambers of commerce and/or visitor information centers. You can also contact the National Mississippi River Parkway Commission (www.mississippi-river.com) or the Minnesota/Wisconsin Departments of Natural Resources (www.dnr.state.mn.us and www.dnr.state.wi.us, respectively).

The *Great River Birding Festival* celebrates the precious natural world and its wildlife. Usually taking place during the second weekend in May, it is a newer festival, but already one of the most popular on the GRR. The festival celebrates eagles, the beginning of spring, and International Migratory Bird Day all in one festival. Guided birding tours and hikes, interpretive programs, and workshops take place in each community.

day afternoons November to March). Even better—at 152 Main Street is the *National Eagle Center*, where volunteer staff care for injured and non-releasable eagles.

On a lighter note, you may recognize the town from Hollywood. Wabasha was the setting for the films *Grumpy Old Men* and *Grumpier Old Men*. The screenwriter happens to be from Hastings, but his grandfather was a Wabasha native.

On Hiawatha Drive, go east through Wabasha, then south out of town, for about 3 miles on CR 30 to County Road 24. Turn left and follow this east, south, and west back to Highway 61, a total of about 5.5 miles. Near the start of the CR 24 stretch, you may want to take County Road 76 2 miles to its dead end at *Teepeeota Point*. Here you'll see the Mississippi and Zumbro Rivers merge and form the ecologically crucial *Kellogg-Weaver Dunes*—700 acres of sand prairie dunes owned by the Nature Conservancy. Virtually every duck species in the Upper Midwest can be found here, along with the semi-rare Blanding turtle, as well as native grasses and wildflowers. A peregrine falcon nesting project has also been established here.

These sandy soils are also perfect for one of the local economic linchpins: watermelons. If you're fond of the luscious fruit, things get down-right bountiful come late August, when everyone and his or her sister seems to be selling the ripe fruit. The town also has a wonderful *Watermelon Festival* the weekend after Labor Day.

Turn left (southeast) on Highway 61 and drive 2 miles to the junction with State Highway 42 just southwest of Kellogg. Believe it or not, this is the location of Minnesota's fourth-largest tourist attraction, and it's one that many folks have never heard of. At the intersection, *L.A.R.K. Toys*, (651) 767-3387, has become a haven for the nostalgic. The largest children's specialty toy store in North America, one can purchase an old-fashioned hand-carved wooden toy. A toy museum also sits on site (with more than 25,000 items) and you can watch a gigantic carousel spin (and watch the carousel's menagerie being carved). Obviously, many a family has spent an entire afternoon here! Generally, March to December the company is open daily, weekdays 9 a.m.–5 p.m., weekends 10 a.m.–5 p.m.

At the junction of Highways 61 and 42, drive northeast a short distance on the road leading into Kellogg. Turn right at the next intersection and go to County Road 84; turn left and drive east and south for 7.5 miles to Highway 61. You can't see it from your vehicle but you're trailing along the Zumbro River, just to the north, as it heads to its confluence with the Mississippi River. The charming little roadway zigs right, then banks left again, then a hard right to the south again. All along here and to the south, you'll find a plethora of winged critters. You'll be elbow to elbow with birders, binoculars in hand, come migration seasons. But even during busy times you can always find an isolated spot to search out sand-hill cranes, meadowlarks, sparrows, finches, owls, and more.

Quick Trip Option. After heading south for 1 mile on CR 84 after the turn, you can take a left turn at Newton Road, which leads to a parking area at Half Moon Lake and, farther south, the larger Maloney Lake. As you head toward it, look to the south; all of this land is part of the *Kellogg-Weaver Dunes State Natural Area*, with large chunks under ownership of the Nature Conservancy thrown in. Since the road dead ends after 3 miles, you'll have to back-track to CR 84 and continue with the regular tour.

Continue southeast on Highway 61 for 3 miles to *Weaver Bottoms* on the left. This is another sublime slice of creation, location of one of the Midwest's largest tundra swan concentrations from mid-October through November, though there's a laundry list of other species, including rare ducks, American white pelicans (July to September), and more. Mile marker 45 on Highway 61 has a pull-off spot (look for the cemetery) from which you can explore.

From mile marker 45 to Minnieska, an astonishing number of bird species have been spotted; state record numbers of gulls and terns have passed through this area.

Continue southeast for 6 miles to *John Latsch State Park* on the right. The prominent tri-headed bluff line above you was well known to steamship captains, who used the rocky heights as navigation markers and who named the three bulbous outcroppings Faith, Hope, and Charity. Today you, too, can huff and puff your way up the 500-foot rise of Mount Charity for a stunning view of the river valley.

Continue southeast on Highway 61 for 13 miles to Huff Street on the west edge of Winona. Dubbed "The Island City" because of its cozy setting on what is very nearly an island amidst a handful of lakes, Winona lives up to the name. Bluffs tower over the city and beckon travelers to climb them. Eddies and sloughs harbor a zoological convention. Over 100 buildings are listed on the National Register of Historic Places and create an Old World feel as you wander through several districts.

Those castellated bluffs draw one's eye. The dolomite limestone actually helped establish the city (it was rumored to equal the finest limestone in Italy); quarrying took place so feverishly that even a couple of Winona's most recognizable natural landmark bluffs—then and now—were blasted and disfigured before public outcry halted the practice. At Huff Street, look for signs directing you to the right, up to *Garvin Heights*. The road snakes and coils and rises steeply, nearly 600 feet.

The reward? Views for miles and miles and miles from several overlooks. Farther to the southeast is the grand dame of Winona's bluffs. *Sugar Loaf* is slightly shorter but certainly more impressive—so much so that Native Americans worshipped at its base and the city now lights it up at night.

Turn left (northeast) on Huff Street and proceed to E. Second Street in downtown Winona. Turn right and go a few blocks to the *Winona Convention and Visitors Bureau.* The facility, 67 Main Street, (507) 452-2272 or (800) 657-4972, (www.visitwinona.com), has everything you'll need to point you in the right direction. The detailed maps alone are worth a stop.

In a land of Norwegians, Winona provides an ethnic change of pace—the largest concentration of Kashubian Polish culture in the United States. The *Polish Cultural Institute*, 102 Liberty Street, (507) 454-3431, is less than a half mile east of the visitor center via East Second Street. Housed in an erstwhile lumber company's complex, the Polish Museum, as it's locally known, features samples of fine embroidery work for which Poles are noted. A good time to visit the museum is in October, when the *Smaczne Jablka*, or Tasty Apples Festival, is held. Tables creak with the weight of delicious homemade pies and cakes. Hours are weekdays, 10 a.m.–3 p.m., Saturday, 10 a.m.–noon, Sunday, 1–3 p.m.

As you walk to the Polish Museum, along the way you can avail yourself of a self-guided *historical architectural tour* (brochures available from the visitor center). At the corner of Johnson and Third Street is the impressive former armory, which now serves as the home of the *Winona County Historical Society*, (507) 454-2723. Of particular note are the beautiful displays of stained glass; early-nineteenth-century immigrants established Winona as one of the United States' leading markets of stained glass. Kids will love one particularly hands-on exhibit (they can spelunk into a cave mock-up or "pilot" a riverboat, among other things), making it worth a stop for families. Hours are weekdays, 9 a.m.–5 p.m., and weekends, noon–4 p.m.; admission. Architectural mavens can rent an audiotape at the museum detailing Winona's history on a great driving tour. Stop by the *Merchant's National Bank,* Third and Lafayette Streets, to see two precious—and somewhat sizable—examples of Winona's jewel-like stained glass.

As the headquarters of the Upper Mississippi River refuge, the city boasts miles and miles of marshland, sloughs, and bottomland. A trek northwest of downtown along Riverview Drive, then north on Prairie Island Road, takes you through lowlands formed by one big river and a handful of lakes. It also has a nice nature trail and is on an established bike trail. Directly across from downtown Winona's Levee Park is *Latsch Island*, a superb place to linger for a morning or afternoon, and a great wildlife viewing opportunity. There are beaches, but be *very* careful of currents. Note the

Getting a bird-dog's eye view of Winona. Thomas Huhti

unique boathouses on the island. This is private property, so respect limits.

From East Second Street, go north a short distance to Winona Street, turn right and drive across the Mississippi River bridge to State Highway 35 in Wisconsin. Turn left (north) and go about 6 miles to Fountain City. Initially the terrain along Highway 35 seems nothing more than dried up, off-the-river marshland, perhaps agricultural land gone to seed or furrow. But soon you'll see *Lock and Dam 5A*, which has a viewing platform. This spot also hosts what locals proudly claim to be the only floating bar (as in imbibing establishment) on the Mississippi River (though one has to believe that similar places exist along the huge waterway).

As Fountain City approaches, you're greeted by more epic limestone and sandstone rises. The most salient feature is the 550-foot-tall *Eagle Bluff*, the highest point along the Mississippi River on the Wisconsin side. It's not as tall as Winona's chief peaks, but impressive nonetheless.

In Fountain City, the sandstone rises seem to bow down to the mighty Mississippi River, and the town sits cozily ensconced in the shadow of the bluffs. The town is downright attractive—something like an Italian fishing village plunked onto Old Man River's edge. (Though there's a wonderfully bizarre smattering of unique architecture—something Swiss Bavarian, for example, next to a squat fisherman's bungalow.)

In town, one of the strangest Mississippi River highlights has to be the *House with a Rock in It*, as it's unofficially known. In 1995, a 50-ton boulder fell out of the bluffs and crashed into the house. Perhaps symbolic of the live-and-let-live nature of many river dwellers, the owners just shrugged and turned it into a tourist attraction. Hours vary; admission.

Continue northwest on Highway 35 for 12 miles to Buffalo City. Challenging and gorgeous, the road plunges and rises, turns and rolls, and nary a mile goes by without something of interest whipping past your window. If you're making this stretch come evening on a clear day, you're blessed and appreciate the grandeur that can be river life.

Soon you'll roll up to one of Wisconsin's smallest state parks—*Merrick State Park,* where the big river seems to spread almost forever (damming caused the widening yaw). The park features campsites plunked right next to the water in semi-secluded spots.

Just off Highway 35 to the west, Buffalo City was for a long time the smallest incorporated city in the United States. Now it's nearly 1,000 friendly folks, and it makes for a great stop off, if only to experience one of its many city parks. One park contains the original 1861 jail. The town also sports a riverside walking trail.

Drive northwest 6 miles on Highway 35 to Alma. For a burg its size, Alma has to be the longest Mississippi River town, seemingly starting miles and miles south of the town's nucleus. To know when, exactly, you've arrived, keep your eyes open for Twelve Mile Bluff towering above Alma. Riverboat pilots used this as a navigational aid in the nineteenth century.

Alma retains the charm of its 1850s founding by Swiss pioneers, with dozens of century-old buildings dotting the town. The gentrification quotient has remained low; thus, the appeal is wonderfully underdone. Just wandering around the town and lugging yourself up the bluffs on the carved stairs is fun, but you can also use the car to wind up and around the "dugways"—as locals call the bluff country roads backing off the town: fantastic scenic drives. (Easiest spot to appreciate the view would be at *Buena Vista Park* along County Road E behind the town.)

For sights, otherwise, *Lock and Dam 4* has the largest fishing float on the Mississippi River, with over three dozen species of fish caught in the vicinity.

Continue northwest for 9 miles to Nelson. Just north of Alma, at the mouth of the Buffalo River, is *Buffalo Slough,* low wetlands charged with water from myriad sources. Some of the greatest timber piles of Wisconsin's storied lumbering past were found here when jams of logs floated down the Chippewa, Saint Croix, and Eau Claire Rivers collected here. So concentrated were these floats that it caused a virtual monopoly on the northern timber trade, with resulting shoot-em-up disputes between disagreeing participants. This is also the spot you'll find *Rieck's Lake Park,* with some of the state's best wildlife viewing. This is the prime spot statewide to get a view of tundra swans (especially in late fall and early winter).

In Nelson, stop by the fifth-generation, family-owned *Nelson Cheese Factory,* (715) 673-4725, which churns out lots of varieties—you have to get the cheese curds. Tours are offered.

Continue northwest on Highway 35 for 4 miles. At the confluence of the Mississippi and Chippewa Rivers is a superlative jewel—the *Tiffany Bottoms Wildlife Area,* which spreads along the Chippewa River from here for over 12,000 total acres. This region was so rugged (and wet) that it took until the 1930s and its ambitious Depression-era WPA projects that roads could branch into its topographic hardiness. Even today there are more boat landings around these parts than parking lots, and abandoned old roads snake every which way. These can be explored, using caution, of course, and an active respect for private property. The berry picking is great.

Drive northwest on Highway 35 for another 4 miles to Pepin. We've already seen *Lake Pepin* on the Minnesota side; now take in a sunset over the lake from the Wisconsin side. If so, you'll realize why William Cullen Bryant once sat here and pondered, impelling him to write, "Lake Pepin ought to be visited in the summer by every poet and painter in the land." Perhaps owing to this splendorous beauty, Wisconsin and Minnesota actually quibbled for decades over where precisely the river channel—and thus, the state boundary—lay. Pepin is actually quite wide by Great River Road measures, backing well off the river and seemingly lacking the usual crenellated, sentinel bluffs.

Many visitors are drawn to the area because author Laura Ingalls Wilder, of *Little House on the Prairie* fame, was born near here in 1867. To commemorate the event, a wayside park and replica of the cabin she was born in are located about 7 miles north of Pepin on County Road CC.

Continue northwest for 7 miles to Stockholm. Up the road sweeps, followed by a gut-busting descent. One mile southeast of town, you can see the river valley from a historic overlook where Nicholas Perrot built a fort in 1686 and laid claim to all of the Mississippi's drainage, "no matter how remote."

Stockholm was almost named "Swedenburg" when it was founded, but this was too close to a religious movement at the time, so the Scandinavian capital's name had to do. This Stockholm may seem downright vacant, yet spend a few minutes and you'll discover how much there actually is here.

Start at the old post office, underneath which you'll find the *Swedish Institute,* home to immigrant memorabilia and lots of nineteenth century artifacts. Then, you just wander about. Splendid little gardens, a great source of local pride, are everywhere. Shops here specialize in artisanry and, especially, Amish crafts. The town hosts annual art fairs that have become huge events.

Drive north on Highway 35 for 14 miles to Bay City. North of Stockholm, the Great River Road turns practical, forsaking the eye-level grandeur of earlier miles. Not boring, simply efficient.

Replica of the cabin Laura Ingalls Wilder was born in near Pepin. Thomas Huhti

About 5 miles along, tiny Maiden Rock, the story goes, was named in honor of a Native American "maiden" who preferred a plunge off a local bluff to an arranged marriage. Much happier is its reputation today as another artist haven. Anglers also love the trout landed from the Rush River north of town.

Quick Trip Option. Just south of Maiden Rock, you can take a jaunt east on County Road AA to 20th Avenue, an official Wisconsin rustic road. North of town, you can make a lovely loop along the Rush River by turning right on 385th Street, paralleling the river to the bridge, then returning via County Road A (an official scenic drive highway). This has some of western Wisconsin's best birding spots.

Bay City is a hardy little town. West of here is Trenton Island, a place that is perhaps even hardier (though some prefer to tack on "fool" before that adjective). That's because the big old river regularly wades in and swallows up the island, yet none of the 100 or so residents wants to leave, even with official state/local/federal "suggestions" that they do so. Stop by and get an appreciation for the can-do pioneer ethic.

Continue northeast on Highway 35 for 23 miles to Prescott. From a few vantage points in town you get a bird's-eye view of the mighty sister rivers—the disparately colored Saint Croix and Mississippi Rivers (the steely blue Saint Croix clashes with the Big Muddy) as they meld into one giant behemoth rolling southward.

This, the state's westernmost community, was among Wisconsin's original settlements, platted by a freelance Indian agent acting as intermediary for controlling interests back East and profiteers in Saint Paul. Given its strategic location, its ultimate survival was assured.

Right near the junction of U.S. Highway 10 and Highway 35 at 233 Broad Street North in downtown Prescott sits the *Prescott Welcome and Heritage Center,* (715) 262-3284 and (800) 4-PIERCE. In addition to travel information, it has lots of exhibits on local history.

Prescott has really but one "sight," but it's a good one. *Mercord Park* sits high above the town and offers commanding views of the two rivers. In the park you'll also find a restored bridge gear house from the original bridge spanning the river here. Generally someone is around here May to October, Friday–Sunday afternoons.

From Prescott, take U.S. Highway 10 west for 3.5 miles to U.S. Highway 61. Turn left (south) and proceed 2 miles back into Minnesota and downtown Hastings.

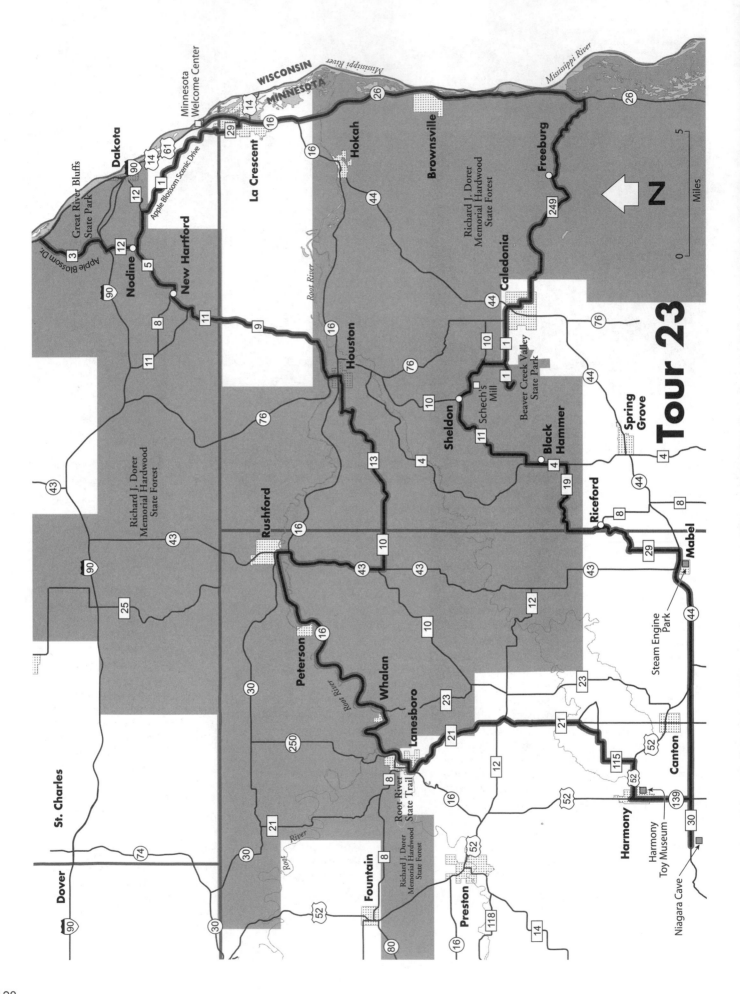

Tour 23

128

Tour 23
Old Order Amish, Apples, and Valleys

La Crescent—Houston—Rushford—Lanesboro—Harmony—Mabel—Caledonia—Brownsville—La Crescent

Distance: approximately 155 miles

This tour represents a thumbnail-sized piece of our map, but what a treat this tiny corner of Minnesota offers. We experience one of the shortest but most gorgeous scenic drives in the state (apple blossoms everywhere!), fabulous parks, a chapter of the Laura Ingalls Wilder saga, classic undulating bluff-lined valleys, and, to top it all off, a visit to Minnesota Amish country.

The scenery itself provides a geological education. During the ultimate glacial epoch, southeastern Minnesota was inexplicably "saved" from the ravages of the bulldozing glacial advances. Somehow, the walls of ice wrapped completely around the area. The resulting "Driftless Area" sports the variegated heights other Midwestern areas now lack, along with the resulting deep valleys and gorges caused by melting ice. Millennia after millennia of accidental land-forming processes has resulted in splendid driving, as the tiny roads rise and dip in a soothing regularity.

Start your tour at the junction of State Highway 14/61 and I-90 a few miles north of La Crescent. Here, at the *Minnesota Welcome Center,* is the best place in the area to start this lovely tour. In addition to providing the usual collection of informative travel literature, the center has a nice outdoor viewing platform with tables and telescopes to get an eyeful of Mississippi River traffic to the east.

From the welcome center, drive south on Highway 14/61 for about 2 miles to North 4th Street in La Crescent (look for a convenience store on your right). Turn right and drive a short distance to North Elm Street (also County Road 29). Turn right (north) and look for the first of many apple-adorned signs for the *Apple Blossom Scenic Drive.* This 17-mile drive to the north of La Crescent is packed with gorgeous scenery. It's so nice that many folks never finish the tour, so enraptured are they by the scenic mileage.

Apples as an economic staple in Minnesota? Around here, one can't help but notice the family farms dotted with apple trees. During blossom season (usually mid-May), to the horizon one sees undulating hills dotted with trees splashed with

color. Over three dozen varieties are available. During the third week of September, the *Apple Festival* runs concurrent with the harvest at the Abnet Field grounds on the south side of La Crescent, when orchard tours supplement the King Apple Grande Parade.

Apples dominate the scene around here. As the road goes up, however, other agricultural pursuits arise. Contented cows chew cud beside apple-red barns. Dense stands of trees are numerous; it was trees and their timber that originally drew the first settlers, after all. A couple of miles north of La Crescent, pull off into a parking area for a superb view of the Mississippi River and Lake Onalaska. This big river lake is dotted with windsurfers and sailboats. Also scan the horizon for migrating waterfowl, including tundra swans.

Follow the Apple Blossom Drive along CR 29, which becomes County Road 1 in Winona County, then left on County Road 12 to its junction with County Road 3; turn right on CR 3 and follow it north to its terminus at Highway 61. Along the way, *Great River Bluffs State Park* lives up to its name on a prominent perch overlooking the Mississippi River. Wandering along the many trails snaking the grounds, you'll come upon a number of overlooks with dramatic vistas, especially in October. Birders go batty over the plethora of songbirds, wild turkeys, eagles, and hawks, too.

Backtrack on CR 3 to CR 12, then drive south about 2 miles to Nodine. There, turn right on County Road 5 and take it to County Road 8 at New Hartford. Drive west on CR 8 a short distance to Township Road 2. Take

Bobo's Favorite Rest Stop

The Minnesota Welcome Center north of La Crescent was a hit with this author's yellow lab, Bobo. This huge pooch often takes up half of the few square feet of animal areas at most rest stops, many of which offer neither tables nor shade trees. Here, a seeming acre-plus of tree-studded leg room offers lots of joyful sniffing. Bobo has also met many a mammalian representative of the "gopher" state here!

He also can get a lot of exercise in by walking a quarter mile down to the area along the Mississippi and its sloughs to Lock and Dam No. 7. Along the way there are sandbars, canoe and boat landings, piers, and rough fire pits to be explored. (Bring mosquito repellant.) Obviously, Bobo isn't welcome at the lock and dam (river currents are too dangerous to dog-paddle in). A parking lot is there, along with a viewing platform for up-close-and personal views of the mammoth ships gracefully slipping beneath as they're raised eight feet in the lock-through process.

this southwest to County Road 11, which becomes County Road 9. Follow this road into Houston and the junction with State Highway 16. (The total distance from Nodine is about 13 miles.) CR 11 and CR 9 follow aptly named Silver Creek, glistening a metallic sheen in the summer sun. Once an important port on the Root River, Houston later became known for dairy and poultry, along with the dozens of springs. Today most visitors know it as the eastern terminus of the 36-mile-long *Root River Trail*, where bikers pass by limestone ridges, wildflowers, and classic railroad trestles.

The best place to stop is at the *Houston Nature Center*, 215 West Plum Street, a block north of Highway 16, (507) 896-HOOT. The facility is legendary as the home of Alice the owl (a rehabilitated injured owl). The center has also replanted more than 100 varieties of native grasses and flowers to reconstruct once-lost prairies. The bluebells are spectacular! Hours are Memorial Day weekend to Labor Day, Thursday–Monday, 9:30 a.m.–4:30 p.m. (until noon Thursday and Sunday).

From Houston, drive west on Highway 16 for 1 mile to Poppy Road; turn left and go a short distance to County Road 13. Turn right (west) and drive for about 11 miles to State Highway 43 (a few miles before Highway 43, CR 13 becomes County Road 10). Along the way, you pass by the *Wet Bark Recreation Area*, part of the Richard J. Dorer Memorial Hardwood State Forest. Hiking and ski trails pass by and along lovely overlooks; some loops rise over 300 feet.

Turn right (north) on Highway 43 and drive 6 miles to State Highway 16 in Rushford. Just west of town, off State Highway 30, lovely *Magelssen Bluff* has a natural area and park, with a 50-foot Christmas tree atop the bluff. The town also has an old flour mill two blocks west of Rush Creek off the Root River.

La Crescent's Apples

Starting in the 1850s, raspberry and strawberry production began to be buttressed by a newcomer: apples. Playing Johnny Appleseed was one John Harris, who showed up in 1856 and planted the first trees on the west side of La Crescent. His secret to success? Likely a combination of the big river's microclimate and Lake Onalaska ameliorating bitter winters and spring, along with the long bluff lines protecting flora in their lee sides. Harris insisted, however, that the clay and sandy loam soil also played a part. Within a decade, Harris had nearly two dozen apple varieties being displayed at fairs and the industry was off and running. His wasn't an immediate success—he was still nearly wiped out in harsher winters—but he proved apples could thrive in the area. For this he's often called the "godfather" of Minnesota's horticulture industry.

Sign marking one of the loveliest drives in the state. Thomas Huhti

Turn left on Highway 16 and follow it for about 15 miles into Lanesboro. On this superbly rollicking ride, the road mimics every move of the squiggly Root River. And the topography, even for such a forested state, hints at something special. Another tidbit: Locals like to tout the fact that a lack of standing water around here, along with multifarious bird species, makes the place uniquely mosquito-free in summer.

Three biological zones interconnect in these parts. Classic woods meet prairie, with a touch of oak savannah. As the road rises and falls through tiny Peterson and Whalan toward Lanesboro, it's hard not to notice an ethnic addition to the usual mix of Norwegians, Irish, and German/Dutch. The Old Order Amish are focused mostly around Harmony farther south, but the clippety-clop of horse-drawn carriages is prevalent hereabouts too.

Lanesboro defines quaint, with the carefully preserved structures downtown in toto on the National Register of Historic Places. This town of fewer than a thousand full-time residents has been named to nearly half a dozen national "best of" lists for historic preservation, arts support, and even outdoor sports. First stop for many people is at the *Lanesboro Area Chamber of Commerce*, 100 Milwaukee Road, (800) 944-2670 (www.lanesboro.com). Downtown, wander about *Sylvan Park*, where the Amish sell baked goods, produce, and handicrafts. Other park sections sport spring-fed trout ponds, a stone dam, campground (with a

A common scene in Amish country. Thomas Huhti

cool, free library lending office), and lots of gurgling waters.

In the vicinity of the park, stop by the *Cornucopia Art Center*, where more than 70 artists show their works; within this structure the *Commonweal Theatre Company*, (800) 657-7025, performs throughout the year.

Don't forget too that Lanesboro is a recreation hub, with biking along the Root River Trail, and canoeing on the Root River.

At the junction of Highway 16 and County Road 21 on the south edge of Lanesboro, turn left (south) on County Road 21. Follow this for about 9 miles to County Road 115. Turn right and follow the road west and south to U.S. Highway 52, a total of about 3.5 miles; turn right (west) and drive 2 miles to Harmony. The roll from Lanesboro to Harmony is a beaut—classic agrarian stretches, typical southeastern Minnesota bluff country hillocks, and stand after stand of oak, maple, and hickory trees. You can stop your car every mile here, hop out, and start counting the wildlife. Nearly 50 bird species have been spotted along the route. But don't forget to take it slow and be alert. These parts are populated by many Amish and buggies and horses are ever-present.

There's an interesting story behind Harmony's melodious name. Apparently, just after the town was formed, a community meeting to choose a name devolved into an acrimonious shouting match. One man purportedly stood and pleaded, "Let us have harmony!" The crowd was struck silent by its appropriateness and, well, the rest is history!

The *Harmony Visitor Information Center*, 15 Second Street NW, (800) 288-7153 (www.harmony.mn.us), is right off Highway 52. With so much to do and so little time, these folks help make the most of it. They can, for starters, provide an exhaustive list of organized tours to Amish settlements. Most tours take in a few Amish farms to see centuries-old farming and handicraft methods up close. (The handcrafted woodwork and quilts are pricey but one of the best souvenirs in the state. If you're short of cash, try some delicious baked goods.) Guides are well versed in the cultural aspects of the Old Order and its unique lifestyle, so if you know little about the Amish, it's a good opportunity to get a crash course—and a lovely drive in the countryside. *Note: Sundays are days of rest for the Amish and tours are not offered.*

Two long-running tour operators are *Michel's Amish Tours,* 45 Main Avenue, (800) 752-6474; and *Amish Country Tours,* (507) 886-2303, in the depot on the village green.

The *Harmony Toy Museum*, 30 Main Avenue South, (507) 867-3380, is a cheery little place. And who wouldn't be happy when wandering around the aisles with shelves chock-full of some 4,000-plus toys, historical photographs, and even the occasional farm implement.

In keeping with the rest of the town, recreational opportunities are rooted in the past. Nothing beats a roll around the old-fashioned wood-floored rink at *Harmony Roller Skating Rink* downtown. Even better is the gracefully aging *Jem Theatre* along Main Avenue. This renovated 1940 grand dame is the county's only movie palace.

A wonderful bike trail is the *Harmony-Preston Valley State Trail* stretching north to Preston (from where you can pedal east along the Root River State Trail). One caveat: The 3-mile stretch right in the middle of this ride is steep and difficult.

From Harmony, drive south on State Highway 139 (Main Avenue) for 2.5 miles to Niagara Road (County Road 30). Turn right (west) and drive 2.5 miles. One of the largest caves in the Midwest, *Niagara Cave* boasts a 60-foot waterfall, ancient fossils, even a crystal wedding chapel. Kids love to drop coins into the eerily deep wishing well. The cave's terra firma center, (507) 886-6606, also offers guided tours, picnic grounds, and more. Tours are given every half hour, 9:30 a.m.–5:30 p.m., May–September, reduced hours April and October; admission.

Return east on CR 30 and drive about 15 miles to Mabel, being joined by State Highway 44 halfway along. You can't overlook a place named Mabel, can you? And you certainly can't ignore this town of about 700 after seeing its moniker: "Rural America's Steam Engine Capital." That's not just a lot of hot air either. *Steam Engine Park* is a must-see for its steam engine museum, a thrilling collection of old-fashioned steam-powered agricultural equipment. These monstrosities

The Gentle People

No one knows for sure just how many Amish live in the Midwest. (Hereafter, "Amish" will be used to describe both Amish and Mennonites, with whom Amish are often confused.) Conservative efforts peg the number at close to 100,000, mostly in Ohio, Indiana, and Wisconsin. Minnesota has a large number in its southeastern counties; Harmony's is by far the most concentrated. Families began relocating here in the early 1970s and, at present, approximately 100 families now live in the area. The community has seven one-room schoolhouses.

The base of Amish culture is the community, with two overriding tenets: separation and obedience. The outside world isn't "evil," but it does have a negative influence and distracts one from true actions. Obedience is even more important. The Amish follow an oft-misunderstood idea called *gelassenheit*, loosely translated as "yielding" or "submission." This forms a core to the Ordnung ("Order"), the unwritten set of social mores that one must strictly adhere to or risk being shunned.

Many kinds of Amish exist. Old Order Amish are more conservative, but increasingly progressive communities are taking hold. For example, some will ride in cars, though they won't drive them. Some will use electricity, if it isn't theirs. Some own property. All Amish still cultivate the ethic of hard work, thrift, and community support.

A note on Amish etiquette: **Although the Amish are friendly and curious of outsiders, their privacy must be respected. The Amish view a photograph as a potential for graven images (a Biblical taboo) and, worse, self-pride.**

More important: *slow down*. Always assume there's a buggy with a family and young child in it just over the next hill or around the next bend.

are so imposing that kids (and maybe some adults) can get spooked a bit. Try to get here in late-September for *Steam Engine Days*, when the whole place fires up under a wood-smoke-colored sky; the machines thresh and chop wood in a cacophonous fury.

Quick Trip Option. Norwegian-Americans (or anyone interested in things Norskie) may want to head to Spring Grove, the first Norwegian settlement in Minnesota. In addition to the requisite Viking statue, there's also Norwegian rosemaling on pretty much every window box in the area—and the water tower. Cute gingerbread buildings house a variety of shops. Spring Grove Soda Pop is quite popular. Stand there drinking a bottle and you'd swear you're in 1930. A mom-and-pop team started the shop in 1895, and now the diminutive factory produces a whopping eight flavors. The factory still sells by the bottle. Spring Grove is located about 6 miles east of Mabel on Highway 44.

Drive east of Mabel on Highway 44 a short distance to County Road 29. Turn left (north) and follow this road 5 miles to Riceford (as it bends sharply to the northeast) along Riceford Creek. Along the way you'll pass signs to *Sportsman's Park*, with an old mill pond and a stream offering up trout. CR 29 is dead-eye straight in the beginning, but it starts whipping curves at you three miles out, with super views of the creek valley. The highway bridge in Riceford is a perfect place to park and admire the beauty of small town America. To the northwest of Riceford, there are said to be the remains of an old logging-era settlement; it's difficult to find, however.

Drive north out of Riceford for 2 miles to County Road 19; turn right (east) and continue for 3.5 miles to County Road 4. Turn left (north) and proceed 2 miles to County Road 11 just north of Black Hammer. You'll cruise along the Yucatan Valley, then past the "Black Hammer Stone Lady," a stone formation atop a tree-topped promontory shaped like a hammer (it's not easy to spot). Two miles past that is the 125-year-old Black Hammer Lutheran Church.

Turn right on CR 11 and follow its meandering path for about 6 miles in a northeasterly direction to County Road 10 in Sheldon. Turn right and go for about 2 miles. Just outside Sheldon, you'll want to visit *Schech's Mill*. This structure is Minnesota's only extant water-powered gristmill, a big deal considering the millstone and four stone burrs are original. The exteriors are built of locally quarried limestone. Note that this is private property, not part of Beaver Creek State Park. Tours are only available for a fee; call (507) 896-3481, for information.

Drive on CR 10 to where it turns left (east). Continue straight south for about 1 mile to

One of the monster machines at Steam Engine Park in Mabel. **Thomas Huhti**

County Road 1; turn right (west) and proceed into *Beaver Creek Valley State Park.* With 25-foot-high sandstone and dolomite bluffs suddenly rising from nowhere, this park, (507) 724-2107, offers rugged hiking and spectacular views. Don't mess around during rains however. Flash flooding can be dangerous on the generally tranquil Beaver Creek. South- and west-facing slopes are known for their residual patches of native southern Minnesota prairie plant species. In addition to the many critters dashing through the undergrowth are several rare birds, including many not found elsewhere in the state. You may even be lucky enough to spot the timber rattler in the park. They're not often sighted, but if you do, leave it alone; the species is endangered and protected.

Drive east on CR 1 for 4.5 miles to downtown Caledonia, where it becomes Kingston Street. Turn left (east) onto Main Street, go a few blocks to Winnebago Street, turn right and drive to Adams Street on the southeastern edge of town. Turn left and head east on what becomes County Road 249 to Freeburg, about 7.5 miles away. At the east edge of Caledonia sits a *pioneer village,* a collection of extant village and homesteader structures relocated on site.

Farther along, the road follows the contours of one of the forks of the Crooked Creek, which winds wickedly through a gorgeous valley with the same name. So take it slow. Besides the curves,

wild turkeys seem to pop out every half mile. Up on the bluff lines are old logging trails and dilapidated structures.

At Freeburg. *Saint Nicholas Church* here dates from 1868. Of particular interest is the fossil stone cross in the graveyard.

Continue east on CR 249 for about 4.5 miles to State Highway 26. The area east of Freeburg along CR 249 is dotted with historic log structures. Feel free to disembark and nose around!

At Highway 26, turn left (north) and cruise for 8 miles to *Brownsville.* Not much occupies us for the first 12 or so miles, but there's our old friend, the Mississippi River, off to the right. This is part of the Upper Mississippi Refuge, and, in season, an absolute army of tundra swans (and eagles) can be spotted on these stretches.

Brownsville is one of the state's oldest Mississippi River towns. The town church is listed on the National Register of Historic Places. Bluff caves above the town were used for apple preserving in hot months.

Continue north on Highway 26, which blends into State Highway 16, then into State Highway 14/61. Follow this to its junction with I-90 north of La Crescent, where we began. From Brownsville, the total distance is about 12.5 miles.

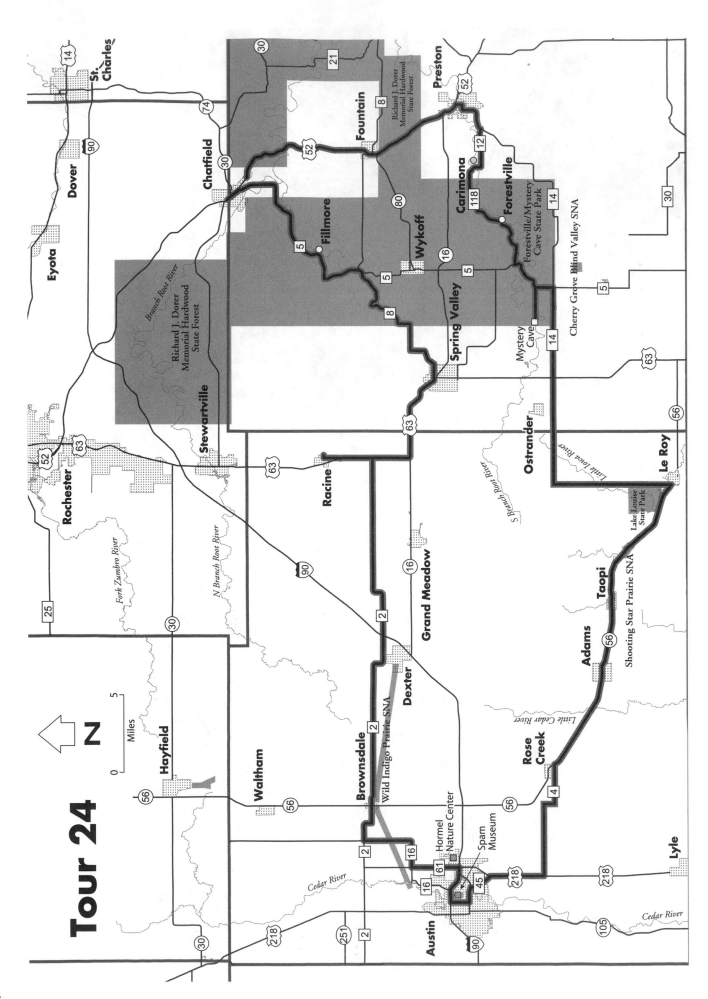

Tour 24

N

Miles
0 5

St. Charles
14
Dover
90
Eyota
90
74
30
Chatfield
30
52
Fillmore
5
Fountain
21
8
Richard J. Dorer Memorial Hardwood State Forest
52
80
Wykoff
5
5
Carimona
118
12
Preston
52
Forestville
14
Forestville/Mystery Cave State Park
Cherry Grove Blind Valley SNA
5
Spring Valley
16
5
8
Mystery Cave
14
63
Rochester
52
63
Branch Root River
Richard J. Dorer Memorial Hardwood State Forest
Stewartville
Fork Zumbro River
25
30
N Branch Root River
63
Racine
63
16
90
S Branch Root River
Ostrander
63
56
Le Roy
Little Iowa River
Lake Louise State Park
56
Hayfield
Waltham
56
56
Grand Meadow
16
2
Dexter
Wild Indigo Prairie SNA
2
Brownsdale
2
16
Shooting Star Prairie SNA
Taopi
Adams
56
Little Cedar River
Rose Creek
56
4
Hormel Nature Center
Spam Museum
61
16
45
2
16
218
218
Lyle
Austin
218
90
251
2
105
Cedar River
Cedar River
30
218

134

Tour 24
Valleys to Prairies . . . and Spam

Preston—Forestville/Mystery Cave State Park—Lake Louise State Park—Le Roy—Taopi—Austin—Racine—Spring Valley—Chatfield—Fountain—Preston

Distance: approximately 135 miles

What a difference a tour makes. Tour 23, which takes in an area east of this one, is dominated by the rolling hills of the Driftless Area and the snaking Root River. Old Order Amish, owls, and acres of bluebells are some of the highlights.

Here, those tucked-away valleys give way slowly, eventually settling down in the flat, open-air prairie expanses. Travelers will find long horizons and impossibly large skies, with the occasional munching bison thrown in, as they travel westward to Austin. For attractions, how about a fascinating mélange of bluff country recreation and geography, the route of Laura Ingalls Wilder, culminating with a pilgrimage to the home of that most American of foods: Spam.

Start your tour in downtown Preston on Fillmore Street. The location of this town, population 1,500, on the Root River is ideal for dams, mills, waterpower, and transportation, all of which contributed to its founding in the late-nineteenth century. Root River tributaries still support the economy today, only instead of timber and flour mills, it's game fish that draws folks today. Throw a dart at an area map and you'll likely hit a blue-ribbon trout stream. In fact, *Outdoor Life* has tabbed this region one of the top 10 trout areas in the country. This would naturally be why an oversized trophy trout sits right along the road in town. Try to visit in mid-May for the *Trout Days* festival, when, in addition to myriad fishing competitions, kids can watch the great fish-themed floats during the parade.

Anglers aren't the only ones drawn to the natural highlights. Preston is also a hub for bikers and hikers who embark from town on not one but two state trails: the *Root River State Trail* and the *Preston-Harmony State Trail*. The Root River trailhead is located four blocks south of State Highway 16 just off Pleasant Street.

Drive west on Fillmore Street (also County Road 12), then turn south and follow the road for about 5 miles southwest to tiny Cari-

A tribute to what draws many people to the Preston area. Thomas Huhti

135

Two nineteenth-century structures in Forestville/Mystery Cave State Park. Courtesy of Forestville/Mystery Cave State Park.

mona. Turn left (west) on County Road 118 and proceed for another 5 miles to the entrance to _Forestville/Mystery Cave State Park_. The park, (507) 352-5111, is a part of one of southern Minnesota's most visited (and most varied) attractions. Itself part of a larger state land area, the park houses the remaining structures of an 1800s homesteading community. In its heyday after the Civil War, the town had well over 100 residents. Sadly, the railroad squashed its plans, and by the turn of the twentieth century, most residents had decamped. Today costumed guides lead visitors about the restored Meigher General Store, where clerks still "stock" the shelves with period consumables. Later, the well-to-do general store proprietor's house and grounds are worth a stop-off. Also, have a chat with the workers toiling in the gardens. Hours are Memorial Day weekend–Labor Day, Tuesday–Friday, 10 a.m.–5 p.m.; Saturday, noon–6 p.m.; Sunday, noon–5 p.m.; weekends only in September and October; admission.

From Forestville State Park, continue west on CR 118, then County Road 5, about 5 miles, following the signs to _Mystery Cave_. As you drive, you'll experience a topographical hodge-podge: limestone bluffs, hills, valleys, apple orchards, agriculture, and trout streams. You're also in a transition between two biotic "zones"—tall-grass prairie and deciduous forest. An amazing diversity of flora and fauna is apparent, even from the road. Rare glacial snails share the park with endangered timber rattlers; both are well outnumbered by white-tailed deer. Over 175 species of

birds have been spotted within the two parks, including the more pervasive wild turkey. Listen, too, for the sonorous night call of owls.

Minnesota's southeastern region is populated by freakish "karst" geological formations—sinkholes, soaring outcroppings, and the like. No place best typifies this oddball landscape better than _Mystery Cave_, (507) 352-5111. The longest cave in Minnesota at well over 13 miles (passages strike out every which way), the subterranean chamber of weird and wonderful is well worth a visit. Eerie dripping punctuates the silence. Intermittent floodlights reveal turquoise-hued pools. Look for fossils in the walls. During dry summers the entire South Branch Root River above it will sink into the caves through its gravel beds. It is a cool 48 degrees, so dress warmly. One-hour tours are available constantly (10 a.m.–4 p.m., until 5 p.m. in summer); two-hour, three-quarter-mile tours are available summer weekends only; admission.

From Mystery Cave return east to CR 5, turn right (south) and go about 1 mile to County Road 14. Turn right and drive west, then south, for 16 miles to _Lake Louise State Park_. As you leave the Mystery Cave area, look about you: This area was heavily mined for iron, and residuals can be seen in the bluff sides.

Lake Louise Park, (507) 324-5249, perhaps best represents this tour's fascinating diversity in flora. In one short drive one can experience woodland oak and maple/basswood forests mixing with prairie and savanna. Come spring and summer, photo hounds descend on the park for its carpets of wildflowers—you'll swear you were in nineteenth-century Minnesota. The 6 miles of hiking trails are relatively flat and easy. And finally the lake, the only one in the area, is sure to be a big hit with the kids. A recently completed 12-mile paved recreation trail runs west from the park to Taopi.

From Lake Louise State Park, drive south on CR 14 for 2 miles to Le Roy. This town of fewer than 1,000 people is one of four communities along Highway 56 from here to Rose Creek to the west that features legendary Prairie School architecture, designed by devotee students of Frank Lloyd Wright's school. Here, the *First State Bank* right downtown (can't miss it in this burg) is a shining example of Wright's influence.

Le Roy is also the proposed eastern terminus of a paved recreation trail from Le Roy to Austin. The so-called Shooting Star State Trail would parallel (for 28 miles, anyway) State Highway 56—the auto version of the same name. Both take in gorgeous wildflowers, architecture, and a look at prairie land that exists *almost* as it did in the nineteenth century.

In Le Roy, turn right (west) on Highway 56 and go about 8 miles to Taopi. In the early twentieth century, this tiny community was a hotspot of the suffrage movement; virtually all the town's leaders and the majority of business owners were women. Granted, it's a thumbnail-sized community, but progress is progress. Today, it has an amazing draw for nature lovers. Just west of the hole-in-the-wall post office (the state's smallest operational postal center) is a parking area for *Taopi Prairie.* This mile-long "strip prairie" is one

of the state's last native prairie and oak savannah stands. Wander the path and look for big bluestem, prairie coneflower, blazing star, and showy goldenrod, among others. Take your camera.

Continue west for 12 miles on Highway 56 to State Highway 4 in Rose Creek. Turn left (west) onto CR 4 and drive 7 miles to U.S. Highway 218. Turn right (north) and proceed for about 3 miles to County Road 45 (10th Drive SE) just south of *Austin.* Follow CR 45 for slightly more than 1 mile to East Oakland Ave; turn left (east) and go a short distance to Main Street. Turn right and go 3 blocks. Take the picturesque drive through the carefully gentrified downtown proper area of Austin, which spreads casually along the banks of the Cedar River, two of whose bights form lovely lakes in the town. At 329 North Main Street, the *Austin Convention and Visitors Bureau,* (800) 444-5713 (www.austinmn.com), has all the information you need on the wheres and hows of this community.

Though the town is attractive in its own right, when speaking of Austin, the names Hormel and its world-famous product, Spam, are inextricably linked. Hormel Foods Corporation has been an economic anchor of southern Minnesota for nearly a century.

Consider these Hormel factoids: The massive plant's nine-story canning tower was for a long time the tallest building in the region; the company sucks in raw materials from hundreds and hundreds of miles away; the company turned profits even during the Great Depression; and of course, Hormel invented the famous product, Spam. This

Minnesota's smallest post office in Taopi. Thomas Huhti

venerable product is the top reason that so many road trippers flock to this town today. (See the sidebar "It's a Spam, Spam, Spam, Spam, Spam World" on this page.) The unofficial moniker of Austin is, of course, Spamtown.

From the convention and visitors bureau, consider a short (in distance) walking tour. First, walk north to 4th Ave NW and turn left. Walk west two blocks. The name Hormel still comes into play here. The *George Hormel Historic Home*, 208 NW 4th Avenue, (507) 433-4243, is the erstwhile home of the founder of Hormel foods. Gazing at this mansion, one can appreciate how successful his diminutive 1887 butcher shop became. Of course, the interiors are spectacularly ornate, with original furnishings and detailing. Don't miss the rare and intricate honeycombed woodwork. Hours are daily 10 a.m.–4 p.m., June–August, weekdays only the rest of the year; admission.

Walk east past North Main Street to 125 Northeast 4th Avenue. The eye-catching *Paramount Theatre*, (507) 434-0934, opened in 1929, is a Spanish Colonial gem designed for vaudeville and first-run movies. The interiors are magnificent; you actually feel yourself part of Spain. Tours are available by appointment only.

Here's a local secret. Austin has plenty of history and culture, but a favorite place to relax (or duck away from a downpour) is to head two blocks east to the *Austin Public Library*, (507) 433-2391. This gorgeous, $4 million new library spreads across more than 26,000 acres overlooking a millpond. Glass-enclosed "porches" overlook the sparkling waters and make for a lovely place to peruse a newspaper (and, for the modernists, there is Internet access).

Return to your car. Drive north on North Main Street approximately 10 blocks to the *Spam Museum*. Opened in 2001, the "museum," 1937 Spam Boulevard, (800) LUV-SPAM (www.spam.com), gives long-overdue recognition to one of the world's most famous brand names. Even for vegetarians, this place has to be experienced. In fact, the whole tongue-in-cheek spirit of the place is a delight. Master of satire and irony, comedian Al Franken, pops up as a Spam quiz-show host; the hilarious Monty Python's Flying Circus "Spam Skit" is re-created to peals of laughter; the management has even given a funny nod to "spam e-mail"—with their own cyber Spam-café! On the more product placement side, you can suit up and "make" Spam and learn the history of this amazing canned product. Hours are Monday–Saturday, 10 a.m.–5 p.m.; Sunday, noon–4 p.m.; free.

From the Spam Museum, travel north on Main Street a short distance to 15th Avenue NE. Bear right and follow signs to I-90. Travel east on I-90 two exits to 21st Street NE. Exit and travel north to the *Hormel Nature Center*. Nature lovers will adore this special nugget, (507) 437-7519, just a hop off the interstate. The nearly 300 acres offer 9 miles of lovely strolling along trails winding through native Minnesota prairie, hardwood forest, and wetlands. Trails are maintained for cross-country skiing in winter; one is handicapped accessible. Many streams gurgle through the property, perfect for canoeists who want to spend a lazy day paddling. Families will love the exhaustive offerings of naturalist-led programs and activities; travelers report the interpretive center's staff to be informative and helpful. Hours for the interpretive/information center are Monday–Friday, 9 a.m.–noon and 1–5 p.m.; Sunday, 1–5 p.m.; trail hours are 6 a.m.–10 p.m., daily.

Travel north on 21st Street NE (County Road 61) to County Road 16. Take that north, east, and north for 7 miles to County Road 2. Turn right (east) and drive 2.5 miles to Brownsdale. Any science or astronomy buff, or anyone who's seen the uplifting movie *October Sky* (about budding rocket scientists in the post-*Sputnik* era) will appreciate this community's little-known contribution to rocketry. On January 15, 1957, high school students from Austin's Pacelli High School launched a 4-foot-10-inch rocket to an altitude of 1,642 feet—with a live mouse inside. A later rocket climbed to 3,250 feet. Sadly, both mice died. The first launch was noteworthy because it predated *Sputnik* by nine months. This Minnesota craft didn't reach orbit, but it was one of the first rocket launches of its kind in the United States. David Brinkley and ABC News visited and brought the small community ever-so-brief fame.

It's a Spam, Spam, Spam, Spam, Spam World

Let us consider for a moment Spam. No joke! What better representation of Americana than this lovingly processed food?

Come on: You know you love it. Even self-professed foodies crave this wonderfully gelatinous comfort food. Who doesn't feel the pangs of Midwestern nostalgia for a sandwich of fried Spam on white bread with lettuce and mayo?

Spam has entered our American food consciousness as perhaps no other has. It predated the global tentacle reach of McDonald's by a generation. Even in these fat-freak-out days of dieting, Spam holds on strong (perhaps due to a combination of people tired of being preached to about lower fat intake or those dedicated to the thankfully-fat-friendly Atkins diet). Every small-town American can likely recall lunches of Spam, but World War II soldiers probably loathe it as much as love it. Part of Army rations, Spam found its way, perhaps inexplicably, into the diets of South Pacific islanders, where even today it remains a diet mainstay. Who can forget Monty Python's famous skit, wherein they, dressed as Vikings, simply sang, "Spam, Spam, Spam, Spam . . . " ad nauseam. You want global reach? What do you call those ever-present e-mails in your computer inbox? There's the grudgingly respectful mark of a well-known product.

Continue east on CR 2 for 20 miles all the way to U.S. Highway 63. Turn left (north) and travel for 2 miles into tiny Racine. Turn east off Highway 63 onto Main Street and travel until you see a city park (at Oak Avenue). Turn right after the park and travel two blocks. Here is *B.E.A.R.C.A.T. Hollow,* (507) 378-2221, and before you ask, the name means "Beautiful, Endangered, and Rare—Conservation and Therapy." This farm cares for orphaned and injured wild animals and allows the animals to recuperate, while allowing humans an interactive and educational opportunity. There are lots of bears but also some magnificent lions and tigers. Among the highlights are the world's largest black bear and a 1,200-pound tiger! Mini-train tours are led by the very nice owner and are lots of fun. Hours are Wednesday–Sunday, 11 a.m.–5 p.m., May 15th to Labor Day; admission (pricey, but worth it).

Return south on Highway 63, then east, and drive into Spring Valley, for a total of about 9 miles. Spring Valley is a lovely riverside town best known today for its historical connection to the famed scribe of the *Little House on the Prairie* books, Laura Ingalls Wilder. The local Methodist church, now a museum, is where Laura, Almanzo, and Rose Wilder attended services in 1890 and 1891. Operated by the Spring Valley Historical Society, (507) 346-2763, the museum houses memorabilia of regional history in addition to photos of the Wilder family. Note also the gorgeous Italian stained glass windows—some of which date from 1715. Hours are Monday–Saturday, 9 a.m.–5 p.m., June–August; Sundays only in June and October. Across the street, at 220 Courtland, the society also operates the *Pioneer Home Museum,* a nicely preserved structure built in 1865 that contains furniture and artifacts from the period.

Spring Valley is also in close proximity to Forestville/Mystery Cave State Park (see above). As such, wildlife viewing is superb. The best time to come is mid-May, when Spring Valley's *Bird Fest* includes guided walks by ornithologists. You won't find a better way to gain knowledge about the area's bountiful nature.

From Highway 63 in Spring Valley, turn left on Farmer Street and follow it east as it becomes County Road 8. Take this for about 10 miles to tiny Fillmore, where CR 8 splits off to the right. Continue north on County Road 5. All the way from Spring Valley, the road rolls incredibly, bends and twists suddenly, with amazing vistas all around you. (An incredible number of streams seem to gurgle next to the road.) All along here, you'll see more evidence of the area's unique karst topography.

Take CR 5 for about 11 miles to U.S. Highway 52; turn left (north) and drive a short distance into downtown Chatfield. This pleasant community is known as "Bandtown" for its rollicking brass band which tours through town occasionally during summer in their bandwagon. It's great fun if you happen to be in town during a "performance." If not, free concerts are offered Thursdays at 7:30 p.m., mid-June to mid-July. At the intersection of Highway 52 and County Road 2/30 downtown sits a *tourist information kiosk* and, nearby, a couple of tiny *museums.* The town's information providers can give you lots of tips on local scenic drives in every direction from downtown (they have many). However, unique is the *Haven Wall* on Winona Hill, built with stones from around the world. To get there, drive one block northwest of this intersection, then turn right and follow the road to the right past a bed and breakfast.

From Chatfield, drive south on Highway 52 for 8 miles to Fountain. "Sink Hole Capital of the USA," the signs around here proclaim. Yes, you're still in the heart of karst country, and the limestone caverns dotting the countryside also offered up numerous springs and, well, "fountains" used by early settlers. The easiest to see is right on the outskirts of town near the welcome sign; another is near the Root River State Trail trailhead off County Road 8—this one has a great viewing platform standing above it. At the junction of Highway 52 and CR 8, the *Fillmore County History Center,* (507) 268-4449, has one of southern Minnesota's largest collections of antique agricultural equipment, with more than 40 vintage Oliver tractors on site. In addition, the center has everything from nineteenth-century handmade tools to airplanes. Hours are summer, Monday–Friday, 9 a.m.–4 p.m.; weekends 1–4:30 p.m.; weekdays only the rest of the year.

From Fountain, drive south 6 miles on Highway 52 to return to Preston.

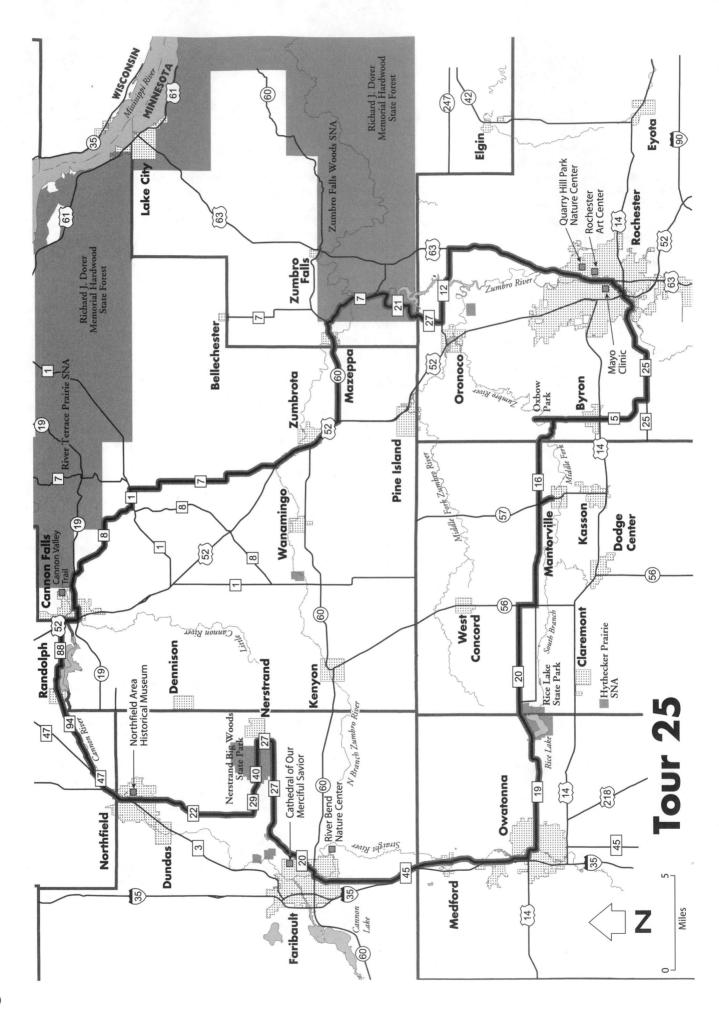

WISCONSIN

MINNESOTA

Mississippi River

61

35

61

63

60

Richard J. Dorer Memorial Hardwood State Forest

Richard J. Dorer Memorial Hardwood State Forest

247

42

Elgin

Eyota

90

Lake City

Quarry Hill Park Nature Center

Rochester Art Center

Rochester

14

52

River Terrace Prairie SNA

1

Bellechester

7

Zumbro Falls Woods SNA

Zumbro Falls

7

21

12

27

63

Zumbro River

63

19

Mazeppa

60

52

Oronoco

52

Zumbro River

Oxbow Park

Byron

Mayo Clinic

25

7

Zumbrota

52

Pine Island

5

25

14

19

7

1

8

Wanamingo

Middle Fork Zumbro River

Middle Fork

16

57

Mantorville

Kasson

Dodge Center

Cannon Valley Trail

8

1

52

8

60

Middle Fork

West Concord

56

Claremont

Hythecker Prairie SNA

56

Cannon Falls

52

Randolph

88

19

Dennison

Little Cannon River

Nerstrand

Kenyon

60

20

Rice Lake State Park

South Branch

Rice Lake

47

94

Cannon River

Northfield Area Historical Museum

Nerstrand Big Woods State Park

27

40

29

27

Cathedral of Our Merciful Savior

River Bend Nature Center

N Branch Zumbro River

19

14

218

47

22

Owatonna

45

Northfield

Dundas

3

20

45

35

Medford

14

35

Faribault

Cannon Lake

60

Straight River

Tour 25

N

0 5 Miles

Tour 25
Big Medicine and River Valleys

Rochester—Mantorville—Owatanna—Faribault—Nerstrand-Big Woods State Park—
Northfield—Cannon Falls—Zumbrota—Rochester

Distance: approximately 160 miles

The highlight of this tour is hardly found on a country road, but it's something every visitor to southern Minnesota should experience: the Mayo Clinic in Rochester. This behemoth facility is the economic anchor for a region and draws "visitors" from around the world. What they discover is a city with a small-town flair, a lovely amalgam of history and modernity.

However, back on those blue highways, we discover so much more in this amazing area. In a grand counter-clockwise swoop we take in some of southern Minnesota's grandest natural splendor, a couple of its most precious and historically maintained communities, along with more classic rolling countryside vistas.

And, of course, from here we can already feel the pull of the Minnesota River. We won't taste it yet, but the tiny tributaries that feed it along our route reveal part of its history. Exploration and settlement routes have become, for us, a splendid drive!

Start your tour in downtown Rochester. No matter which direction you come from, all roads (and plenty of signs) will lead you toward the world-famous Mayo clinic downtown. The best place to begin your tour is at the *Rochester Convention and Visitors Bureau*, 150 South Broadway, Suite A, (800) 634-8277 (www.rochestercvb.org). Plan to park your vehicle in one of the area's plentiful lots, so that you can be ready for a short (in distance, not necessarily time) *walking tour* of this progressive city.

Perhaps no urban center better represents a superlative mixture of medium-sized city with small-town flavor than Rochester. The streets are wide, rarely congested, and *clean*. Greenspace carpets the entirety. The economy booms along, even in the swoons of the late 1990s. This is due mostly to two major employers: IBM (the largest IBM complex under one roof) and the legendary Mayo Clinic. Numerous national media have crowed about the livability status of the city, and it perennially ranks among the favorite places to live in the United States.

From the Convention and Visitors Bureau, walk three blocks west, then one block north to the entrance to the Mayo Clinic. Heads of state, kings, celebrities, and the fabulously wealthy often fly in to Rochester's *international* airport for state-of-the-art technology and cutting-edge medical research at the renowned *Mayo Clinic*, (507) 284-9258. Serving the common folks as well, this enormous complex dominates the heart of downtown, in spirit as much as size. This, the world's largest interconnected medical facility (more than 47 buildings), has been leading the world in medical research since its inception. Public tours and video presentations are given weekdays at 10 a.m.; a public tour of the facility's extraordinary art and architecture is offered Tuesday–Thursday at 1:30 p.m.; free, though phoning first is recommended.

From the Mayo Clinic, return to your vehicle. Drive north on 1st Avenue SE two blocks to Center Street. Turn right and drive to the Mayo Civic Center. Rochester is a city for art mavens, and nowhere is that more in evidence than at the state-of-the-art event facility, the *Rochester Art Center*, 320 East Center Street, (507) 282-8629. It has benefited greatly from local philanthropy, notably the Mayo Clinic, with exhibitions by national, regional, and some local artists. Hours

The Mayo Clinic Story

The Mayo Clinic began in Rochester's Saint Mary's Hospital. In 1863, William Mayo moved to Rochester to act as medical examiner for U.S. soldiers. Years later as the community grew, he assisted in forming Saint Mary's, along with his two sons and a local parish.

This evolved from a private practice into what effectively was the nation's first private integrated group practice, wherein teams collaborated on a treatment. Notable accomplishments include:

—First centralized patient record system.
—First pneumatic patient record delivery system.
—First blood bank in 1933.
—1950 Nobel Prize for discovering cortisone.

Today, the facility administers to 1.5 million visitors, so many from around the world that its brochure is printed in Arabic, Greek, and Spanish. Over 18,000 employees show up for work here, including 2,000 doctors and researchers. Yes, this has resulted in major dollars for the city. Philanthropy is booming in Rochester—everything courtesy of Mayo money.

Sculpture in downtown Rochester's Peace Plaza. Tim Bewer

are Tuesday–Saturday, 10 a.m.–5 p.m. (until 9 p.m. Thursday); Sunday, noon–5 p.m.; free.

Amid the tall buildings in downtown Rochester, check out Peace Plaza, the city's premiere outdoor relaxation spot. Here, a fountain and a sculpture by Charles Gagnon depicting linked doves provide an oasis of tranquility to the surrounding hubbub.

From the art center, continue east on Center Street and follow it for 1 mile to where it joins 4th Street SE. Drive for 1 mile to East Circle Drive and turn left (north). Go for about 1.5 miles and look for signs to the *Quarry Hill Park Nature Center.* This getaway, 701 Silver Creek Road NE, (507) 281-6114, offers a pleasant,

relaxing respite from the subterranean subway walking systems of the Mayo Clinic. The 270 acres of meadow, flood plain, and upland forest sport 5 miles of trails. Families will love the nature center, which has interactive displays and exhibits on regional flora and fauna. Hours are Monday–Saturday, 9 a.m.–5 p.m.; Sunday, noon–5 p.m.; free.

Return south to 4th Street SE and drive west across town about 3 miles to 7th Avenue SW. Turn left (south) and go less than 1 mile to 10th Street SW. Turn right and watch for signs to the *Plummer House of the Arts.* This 49-room mansion, 1091 Plummer Lane SW, (507) 281-6160, was built for a wealthy doctor. The lavish interiors are worth a look (many innovations—for the period—were built into the 1921 structure). Many people enjoy the 11-acre grounds more, with gardens, bird trails, a water tower, and even its own quarry. Grounds are open to the public year-round; self-guided house tours are available Wednesdays in summer from 1–5 p.m., along with the first and third Sundays of every month 1–5 p.m.

From the Plummer House, return east to 7th Avenue SW; turn right (south) and go a short distance to Memorial Parkway. Turn right (west) onto 12th Street SW, which becomes County Road 22, then County Road 25. Follow that to Bamber Valley Road (County Road 8). Turn left (south) and go to Mayowood Road (County Road 125) and turn right. Drive to *Mayowood.* Total distance is about 3.5 miles. Architectural and design enthusiasts must make a pilgrimage to this splendid 1911 mansion, (507) 282-9447, and surrounding grounds of Dr. Charles Mayo. The crown jewel of Mayowood is the stately "house," with four dozen rooms laden with antiques and original furnishings and fixtures. The detail work within the rooms is breathtaking, even to those who don't know floorboards from wainscoting. Touring the immense house can take half a day, but be sure to leave enough time to wander the spectacular grounds. Gardens and terraces spread out through the 3,300 *acres*, leading to Mayowood Lake and the Zumbro River (check out the remnants of the dam, which was constructed to power the huge home). From the river, the view of the stately mansion is still impressive. Tours are given Tuesday, Thursday, and Saturday, early May to mid-October; admission.

From Mayowood, drive west about a half mile to County Road 25. Turn left (west) and go about 5 miles to County Road 5; turn right (north) and travel about 7 miles to County Road 105. Follow that north a short distance to *Oxbow Park.* Soon after departing Mayowood, you'll need to creep along slowly. The vistas are lovely, to be sure, but mostly the road necessitates it—rising and falling, curling around a stand of trees or pond every hundred yards. Appreciate it.

In the spring, wildflowers creep to the sides of the road; in fall the colors of the trees are grand. Myriad creeks and streams disappear under the road. Oxbow Park features hiking trails and a chance to wander among the meadows of native Minnesota flora and visit the zoo with a catalog of indigenous Gopher State fauna. Open daily 7 a.m.–10 p.m.

Return south to CR 5 and turn right (west). Take that road (it changes to County Road 16 in Dodge County) for about 7 miles to State Highway 57. Turn left and proceed into Mantorville. History buffs tout their love of this attractive, time-locked town. You'll understand quickly as the road descends gracefully into the downtown. Extraordinarily well-preserved architecture gives the place a daguerreotype feel. Better—it's all nestled into a picturesque crook of the Middle Fork of the Zumro River.

The downtown's entire 12-block stretch is listed on the National Register of Historic Places. Most is built of Mantorville limestone; soft and nearly malleable, it hardens beautifully over time. Stop by virtually any business to pick up free brochures on *historical walking tours*. Short on time? Head immediately to the *Dodge County Courthouse* on Main Street (can't miss it), purportedly the oldest in Minnesota. Just across 6th Street is the *Restoration House*, (507) 635-2131, reconstructed along with other buildings on the block to its original 1850s style. Also of interest is the three-story log house in the rear. Open May to October, Tuesday–Sunday, 1-5 p.m.; admission. You could easily spend all day here, so plan your time wisely.

Return to CR 16 and turn left (west). Drive about 7 miles to State Highway 56, turn right (north) and go about 1 mile to County Road 20. Turn left (west) and proceed for 8.5 miles to *Rice Lake State Park*. This stretch is almost a straight shot from CR 16, but along the way a few quick country road turns lie in wait, so take care. About halfway, just past Eden, the jaunt onto Highway 56 leads to a couple of *wildlife viewing* areas. A quick poke around, however, may reveal nothing more than a few nervous squirrels.

Once the site of a pioneer village, *Rice Lake State Park* is part of a mostly lost oak savannah—the Southern Oak Barrens, which once covered nearly 10 percent of Minnesota. A tiny parcel within the park remains untouched. Birders adore this place; a phone-book-sized list of avian species is available.

Continue west for 9 miles on County Road 19 (the number changes when CR 20 crosses into Steele County) to Owatonna. The name that rolls like a line of poetry comes courtesy of the daughter of legendary Dakota chief Wabena; the young girl drank from a nearby spring and was purportedly cured of a malady. You can visit the memorial to the young princess and other travelers who came to imbibe the salubrious waters at *Mineral Springs Park*, just northeast of the downtown area (take Grove Avenue north to Fremont Street; turn right, then left onto Cherry Street and follow signs).

At Cedar Avenue in Owatonna, turn left (south) and go about 3 blocks to Broadway Street. There you'll find an architectural wonder (among several others): the *Norwest Bank*, 101 North Cedar. This 1908 blood-red brick edifice was designed by famed architect Louis H. Sullivan. Visit in the morning and then the evening, if possible, and note the gorgeous colorings as the sun is reflected. Sullivan himself credited this building with rejuvenating a flagging design career, and you'll understand why.

Return north on Cedar Avenue to CR 19; turn left on Glendale Street and go a short distance to State Avenue. You'll arrive at a one-of-a-kind attraction, the *Minnesota State Orphanage*, 540 West Hills Circle, (507) 451-2145, now a museum that sits on 329 quiet acres. Built in 1885, the facility had over 13,000 children pass through it. Of special note is the amazing self-sufficiency of the place. A subdued highlight is the eerie cemetery memorial to the unfortunate children who never found their way out. Open weekdays 8 a.m.–5 p.m.; weekends 1-5 p.m.

Drive north on State Avenue a few blocks to Hoffman Drive (County Road 45). Turn left (west). This velvety county road parallels I-35, but what superb scenery those mad interstate travelers miss! It seems we drive into an oil painting as we roll. A spiderweb of creeks spills into the Straight River, our trip's watery accompanist.

Proceed for about 16 miles to Faribault, where CR 45 becomes Willow Street. Follow it to First Street NE (State Highway 60) near the downtown area. This community of about 20,000 residents, perched on a rolling aerie above the converging Straight and Cannon River Valleys, is lovely, with bridges seemingly everywhere, and town streets dipping and bending as the topography dictates.

Fur trader Alexander Faribault established a large outpost here and, in 1853, erected one of Minnesota's first frame houses. The renovated structure, at 12 First Avenue NE, is open for tours. Because of Faribault's generosity and far-sightedness, Minnesota's first Episcopal parish was established nine years later. The *Cathedral of Our Merciful Savior* is located nearby at 575 Second Avenue NW, (507) 334-7732; open weekdays, 8 a.m.–noon. Here, Bishop Henry Whipple became legendary for his attempts to protect native Sioux rights. He helped change U.S. policy toward the Sioux with his rather forceful communications with Indian agents and the U.S. federal government. Thankful Sioux com-

The restored Faribault House, Faribault. Tim Bewer

munities donated numerous gifts, many of which are found inside the church.

In turn, the church and Faribault's financial largesse drew a sophisticated crowd of settlers. Scholasticism and culture flourished, resulting in the town being dubbed the "Athens of the West."

Take Highway 60 east, cross the bridge and follow the brown signs to *River Bend Nature Preserve.* This 600-acre preserve of bits and pieces of native flora provides a sense of tranquility right on the outskirts of town. From an interpretive center housing exhibits on the region's natural and human history, eight miles of trails strike out into the meadows and woodlands.

Return to Highway 60 and turn left, then make a quick right onto County Road 20. Follow that northeast for 4 miles to County Road 27 in Cannon City. Bear right onto CR 27 and follow east, then north, for 7 miles to County Road 40. Turn left (west) and follow the signs to *Nerstrand Big Woods State Park.* Prairie Creek tumbles somnolently through lush, dense greenery, for all the world appearing like a rain forest's triple-thick canopy. Nerstrand Big Woods State Park, (507) 334-8848, is superb—due primarily to its location—plunked amidst one of Minnesota's last remaining sections of "Big Woods" topography. But it isn't simply the massive umbrellas of trees that are so inspiring. Mile after mile of easy to moderate trails wend over hills and into valleys, bypassing a handful of calendar-quality cascades. Still, those trees—an ecological laundry list of basswood, elm, ironwood, and green ash in particular—do dominate. Carpets of more than 50 varieties of wildflowers dot the treeless patches. With all the foliage producing blessed isolation, the camping is superb, despite the park's popularity.

Return to CR 40 and turn right (west). Go 4 miles to County Road 84/29, turn right (north) and drive 4 miles to the junction with County Road 22. Bear right and drive 2 miles to the merger with State Highway 246. Go north 3 more miles into downtown Northfield, where Highway 246 becomes Division Street. After the state park, massive swatches of greenery are quickly replaced by agricultural patchwork. The road passes over glacial drift accumulated atop Platteville limestone, the car rocking gently as the road rises and falls.

Northfield was once described as a "city of cows, colleges, and contentment." The town is certainly lovely, rivaling Mantorville, with an equal number of grand, historic structures lining the downtown streets. The city has much to offer. So the first stop should be at the *Northfield Area Chamber of Commerce*, 205 Third Street West, (800) 658-2548 (www.northfieldchamber.com), just west of Division Street South in the central district. Definitely pick up their excellent maps of local tours.

It is, however, higher education that best represents Northfield to many. This haven of learning hosts two renowned liberal arts colleges: *Saint Olaf,* 1520 Saint Olaf Avenue, (800) 275-6253, and Carleton, 1 North College Street, (800) 995-CARL. *Carleton* was founded in 1866 by the Congregational Church and likes to quote others who declare it the "Harvard of the Midwest" (as do many other liberal arts colleges). It may have a claim, though, drawing more National

One of several lovely falls at Nerstrand Big Woods State Park. Thomas Huhti

Merit Scholars than any other U.S. liberal arts college. Saint Olaf was established in 1874 to assist Norwegian immigrants.

Located just north of the downtown area, both have picturesque campuses well worth a visit. You can find an art gallery at each. Saint Olaf's superb views of the Cannon River Valley lure postcard photographers, while Carleton is proud of its arboretum and twin lakes. The music and theater departments of the colleges are top-notch, and performances of one sort or other are ongoing year-round. Saint Olaf's Christmas pageant and concert is nationally renowned.

From Division Street in Northfield, go west a block or two to Dahomey Avenue (also State Highway 3). Turn right and travel north for about 1.5 miles to County Road 47. After 1 mile, take a quick right onto County Road 94 and drive for another 6 miles to County Road 88 in Randolph. Proceed east on 88 for 4.5 miles to U.S. Highway 52. Take your time and enjoy the route. These are the real blue highways: impossibly narrow—but well-maintained—county roads once designed for lumbering wagons laden with farm-to-market produce. Even the most precise gazetteer cannot capture the, well, squiggles of the attempts (or resignation) of the highway department to emulate Mother Nature. The first stretch of road follows the Cannon River; while east of Randolph, you'll pass Lake Byllesby (with a great regional park on its east shore).

Turn right (south) on Highway 52 and go 1 mile to State Highway 19. Turn left and go a short distance to downtown Cannon Falls. The town sits in the crook formed by the merging of the Big Cannon and Little Cannon Rivers. Early voyageurs dubbed these the Rivers of Canoes (*cannon* is a mispronunciation of French canots, or "canoe").

What with this nomenclature, it's no surprise to see cars bedecked with paddle craft around here. The Cannon River is, in fact, one of seven in the state's Wild and Scenic system. Outfitters have all the gear you need. Just be forewarned: During high water—not uncommon—this river can be unforgiving, so know before you go.

Right in town, just west of the junction of Highway 19 (Main Street W.) and County Road 20, right in town, is the trailhead (and a parking lot) for the *Cannon Valley Trail*, which stretches east 20 miles to Red Wing. Just over 3 miles east of Cannon Falls, a turtle nesting site is a spring treat. Otherwise, expect to encounter lots of prairie vegetation and grouse.

From Cannon Falls, head east on Highway 19 for about 2.5 miles to County Road 8. Turn right (south) and drive for about 7 miles to County Highway 1 in tiny White Rock. Turn left (east) and go a little more than 1 mile to County Road 7. Mile upon mile of greenery interspersed with agricultural mazes is the typical view in these parts, but gorgeous nonetheless. There was no evidence of a white rock near

Jesse James and the Northfield Raid

In September 1876, the James-Younger gang stormed into Northfield and attempted to rob a bank. What they didn't expect was the citizenry fighting back; two locals and two robbers died in the exchange. Jesse and Frank James escaped, but a posse collared the rest of the gang, who spent many a year in Stillwater State Prison. The town fetes this heroic stand the weekend after Labor Day with the Jesse James Days. More information is available at the *Northfield Area Historical Museum*, 408 Division Street, (507) 645-9268. Here and at the chamber of commerce you can pick up a great driving tour brochure detailing the gang's activity throughout the region.

145

White Rock, but the kids will have fun looking for it nevertheless.

Turn right (south) on CR 7 and proceed for 10.5 miles to U.S. Highway 52. Turn left and continue south for 3 miles to West Fifth Street. Turn left (east) and drive a short distance to Main Street in Zumbrota. Turn left and go north a few blocks to West Second Street. Turn left, go one block to West Street, then turn right. You should be at Minnesota's only remaining original covered bridge. The *Zumbrota Covered Bridge* is proudly ensconced in a 65-acre park of the same name. Well-restored, the bridge actually shares its spot with two other original county historical nuggets: a Milwaukee Railroad depot and a classic one-room schoolhouse. Covered bridge fanatics should clear their slates the third Saturday in June for the *Zumbrota Covered Bridge Festival*, with band concerts, a street dance, flea market, and bingo.

Return to Main Street and head south to Highway 52/State Highway 60 on the south edge of town. Bear left on Highway 60 as it turns to the east, **and take that for about 7 miles to County Road 7 east of Mazeppa. Turn right (south) on CR 7** (a wildlife viewing area comes up quickly) **and drive for about 4 miles to County Road 21. Follow CR 21** (which becomes County Road 27 in Olmsted County) **for about 6.5 miles to County Road 12.** It's a lot easier to roar down U.S. 52 to return to Rochester, but where's the fun in that? As the crow flies, Zumbrota is about 20-odd miles to Rochester, but this route will really give quite a ride. CR 21, you'd swear, seems designed by a sadist, whipping around river bights haphazardly (not dangerously, just ambitiously). And every half mile seems to lead to a public access to a campsite, a boat/canoe launch, or fishing hotspot. To the left, the snaking Zumbro Lake (actually a wide part of the Zumbro River) is the reason for the many of the road's twists and turns.

Turn left (east) on CR 12 and go for 5 miles to U.S. Highway 63. Turn right (south) and head back to downtown Rochester, approximately a 10-mile stretch.

Tour 26
The Forgotten Minnesota River

Mankato—Kasota—Saint Peter—Le Sueur—Henderson—Jessenland—New Prague—
Montgomery—Waterville—Elysian—Madison Lake—Mankato

Distance: approximately 135 miles

This is the first of our two tours of the Minnesota River Valley, one that runs roughly north and south between Mankato and New Prague. The roads are sparsely traveled, evidence that most travelers miss the north-south segment, opting instead to traverse the east-west stretch (see Tour 17). Even a few natives of Minnesota have raised an eyebrow in modest surprise when told that the Minnesota River does indeed flow south to north from Mankato. Thus, this segment of the river is indeed a forgotten one.

Yet people miss a great deal in bypassing this stretch. A short list: the NFL, Nobel laureates, superb recreation trails, virgin prairies and residuals of exploited geology, epicenters of Swedish and Czech-Minnesotan culture, and more steely-hued, pleasant lakes than you could count in a day. Surely everyone will find something of interest on this route. Sandwiched within are some lovely roads and, thankfully, not too many miles.

Start your tour in downtown Mankato, on Riverfront Drive, near East Mulberry Street. At the confluence of the Minnesota and Blue Earth Rivers, it's not surprising that the city named by the Dakota for the cerulean-hued banks—mistakenly thought by French explorers to contain copper—lay at a crucial transportation junction point for early *voyageurs* blazing trails westward and the settlers who followed. Searching for the fecundity of home, they certainly found it along this elbow-shaped river valley.

Near the intersection of Riverfront Drive and East Mulberry Street, follow the signs to the railroad depot, home of the *Mankato Area Chamber and Convention Bureau*, 112 North Riverfront Drive, (800) 657-4733 (www.mankato.com). If for nothing else, the facility should be visited just for the excellent maps of the many recreational trails found in and outside of Mankato.

Quick Trip Option 1: For what might be the best views of the Minnesota River in this whole tour, jog north from the visitors center on River Front Drive and turn right onto Main Street. Immediately turn left and cross the river on Veteran's Memorial Bridge. This road becomes Belgrade Avenue. Follow this for approximately eight blocks and bear left onto Lee Boulevard (the City Hall and library are on your left side at the junction). Immediately turn right onto Lookout Drive and start looking to your left. This very short (no more than a mile) road wends along the Minnesota River and climbs up to some pull-offs with spectacular views.

Drive south from the visitor center on Riverfront Drive for about 1.5 miles and you'll see *Sibley Park* on the right. After checking out the downtown scene, the park is a great place to view an almost limitless array of Minnesota flora in a gorgeous arboretum. Kids, however, yawning at the rainbow of colors, may instead be more satisfied by the petting zoo! Others may prefer to just loll in the picnic grounds, watching and photographing the confluence of the two ambitious rivers (try to notice the distinctive colorations that impelled the French to send samples back to France, in hopes that analysis would reveal copper riches). Open daily 6:30 a.m.–10:30 p.m.

Truly, many travelers wind up spending more time than they thought here, lounging on picnic benches or dipping their feet into the cool waters from the banks. If that's not enough, you can really get a view of the Minnesota River on a mile-long trail that stretches to Veterans's Memorial Bridge downtown.

OK, but let's be honest. Say "Mankato" to natives of the Gopher State and they'll likely think of Vikings, not copper or French explorers. No, it isn't a Norwegian enclave, but rather the summer *training camp site* of the NFL's Minnesota Vikings. During summer training camp, everyone, it seems, is garbed in purple and gold. Generally, these start up in late July and early August and run twice a day six days a week at Mankato State University. Do double-check everything with the visitor center first as things change often, especially due to warm weather. To get to the practice facilities from the visitors center, drive south on Riverfront Drive to County Road 16 (Stoltzman Road) and follow this to Stadium Road. Turn left and follow this to the field.

History buffs may wish to visit the *Blue Earth County Heritage Center*, 415 Cherry Street, (507) 345-5566, which focuses mostly on the industrial and agricultural history of the county in a spiffy new gallery. Hours are Tuesday–Sunday, 10 a.m.–4 p.m.

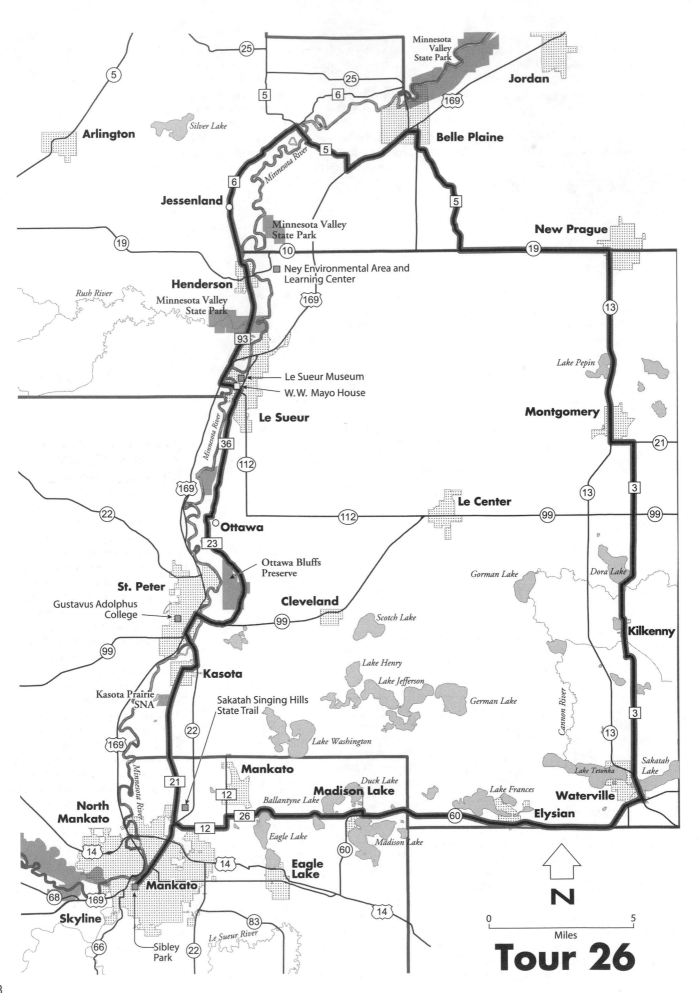

25

5

Arlington *Silver Lake*

25

5   6

169   **Jordan**

Minnesota
Valley
State Park

5   **Belle Plaine**

5

Jessenland

6   *Minnesota River*

New Prague

19   19

Minnesota Valley
State Park

10

13

Ney Environmental Area and
Learning Center

Henderson

Rush River

Minnesota Valley
State Park

169

Lake Pepin

93

Montgomery

Le Sueur Museum
W.W. Mayo House

21

Le Sueur

36

112

3

Minnesota River

Le Center

99   99

13   99

22

112

Gorman Lake   *Dora Lake*

Ottawa

23

Ottawa Bluffs
Preserve

Cleveland

Scotch Lake

Kilkenny

St. Peter

Gustavus Adolphus
College

Lake Henry

Lake Jefferson

Cannon River

99

Kasota

German Lake

Kasota Prairie
SNA

22

Sakatah Singing Hills
State Trail

Lake Washington

13

*Sakatah
Lake*

169

21

Mankato

Lake Tetonka

Duck Lake

**North
Mankato**

12

Madison Lake

Ballantyne Lake

Lake Frances

Waterville

26

60   **Elysian**

3

12

14   *Eagle Lake*

60   *Madison Lake*

14   14

Minnesota River

**Eagle
Lake**

N

68   169

Skyline

83

0   5

66

22   *Le Sueur River*

Miles

Sibley
Park

Tour 26

The history of Mankato can be appreciated in a somewhat different way. Those who can recall their first childhood forays into literature may recall the names Betsy and Tacy, two childhood best friends who lived on Hill Street in a town called Deep Valley. The author was Maud Hart Lovelace, a lifelong Mankato resident. In all, Lovelace penned a baker's dozen novels with the two precocious heroines, whose tales were eagerly devoured by generations of young readers. Locals will tell you that, of course, Deep Valley was Mankato and Hill Street was actually Center Street, west of the Minnesota River. (You can get there via Belgrade Avenue; see the Quick Trip Option above for directions to Belgrade Avenue.) At the top of Center Street, a stone bench bears a plaque honoring the author. The houses of the real girls upon whom Betsy and Tacy were based can also be seen. Betsy's house is at 333 Center Street; at 332 Center Street is Tacy's former home. The latter has already been purchased by the county historical society and is under renovation. Ultimately, it will be a history and interpretive center detailing not only the fictional characters' lives, but also how Mankato itself came alive through the books. If you're interested in tours, contact the historical society at (507) 345-8103.

Recreation buffs may be surprised to find it a hotbed of outdoor activities. Sublime *recreation trails* are everywhere throughout the downtown, and stretching throughout the region. The other popular county tour is the 13-mile Red Jack Trail to Rapidan. The trail passes by Mount Kato—excellent skiing—and a picturesque railroad trestle. You can find the trailhead at West High School, across U.S. 169 from Sibley Park.

Return to Riverfront Drive and drive north, going through the downtown and eventually passing U.S. Highway 14. After that, take the road, which is Lime Valley Road, for about 3 miles to its junction with County Road 21. After the road passes through Mankato and passes over (and under) a series of train tracks, the prairie suddenly seems to appear from nowhere. Along the way, you'll pass the trailhead for the 40-mile-long *Sakatah Singing Hills State Trail*, stretching to Faribault through Sakatah Lake State Park. One of the most popular of Mankato's many trails, it features a dizzying array of bluffs, river paths, and challenging off-road options.

Continue on CR 21 for about 1.5 miles to County Road 101. Turn left (west) and drive about another 1.5 miles. A geological wonderland indeed awaits. The *Kasota Prairie Scientific and Natural Area* is a lovely hodgepodge of geology and topography set upon a modest terrace sculpted 70 feet above the Minnesota River Valley. The temperature literally cools as you gracefully crest the rise and wisp through the tall grasses. Moist meadows, oak woodlands, and hardwoods thrive in the nutrient-rich, silty soils deposited by the Glacial River Warren. You can wander down to

the widening river and watch it chug by. Needless to say, an explosion of wildflowers draws photographers in spring. Get out of the car for a spell and scout outcroppings of the local specialty—yellow limestone. (Mining does still go on in the region, though much less so than a century ago.)

Return to CR 21 and continue north for 3 miles into tiny Kasota. Almost immediately you pass *Seven Mile Creek Park*. Should you require still more traipsing in a riverine paradise, here's a good spot. If the previous prairie offered a bit of isolation from the real world, this place will allow you to be gloriously alone. You might feel as if you've had enough of river views for a spell, but you'll change your mind as you hear the singing in full delight.

The distinctive golden-Lab-colored limestone, common to the area, is still mined and processed at a plant on the outskirts of Kasota. The town center sports a park full of this sturdy and fetching stone—some of the stones are Paul Bunyan-sized.

Just east of Kasota, turn left onto State Highway 22 and drive north 3 miles to Saint Peter, where the road becomes Minnesota Avenue. This charming burg was, believe it or not, almost the capital of Minnesota. A complicated process of bureaucratic pork resulted in the town being proposed as a mini-Saint Paul. Proverbially counting their chickens, locals happily erected a new capitol. At the last minute, however, the legislature turned them down. The building still sits at the corner of 3rd and Walnut Streets. Still, the town can proudly boast that it's one of the state's oldest settled communities.

Go north on Minnesota Avenue to College Avenue, turn left, and go a few blocks up the hill. You'll arrive at the lovely campus of *Gustavus Adolphus College*, 800 West College Avenue, (507) 934-2160, a private liberal college of Swedish/Lutheran heritage plunked downtown overlooking the Minnesota River. Christ Chapel is unmistakable, beckoning with its soaring spire. Linnaeus Arboretum features native Minnesota species of flora but the founders even found a way to transport a host of plants native to Sweden as well. Around the arboretum is a noted collection of sculptures, each linked to the next by a footpath.

Perhaps most unique to the college is Nobel Hall, named in

The Julien Cox House in Saint Peter. Tim Bewer

Ottawa

Ottawa was founded in 1853. On a long strip of land tracing the Minnesota River, it hit a peak in the antebellum period, but within two decades it had inexplicably declined. Six properties do remain and are smashing examples of homestead stone construction. You'll pass by the Ottawa Methodist Church, an 1859 beauty and one of Minnesota's oldest Methodist churches. Also of note is Burr Oak Park; the town's founding families built a park before they platted the town!

honor of Alfred Nobel, the Swede who created the Nobel Prize. A gallery within details each of the Nobel laureates in history. Annually, a conference of previous winners is held. It's a fascinating piece of international intellectual and peaceful pursuits in the heartlands.

Saint Peter's *Julien Cox House*, 500 North Washington Avenue, (507) 934-4309, was built by the town's first mayor (and later state senator). The lovely 1871 Carpenter Gothic-Italianate structure is open for tours weekends in summer but times vary. Also impressive, but in an entirely different way, is the *Saint Peter Regional Treatment Center Museum*, 100 Freeman Drive, (507) 931-7270, the first psychiatric treatment facility in Minnesota. Today the aging building houses a small museum that offers a glimpse into the quite shocking field of "psychiatry" in the late nineteenth century. Tours are offered by appointment only.

For lovely river views, check out *Riverside Park* along Front Street, near the Saint Peter Chamber of Commerce. It has an artesian-fed pond, and kids are encouraged to

fish. Lots of hiking trails also snake out into the lands fronting the river.

Return to Minnesota Avenue, turn left and go a short distance to Park Row Street (County Road 23). Drive east, then north, for about 7 miles to Ottawa. You sweep around a major bight of the Minnesota River in a reverse *c* and through lowlands seeping with oak and swamp vegetation. The big old river provides ample water for blue-ribbon trout fishing. A former DNR fish hatchery pond, in fact, is still stocked annually by the state with trout. Families are encouraged to let kids toss a line.

Two miles south of Ottawa your eyes cannot help but wander to the left side of the road. Something, your visual cognition tells you, is special here. True, the *Ottawa Bluffs Preserve (Bluff and Fen)* is important enough for the Nature Conservancy to have purchased it for preservation. Thirty acres are dry mesic prairie; 40 more are hardwood with gurgling springs. A fen is found where the bluffs meet the water—a truly inspiring place.

Just north of the preserve is a seemingly incongruous sight: the hulking outline of a silica-sand extraction plant (sand and gravel are mined nearby). Ugly? Sure, but it provides crucial jobs and, in fact, is an effective use of an ex-mine site.

Head east out of Ottawa a short distance on CR 23 to County Road 36; turn left (north) and go for 5.5 miles to Bridge Street in Le Sueur. Pierre Charles Le Sueur, famed French *voyageur,* in the late seventeenth century became one of the first Europeans to travel this waterway. This spot was among his favorite due to its lack of water obstacles and natural beauty. Le Sueur may ring a bell, as it was once home to the Green Giant food company in its heyday. You'll definitely want to stop by the *Le Sueur Museum*, 709 North 2nd Street, (507) 665-2050, home to an amazing collection of Jolly Green Giant memorabilia. Kids adore having their pictures taken with the myriad images of the big old green giant himself. Hours are weekdays, 9 a.m.–noon and 1–4:30 p.m.

Parents are more taken with the *W. W. Mayo House*, 118 North Main Street, (507) 665-3250, originally built and resided in by one of the founders of the Mayo Clinic. Later, the owners of the Green Giant company lived in the painstakingly-restored mansion. Hours are summers, Tuesday–Saturday, 10 a.m.–4:30 p.m.; admission. Both the Le Sueur Museum and the Mayo House are located north of Bridge Street.

Quick Trip Option 2: Le Sueur isn't all green giants and vegetables. Don't forget that the town site was in part picked due to its near-perfect riverside location. Those still hankering for a lazy river day have two nice options close to Le Sueur. A quarter mile west of Le Sueur's center is *River Park*, a superb local park with more than 80 acres of nature trails, picnic areas, camping, and, of course, a great deal of Minnesota River tranquility. Even better, some believe, is *Chamberlain Woods Scientific and Natural Area*, 3 miles south on County Road 36, then a quarter mile west on Township Road. Here you'll find 250-plus acres of deciduous forest (and a mélange of other biotic zones) backing gently off the river. Critters abound here.

From Le Sueur, take Bridge Street (State Highway 93) west, then north for about 6 miles to Henderson. You skirt the banks of the Minnesota River here, with views of spectacular bottomlands. The sights are splendid: alternating marshy swales, steely blue waters, and numerous stands of hardwoods. Suddenly, the greenery gets downright busy as you whip through the edges of the *Minnesota River Valley State Recreation Area*. Many public exits are found along here; feel free to stop and snoop for lovely water vistas and great birding opportunities.

Turn right (east) on State Highway 19 and drive 2 miles to the lovely *Ney Environmental Area and Learning Center*. The center, (507) 665-6244, is relatively new and expanding, but they have loads of exhibits and activities for families. Look for deer, turkeys, and eagles on the approach.

On the way back to downtown, turn left onto Hen Station Road (County Road 34) and go a half mile to the twin towns of East Henderson and Henderson Station. They were once known as Clarksville, but later abandoned before being rechristened as the separate towns. A few of the original buildings still retain a sense of history.

Ditto with Henderson proper. Much of the downtown district is on the National Register of Historic Places, and it's in decidedly better shape than East Henderson.

Return to Henderson and turn right (north) on County Road 6; take that for 3 miles to Jessenland. We roll by a picturesque county park. The road bends to the west, away from the river, before beginning a mighty swing eastward, as if it missed its partner. As the tree density rises, the road suddenly winds its way into Jessenland. Note the town hall; built in 1905, it also doubled as the local schoolhouse. The town's *Saint Thomas Catholic Church* was Minnesota's first Irish agrarian parish.

Continue northeast for 5 miles to County Road 5. Turn right (southeast). One cannot mistake the local landmark, the "Avenue of Trees," right atop the nearby Minnesota River. These large rows of proud cottonwoods mark the spot where the original road constantly flooded. Even ferries had to stop running the river in even moderately rainy periods. Thankfully for us, the current bridge was built. As you cross, it isn't hard to imagine a swollen Minnesota River getting its anger up, making travel hazardous a century (or less) ago.

Drive east on CR 5 for approximately 12 miles to State Highway 19. Turn left (east) and drive 7 straight miles to the heart of New Prague. Initially, that odd feeling in your gut is understandable. After the first half of our tour, you've likely developed a habit for water. Don't, worry, though. A few miles through the farm fields east of the Minnesota River will get you back into the swing of things. (For those seriously craving a dose of water, you do cross over . . . one, two, *three* ribbony creeks and streams that languidly flow toward the Minnesota River.)

The heart of Bavarian Czech culture in Minnesota, New Prague is so proud of its heritage that a most prominent spot on the town's Web site is devoted to the local polka music organization. Visitors love the town's eastern-European-style brick edifices, perhaps best represented by the stylings—inside and out—of *Schumacher's New Prague Hotel*, 212 West Main Street, (952) 758-2133. This is a fantastic place for Old World stick-to-your-ribs fare. You may even get to experience an oom-pah concert.

Wander the downtown. The low-key, friendly atmosphere is a great way to take in a walking tour. Notice the 10 murals adorning building sides detailing the immigration history of the town. In front of the local library sits a 13-foot-tall wooden sculpture donated by a Czech artist whose son was an exchange student in the city. Plan to be in town the third Saturday in September for *Dozinky*, a Czech harvest festival.

Drive west on Highway 19 (Main Street) to 4th Avenue SW, which is also State Highway 21/13. Turn left (south) and follow this for 7.5 miles to Boulevard Avenue (County Road 57) in Montgomery. Turn left (east). In its entirety, the route is known as the "Czech Memorial Highway." If New Prague claims to be the heart of Czech culture, locals here may beg to differ. They'll absolutely insist—politely, of course—that you come for one of the oldest street festivals in the state (begun in 1929): *Kolacky Days*, every year in late July. You haven't experienced Minnesota Czech life until you've eaten a *kolacky* and participated in the festivities, which include dancing, games, and all the other hoo-ha of a small town food fete.

Pronounced "ko-latch-kee," the humble delicacy is a fruit-filled pastry. The Czechs make the world's best, and this town claims the top spot. You can get everything from apple to prune, which is the favorite of purists.

Drive a few blocks east on Boulevard Avenue to 5th Street NE (County Road 3). Turn right and drive south for 16 miles to State Highway 60 just south of Waterville. Certainly named well, Waterville is plunked almost precisely between Sakata and Tetonka Lakes—and locals love to point out that there are 48 other lakes within a 25-mile radius. (It certainly seems so as you drive these roads.)

Turn left (east) on Highway 60 and proceed for about 3 miles to *Sakatah Lake State Park.* This lovely 800-acre park, (507) 362-4438, sits beside the lake of the same name. Trails wend around the lake, and the park is also on the Sakatah Singing Hills State Trail, which runs about 40 miles between Mankato and Faribault. Part of the longest recreational trail in the state, this stretch has sublime sights all along the way. From the east end of Lower Sakatah Lake to the west end of Lake Tetonka are 11 uninterrupted miles of water. So rife are bullheads that Waterville hosts an annual *bullhead festival* the second weekend of June. The state record for largemouth bass hails from Lake Tetonka, by the way. And bravo to this park for the bike-in-only campsites.

Drive west on Highway 60 for about 8.5 miles to Elysian. In the midst of the so-called "Lakes Region," you can't help but notice all those inviting pools of water whipping past the car. The car splits two baby lakes, then a third to your left, signaling the arrival in Elysian, the de facto capital of the Southern Minnesota Lakes Region (www.mnlakes region.com). The highway crosses over endless creeks, all of which feed the ever-present lakes. In Elysian, Lake Frances to the northwest seems large enough by most standards, but is dwarfed by massive Lake Elysian, which unfurls itself ever so slowly to the southwest.

The *Le Sueur County Historical Society Museum,* at 4th and Frank Streets, is open sporadically. If it is open, check out the state's most com-plete prehistoric bison skull. Science buffs will insist, however, that the coolest thing on display is one of the world's only micro-meteorite detectors (the other is at Temple University). While at the museum, ask for the story on the James Gang's ride into town while on the lam. Also get directions to *Klondike Hill* north of town. The tallest spot for three counties, it has stellar views of the lakes region. It was also used as a camping spot by the James Gang outlaws.

Continue west on Highway 60 for 7 miles to Madison Lake (the town and body of water). When you finally pass Lake Frances west of Elysian, another huge and glorious lake pops up a few miles later on your left. That would be Madison Lake. Native Americans dubbed it "Spirit Lake."

Quick Trip Option 3. Probably, the most fun thing to do in Lake Madison is circle the big old lake of the same name. On the west end of town, take a left turn off Highway 60 onto Park Road and trace the edge of the lake all the way to County Road 17, then head east and follow County Road 48 north. You could do it easily in an hour, while not missing a thing. There are plenty of county parks along the way. *Bray Park* is especially worth a visit, with a blacktop walkway through virgin timber.

From Madison Lake, take County Road 26 west for about 5.5 miles to County Road 12 just west of Eagle Lake. Turn left and drive south, then west, for 3 miles to Lime Valley Road just north of Mankato. Turn left (south) and travel 2 miles back into downtown Mankato and Riverfront Drive.

Tour 27
Germans, Dakotas, and "Little Yellowstone"

New Ulm—Fort Ridgely State Park—Morton—Birch Coulee Historic Site—Redwood Falls—Lower Sioux Indian Reservation—Gilfillan—Sleepy Eye—New Ulm

Distance: approximately 100 miles

This tour, the second of our Minnesota River Valley wanderings, is the part that gets most of the credit, not to mention auto traffic. Many people forsake the Mankato loop of Tour 26, for whatever reason, and instead focus on the east-west stretch. This tour is the more heavily traveled, and there are good reasons for its popularity. Simply put, it offers concentrated doses of culture, ethnicity, and history, all within a day's driving distance.

And of this tour, New Ulm is the unquestionable queen. Many travelers drift into this Euro-style town and never really see much else along the river, so lovely and full of sights is this German enclave.

In this heavily Norwegian state, New Ulm equals German, German, and more German. From Teutonic heroes scowling protectively from hills overlooking the town, to traditional butcher shops dispensing myriad sausage, to nearly monthly German festivals (not to mention a brewery), New Ulm is a bit of *Deutschland* in the heartland.

Should we manage to depart New Ulm's loveliness, we trace the history of settlers as they spread westward along the river. Within 30 miles we juxtapose successful immigrant stories with tragic treatment of Native Americans as the country grew. On a more positive note, what follows is a visit to one of the best city parks (in addition to Duluth's skyline parkway) you'll ever see: Redwood Falls's Alexander Ramsey Park.

Begin your tour in downtown New Ulm. New Ulm *is* German, from the Teutonic flair of the downtown buildings to the glockenspiel standing proudly above the downtown, not to mention the German warrior standing sentinel on an aerie overlooking the town. A casual, gentrified Old World look and feel, a gorgeous state park, not to mention one of the Midwest's most famous local beers . . . all of this translates into must-see status for road-trippers. You'll be shoulder to shoulder with other travelers on any summer day. An admission:

Example of New Ulm's imposing Germanic architecture. Thomas Huhti

153

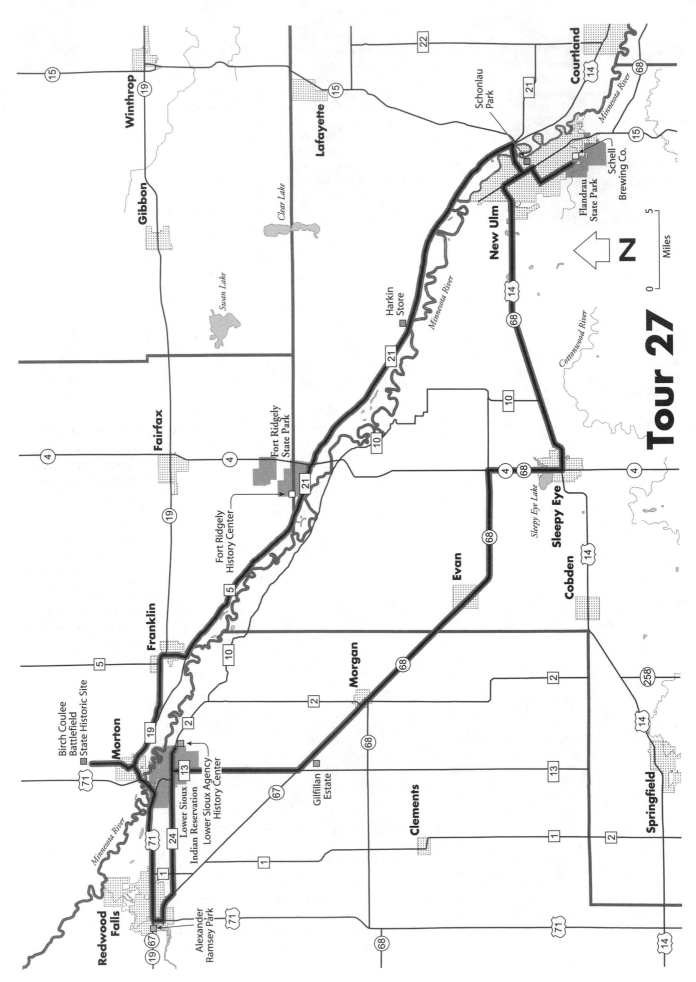

Winthrop
Gibbon
15
19
Lafayette
22
21
15
Schonlau Park
Courtland
14
68
Minnesota River
New Ulm
Schell Brewing Co.
Flandrau State Park
15
N
Miles
5
0

Clear Lake
Swan Lake
Harkin Store
Minnesota River
14
68
Cottonwood River

Tour 27

Fairfax
4
4
Fort Ridgely State Park
Fort Ridgely History Center
21
10
10
Sleepy Eye Lake
Sleepy Eye
4
68
4
19
5
Evan
68
Cobden
14

Franklin
5
10
Morgan
68
2
258
2

Birch Coulee Battlefield State Historic Site
Morton
71
19
2
Lower Sioux Indian Reservation
Lower Sioux Agency History Center
13
Gilfillan Estate
68
67
Clements
13
14
Springfield

Minnesota River
71
24
1
Alexander Ramsey Park
1
1
2
71
Redwood Falls
19
67
71
68
68
14

154

one tour could not in any way capture all that New Ulm has to offer. The following are the most popular favorites and/or absolute must-sees.

Thus your first stop should be the *New Ulm Area Convention and Visitors Bureau*, 1 North Minnesota Street, (507) 233-4300 or 888-463-9856 (www.newulm.com). Arguably the most efficient operation along the Minnesota River, the CVB has superb materials for travelers and an engaging staff.

Be certain to pick up well-made and handy *walking tour* brochures. This gives the details on the two most prominent features of New Ulm's "skyline." A few blocks north of the CVB and within easy walking distance is the *glockenspiel* in Schonlau Park, at 4th Street North and North Minnesota Street. It's one of the world's few free-standing carillon towers; this one has two tons of bells, the heaviest at 595 pounds.

From the CVB at the corner of Minnesota and Center Streets, go south on Center about 1 mile to Hermann Heights Park. There, you'll find New Ulm's other major claim to fame, the *Hermann Monument*, an imposing statue looking menacingly from atop a bluff, dares anyone to threaten the town. This statue towers 102 feet high and represents the liberation of Germany from Rome in AD 9. (The picturesque Hermann Heights Park beneath Hermann's malevolent stare, by the way, is one of the nicest picnic spots anywhere along the Minnesota River.)

At Hermann Heights Park on Center Street, look for Summit Avenue leading southward. Take that for about 1 mile to the entrance to *Flandrau State Park*. This 1,000-acre park, 1300 Summit Avenue, (507) 233-9800, along the Cottonwood River is packed with folks, given its proximity to a tourist hotspot. Still, its backwoodsy trails and sand-bottomed, filtered swimming pool (really!) are worth a stop. Tranquil camping is topnotch here, with 36 rustic sites. Trails lead up and over some relatively ambitious rises; some 60 species of birds can be spotted from trails. Open 8 a.m.–4 p.m. daily.

Go north a short distance on Summit Avenue to 10th Street S.; turn right and go to S. Broadway Street; turn right and go about 1 mile to 18th Street S. Turn right and follow the road left onto Washington Street S., then Schell Road. Tired of museums and—if that's possible—natural wonders? New Ulm's got a wonderfully different kind of stop, *August Schell Brewing Company*, 1860 Schell Road, (507) 354-5528, the second-oldest family owned and managed brewery in the U.S., dating to 1860. Breweries were always big in German New Ulm, but Schell's founder had one big advantage; he was on friendly terms with the Dakota. And during the Dakota Conflict of 1862, all the other breweries were torched. The business naturally boomed. Today the grounds are

lovely, with a gorgeous mansion, floral gardens, and deer park. Tours are available (Memorial Day weekend to Labor Day, 3 and 4 p.m., plus 1 and 2 p.m. weekends; reduced off-season hours). Even if you arrive when they're not offered, the tranquil atmosphere makes for a nice stop. By the way, Schell's makes 15 varieties of outstanding, special-crafted beers, plus less potent beverages like root beer.

Return to South Broadway Street (State Highway 15), turn left and drive north back through town. Follow Highway 15 as it turns east and take it for about 1.5 miles across the Minnesota River to County Road 21. Turn left (west) and travel 9 miles to the Harkin Store. Once past town, the roadway follows the snaking and looping Minnesota River, which dances near the road, then lurches away, but its presence is always there.

What today are pastoral agriculture and fallow lands adjoining the flowing Minnesota River were once platted dirt streets of West Newton, a thriving pioneer town whose heart and soul was the *Harkin General Store*, (507) 354-8666, built in the 1870s. In 1873, the railroad bypassed the river community, sucking much of its life. The following year, a grasshopper invasion devastated the remaining homesteads. Still, the general store hung on until 1901 and the advent of rural-free mail delivery.

Today, wander about Harkin's atop the creaky floorboard—like everything else, they're original—and sniff. Yup, the administrators of this living museum like to tout its olfactory historic accuracy. True enough, the aged bottles lining the shelves still hold the camphor, oils, and spices and aromas do tell of a century and a quarter of time. Hours are daily except Monday, 10 a.m.–5 p.m., Memorial Day weekend through Labor Day, and during New Ulm's Oktoberfest; admission.

Drive northwest on CR 21 for 4 miles. Here you'll see signs pointing out the site of the erstwhile *Little Rock Trading Post Site*. Built in 1834 by Joseph LaFrancoise, a *vouageur* who acted as interpreter and negotiator between the Lakota Sioux and the United States, the post was a crucial conduit for commerce and communication. Not much remains, but the site still has a genuine historic feel to it. The river views are superb as well.

Drive 5 more miles northwest to State Highway 4; turn right and go a short distance. *Fort Ridgely State Park* tells the somewhat odd tale of a little fort that could. Built in 1853 almost as an afterthought by the U.S. Army—incompetently

Everybody Polka!

Given the German heritage, *gemuetlichkeit* (basically, "spirit of bonhomie, friendliness, a party attitude," all rolled into one) is free flowing around here. Much of the German influx was specifically Bohemian, which was heavily Czech influenced. This may explain the preponderance of good time oom-pah polka music in New Ulm (the polka was born in Czech Bohemia). Evidence of that is station KNUJ AM 860—all polka music, all the time. They have great CDs and tapes for sale, too.

The Schell Brewing Company—after nearly 150 years in operation, still going strong. Thomas Huhti

placed and planned, some have said—Fort Ridgely wasn't intended for defensive purposes. But that's what troops were forced to do in 1862 during the Dakota Uprising. Not one but two massive attacks were repelled, astonishing the Dakota, who had anticipated overrunning the fort and taking control of the entire valley. The contiguous state park has a campground and plenty of rolling hills snaked with hiking trails, and, strangely enough, a golf course.

New Ulm Festivals

Anytime you show up in this town, some shindig is going down. The following are just the highlights; for details, consult the Web site www. newulm.com

Fasching (German for "German Mardi Gras") takes place in early February; a celebration designed to chase away lingering winter blues, is has great German food and music, dancing, and a costume contest. A highlight is the Concord Singers, a local choral group of some renown. In June, Flandrau State Park hosts an open house at its *Flandrau Fest,* with lots of water-based events, music, food, and more.

One of the most respected ethnic festivals in North America is New Ulm's *Heritagefest* the second and third weekends of July. Continuous European entertainment takes place on five stages, food and spirits flow, and lovely costumed characters appear everywhere. These are the traditional *Narren,* locals dressed in amazingly detailed mythical or invented figures' dress (the hand-carved masks are remarkable). The kids have their own special ethnic activities center.

Being a German town, you'd be surprised if there weren't an *Oktoberfest,* and, of course, there is, held the first two weekends of October. More omm-pah music than you ever heard in your life, a river of beer, and German fare that'll keep you sated for a week.

The visitor center/history center, (507) 426-7888, is open May 1 to Labor Day, Tuesday–Saturday, 10 a.m.–5 p.m.; Sunday, noon–5 p.m.; an admission sticker is required.

Return to CR 21, which changes to County Road 5 after about 1 mile. Continue northwest on CR 5 for about 11 miles to State Highway 19 just north of Franklin. Turn left (west) and go about 5 miles to County Road 18 in Morton. Turn right and drive north 2 miles on to County Road 2. You'll see signs pointing out the *Birch Coulee Battlefield State Historic Site.* Here on September 22, 1862, a party of 150 soldiers was ambushed by Dakota Sioux during the Dakota Uprising. For a day and a half, the battle raged, with so many casualties on both sides no one ever tallied up the dead. Scouts finally slipped away and alerted Fort Ridgley, which dispatched reinforcements, finally quelling the battle.

Quick Trip Option. A mere 15 miles north of Morton on U.S. Highway 71 is the town of Olivia. You're in the heart of corn country here, and for proof look no farther than the Giant Ear of Corn in the town's Memorial Park. This is without question a cool photo-op. The park has free camping, too. Speaking of free, during late July's Corn Capital Days festival, the town also doles out—free!—all the corn you can eat.

From the battlefield, return to Morton, then follow Highway 19 (also U.S. Highway 71) west 5 miles into Redwood Falls. On your way back through Morton, you may want to continue your trip into the area's eventful past. The town has a quaint *historical museum* and two *monuments* to the Dakota Conflict of 1862.

Although a town with a name right out of the movies, no one seems to have heard of Redwood Falls. But there are great reasons to stop. And you can find out more at the *Redwood Area Chamber and Tourism Office*, 200 South Mill Street, just south of Highway 19 (Bridge Street).

One of them is a true state treasure, *Alexander Ramsey Park*, the state's largest municipal park. Turning north off Highway 19 on the west side of town, you're initially underwhelmed: "Not another park by a river." Yet this one is different. The park seems to just go on and on—over 217 acres along the Redwood River are subsumed by the park's borders. But size matters less than what lies therein—bending, dipping roads bypass sheer rock, bridges wisp you literally feet above splendid rapids and past semi-thunderous waterfalls. (Be sure to stop at Zeb Gray Overlook area.) Hiking trails, ski trails, fishing—recreational opportunities at every bend in the road. Eventually, the road bypasses a golf course and a great zoo. Hop out and say hello to the penned-up bison. Spend the day hiking along the rarely overpopulated trails, then pitch a tent in the spacious campground. All of this is probably why locals tout it as the "The Little Yellowstone of Minnesota."

On the west edge of the park stands the *Redwood County Museum and Minnesota Inventors Hall of Fame*, (507) 637-3329. Interestingly enough, these grounds were once the country's poor farm. Two floors of relics could require most of a day to poke around. Besides the oddball inventions of Gopher State geniuses, you'll find a one-room schoolhouse and fun wildlife exhibit. The only problem is—it seems to be open irregular hours. If you're *really* looking for local tidbits, ask at the museum about the location in the northern part of Redwood Country for the birthplace of Sears, Roebuck, and Company (which is somewhere, they say, along County Road 101, though this author, despite half a morning, never did find it).

On West Bridge Street in Redwood Falls, go to Mills Street and turn right. Take that, which is also State Highway 67 south, then southeast for about 1.5 miles to County Road 24. Turn left (east) and drive 5 miles to the junction with County Road 2; continue east on CR 2 for 3 miles. You'll come to the *Lower Sioux Agency*, (507) 697-6321, established in 1853 as a link in the chain of U.S. government administration of former Sioux lands, which had been ceded in 1851. This was a distribution point for barter and goods the U.S. government owed the Sioux. Today you'll find an 1861 warehouse looking pretty much as it did then, one imagines. An interpretive center relates the history of the site and 3 miles of trails wend along the Minnesota River. All told, this site gets kudos for representing the true history of the place—the good and the bad in the at-times nasty relationship between the federal government and

the Native Americans. Hours for the interpretive center are May through Labor Day, Monday–Saturday, 10 a.m.–5 p.m.; Sunday, noon–5 p.m.; reduced off-season hours; admission.

Near the agency on CR 2 is the *Lower Sioux Community*, with historic sites dating to the agency's times, including Saint Cornelia's church and a school trading post. Few travelers visit here, but it has some historical exhibits detailing U.S.-Sioux relations.

Backtrack on CR 2 to County Road 13; turn left (south) and go 5 miles to State Highway 67. Turn left (east) and follow the signs to *Gilfillan Estate.* This historic 1872 homestead manor house and adjoining buildings, all restored to former splendor, is worth a weekend-only tour, (507) 249-3451, 1-4:30 p.m., June–September, giving you the opportunity to snoop around antique barns packed with old farm equipment. (The founding family became rich by exporting prized beef to Europe.) The real reason you should come is for the early August *Farmfest*, which some claim is the largest farm festival in the Midwest. Here visitors get a bit of farm history, agricultural economics, rural sociology, and crop development—with a hefty dose of 4H-style fun—all rolled into one.

Minnesota River Valley Scenic Byway

The Minnesota River, the state's "Second River," is the first in the hearts of many Minnesotans. On a map, it looks so inviting—and so easy to follow. This is the intent of the Minnesota River Valley Scenic Byway, which runs from Belle Plaine, southwest of the Twin Cities, to Browns Valley on the South Dakota border.

Should you choose to trace this route in its entirety, however, a daunting task awaits you. Though the road is officially designated a scenic byway by the Minnesota Department of Transportation and signs theoretically do exist, most travelers will find it virtually impossible to follow each miniscule state/county/local road between attractions. You quickly discover that this "scenic byway" is really an alphabet soup of tiny highways, in various states of disrepair or repair, and which may or may not be marked. In addition, the river itself is an unending series of twists and loops and bends, making it impossible for any one road to follow it faithfully for any great distance.

And it's not simply the immense mileage that you rack up. Rather, so many historical and natural sites are found along the way (there are well over 100) that one is simply overwhelmed. Most travelers would need a minimum of three days to experience a small portion of what this grand tour offers.

Despite the feeling of not quite knowing where you're going (or, in some cases, because of it), the trip can be a hoot. Lost along an official scenic byway! Isn't that a part of what road-tripping is all about? So what if you slip off the "path"? If you're enjoying the views and the experience, then you're going the right way. Remember, one way or another, you'll cobble together a route to your "destination." Thus, you've blazed your own trail, just like the explorers did more than a century ago.

Granite memorial in Sleepy Eye honoring the grave of the Lakota chief who lent his name to the town. Thomas Huhti

Continue east on Highway 67 for about 4 miles to State Highway 68 in Morgan. Along the way to Morgan, you can stop in at *RichNes Alpacas,* (507) 249-3631, where if you phone in advance, you can take a tour and the kiddies can pet the cute little fur-bearers.

Follow Highway 68 east, then south, for 14 miles to Sleepy Eye. What a town name—and one that begs for a plausible explanation. Here you

go: The name stems from the droopy peeper of a local Lakota chief, *Ishtakahbah,* who's buried beneath a granite marker at the town's *depot museum.* If you adore railroads and their heritage, plan to make a stop here. A proud statue of the chief stands tall in the downtown today.

Drive east about 13 miles on Highway 68, follow it south, and proceed on Broadway Street back to downtown New Ulm.

Tour 28
Prairies, Lakes, Fossils and the Little House

Worthington—Fulda—Currie—Lake Shetek State Park—Walnut Grove—Sanborn—Jeffers Petroglyphs—Mountain Lake—Worthington

Distance: approximately 175 miles

Road-trippers couldn't ask for a more varied trip than this tour in southwestern Minnesota. Just an hour off Interstate 90, travelers can whip through prairies seemingly from centuries ago, hop aboard trains in a town so small it may not appear on your map, and even visit Walnut Grove, a town that may best represent the ethos of the pioneer American spirit. Little Walnut Grove is the heart and soul of the literary tradition of Laura Ingalls Wilder of *Little House on the Prairie* fame.

But wait. Just down the road from the famous prairie town, we roll up on an intriguing piece of "natural" architecture: a sod house. Perhaps the most fascinating natural history site in the state follows. Jeffers Petroglyphs Historic Site is an unfairly overlooked slice of time locked under the prairie, and many travelers have come away saying it was the most educational—if not favorite—stop in southern Minnesota.

Start your tour in Worthington at the intersection of State Highway 60 and Oxford Street. Plunked attractively around 785-acre Lake Okabena in far southwestern Nobles County, Worthington once shared the same name as the lake ("nesting place of herons"). Lovely Lake Okabena is perfectly situated in a geological landmark dubbed the "Gorge of the Midwest," which captures prairie winds so effectively that windsurfers make pilgrimages here from all over the area.

But it surely wasn't windsurfing that drew Worthington's original settlers. The town grew as a railroad town, but it really took hold with the influx of a particular group of settlers: the National Colony of Toledo, Ohio. The hardy settlers were adamantly opposed to alcohol and other immoral pursuits. Not finding it easy to exist in the more "dissolute" East, they packed up and created their own settlement on Minnesota's prairie. Like other erstwhile Midwestern utopias, not much remains of this intriguing early pioneer settlement.

Worthington's premier and most easily accessed sight is its *Pioneer Village*, (507) 376-3125, about a mile southeast of exit 43 off I-90 on Oxford Street. The historic structures (some 40 all told) were reassembled here from around the county, some dating to the late-nineteenth century. Snooping around extant churches, a bank, a general store, a saloon, and several dozen more quaint buildings makes for a lovely stop off the interstate. Open Memorial Day weekend to Labor Day, Monday-Saturday, 10 a.m.-5 p.m.; Sunday 1-5 p.m.; admission.

On Oxford Street, go a short distance to Milton Street; turn south and drive a couple of blocks to 1st Street. Turn right (southwest) and go less than 1 mile to 12th Street in downtown Worthington. Turn right and go a few blocks. At 407 12th Street, the *Nobles County Art Center*, (507) 372-8245, houses local and regional artists and has monthly art exhibits. Open 2-4:30 p.m. Monday-Friday, and 7-9 p.m. Tuesday evenings.

As this book was being prepared for publication, Worthington was finalizing renovation plans for a historic mansion in town just about a block away. The *Dayton House*, 1311 Fourth Avenue, is an 1890 beauty. And if the interiors match the visual pleasantries of the outside, it'll definitely warrant a stop.

Also in Worthington, look for the *Avenue of Flags*, also known as Peace Avenue. The U.S. flag is displayed prominently alongside those of United Nations' member nations. Worthington erected its monument to peace after being named a World Brotherhood City for being the first U.S. city to adopt a German town—Crailsheim—following World War II.

Go back to the intersection of Highway 60 and Oxford Street and drive about 3.5 miles northeast on 60 to County Road 3. Turn left (north) and drive around 9 miles to County Road 16. Turn right (east) and go 3.5 miles to County Road 1. Turn left (north) and drive 9 miles to County Road 15 in the Talcot Lake area, where CR 1 has become County Road 19). Along CRs 3 and 16, you'll be close to East and West Graham Lakes, which sandwich diminutive Kinbrae. For a nice stop-off, between the two lakes is a *wildlife observation area* teeming with wildlife flitting and creeping about.

Talcot Lake marks the southern end of the nearly 5-mile-long *Talcot Lake State Wildlife Management Area* (the northern edge has Oaks Lake,

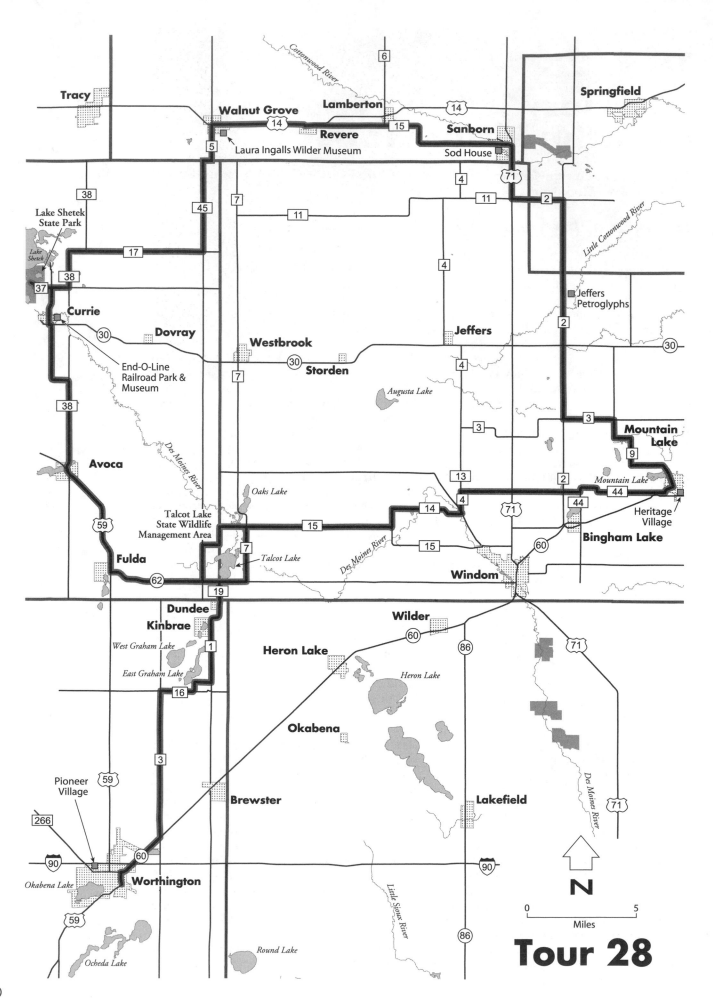

Tracy

Walnut Grove

14

Lamberton

6

Springfield

Revere

15

Sanborn

14

5

Laura Ingalls Wilder Museum

Sod House

71

38

45

7

4

11

2

11

Little Cottonwood River

Lake Shetek
State Park

17

Lake
Shetek

38

37

38

Currie

30

Dovray

4

Jeffers
Petroglyphs

2

Jeffers

30

End-O-Line
Railroad Park &
Museum

Westbrook

7

30

Storden

4

Augusta Lake

3

38

Des Moines River

Oaks Lake

3

Mountain
Lake

9

Avoca

Talcot Lake
State Wildlife
Management Area

13

Mountain Lake

2

44

59

15

14

4

44

Heritage
Village

Fulda

7

Talcot Lake

15

71

Bingham Lake

62

Des Moines River

15

60

19

Windom

Dundee

Wilder

Kinbrae

60

71

1

West Graham Lake

Heron Lake

86

East Graham Lake

16

Heron Lake

Okabena

3

Lakefield

Des Moines River

71

59

Pioneer
Village

Brewster

266

90

60

90

Okabena Lake

Worthington

Little Sioux River

N

59

86

0   5

Miles

Round Lake

Ocheda Lake

Tour 28

End-O-Line Railroad Park and Museum in Currie. Tim Bewer

and both are fed by the languorous Des Moines River). Signs mark public access points along the tiny roads leading into the reserve. Take your boots and binoculars, for there are water hazards, interesting plants, and wildlife everywhere. This area is known for wild turkeys, so keep a special eye out for Tom and family.

From Talcot Lake, return 3 miles on CR 19 to State Highway 62. Turn right (west) and go 7 miles to U.S. Highway 59 in Fulda. Once regarded as the "end of the line" for the railroad, the town was formed along Seven Mile Lake by a shrewd bishop, the aptly named John Ireland, who contracted for some 370,000 acres of land to bring Irish immigrants west. (Germans mostly came, but it was a nice gesture.)

Fulda had some of the nation's first electric lights, which ringed Seven Mile Lake beginning in 1893. (Inconveniently, the carbon bulbs burned out daily!) The historical sights that most interest road-trippers these days are the downtown *Civil War cannon*, and the 1870s-era (nobody's quite sure on the exact age) *Fulda Depot*. Located on Saint Paul and Front Streets, the depot is listed on the National Register of Historic Places and now home to an antique store.

Drive north on Highway 59 for 7 miles to County Road 38 at Avoca. Turn right and drive north for 9.5 miles to Currie. This tiny and out-of-the-way community is definitely worth a visit by railroad buffs (and others even remotely interested in steam engines) for one big reason. It's the home of the *End-O-Line Railroad Park and Museum*, (507) 763-3409. In the late 1970s a local 4H group volunteered to restore an old railroad

turntable in town. One thing led to another and, before they knew it, a whole museum had been born. First stop should be inside at the HO-scale model of the Currie Railroad Yards as they appeared in the nineteenth century. Then wander outside and picture the scene. It's not hard to do, the model is so detailed. Steam trains chug, bells chime, and mini-trains give rides to giggling children. A collection of painstakingly refurbished structures (including a too-cool saltbox foreman's house) is also on site, and definitely worth a look.

Hours are Memorial Day weekend to Labor Day, 10 a.m.–noon, and 1–5 p.m. on weekdays, and 1–5 p.m. only on weekends (last tour at 4 p.m. sharp); admission.

And a bonus: From the site a bike trail sets out to the north all the way to Lake Shetek State Park. A round trip would take most of a morning or afternoon, but the grade is easy; the total distance would come out around 13 miles.

Drive north on CR 38 to County Road 37 and turn left; go about 2.5 miles to *Lake Shetek State Park.* Here you find nearly 1,200 acres of peaceful waterside park, with a huge campground (and quaint log cabin, available by reservation). Stretching your legs or paddling a canoe is a great way to unwind from driving. The miles of trails take in plenty of wildlife, including a host of migratory birds. Also on site is a monument to 15 settlers killed during the 1862 Dakota Uprising. The interpretive center is the best place to start, with natural history exhibits and plenty of maps for striking out along the shores. Call (507) 763-3256.

Return to CR 38 and drive east and north 4 miles to County Road 17. Turn right (east)

Walnut Grove—a must-stop for fans of Laura Ingalls Wilder. Thomas Huhti

and proceed for 7 miles to County Road 45. Turn left and go north for 4 miles, then east a short distance to County Road 5. Cruise north on that for 2 miles to Walnut Grove. There is only one draw in this tranquil community, but it's a biggie. Do Laura Ingalls Wilder, Mary and Almanzo,

Little House Highway

So enraptured are Americans by the virtues that Laura Ingalls Wilder's family seemed to exemplify—hardiness, devotion, loyalty, among others—that historic sites devoted to the author's life have become not only pilgrimage destinations but also officially recognized ones. Yes, various state and local agencies have cobbled together the geographically noteworthy spots of Wilder's life into the "Laura Ingalls Wilder Historic Highway," of which Walnut Grove is arguably the heart and soul. Most of the route through Minnesota is on U.S. Highway 14.

The highway stretches from Pepin, Wisconsin, on the Mississippi River (where one can visit Laura Ingalls Wilder's birth-site cabin), westward to De Smet, South Dakota, where the original Wilder home stood, and where, if you have time, you can visit 16 spots mentioned in her books. (The city also hosts a Laura Ingalls Wilder Pageant the last weekends in June and first two weekends in July. More details later.) Nearly two dozen towns and cities boast historical or literary connections to Wilder along the route.

Walnut Grove, aptly enough, is in the center of the drive, if you take the highway in its east-to-west entirety. In 1874, seven-year-old Laura and her family moved from Wisconsin and their diminutive cabin, to move to Walnut Grove, on the banks of Plum Creek, where they settled. Laura's childhood is recounted in her book *On the Banks of Plum Creek.*

By the way, another Ingalls-centric route is U.S. Highway 52, between Rochester, Minnesota, and Burr Oak, Iowa, where Laura lived for about a year.

Ma and Pa ring a bell? To anyone who's read the famed novels or watched the TV version, this place is nothing less than a pilgrimage to a bygone era. To legions of her fans, Walnut Grove represents a real glimpse into the world of Laura Ingalls Wilder that they only imagined through her books.

The first stop for most in Walnut Grove is the *Laura Ingalls Wilder Museum*, 330 Eighth Street, (507) 859-2358. Just look for the Walnut Grove water tower and head right for it. Six buildings comprise the museum grounds—all original structures relocated here and smashingly restored. An 1890s railroad depot has a quilt made by Laura herself and a collection of memorabilia from the television series. Most visitors find themselves just wandering the grounds thereafter, stopping by the chapel to see a red pew from the original Congregational Church; examining the retouched rooms of an 1890s home; even playing a hand-pump organ in another building.

Another favorite is Heritage Lane, where a huge assortment of pioneer-era equipment can be viewed up close. Check out the covered wagons. The museum structure is open daily 10 a.m.–6 p.m., June–August, reduced off-season hours; admission.

Otherwise, a mile north of town via County Road 5 you can visit the unreconstructed *Ingalls homestead site*. The dugout house (the dugout sod house was typical of the period, with a "dugout" being carved into a hillside and reinforced with sod) is decaying in the grasses. But what a feeling it is to wander the nearly 30 acres around it, all covered by restored native prairie grasses. Admission.

Back in town, the *Congregational Church* where the family attended services is at the corner of 5th and Bedal Streets. At the corner of 4th Street

The Sod House in Sanborn, where you can spend the night. Tim Bewer

and Washington Street is the *school* where Mary, Laura, and Carrie attended class (now a private home, it's unavailable for tours). Finally, at the corner of 8th Street and County Road 20 is the *Masters Hotel*, where Laura once worked (also a private home, it is not open for tours).

And, most precious of all, when you hear the church bell ringing on Sunday morning in the English Lutheran Church, 5th Street and Wiggins Street, pay attention. Charles Ingalls gave his last three dollars to the Congregational Church for a new bell. Now *that* is history.

During the summer, one Laura Ingalls Wilder-themed event or takes place in town. Without a doubt the granddaddy of all Little House events is the *Wilder Pageant* weekends in July. This outdoor drama recounts the life of the Wilder family as they forged a new life on the prairie. Visitors also love the Laura and Nellie look-alike contests and the annual visit by a cast member from the television series.

From Walnut Grove, drive east on U.S. Highway 14 for 5.5 miles to County Road 50 in Tiny Revere. Continue east on CR 50 for 4 miles to Lamberton and County Road 15 (easy to miss). Follow it east for 6.5 miles to Sanborn. You haven't lived until you've spent a night in a sod house, a visitor once joked at Sanborn's *Sod House*, (507) 723-5138, an authentic replica of a housing structure necessitated by the dearth of timber on the prairies. Aesthetically, umm, unchallenging, it certainly has to be regarded as one of the most practical structures for a harsh

homestead life. The sod actually makes for decent insulation. Cooler in the summer and warmer in the winter than log structures, if one can overlook the dwellings' lack of curb appeal, they could make a comeback.

OK, you're probably wondering about the details. In total, over 300,000 pounds of sod was laid in a cross-stitch pattern (the roof itself weighs over 12 tons). Holy cow! Finding the proper grass is difficult itself, as deep root systems are needed to hold things together, and most of southern Minnesota's prairies are just too young today. Surrounding the sod house are restored prairie grasses and wildflowers.

Here's the cool part. If you're looking for the most unique place to hang your hat and send friends a postcard, this is it. The sod house is also a bed and breakfast!

From Sanborn, drive south on U.S. Highway 71 for 3 miles to County Road 11; turn left (east) and drive 3 miles to County Road 2 (along the way, CR 11 becomes CR 21). Turn right (south) and continue for about 5 miles to the *Jeffers Petroglyphs*. Here many find their own personal retreat from the craziness of modern life, a chance to reflect on the larger mysteries of the universe. Somehow, some way, for some reason, prehistoric inhabitants of this area laboriously chiseled more than 2,000 rock carvings into the red quartzite bedrock thrusting up from the glacial till surrounding it. The pictographs are certainly spiritually oriented, but more than that, no one can really say. Even if you're not a fan of paleontology,

One of many rock carvings at the Jeffers Petroglyphs. Tim Bewer

Continue south on CR 2 for about 7 miles to County Road 3. Turn left (east) and drive 3 miles to County Road 9. Turn right and follow the road east and south for 6 miles into **Mountain Lake.** Architecture buffs love this town, because of a couple of distinctive private homes created by noted designer Bruce Goff. One of the strangest homes you'll ever see is the *Jacob Harder House* on Eighth Street between Second and Third Avenues. *Alien* (as in "extraterrestrial") is a word that has been used, perhaps most precisely, to describe this house. That's all that can be said about that structure; the rest will be a surprise.

While in Mountain Lake, work up your appetite, as you have a wonderful place to sate it. Mountain Lake's *Heritage Village,* on the southeast side of town, (507) 427-2023, is a collection of 21 reconstructed and restored local buildings of historical interest. The entire town is steeped in the tradition of its early Russian and German settlers, and Heritage Village certainly reflects that. Open from Memorial Day to Labor Day, 1–5 p.m. While the structures are of interest, be sure to stop at the *Heritage Ayte Shtade* (or "eating place") for a sampling of the hearty fare. Delectable items from meatloaf to cold fruit pie are not found anywhere else. The restaurant is generally open Thursday to Saturday in the evenings, and for lunch on Sundays.

To return to Worthington, you have two options. One is simple and routine, the other a bit complicated and out of the way.

Option One: On the south edge of Mountain Lake, take State Highway 60 for about 42 miles straight back to where you began this tour in Worthington.

Option Two: From the south edge of Mountain Lake, take County Road 44 west for 12.5 miles to County Road 4; turn left (south) and drive 1.5 miles to County Road 14. Turn right and proceed west, then south, for 5 miles to County Road 15; turn right and drive for 10 miles to County Road 19 in the Talcot Lake area. Turn left (south) and go 9 miles to County Road 16 (about halfway CR 19 changes to CR 1). Turn right (west) on CR 16 and go 3.5 miles to County Road 3. Turn left (south) and drive 9 miles to State Highway 60. Turn right and proceed southwest for about 3.5 miles into Worthington.

just wandering the site, striking off from the tepee interpretive center into the native grasses, letting the wildflower blossoms wisp through your fingers, can be a highlight of the tour.

Hours are summers, 10 a.m.–5 p.m. weekdays, until 8 p.m. Saturdays, and noon to 8 p.m. Sundays; reduced hours May and September; admission.

Tour 29
The Pocket—Buffalo and Prairies

Luverne—Blue Mounds State Park—Edgerton—Tyler—Lake Benton—Pipestone National Monument—Split Rock Creek State Park—Jasper—Luverne

Distance: approximately 110 miles

This tour begins with one of the most intriguing of Minnesota's state parks, a land where buffalo roam as they did millennia ago, and a peek at a spot that may have been visited by extraterrestrials. From here we visit an oft-ignored national monument where streams bubble and prairie grasses stand proud and green in an otherwise desolate environment. The winds buffeting our auto indicate a change in topography, and a short hop northward reveals staggering vistas as we climb, ever so slightly, along a massive escarpment provided by eons of geological processes.

Start your tour in downtown Luverne, at the corner of Freeman and Main Streets. "Luverne: Where the buffalo *still* roam," locals like to say in this cheerful little gateway town. Those bison may be up the road a piece in a state park, in truth, but the town does seem locked in a friendly time warp, with the lovingly preserved streetscapes and building facades telling of a tranquil and lengthy history. Luverne is close enough to South Dakota and Iowa to see the respective borders on a clear day. The *Luverne Chamber of Commerce Convention and Visitors Bureau,* 102 East Main Street, (888) 283-4061, has all the information one might need.

Trolling about the downtown, travelers will notice the copper-hued aesthetics. This would be locally famous Sioux quartzite, a heavy and visually pleasant stone quarried for generations in the area. The stunning *Rock County Courthouse*, a couple of blocks north of Main Street on Brown Street, is a magnificent edifice built from the quartzite (with a recent $1 million facelift). The ex-vaudeville venue *Palace Theater,* where the visitors bureau is housed, though wearied, still looks grand with the dark red stone. The stone also adorns the *Carnegie Cultural Center*, Lincoln Street and Freeman, which showcases regional artists.

But if you really want to see a superb example of the stone being used, check out the *Hinkly House Museum,* at 217 North Freeman. It was the home of R. B. Hinkly, a quarry magnate—so you know the stone used in this home is top notch. (An interesting Hinkly House tidbit: Pa Hinkly used to store the explosives for his quarry in vaults in the home's basement. But the blasting caps were at least kept upstairs.)

For a more up close and personal experience with a bison, the Luverne vicinity has a few ranches raising the massive beasts. The visitor bureau has details on tour availability at these private operations.

Take Main Street west for 2 blocks to Kniss Avenue (U.S. Highway 75); turn right (north) and drive for 4 miles to County Highway 20. Turn right and drive east for 1 mile to the entrance to *Blue Mounds State Park.* One of the largest prairie parks in the state—perhaps even in the Midwest and Plains—Blue Mounds, (507) 282-4892, boggles the mind with its natural beauty and ecological uniqueness. Few have left the park not deeply moved. Virgin and restored prairies are splashed with a dizzying array of wildflower colors. (A rarity, even prickly pear cactus is found throughout the park.)

Yet *everyone* comes to see the park's resident bison herd (not buffalo, see the nearby sidebar "Bisons and Buffalos"). The sacred animal to the Native Americans atavistically reigns here again. It's impossible not to feel your breath pause a bit as you climb a hiking trail's rise and, off in the near distance, you see the massive beasts grazing stoically.

Luverne Festivals

Road-trip aficionados also know Luverne for two lovely festivals. For more than half a century, Luverne in late September has hosted a Midwestern favorite: the *Tri-State Band Festival*. A misnomer, really, as the event draws drum and bugle and marching bands from all over the Great Plains and Great Lakes. The first morning kicks off with a rip-roaring parade through Luverne's streets, followed up with field competitions at the high school athletic fields. Sandwiched in between, travelers find a dizzying array of music, demonstrations, crafts, and family-oriented activities.

Another favorite is the relatively young (a mere two decades old) *Buffalo Days* in late May. Celebrating the majestic beasts that once roamed these prairies, highlights of this festival are free tours of Blue Mounds State Park, tractor pulls, parades, waffle feeds, free buffalo burgers, and, of course, a buffalo chip throwing contest.

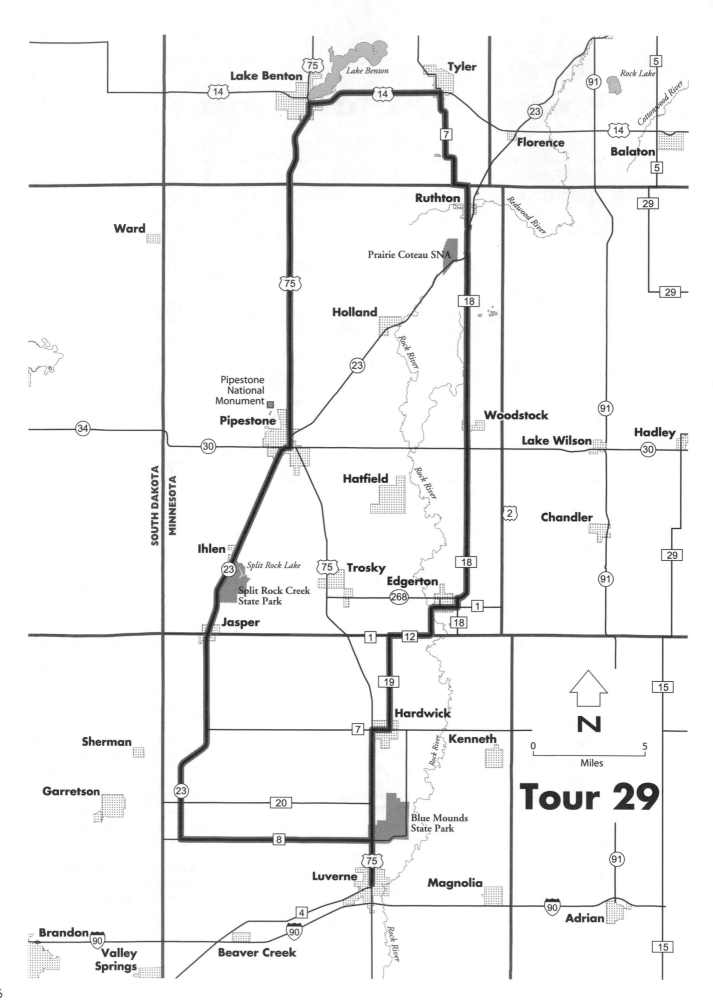

SOUTH DAKOTA

MINNESOTA

Lake Benton

Tyler

Rock Lake

Florence

Balaton

Ward

Ruthton

Prairie Coteau SNA

Holland

Woodstock

Lake Wilson

Hadley

Pipestone National Monument

Pipestone

Hatfield

Chandler

Ihlen

Split Rock Lake

Split Rock Creek State Park

Trosky

Edgerton

Jasper

Sherman

Hardwick

Kenneth

Garretson

Blue Mounds State Park

Luverne

Magnolia

Brandon

Valley Springs

Beaver Creek

Adrian

N

0   5

Miles

Tour 29

The most popular attraction at Blue Mounds State Park, near Luverne. Tim Bewer

The park sits atop a long escarpment of purplish to red Sioux Quartzite, the focal point of which is a prominent, 1.5-mile-long cliff line. This feature is so distinctive that Native Americans used it as a landmark for eons. Unmistakable above the cliffs is Eagle Rock, a 1,730-foot-high aerie from which one can gaze into South Dakota and Iowa.

A lifetime of hiking is found within the park, with footpaths—the majority easy to moderate—wending into prairies or along the at-times-churlish Rock River, and especially in and among the nooks and crannies of the cliffs. (Look for chisel marks in the rock faces where early settlers hacked out stone for building material.)

Writers and artists for generations have spent time within these inspiring prairies. Frederick Manfred, an author noted for his tales of pioneer days and Native American histories, was so moved that he made Blue Mounds his home, living in a teepee structure and attempting to channel the ethos of the place into his books. The park today has preserved his "home" as part of its interpretive center and, in a nice touch, has a lovely reading room with a book collection. This is a splendid place to while away time thumbing pages. But consider adding to your universal karma by donating your vacation reading list (provided you're finished, naturally). And note: At the time of writing, the interpretive center was in initial phases of renovation. When finished, this smashing structure—built partially of local quartzite—will seamlessly blend into the landscape and, better, have loads of information on the park's natural and human history.

Return to Highway 75 and turn right (north). Go for 4 miles to County Road 7; turn right, go 1 mile to County Road 19 in tiny Hardwick. Turn left (north) and continue for 5 miles to County Road 1/12. Turn right (east) and follow CR 1 for about 5 miles to County Road 18 on the southeast edge of Edgerton. The prairie slowly gives way to a mix of pasture and agricultural lands as the highway rises along the Coteau des Prairies. Gophers scamper across the road. Cows chew cud next to gigantic combines as farmers raise index fingers in Midwestern greeting. The grayish soil looks sickly, but glacial till across the ages have given it an astonishing fecundity.

Edgerton. Well now here's a lovely little find. Acres and acres of green surround this sleepy town of Dutch heritage. That explains the working windmill as you approach the town. The region is peppered with modern wind generators, but this one harkens to the Old Country and the original mills of wind. Perhaps it's not as mechanically efficient, but it certainly makes a prettier picture. Better, a couple of diners and cafes in town serve up scrumptious examples of Dutch delicacies.

Turn left (north) on CR 18 and cruise about 23 miles, through Ruthton, to County Road 7. Turn left and follow 7, heading west for 1 mile, then turning right and going north for about 6 miles to U.S. Highway 14 in

Bisons and Buffalos

Strictly speaking, a buffalo is not a buffalo unless it's a water-borne beast. That's right. Zoologically speaking, those great-humped beasts lumbering across the prairies in *Dances with Wolves* or munching contentedly in Blue Mounds State Park are actually bison, as the scientific name—*Bison bison*—indicates. (A precise contrast is better left to the zoologists.) The word *buffalo* comes from an approximation of the French *les boeufs* meaning "cattle" or "oxen." The only real buffalo are found in Africa and East Asia, and in particular Southeast Asia; in other words, a water buffalo is the real thing.

Mystery of Blue Mounds

At the southern end of Blue Mounds State Park sits an oddity no one has ever solved or even posited an in-the-ballpark guess. In a plumb-line-true east to west direction lies a 1,250-foot-long line of rocks. On the first days of spring and autumn, the sun's sunrise to sunset movements are perfectly aligned with the cryptic formation. Guesses hazarded have ranged from the pedestrian Native American sacred ritual site theories and to the ET, alien visitors theories. The Burr Oak Trail leads to the stones; plan for an equinox visit.

Folk High Schools

Tyler was founded by followers of Nikolai Frerik Severin Grundtvig, a Danish theologian who believed in education for all citizens and, in particular, a meshing of patriotism and religion. His followers built five such "folk high schools" in the United States, one of the largest and oldest being Tyler's, built in 1888. Dubbed the "People's College" by locals, it had one major effect: the retention of Danish culture, language, and crafts in a new land.

Tyler. The road continues to climb, it seems, even though by now we've broached the plateau of the Coteau des Prairies highland. Look for whirring (or clanking, or humming) wind farm fans in the distance. For example, about 16 miles north of Edgerton, just north of County Road 8, east of Holland, there are an eye-poppingly large number of the generators—a forest of alien-looking "electricity farmers."

Tyler is Danish to its soul. Travelers' eyes widen as they sweep into town and observe the hues of the Daneland's red and white flag everywhere, and window shutters painted colorfully (and adorned with window boxes of tulips). Many buildings smack of the land of Vikings. Just south of the intersection of CR 7 and Highway 14, and not to be missed, is the *Danebod Church*, 101 Danebod Court, (507) 247-5344, built when the first railroad came to town laden with settlers. More than a church, it has a gorgeous stone hall off to one side. And, a real treat, a folk school keeps alive the folkways of Danish immigrants. Unlike Edgerton, Tyler has no apparent windmills.

It also has something mysterious prowling about. The town, you see, is populated by *Nissemand*, Danish imps akin to Irish leprechauns, and equal in their frolicsome antics—equal parts cheeky mischief and benevolent help. (Here's the key, locals say: The degree of trickery goes down in direct proportion to the amount of food one sets out for them at night.)

Food is the key to visiting Tyler, for sure. One Dane delicacy that garners all the attention around these parts is *Aebleskiver*, or "ball pancake" (or, the local version—"baseball pancake"). That's right, a pancake shaped like a ball. Aebleskiver Days is naturally the local festival of choice, held in late June. Stuff down all the pancake balls your tummy can hold!

Drive west on Highway 14 for 7.5 miles to U.S. Highway 75 in Lake Benton. Named for explorer John C. Fremont's girlfriend, Jessie Benton, Lake Benton is truly a crossroads. Native Americans had used the large lake for navigation and settlement on their way along the Coteau des Prairies. Later, in 1838, the first of many U.S. exploration parties would highlight it as an encampment site. Fast forward to today: The town is crossed by two historic federal highways: 14 (the Laura Ingalls Wilder Memorial Highway) and 75 (the King of Trails). There is a lot going on the area, so you may want to visit the *Lake Benton Area Chamber of Commerce and CVB*, 105 South Fremont Street, (507) 368-9577, before you go exploring.

But Lake Benton for us is the center of Wind Country. This is the crown, as it were, of Buffalo Ridge—the local name for the more melodic Coteau des Prairies. Whatever you call it—it's the highest plateau in the Midwest outside of the Lake Superior Highlands, so prominent in northern Wisconsin and Minnesota. It begins its rise in northwest Iowa and doesn't decline until northern South Dakota. The topography perfectly channels winds along the ridge's epic plateau, and Lake Benton is right in the center.

Over *500* wind turbines can be seen along the ridge, more than 200 alone around Lake Benton. And surprisingly, few people have any idea of this. This, then, is a perfect opportunity to stop by the *Heritage and Windpower Learning Center* on the south side of town along South Center Street

Quick Trip Option. You can get a close-up view of the acres of sleek modern windmills by taking this short tour: From Lake Benton, go west on Highway 14 (past Enron Energy) to County Road 1, 13 miles north to State Highway 19. Then backtrack on CR 1 to County Road 13, follow it east to Highway 75, then south back into Lake Benton. The generators appear in "clumps": nothing for miles, then suddenly an entire horizon full of the space-agey machines. Wind engineers place them precisely where the winds blow through the rises and hollows here. It's truly a spectacle.

Surrounding all of the modern wind machines is prairie land not unlike what greeted the first settlers and explorers centuries ago. Three miles south of Lake Benton via Highway 75 is the *Nature Conservancy Prairie*, a pocket of original prairie resplendent with colorful native grasses and prairie. Butterfly enthusiasts populate the spread, as it's home to a variety of hard-to-find species. More than 25 prairie-dependent species thrive within this expanse of grasses. The Dakota skipper is perhaps most precious; this inch-long straw-colored darter is found only in a few places in the Dakotas, Iowa, and Minnesota.

But wind isn't the only thing of note in lovely Lake Benton. The town's smashing *1896 Opera House*, 225 South Fremont Street, (507) 368-9513, was renovated after the turn of the millennium and offers theatrical productions constantly; if nothing's on tap, just stopping by for a look-see at the interiors is well worth it.

Wind turbines looming over the prairie near Lake Benton. Tim Bewer

From Lake Benton, take Highway 75 south about 18 miles to *Pipestone National Monument* just northwest of Pipestone. The name really says it all. In a region quarrying tough-as-diamond quartzite, it's perhaps ironic that the Native Americans who populated the region preferred the nearly pliable stone lying beneath the glacial till. Early European explorers became enamored of the gorgeous sacred objects carved and chiseled by Native Sioux in this area from a workable soft claylike stone (a bit harder than soapstone, or like the consistency of a human fingernail).

So sacred were the ornamental objects produced here that the site was considered neutral grounds for all tribes; any and all could come and "mine" the stone. Later the Yankton Sioux gained control of the land and sold it to the United States, engendering decades of bitterness and acrimony. In 1937, a national monument was established and today the peacefulness and tranquility has returned.

And what a peace it is, an oasis of green grasses and eye-catching stone rising from what is otherwise harsh, fallow land. Yellows dominate the scene—daisies and yellow goat beards splashing the greenery. Some remnant virgin uplands and tallgrass prairie are sprinkled throughout the few trails.

Then, the stone again. Today Native Americans can, by permit, mine the stone; Inuit from Alaska and northern Canada have come. The Upper Mid-

west Cultural Center sponsors demonstrations of pipe-making by tribal members from time to time. Consider yourself blessed if you get the chance to witness it.

The monument is anchored by an interpretive center. From here, a .75-mile-long trail wends through the gorgeous land. Brooks gurgle, grasses bend in the wind. The noon sun doesn't even seem as hot here as just down the road.

Hours are generally Memorial Day weekend to Labor Day, Monday–Thursday, 8 a.m.–6 p.m.; Friday–Sunday until 8 p.m.; reduced off-season hours; admission.

Return to Highway 75, turn right (south) and drive about 1 mile to the intersection with State Highway 23 in Pipestone. Turn right and continue south and west through town for about 7 miles. You'll arrive at *Split Rock Creek State Park*, (507) 348-7908, a smallish park with campsites, hiking trails (lots of native wildflowers), and of most interest, a quartzite stone dam, built from the stone used to build so much of southwestern Minnesota. It's worth a stop just as a breather prior to the last stretch of miles back to Luverne.

Drive southwest on Highway 23 for 4 miles to Jasper. Southwestern Minnesota is the land of quartzite, and Jasper is the, er, "cornerstone." The

A tranquility-inducing stream at Pipestone National Monument, Pipestone. Thomas Huhti

first quarrying companies moved in and began cutting in 1888, and things have slowed down since. One company survives today, but it's still an impressive sight to see—newfangled wire-cutters shaving away huge blocks of stone. Sadly, due to insurance problems, visitors can no longer visit the quarry site or see operations, except during special occasions, such as mid-July's Quarry Days Festival. Informational videos and exhibits, however, can be seen at the *Jasper Historical Museum,* 102 Wall Street East. It's not open any set hours, but generally nearby shopkeepers will keep an eye out for

visitors and let you in. Most stores also have a brochure on a short *walking tour* of Jasper, allowing a close appreciation of the sturdy stone. Pretty cool—a town built from the same stone that helped found it.

Continue south on Highway 23 for 11.5 miles to County Road 8; turn left (east) and drive 11 miles to Highway 75; turn right (south) and proceed for 2.5 miles to Main Street back in downtown Luverne, our starting point.

Tour 30
The Source of Two Great Rivers

Ortonville—Big Stone Natural Wildlife Refuge—Milan—Lac qui Parle State Park—
Montevideio—Granite Falls—Upper Sioux Agency State Park—Hanley Falls—Madison—
Ortonville

Distance: approximately 165 miles

Lakes may get all the credit in Minnesota (what with the "Land of 10,000 Lakes" moniker and all), but we haven't forgotten the proud old Minnesota River just yet. Southern Minnesota may lack the numbers of lakes dotting its topography, a la its northern cousin, but it has the lion's share of important riverways, from both a historical and ecological perspective.

Our tour begins in the absolute heart of river country. Ortonville lies near the headwaters of two mighty rivers, the Minnesota and Red Rivers, national wildlife refuges on an enormous lake, and an impressive state park that benefits from its setting on a river. We mirror the route of the Minnesota, taking in a geological primer as we roll along. Eons of glacial and riverine machinations reveal themselves in the splendid topography.

We are pulled along the flow of the Minnesota River, but we visit sleepy river towns—a hodgepodge of ethnic immigration—in reverse order of their westward settlement. Red and white for Danes, an added splash of blue tells of Norske pioneers.

Crossing the grand Minnesota, we come upon one of the state's best historic sites, telling the long (and not always happy) tale of European-Native contact, the Upper Sioux Agency State Park.

We finish in Yellow Medicine country—a gorgeous name for a large county stretching from the river all the way to South Dakota. More Native American history is followed in diminutive Hanley Falls by a superb if not mind-boggling collection of antique machinery that rivals any Smithsonian exhibit. In a fitting tribute to the Viking state, we top it all off with a snapshot of Lou T. Fisk, the tongue-in-cheek symbol of Norwegian-Minnesotans.

Start your tour in downtown Ortonville on 2nd Street (State Highway 7). The river valley in which the town is set was on a Native American transportation path, and effigy mounds are still found throughout the region. In the nineteenth century, the town, 50 miles from the nearest trail, relied upon the river for transportation and supplies. Given the ample water supply, agriculture boomed. At one point Ortonville had the state's largest fresh vegetable cannery. The town's sweet

corn production is still legendary, in fact, celebrated annually in August's *Cornfest*.

Once the big river was dammed by the WPA in the 1930s, the town's fortunes took on an entirely different flavor as Big Stone Lake crept toward its borders. Today the 26-mile-long Big Stone is the source of the Minnesota River, and tourism anchors the local economy. Walleye, growing to immense proportions in the depths of the lake, lure in anglers looking for trophies (The town hosts numerous national fishing competitions). The tourist excursion boat *Eahtonka* plies the waters, laden with tourists watching the flora and fauna splashing, bounding, and flying about.

Begin your visit to Ortonville by just lolling with the kids in picturesque *Lakeside Park,* a mere two blocks from downtown on the shores of Big Stone Lake. Also on the lake atop a modest aerie, *Nielson Park* sports tree-shaded hiking trails. Two splendid lookout points offer breathtaking vistas of pumpkin-colored sunsets over Big Stone Lake. The kids may be intrigued by the modest, but eminently worthwhile, *Big Stone County Historical Museum,* at the intersection of U.S. Highways 12 and 75 on the southeast edge of town. It features 100-million-year-old fossils and one of the largest stuffed wildlife collections in the world.

Big Stone Gap

Slightly less than a dozen millennia ago, Glacial Lake Agassiz was held back by the existing continental divide. At one pivotal moment, all that changed, as the lake breached the barrier and roared through, for 3,000 years gouging a channel a mile wide and up to 140 feet deep—today's Minnesota River Valley. So enormous was this "river" of roiling water that its name seems a misnomer—Glacial Lake Warren. Another channel ultimately opened to the north, forming the Red River, lowering Glacial Lake Warren and creating what is today the Minnesota River. Today the residual gap separates Lake Traverse, the headwaters for the Red River, and Big Stone Lake, the source of the Minnesota River.

Quick Trip Option. Here's a short trek to *Big Stone Lake State Park* that gives you a couple of additional options. All you have to do is drive northwest on Highway 7 for a maximum of 18 miles one way. The park is divided into three sections along the highway: the Meadowbrook Area, Overlook Area, and Bonanza Area. The former is the largest and most popular section (and the closest to Ortonville). Its prairie walk is a great way to educate and entertain car-weary kids. Want a grand vista? Ten miles northeast of Meadowbrook

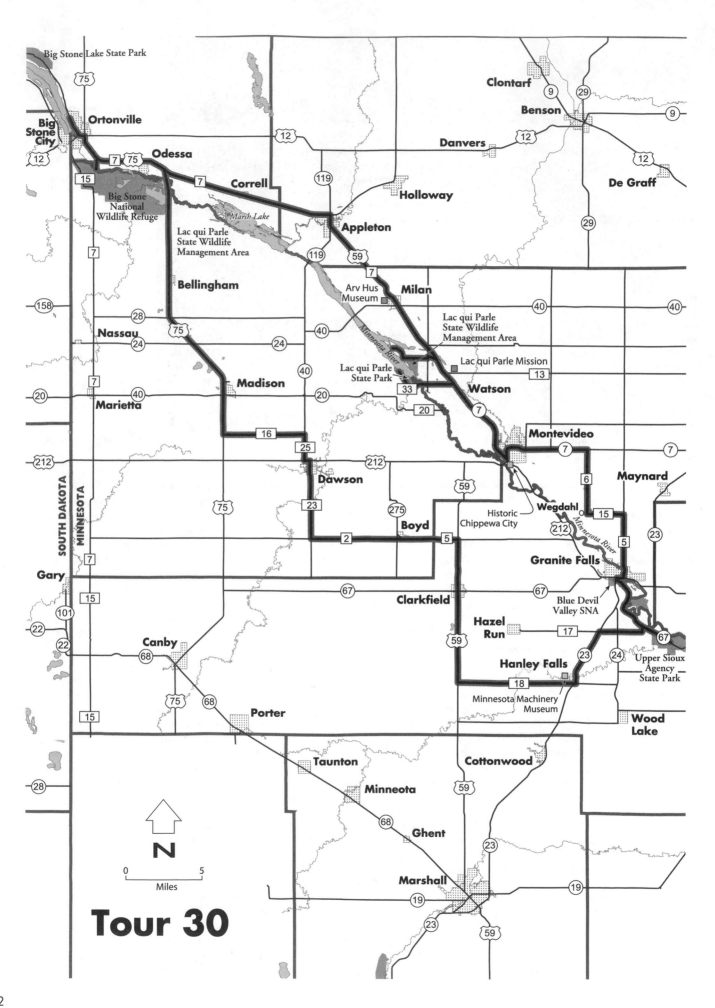

Tour 30

Granite outcropping at aptly named Big Stone National Wildlife Refuge. Thomas Huhti

is the Overlook Area. This rest stop sports a gorgeous view of Big Stone Lake. A mile northwest of the Overlook Area is the Bonanza Area, with the region's best hiking. Woodland and tall grass prairie trails snake out from an interpretive center. View the natural history exhibits in the center, then see it all for yourself on the easy-to-moderate trails. (Hint: Those who are willing to sweat a bit are rewarded with some lovely but smallish cascades.)

In Ortonville, drive southeast on Highway 7 to the edge of town to where the road is joined by Highway 75. Less than 2 miles after that, watch for a turnoff on the right that leads to the *Big Stone National Wildlife Refuge.* This is a must-see for anyone interested in either Minnesota River natural history, or simply nature's bounty. Ten thousand acres are chockablock with streams feeding the river, pothole granite outcroppings providing cover for native fauna (and flora—the rocks actually support cacti), wetlands, residual native prairie cover, and more. The Minnesota River's 11.5-mile flowage through the refuge is virtually invisible from the road, but this stretch is unquestionably one of the highlights of its entire length. Ten thousand years perfectly preserved.

During your visit to the park, consider yourself touched by Mother Nature's hand if you manage to spy some of the free-roaming bison that wander the refuge. It's a birder's haven, too, as its grassland and prairie-floodplain forest transition zone makeup lures umpteen thousand migrating birds—favorite local species include the upland sandpiper, great blue heron, and prairie falcon. And

there are 17 species of duck, more than enough to intrigue hunters who can look, but not touch.

Thankfully for road warriors, an auto tour leads through the refuge. It's a mere 4 miles long, but there are many pull-offs that can lure you into whiling an entire afternoon. Stop No. 1 on the tour has a brochure in the little plastic box; pick one up—you'll be glad you did! (Generally, birding checklists and native flora/fauna catalogs are also available.) Near the rest area along the tour is a footpath easily covered in an hour. Brochure and birding checklists in hand, your ecological knowledge will increase exponentially.

Continue east on Highway 7 for about 19 miles into Appleton. Along the way, you skirt the edge of pinhole-sized Odessa and slough off Highway 75 as it turns to the south. Suddenly you'll see Marsh Lake, and the beginning of another wildlife refuge: the DNR-run *Lac qui Parle State Wildlife Management Area.* An observation point is found on the left side of the road just before County Road 23. Lac qui Parle does, in fact, contain a lake—actually a river lake, where the Minnesota River widens appreciably. Millions of walleye are stocked here, so grab your gear.

Ultimately Highway 7 angles away from the lake and, before we know it, we come out in sleepy Appleton, with nothing much more than lovely Mill Pond Park to hike and camp in.

Continue southeast on Highway 7 (which has been joined by U.S. Highway 59 in Appleton) for about 8 miles to Milan. The Lac qui Parle

Some gorgeous examples of Norwegian rosemaling, an art that the town of Milan is famous for. Thomas Huhti

draw here. A recent addition is a photographic collection. The pictorial representation of the Milan area is a poor-man's auto tour substitute. Also, inquire about William Thompson and the memorabilia the museum houses. Thompson was a local inventor and tinkerer who in 1925 invented a "radio booster," allowing rural radio listeners to greatly improve reception. He would later invent numerous other broadcast devices and help push U.S. broadcasting into the future. Folks at the museum can also give you information regarding a possible visit to a Norwegian Stabbur, a unique sod-roofed log building that's located east of town a few miles.

Drive southeast on Highway 7/59 for 7.5 miles to County Road 13. The road sleepily bends away from any above-average vistas, then briefly returns. And then, just when we thought the wildlife refuges had tapered out, it reappears. The Lac qui Parle Wildlife Management Area's southern unit jumps into view immediately after we depart Milan. Just about any road to your right will lead you into a half-day-or-more exploration of its 31,000 acres of every topographical feature possible, including woodlands, native prairie, and wetlands.

Turn right (west) on County Road 13, then County Road 33, and follow the signs to *Lac qui Parle State Park* (about 5 miles). Situated at the large lake formed by the confluence of a collection of rivers and streams (not to mention the help of dams), the park, (320) 752-4736, is nestled snugly next to the massive wildlife refuge to the west and north, and by woodlands and prairies to the south and east. Five miles of hiking/skiing trails are well worth the effort; every bend and rise proffers another sublime view. Prairie chickens are fairly easy to spot within the park—as are deer. But most birders flock here in migration periods to see the absolute clouds of Canada geese honking cacophonously overhead or on the big lake. This is a major environmental success story: In 1958, the lake had but 150 forlorn geese, and today, a conservative estimate posits the number at around 200,000.

A favorite spot, though, is the *Lac qui Parle Mission*, on CR 13. A simple rebuilt church, it was here where Protestant missionaries first settled— the first such site in Minnesota—near a large Dakota village, in the 1830s. The Bible was painstakingly translated into Dakota. A few exhibits detail the missionaries' history with the Native Americans. But more than the architecture or informational displays is the solitude and peace of the little church. It's a place to sit, take a breath, and ponder. The chapel is open late April to Labor Day, 8 a.m.–8 p.m., (320) 269-7636; free.

Return to Highway 7/59 and go about 7 miles to where the road separates on the southwest edge of Montevideo. At the junction is *Historic Chippewa City*, a turn-of-the-twentieth-century village with 23 buildings that were either relocated from other locales in the county or erected on site.

Wildlife Area seems to fade in tiny increments as we roll toward Milan. With a name that conjures up thoughts of wine and romance in northern Italy, this cheerful burg is actually Norwegian to the core. Norwegian flags are aflutter everywhere and tasteful Norwegian-themed murals adorn downtown walls. Rosemaling, that lovely special craft of wood painting, is elevated to a high art by local artisans, many of whom have small shops downtown. Milan Village Arts is a cooperative with superb examples of Norwegian folk arts. They also offer classes in weaving, silversmithing, rosemaling, and more.

All of this can be experienced at the *Arv Hus Museum*, (320) 734-4868, along Main Street. A particularly nice exhibit details *hardanger*, a Norwegian special weaving. But artistry isn't the only

A classic Minnesota River scene. Thomas Huhti

Visit a gazebo, an old church, a one-room schoolhouse, a general store, and two dozen other buildings. Located where Highways 7 and 59 separate just west of Montevideo, (320) 269-7636; open summer weekdays 9 a.m.–5 p.m., from 1 p.m. weekends; admission.

Otherwise, Montevideo certainly seems to have more acreage of parkland than any other city. Parks are prevalent, perhaps understandable as the Chippewa River joins the Minnesota River in town. A picturesque hiking/biking trail follows sections of both rivers.

From Montevideo, take Highway 7 east through town and go for about 6 miles to County Road 6; turn right (south) and drive for 5 miles to County Road 15 on the outskirts of Wegdahl. Turn left. Exiting Montevideo, the riverine world melts away and we return to more typical Midwestern landscapes: geometric carpets of agricultural fecundity, behemoth tractors gracefully chugging to the highway shoulder to let you pass, a flatness taking full advantage of the 2.5-mile-to-the-horizon limit. Eventually, outside Wegdahl, we arrive at a marvelous example of pioneer stick-to-itiveness, the *Swensson Farm Museum,* (320) 269-7636, with a 22-room brick farm home, an 1880s timber frame barn, an extant grist mill, and family burial plot. Open Sundays, 1–5 p.m., in summer (though calling first is a good idea); admission.

Drive east on CR 15 for 3 miles to County Highway 5; turn right (south) and go 5 miles into downtown Granite Falls. Once in town, **follow CR 5 south through a labyrinth of streets (Center and Lincoln are good bets) to State Highway 23. Turn right and proceed to the junction with State Highway 67.** This town is home to—in the words of local boosters—the "Oldest Rock in the World." Here Glacial Lake Agassiz and Glacial Lake Benson once met, and when the waters receded, a rock was exposed. At two to three billion years old, the rock may justify the claim.

Should you wish to peruse this geological highlight, simply head for the *Yellow Medicine County Historical Museum* downtown at the junction of Highways 23 and 67, (320) 564-4479. Park and ogle the big old stone. Poking around the historical museum is also fun. In addition to lots of geological wonders, you'll find Native American artifacts, a reconstructed log cabin, an original church, and more. Open mid-May to mid-October, Tuesday–Friday, 11 a.m.–3 p.m.; weekends from noon to 4 p.m.

A short stroll from the museum brings you to the *Blue Devil Valley Preserve,* a 35-acre Nature Conservancy tract, on County Road 39, just off Highway 23. One of five such areas in Minnesota, it features more examples of the Morton gneiss—the same type of rock as the granddaddy across the street. The preserve takes its name from the "blue devil," a.k.a the five-lined skink, an endangered lizard that uses the antediluvian stone for cover. (The lizard is one of only two indigenous lizard species in Minnesota.)

Looking for another shot of history? At 169 South 9th Avenue sits the *Volstead House.* This was the domain of Andrew J. Volstead, author of the

Congressional act that led to Prohibition in the 1920s. To be fair, he also penned an act that brought about farmer cooperatives. Hours are generally Monday–Thursday, 8:30 a.m.–4:30 p.m.

Drive southeast on Highway 67 for 8 miles to *Upper Sioux Agency State Park.* Pay special attention while making the short drive to the park—the route is both lovely and winding. At the junction of the Minnesota and Yellow Medicine Rivers sits this historically—and ecologically—significant site. Virtually every habitat type is found here, from prairies to woodlands to wetlands. Unique for our tour is a series of modest bluffs that allow for a more strenuous leg stretch after much driving.

Before or after hiking the many miles of trails, stop at the park's interpretive center. The Upper Sioux Indian Agency was instrumental in U.S.-Sioux relations and fell victim to hostilities during the 1862 Sioux uprising. One of the agency's remaining buildings has been restored, and the interpretive center has excellent educational displays on this sad chapter of U.S. history.

And there's one more pleasant thing. The state park has a campground, the highlight of which is a genuine teepee available for visitors to camp in!

Return northwest on Highway 67 a short distance to County Road 17; turn left (west) and follow it for about 4 miles to Highway 23. Turn left (southwest) and go for 5 miles into Hanley Falls. Up to now, the trip has been full of natural, historical, and ethnic wonders; now it's time for something completely different. In Hanley Falls, the *Minnesota Machinery Museum,* a block west and two blocks north of Highway 23, (507) 768-3522, is home to antique tractors, tools, vintage autos, steam engines, and just about every type of antique something or other imaginable. It's absolutely astonishing how much, well, stuff, this place has. Just try and figure out what half of the implements were used for! Awesome fun at the second weekend in August's *Pioneer Power Threshing Show and Old Timer's Reunion.* Hours are generally May to September, Wednesday–Monday, 1-5 p.m.

From Highway 23, turn right (west) on County Road 18 and drive 9 miles to U.S. Highway 59. Turn right (north) and go 7 miles to tiny Clarkfield. Any shopaholics in your group? Make this a pilgrimage stop then, as Clarkfield is known for its excellent antique shops. While the antiquers browse, perhaps the rest can head for Orras and North Parks, two lovely spots, for some down time.

Continue north 4 miles on Highway 59 to County Road 5. Turn left (west) and drive 11.5 miles to County Road 23 (CR 5 changes to CR 2

in Lac qui Parle County). Along the way, take note of Boyd, a small community that knows how to throw a big party. Make sure to stop in June for the annual Boyd Good Time Days festival, the longest running community festival in the United States.

Turn right (north) on CR 23, then drive north 6 miles to Dawson. Another Scandinavian enclave, Dawson is a cheeky thrill, what with its population of gnomes scattered throughout town. Well, they're really statues, but when you turn your back, you'd swear they'd moved! Beautifully carved, they make for great photo ops.

Continue north 2 miles on CR 25 to County Road 16, turn left (west), and drive west 6.5 miles to U.S. Highway 75. Turn right (north) and follow it for 3.5 miles into Madison. One could call this stretch the "gateway to the prairies." Driving northwest, the road rolls through the foothills of Buffalo Ridge, an epic rise that we encountered in Tour 29. As you drive west, it is said that the elevation change in 15 to 20 miles is approximately the same as that from the Gulf of Mexico to this area.

The Madison area is unique for having the only salt lake in southwestern Minnesota. *Lac qui Parle County Museum,* on Highway 75, (320) 598-7678, has an old schoolhouse, an astonishingly large doll collection, an extant log cabin, a mock-up of an old township row, and a large-game exhibit. The museum has more recently been adding information and memorabilia from local boy Robert Bly. A poet and writer, Bly gained fame in the 1990s for his work promoting—some say starting—a "men's movement." The highlight for Bly fans is the one-room schoolhouse he once used as his study. Open May–October, Monday–Saturday, 9 a.m.–4:30 p.m., Sunday, 1:30-5 p.m.; free.

But the real reason folks come to Madison is lutefisk, or, rather, Lou T. Fisk. You're in another Norwegian haven here, and among the many chainsaw-carved statues dotting the downtown, by far the most popular—always crowded by photo seekers—is Lou T. Fisk, a huge codfish. Say the name fast and you have lutefisk—that "delicacy" of Norwegian communities everywhere.

For the uninitiated, lutefisk is basically codfish cured in lye, then boiled. Generally it's also served with lefse, a Norwegian hard potato flatbread. It's a gelatinous mess, and the smell can make even proud Vikings blanch. Love it or hate it, this is the place to try it. Madison proudly bills itself as the "Lutefisk Capital of the U.S.!" Come during early November's *Norskefest* and give it a shot yourself.

Follow Highway 75 north and about 25 miles back to Ortonville. When Highway 7 splits off to the left, follow it back into the downtown area, where we began this tour.

More Great Titles From Trails Books & Prairie Oak Press

Activity Guides
Great Cross-Country Ski Trails: Wisconsin, Minnesota, Michigan & Ontario, Wm. Chad McGrath
Great Minnesota Walks: 49 Strolls, Rambles, Hikes, and Treks, Wm. Chad McGrath
Great Wisconsin Walks: 45 Strolls, Rambles, Hikes, and Treks, Wm. Chad McGrath
Paddling Illinois: 64 Great Trips by Canoe and Kayak, Mike Svob
Paddling Southern Wisconsin: 82 Great Trips by Canoe and Kayak, Mike Svob
Paddling Northern Wisconsin: 82 Great Trips by Canoe and Kayak, Mike Svob
Wisconsin Underground: A Guide to Caves, Mines, and Tunnels in and around the Badger State, Doris Green
Minnesota Underground & the Best of the Black Hills: A Guide to Mines, Sinks, Caves, and Disappearing Streams, Doris Green

Travel Guides
Great Little Museums of the Midwest, Christine des Garennes
Great Minnesota Weekend Adventures, Beth Gauper
The Great Wisconsin Touring Book: 30 Spectacular Auto Tours, Gary Knowles
Tastes of Minnesota: A Food Lover's Tour, Donna Tabbert Long
Wisconsin Lighthouses: A Photographic and Historical Guide, Ken and Barb Wardius
Wisconsin Waterfalls, Patrick Lisi
Wisconsin Family Weekends: 20 Fun Trips for You and the Kids, Susan Lampert Smith
County Parks of Wisconsin, Revised Edition, Jeannette and Chet Bell
Up North Wisconsin: A Region for All Seasons, Sharyn Alden
Great Wisconsin Taverns: 101 Distinctive Badger Bars, Dennis Boyer
Great Weekend Adventures, the Editors of Wisconsin Trails
Eating Well in Wisconsin, Jerry Minnich
Acorn Guide to Northwest Wisconsin, Tim Bewer

Nature Essays
Wild Wisconsin Notebook, James Buchholz
Trout Friends, Bill Stokes
Northern Passages: Reflections from Lake Superior Country, Michael Van Stappen
River Stories: Growing Up on the Wisconsin, Delores Chamberlain

Home & Garden
Wisconsin Country Gourmet, Marge Snyder & Suzanne Breckenridge
Wisconsin Herb Cookbook, Marge Snyder & Suzanne Breckenridge
Creating a Perennial Garden in the Midwest, Joan Severa
Wisconsin Garden Guide, Jerry Minnich
Bountiful Wisconsin: 110 Favorite Recipes, Terese Allen
Wisconsin's Hometown Flavors, Terese Allen

Historical Books
Prairie Whistles: Tales of Midwest Railroading, Dennis Boyer
Barns of Wisconsin, Jerry Apps
Portrait of the Past: A Photographic Journey Through Wisconsin 1865-1920, Howard Mead, Jill Dean, and Susan Smith
Wisconsin: The Story of the Badger State, Norman K. Risjord
Wisconsin At War: 20th Century Conflicts Through the Eyes of Veterans, Dr. James F. McIntosh

Gift Books

The Spirit of Door County: A Photographic Essay, Darryl R. Beers

Milwaukee, Photography by Todd Dacquisto

Duck Hunting on the Fox: Hunting and Decoy-Carving Traditions, Stephen M. Miller

Spirit of the North: A Photographic Journey Through Northern Wisconsin, Richard Hamilton Smith

Ghost Stories

Haunted Wisconsin, Michael Norman and Beth Scott

W-Files: True Reports of Wisconsin's Unexplained Phenomena, Jay Rath

The Beast of Bray Road: Tailing Wisconsin's Werewolf, Linda S. Godfrey

Giants in the Land: Folktales and Legends of Wisconsin, Dennis Boyer

For a free catalog, phone, write, or e-mail us.

Trails Books

P.O. Box 317 • Black Earth, WI 53515

(800) 236-8088 • e-mail: books@wistrails.com

www.trailsbooks.com